What reviewers said about the fi

"… a vivid and scholarly account of … a desperate and extraordinary night battle, written by a master of the military techniques of the day. … an enjoyable and compelling read."

Piers Mackesy, author of *The War for America, 1775-83, War Without Victory: The Downfall of Pitt* and *British Victory in Egypt, 1801*

"An excellent tactical study of a Napoleonic period battle."

Professor David Chandler, author of *The Campaigns of Napoleon* and *The Art of War in the Age of Marlborough*

"*Where Right and Glory Lead!* is how military history should be written – deeply and carefully researched, salted with common sense, and put into a prose that stands you in a firing line that is fraying thinner by the minute.…"

John Elting, author of *Swords Around a Throne: Napoleon's Grand Armée* and *Amateurs to Arms: A Military History of the War of 1812*

"…an exercise in military history at its best."

Dennis Showalter, *History Book Club*

"… read Donald Graves's brilliant and exciting and sometimes surprising interpretation of the greatest battle ever to have taken place on Canadian soil."

Michael Power, *Brock Review*

"Donald Graves's history is anything but dry, and his insights are extremely valuable. This book is a must!"

Mike Vogel, *Buffalo Evening News*

"… comprehensive and compelling.… Meticulously documented, cogently argued, this book alone will secure Graves's reputation among military historians."

James Elliott, *Hamilton Spectator*

"… a matter of celebration to find a superb history of one such battle.… an excellent example of the 'sharp end' of military history."

Barry Gough, *Canadian Military History*

"… a complete account of the battle in a highly readable style."

Ian McCulloch, *The Beaver*

"… fair treatment of both sides in the Lundy's Lane encounter … should earn this book a 'definitive' treatment for years to come."

David Skaggs, *Journal of the Early American Republic*

Battle of Lundy's Lane, 25 July 1814
This imaginative mid-19th century engraving is inaccurate in many details but is notable for the presence of the clouds of smoke which covered the area of the battle obscuring vision and causing many errors of identification. (Courtesy, National Archives of Canada, C-12094)

Front cover
The Battle of Lundy's Lane, 25 July 1814
Detail from engraving by William Strickland, first published in the *Portfolio*. See page 156. (Courtesy of the National Archives of Canada, C-4071)

Where Right and Glory Lead!

THE BATTLE OF LUNDY'S LANE, 1814

DONALD E. GRAVES

ROBIN BRASS

Toronto

This book was first published in hardcover in 1993 by the
Nautical & Aviation Publishing Company of America,
Baltimore, under the title *The Battle of Lundy's Lane: On the
Niagara in 1814*. This paperback edition includes revisions as
well as a number of additional photographs.

This revised paperback edition published 1997 by Robin Brass Studio
10 Blantyre Avenue, Toronto, Ontario M1N 2R4, Canada
Fax: (416) 698-2120 / e-mail: rbrass@astral.magic.ca

Printed and bound in Canada by AGMV, Cap-Saint-Ignace, Quebec

Canadian Cataloguing in Publication Data

Graves, Donald E. (Donald Edward), 1949–
    Where right and glory lead! : the battle of Lundy's Lane, 1814

Previously published under the title: The battle of Lundy's Lane :
on the Niagara in 1814.

Includes bibliographical references and index.
ISBN 1-896941-03-6

1. Lundy's Lane (Niagara Falls, Ont.), Battle of, 1814. I. Title.
II. Title: The battle of Lundy's Lane.

FC446.L8G73 1997   971.03'4   C97-930502-0
E356.L9G73 1997

DEDICATED

TO

CAPTAIN DANIEL SPRINGER

1ST MIDDLESEX REGIMENT, MILITIA OF UPPER CANADA

PRESENT AT

LUNDY'S LANE, 25 JULY 1814

AND

TO HIS DESCENDANT

MATTHEW DYLAN EDWARD GRAVES

WHO COULDN'T CARE LESS ABOUT MILITARY HISTORY

BUT

LIKED HIS DAD'S BOOK

Contents

LIST OF MAPS

Preface

This book is an account of a battle that took place on 25 July 1814 near the falls of Niagara. The battle of Lundy's Lane, as it is now commonly known, was fought between an American army commanded by Major General Jacob Brown and a British army commanded by Lieutenant General Gordon Drummond. After New Orleans, it was the single bloodiest military action of the War of 1812; but, unlike New Orleans – a very one-sided engagement – the opposing forces at Lundy's Lane both suffered heavy casualties. These losses are an indication not only of the ferocity of the fighting but also of the fact that Lundy's Lane was a vicious, confusing battle fought largely by regular troops. Even worse, much of it took place in the dark, a unique occurrence in 1814.

Lundy's Lane was the major engagement of the Niagara campaign of 1814. Launched as the war entered its third year, this campaign offered perhaps the last best chance for the United States to obtain military success in a conflict that up to then had not gone well for President James Madison's administration. What set the campaign of 1814 apart from previous American operations was that, in Jacob Brown's Left Division, the United States possessed the best led, best trained and most experienced military force it was to field during the war. In nearly four months of hard and costly fighting, in triumph and adversity, this division established an admirable record and its veterans were to dominate the postwar American military for nearly half a century. With some truth it can be said that the birth of the modern U.S. army occurred not at Valley Forge in 1777-1778 but along the Niagara in 1814.

In their time the men of Brown's army were lauded by their fellow citizens, one contemporary remarking that they had done "honour to their country and given an imperishable name to the character of the American soldier." Now, their achievements are nearly forgotten – mention of the War of 1812, the "Second War of Independence," in the United States today is more likely to evoke images of "Old Ironsides," the "rocket's red glare" or Kentucky riflemen slaughtering Britons by the hundred at New Orleans than it does the hard-fought Niagara battles of 1814.

Things are somewhat different in Canada where, in a great national legend that prevailed well into the twentieth century, the War of 1812 was viewed as a heroic contest that cast "British" North Americans against superior numbers in a desperate struggle to preserve their independence and institutions. Lundy's Lane, often called the "Gettysburg of Canada," played a central role in this myth and it was remembered and celebrated long after it took place. What many Canadians often conveniently overlook, however, is that the hardest fighting in both the battle and the war was done by British regulars who also suffered the heaviest casualties. Another overlooked fact is that there were Canadians on *both* sides at Lundy's Lane.

As a Canadian and the descendant of men who fought for their Crown both at Lundy's Lane and in the Revolutionary War, I have tried hard to be as objective as possible in the pages below but, as so much of the sheer weight of evidence is American in origin, I have presented the American side in more detail. Maintaining objectivity is not as difficult as it might seem as the War of 1812 was like a civil war between two branches of one great family. There were fewer differences between the men of 1814, particularly between Americans and Canadians, than there are today. The contending armies at Lundy's Lane shared a common language, a common heritage, a common organization and an uncommon obstinacy in combat.

Since the day it was fought, Lundy's Lane has been the subject of controversy. This is partly due to the fact that both sides claimed victory and partly the result of postwar disputes between American officers which were played out in the press and before military tribunals. The officers of Brown's army were, sadly, a litigious bunch; the campaign of 1814 gave rise to no fewer than five courts martial and one court of inquiry. I have taken full advantage of the excellent evidence contained in the lengthy transcripts of these proceedings. In the course of my research I also uncovered a surprising number of diaries, journals, memoirs and reminiscences left by the men who fought in the battle. As historical evidence these accounts vary widely in quality but even the least credible serve to put a personal face to the horror of war. For this reason, where information has been readily available, I have attempted to recount the postwar fate not only of the senior officers of both armies but also of those participants who left important or lengthy accounts of the action.

I began writing this book with the intention of making a detailed analysis of a Napoleonic period military action but I feel that I have written not so much an account of a battle as I have an account of soldiers in battle. This was to be expected, for in war it is the human element that is always the most interesting, most unchanging – and most important. Both armies which fought at Lundy's Lane possessed their proper allotment of heroes, cowards, dullards and sages – and simple men just trying to do their simple duty. Although the soldiers of 1814 are far removed from their modern counterparts in matters of tactics, weapons and uniforms, in terms of their hopes, fears, aspirations and all other attributes of the human condition, they are much the same. This is a commonplace but it is too often forgotten. Concerning the importance of the human element in war, perhaps the Greek Xenophon said it best when he wrote that "not numbers or strength bring victory in war; but whichever army goes into battle stronger in soul, their enemies generally cannot withstand them."

On a warm summer's evening, one hundred and seventy-eight years ago, two armies, strong in soul, encountered each other near the falls of Niagara. The result was one of the most bitterly-contested battles ever fought on the North American continent.

DONALD E. GRAVES
Ottawa, Canada
25 July 1992

Preface to the Second Edition (1997)

The happy circumstance of having a second edition of my study of Lundy's Lane appear only a few years after the first came out in 1993 has allowed me to revise, and hopefully improve, the text. Thankfully, there were few corrections to be made.

I am very pleased about being able to restore the original title of this work and I offer an apology to my regiment, the Royal Canadian Artillery, whose motto, *Quo fas et gloria ducunt* ("Where right and glory lead"), I have co-opted. I should add that this is also the motto of the Royal Artillery who played such a prominent part in the battle.

The last few years have witnessed a steady stream of publications concerning the War of 1812. I have incorporated much of this new material into the notes below and have included others in an addendum to the bibliography.

I am happy to be able to add that, since the first edition of this book appeared in 1993, the battlefields of Chippawa and Lundy's Lane have been acquired for preservation as historic sites. Neglected for many years, they were threatened by development. They will now be preserved as a permanent monument to the men fought and the many who died on these hallowed grounds. Lest we forget.

DONALD E. GRAVES.
Almonte, Canada
Dominion Day, 1996

A Note on Terminology and Time

The fact that Lundy's Lane was an engagement between two English-speaking armies posed a particular problem – common surnames. Two officers named Drummond and two named Scott played prominent roles in the battle. To avoid confusion, a reference in the text to Drummond, without any further elaboration, will always mean Lieutenant General Gordon Drummond of the British army while, similarly, a reference to Scott will always mean Brigadier General Winfield Scott of the American army. To differentiate, references to Lieutenant Colonel William Drummond and Colonel Hercules Scott will always include their Christian names.

In 1814 both the American and British armies used numerical designations written in figures for, respectively, their infantry regiments and battalions. As the reader might find this puzzling, figures were retained for the designations of British units while words have been used for those of American units – thus, the British 1st Regiment of Foot but the American First Infantry Regiment. On this head, it might be well to add that during the War of 1812, an American infantry "regiment" and a British infantry "battalion" were much the same thing – a permanently organized unit of between five hundred and one thousand men. For the British army, I have used the terms "battalion" and "regiment" interchangeably as they were used in 1814.

Another problem of terminology peculiar to the Niagara campaign is that it was fought between the American Left Division and the British Right Division – terms that derived from the way the opposing nations faced on the map of North America. The United States, facing north, called its westernmost field formation the Left Division while Britain, facing south, named its the Right Division. To further confuse matters, there was also an American Right Division and a British Left Division but when they are mentioned below, they will be preceded by their national designations.

Both armies used the term "militia" for their non-regular troops. To avoid confusion, I have generally used the term "Volunteers" for American non-regulars while retaining "militia" for Canadian non-regulars.

Variations in the spelling of place names also caused some problems. After much vacillation, I opted to retain the modern spelling of Sackets Harbor and Chippawa throughout, except in quoted text.

Lundy's Lane occurred near the falls of Niagara and while most readers will be familiar with this great natural wonder, they may not be as familiar with the surrounding area. The Niagara river (actually a strait) flows northward from Lake Erie to Lake Ontario. Thus, downstream on the Niagara is to the north, upstream to the south; the left or west bank of the river is Canadian while the right or east bank is American. In 1814, a road ran along the length of the Canadian side from Fort Erie to Newark (present-day Niagara-on-the-Lake). This route was known as the river road except for that portion of it between the villages of Chippawa and Queenston where it was called the Portage road as it formed the means of bypassing the obstacle to navigation posed by the falls. This terminology has been retained throughout the text.

A difficulty faced by all historians who investigate military actions is time. In combat, time is a relative thing – seconds drag on for minutes, minutes flash by in seconds – and the historian trying to establish accurate times for the events of a battle, based on participants' accounts or other evidence, faces a difficult task. When dealing with an early nineteenth century military action, this task is made doubly difficult as global time zones did not exist in 1814; watches were set to a local time that might change within a distance of fifteen miles. There is one thing, however, that all participants agree happened during the battle of Lundy's Lane – shortly after it commenced, the sun went down. The time of sunsets can be accurately established and, at my request, the Herzberg Institute of the National Research Council of Canada used their computer banks to ascertain that on 25 July 1814 the sun set in the vicinity of the falls of Niagara at 7:46 P.M., Eastern Standard Time, give or take one minute. There was, of course, no standard time in 1814 but, using sunset at 7:46 P.M. as a benchmark and relating other happenings to it, it was possible to work out a fairly accurate sequence of events and also to provide approximate times for those events. The emphasis is on the word approximate.

Acknowledgements

It took about six hours to fight the battle of Lundy's Lane. It has taken about six years to write this book and it would never have been completed without the help of numerous individuals and institutions. I can never truly repay them for their assistance, the best I can do is to acknowledge *some* of the debts I owe.

Space restrictions preclude a complete listing here of the archives, libraries and historical societies whose staff have assisted me over the years but the names of most can be found in the list of abbreviations at the back of this book. I would like to thank them all for their patient and professional responses to my numerous inquiries. In particular, however, I would like to emphasize my debt to Timothy Dubé of the Manuscript Division, National Archives of Canada, who fielded many complicated questions and drew my attention to obscure sources I might otherwise have missed.

I am fortunate to be employed at the Directorate of History, Department of National Defence, Canada, for there is no better professional environment for a military historian, or author, in this country. Over the past six years, my superiors, Dr. W.A.B. Douglas, Director, and Doctors Roger Sarty and Steven Harris, Senior Historians, have given me nothing but encouragement to complete this book while my colleagues have provided me with critical, yet positive, analysis of my work. Three of my comrades warrant special mention. Mr Réal Laurin, staff librarian and ex-sergeant, who runs a tight ship and rightfully brooks no nonsense from mere academics, responded cheerfully on his own time to my pleas for guidance in the complicated world of bibliographic search techniques. On European battlefield tours with units of the Canadian Forces, Dr. William J. ("Old Bill") McAndrew not only tried to teach me an eye for the ground but also demonstrated the shortcomings of traditional academic methodology when analyzing combat and combat stress. My thanks are particularly due to Brereton ("Gentle Ben") Greenhous, whose sunny disposition and considerate nature have always rendered him a tower of strength to his co-work-ers, and who descended upon my prose like a wolf on the fold. The result is a much shorter, much better, book.

During the past six years, old friends and fellow travellers have repeat-edly came to my aid. Brian Dunnigan, executive director of Old Fort Niagara, Youngstown, N.Y., responded to questions concerning the history of the Niagara peninsula and helped me locate many illustrations. Stuart Sutherland of Toronto put at my disposal the results of his personal research into the British officer corps of the War of 1812. Dr. John Houlding, author of the masterful *Fit for Service: The Training of the British Army. 1715-1795* (Oxford, 1981) read my early drafts and advised me on the complexities of musket period tactics. Douglas Hendry, formerly with the Public Record Office, undertook painstaking research for me in that institution's arcane record systems. James Gooding and Joyce Eakin-Gooding of Museum Res-toration Service patiently put up with requests for bibliographic and picto-rial material. Dennis Carter-Edwards of the Canadian Park Service pro-vided me with the journal of the British command engineer at the siege of Fort Erie while André Gousse of the same organization ransacked his pic-ture files for my benefit. Judith Saunders, curator of Old Fort Erie, assisted me with questions concerning that post and the siege of August-September 1814. Finally, I must not forget my old comrade "in harms", René Chartrand, who gave me the benefit of his extensive knowledge of military uniforms and military art. This is also an opportune time to thank *mon vieux ami* and "the good woman Luce" for sharing, these many years past, the warmth of their home with a cynical young cowboy just in from the west.

Military critics are tough critics and early drafts of my work received the "death of a thousand cuts" from three good soldiers and good historians. Lieutenant Colonel (Retd.) Gordon Rudd, U.S. Army, emphasized that enlisted men always complain and only a civilian like me would think such complaints, even if written down, constitute believable evidence. Colonel John Elting (Retd.) U.S. Army, prolific historian and friend, found some shocking lapses in my logic. Colonel John, who is "Old Army" in every way, also shared with me the difficulties of bringing a horse-drawn artillery bat-tery into action. The comments of my late friend, Brigadier General J.L. Summers, MC, CD, Canadian Army (Retd.), were, as usual, to the point and I have tried to obey his injunction to provide maps that show "where all your little men are going."

The writing of this book resulted in an unexpected side benefit – it brought me into contact with four fellow students of the War of 1812 from the United States and our mutual interests have developed into fine friendships. I am particularly indebted to Dr. John C. Fredriksen of Salem, Mass., whose knowledge of American manuscript sources of the war is unparalleled, and who responded magnificently to my many desperate requests for assistance. I am also extremely grateful to three other authors who opened their files to me and contributed in other positive ways to the writing of my own: Dr. John Morris of Garrettsville, Ohio, working on a biography of Jacob Brown; Patrick Wilder of Oswego, N.Y., author of *The Battle of Sackett's Harbor, 1813*; and Colonel Joseph Whitehorne, U.S. Army (Retd.), of Front Royal, Va., author of *While Washington Burned: The Battle of Fort Erie*. I must also pay my respects to Joan Morris, Katrina Wilder and Ellen Whitehorne who have patiently put up with the disruptive presence in their homes of a lanky monomaniac from the north country.

Even for military historians there is more to life than writing and I would like to express my appreciation to Wilf and Peggy Greaves for many hours of unpaid babysitting and homecooked meals that let me get on with my work at crucial moments.

Finally, I want to thank Sherry who displayed a quality of patience that goes far beyond the call of duty. For too many years she, Willy, Erica and the late Daisy the dog have been forced to share their home with the uninvited ghosts of the American Left and British Right Divisions. They can now be laid to rest.

Acknowledgements for the Second Edition (1997)

I would like to take the opportunity to thank both those persons who pointed out minor errors in the first edition and those who provided me with additional material that I have incorporated. In particular, I would like to acknowledge the assistance given by Dennis Carter-Edwards, Bill Chearos, Robert Foley, Bill Gray, Robert Henderson, Dennis Gannon, Robert Malcomson, Mikhail Murgoci, Jesse Pudwell and Esther Summers. I would particularly like to thank Mr. Nicholas Riall of the United Kingdom for providing a portrait of his distinguished ancestor, Major General Phineas Riall.

I committed a grievous error in the acknowledgements of the first edition when I neglected to thank Bill Constable, who drew the tactical maps in this book. I take this opportunity to rectify that unforgivable omission.

D.G.

John Crysler's Fields, 11 November 1813

It had rained throughout the night and dawn brought a grey morning with a cold east wind. As stiff-fingered drummers beat "Reveille" in the camp of Major General James Wilkinson's army on the Canadian shore of the St. Lawrence River, wet, shivering men threw off sodden blankets and eased to their feet. Three weeks before, Wilkinson and his troops had left Sackets Harbor at the eastern end of Lake Ontario in a flotilla of small boats to move against Montreal and it had been bad weather and tough going all the way. British gunboats had hounded the flotilla's rear while Canadian militia had sniped at it from the banks.

It was now 11 November 1813 and they were camped about eighteen miles below Ogdensburg, New York. The previous day, Wilkinson had detached a force to clear the Canadian shore ahead to prevent such harassment and he now waited for the report of its commander before proceeding further. Around 10:30 A.M., a messenger arrived with the expected word and orders were issued for the men to re-embark, but at the same time confusing reports began to filter in that a British force was advancing on the camp by land from the west. Wilkinson ordered Brigadier General John Boyd to take his own and two other brigades and "march upon the enemy."[1] Boyd moved out in the early afternoon and it was not long before the sounds of musketry and artillery fire were heard.

The firing continued for some time. Thirty-four-year-old Captain Mordecai Myers from New York, whose company of the Thirteenth Infantry had been left behind to guard the boats, listened to it with concern as he was anxious to join the his regiment fighting with Boyd. He was therefore quick to respond when an aide rode up and ordered him to form his company and march to the sound of the guns. Moving westward through a wood, Myers and his men emerged into a cleared area to find themselves on the edge of a pitched battle. Here they met Boyd who exhorted them to "Rush on, my 'jolly snorters,' you are wanted!"[2] Instead, the experienced Myers halted for a few moments to let his men "go into action coolly" and then, forming them in line, advanced slowly across the wet, muddy fields. He shortly encountered remnants of the Twenty-Fifth Infantry, running "helter skelter" from the fight. Calling out to the Twenty-Fifth's commander, Lieutenant Colonel Jonas Cutting, to find out what was happening, Myers received the reply: "My men will not stand!" "But," the young officer coldly snapped back, "you are leading them!"[3] Mordecai Myers and his men had arrived at the tail end of what later became known as the battle of Crysler's Farm.

For more than two hours, Boyd, with about two thousand men, had been trying to dislodge a smaller force of British and Canadians from the farm of Canadian John Crysler. The British commander, Lieutenant Colonel Joseph Morrison of the 89th Regiment of Foot, possessed a good eye for terrain and had chosen his position wisely. His right flank was secured by the river, his left by woods, and his front was broken by a series of ravines behind which he placed his three artillery pieces and two regular infantry units, the 49th and 89th Foot, in line. Using the superior discipline of his troops, he had fought off a series of disjointed and clumsy American attacks that withered away in the face of concentrated artillery and musket fire. The enemy "advanced quickly at the *pas de charge à la Française*," one British participant smugly recalled, "which was quickly changed by a well-directed fire from our field-pieces, to one more comporting with the dignity of the American nation."[4]

In response to the disciplined enemy volleys, Boyd's men "dodged behind stumps and opened individual fire."[5] Frantic officers attempted to get their men back into line but they persisted in seeking any available cover. Their fire was ineffectual, one British officer remembered it as being "heavy, but irregular."[6] Lieutenant Colonel Eleazar W. Ripley of the Twenty-First Infantry tried to form his men in ranks but they persisted in "shooting until their ammunition was exhausted, whereupon they could not be prevented from retiring."[7] As Boyd had brought no reserve ammunition forward, the Americans began to edge back as their cartridges ran out – at first single men, then twos and threes and, finally, whole regiments retreating in some disorder.

Seeing the Americans begin to waver, Morrison ordered an advance. Marching slowly, five companies of the 49th Foot dressed in grey greatcoats because of the weather and six companies of the 89th wearing the more traditional red coats moved forward in line. Their progress was impeded by the wet, ploughed ground and the split rail fences which criss-crossed it – but it was relentless. The American artillery (which had come late into action) fired on them, inflicting heavy casualties. In the space of ten minutes the 49th "lost eleven officers out of eighteen and men in proportion" but, reforming its ranks, advanced directly on the guns.[8]

Left without infantry support, the American gunners ceased firing as the British approached and began to limber up their guns for a withdrawal. To buy them some time, a squadron of the Second U.S. Light Dragoons charged at the right of the oncoming British line. Lieutenant Colonel Charles Plenderleath, commanding the 49th, promptly wheeled his right flank company to face the oncoming horsemen and it "poured in a volley" which left "many saddles emptied ere they went right about."[9] The dragoons' sacrifice was not in vain; all but one of the American guns were saved.

The late afternoon sky grew dark as the rain threatened to return. Covered by a scratch force that included Myers's company of the Thirteenth, Boyd withdrew to the camp leaving more than a hundred dead behind on John Crysler's fields. For the first time during the War of 1812 the United States regular army had met British regulars in a major pitched battle in the open and the result was a conclusive demonstration that raw courage was not enough to beat discipline and training. Although acknowledging the individual bravery of their opponents, British and Canadian officers who fought in the action did not form a very high opinion of the military prowess of "Cousin Jonathan," their condescending term of derision for that uncouth, bumbling, country relative who had the temerity to declare war on his betters. "This was Jonathan's debut on the open plain," one sneered, "and I think, for the future, he will prefer his old mode of acting in the bush."[10]

In the following summer of 1814, however, many of these same officers would be given good cause to revise that opinion by a far bloodier battle fought within earshot of the falls of Niagara and along a once-quiet country lane – Lundy's Lane, the locals called it.

This is the story of that battle ...

PART I

Background
to a Battle

CHAPTER 1

"A Mere Matter of Marching"–
The Coming of War

*The acquisition of Canada this year
as far as the neighbourhood of Quebec
will be a mere matter of marching.*
THOMAS JEFFERSON, 1812

Young Jarvis Hanks of the Eleventh Regiment of Infantry, United States Army, found it quite a chore to keep up as his unit marched from French Mills, New York, toward Sackets Harbor in February of 1814. An unseasonable thaw had transformed the roads into a quagmire that made the going tough for a fourteen-year-old drummer boy with shorter legs than his adult comrades – and those short legs clad in a pair of breeches Jarvis had tailored himself out of an old blanket. But Drummer boy Hanks was inured to the rigours of military life and passed the time by "associating with the most lo-quacious of my comrades" so that "the pleasures of friendly converse, soon diverted my mind from the present troubles of marching and privations."

Jarvis Hanks had been beating the drum for three years for his own pleasure when an army recruiting party arrived in his sleepy little village of Pawlet, Vermont, in the spring of 1813. An imaginative lad, he immediately became "fired with ardour in anticipation of a soldier's career" and "a desire to engage in the service which was not to be relinquished." An obliging officer confidently assured his anxious and doting parents that such a child "would not be compelled to go into battle" but would be retained for recruiting purposes. So it came to pass that, six months short of his fourteenth birthday, Jarvis Hanks enlisted in the regular army for the duration of the present war between the United States and Great Britain.

He shortly discovered, as have so many, that a soldier's life did not measure up to the scenes of glory played out in his imagination. He was soon "sorry enough" that he "had exchanged the comforts of my mother's cupboard" for greasy, raw pork and was surprised to see that the army had "no special regard" for the Sabbath, which in camp was a day like any other. As for sleeping arrangements, he quickly learned to appreciate the "soft side of a pine board." Jarvis Hanks also experienced the grim side of military life, watching with horror as a sixteen-year-old convicted deserter was "launched into eternity" by a hangman's noose. In November 1813, as he stood in the ranks as his regiment exchanged volleys of musketry with British regulars at Crysler's Farm, he wryly remembered the recruiting officer's promise that he would not have to go into battle.

But the army wasn't all bad. For one thing, he liked beating his blue and red drum with its fierce, patriotic eagle emblem painted on the shell. For another, he got a ride in one of the new steamboats. And then there was the whisky ration. Young Hanks had "no love for fire water" and drank his daily gill once only "to test his mettle" but an older comrade, Jemmy Thompson, did have a liking for the stuff and was only too glad to relieve Jarvis of the necessity of downing it. In return Jemmy cooked his victuals, washed his clothes, "hooked anything that was wanted" and generally kept an eye on the lad. After ten months with the Eleventh Infantry, Jarvis was comfortable with military life and might have come to like it even more if his soldier friends hadn't kept getting killed in the war.[1]

In the memoir of his experiences that he left for his descendants, Jarvis Hanks never expressed much interest in the origins of this war. Indeed they are still a matter of some dispute among historians but most are agreed that the roots of the War of 1812 can be traced back to the 1783 Treaty of Paris which marked the conclusion of the Revolutionary War between Great Britain and her former colonies. The treaty ended the fighting but did not establish good relations between the two former enemies nor did the signatories live up to its terms. When the new American government failed to compensate the Loyalists, those former citizens who remained true to the British connection, Britain had a convenient excuse to retain her military posts in the northern territory of the new republic.

In the early 1790s, the Indian nations of the northwest, the region around the upper Great Lakes, formed a military confederacy to resist the encroaching tide of American settlement. This confederacy defeated several military expeditions sent against it, and many Americans suspected that it was being actively encouraged and supported by Britain. The growing tension between the two countries was lessened by the American victory over the Indians at the battle of Fallen Timbers in 1794 and a resulting treaty with the confederacy pushed the borders of American settlement north and west. Cooler heads also prevailed in diplomatic circles and the United States and Great Britain signed the Jay Treaty that same year to end their differences and regularize their relations. In accordance with the terms of this treaty, the British evacuated the posts they had maintained on American soil since 1783.

New sources of friction arose, however, fuelled by the global conflict between France and Britain that began in 1793. American shipowners were caught in the middle when both Britain and France passed a series of embargoes forbidding ships that traded with one nation from trading with the other. To force both belligerents to recognize American maritime rights, the United States Congress passed a series of legislative acts between 1806 and 1810 that restricted American trade with both nations. These measures proved more harmful, however, to the economy of the United States than they did to either Britain or France.

American frustration was further increased by the actions of the Royal Navy. Desperate for wartime manpower, British warships frequently boarded American vessels looking for deserters, and although American seamen carried identification papers, British naval officers often refused to recognize them. Between 1803 and 1807 many Americans (estimates run as high as a thousand per year) were impressed into the Royal Navy to languish in the lower decks of His Majesty's warships. In 1807, to add insult to this injury, HMS *Leopard* fired into the unprepared American frigate, USS *Chesapeake*, after she had refused to allow the British crew to board her and search for deserters serving in her crew. Although British officials disavowed the action and (after a lengthy delay) made restitution, the incident stoked a growing American resentment of Great Britain.[2]

Resentment turned to anger when there was a recurrence of trouble in the northwest caused by the creation of a new Indian confederacy under the charismatic Shawnee chief Tecumseh. President James Madison sent a force of regulars to the area which, in November 1811, dispersed the confederacy at the battle of Tippecanoe. When Tecumseh and the survivors of the battle sought refuge in Canada, it heightened American suspicions that the British were behind the unrest on the frontiers and a growing number of Americans began to talk seriously of war with Great Britain.

Against this sombre background, the Twelfth Congress met in November

1811. The mid-term elections of 1810 had seen the rise of a new "war hawk" faction within the governing Republican party that dominated Congress, especially the crucial House Foreign Relations Committee, which, in response to Madison's call to "put the nation in armour," tabled a report on 29 November 1811 calling for measures to prepare for war.[3] Although the opposition Federalists urged caution and the New England states were generally against hostilities, a nationalistic mood was sweeping the country. Congress passed legislation increasing the size of the American military establishment and by the spring of 1812 the republic was actively preparing for war.

At the last moment British leaders awoke and took long overdue steps to appease the United States. The Royal Navy was ordered to respect the rights of American ships and sailors and to stop violating American waters. Britain also offered the United States a share of European trade and on 16 June 1812 went further and suspended the Orders-in-Council that governed her embargoes, eliminating many of the restrictions that had been so damaging to American commerce. It was too late, a decade of insensitivity had hardened attitudes in Washington and President James Madison rejected these overtures Two days later Congress, with the rallying cry "Free Trade and Sailors' Rights!," declared war on Britain.

The United States, with its small regular navy, had no prospect of challenging Britain's overwhelming strength on the high seas. Madison and his cabinet therefore decided that their best option was to bring America's superior numbers to bear on the British colonies in Canada. Their acquisition would destroy the Indian threat and give the United States an important bargaining chip in any peace negotiations. There were also economic considerations. Madison believed that Napoleon's Continental system, which closed European ports to British trade, would ultimately prevent Britain from trading with Scandinavia, the traditional supplier of the masts and timber necessary to maintain the Royal Navy. If that happened, Britain would be dependent on her North American colonies for this vital resource and, if deprived of those colonies, she would have no choice but to accept American terms for trade if she wished to retain an empire based on maritime communications. Thus, the Canadas were not only a convenient theatre of war for the United States; they were a prize worth fighting for.[4]

American leaders were confident. Former President Thomas Jefferson predicted that the annexation of Canada was a "mere matter of marching."[5] And marching it would have to be, for in the face of British sea power,

American armies would have to move by land. But in the rush to war the United States had not considered the difficulties of mounting a campaign on her northern frontier. To permit an army to operate in that area, supplies would have to be transported over a considerable distance, a laborious and time-consuming business as there were few roads and the major north-south water routes involved lengthy and difficult portages. Compounding these problems were long winters, short summers and heavy precipitation which curtailed the campaigning season and adversely affected the health and mobility of armies. There was also the problem of the Great Lakes. A successful invasion must depend on obtaining control of lakes Erie, Ontario and Champlain, but at the outbreak of war only Britain had a substantial naval presence on these lakes – the Provincial Marine, a small colonial fleet.[6]

The importance of naval power on the lakes was not apparent to Madison's cabinet in Washington when they planned their first campaign against the two British colonies of Upper and Lower Canada. On the map, they seemed easy targets as their communications and logistics paralleled the border and were vulnerable at several points. Throughout the spring and summer of 1812, before the declaration of war, Madison and his cabinet had consulted with various military leaders and decided that major operations would be mounted against Montreal and across the Detroit river with diversionary attacks against Kingston at the eastern end of Lake Ontario and the Niagara at the western end. If successful, these operations would conquer the province of Upper Canada, isolate the western Indians, gain control of the Great Lakes, take Montreal and put the United States in a position to mount an attack the following year against Quebec City, the capital of British North America.[7]

It was an ambitious plan, requiring careful preparation and a large, well-trained military force. But the United States did not possess such a force. Always small, the American army had suffered from years of neglect by administrations who preferred cheaper, more numerous militia over a more expensive permanent force. In preparation for war, Congress had tripled the army's strength on paper but recruiting was hampered by the unpopularity of the regular service. Against Canada Madison favoured the use of militia and in the spring of 1812 called for fifty thousand volunteers; the response was so disappointing that the government belatedly turned to increasing the regular force. The army's numbers grew only slowly, and by the outbreak of war it consisted of no more than twelve thousand men, about one-third of its authorized strength of thirty-five thousand.[8]

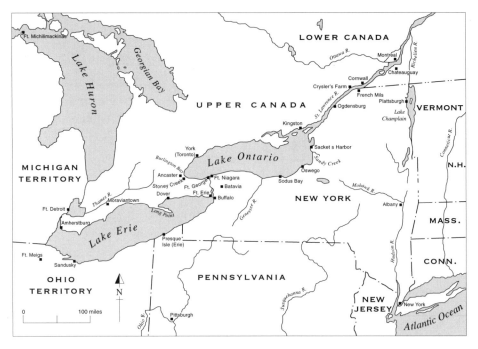

The northern theatre of war, 1812–1815

Numbers were not the only problem. From top to bottom, the army lacked leadership. The Secretary of War, Dr. William Eustis, a man obsessed with detail, proved incapable of mobilizing the republic and the provision of war materiel became muddled in administrative chaos. Ignoring advice to mix the prewar regulars and new recruits within each unit, Eustis left most of the old regiments in their garrisons in Louisiana and the west and attempted to invade Canada with newly raised units.

To command them the government had no choice but to appoint aging veterans of the revolutionary war or politically-connected militia officers as generals. At an average age of fifty-five, these leaders did not inspire confidence – one prewar officer sardonically (and prophetically) remarked that "it is only after several of us who have some knowledge of military business are sacrificed, that men will be placed to lead who are now in the ranks or in obscurity."[9] Even worse, many of the junior officers, who had obtained commissions because of political connections, proved to be "men of no talents for military life" who were "lazy, drinking gamblers and a "dead weight."[10] The United States thus entered its first major war with an army that was untrained, under strength and poorly led.[11]

The defence of Canada was the responsibility of forty-five-year-old Lieutenant General Sir George Prevost, a veteran of considerable service. To defend the nearly half million inhabitants of British North America against the United States with a population of six million, he had only 8400 British regulars and fencibles, or Canadian regulars, thinly spread from Halifax on the Atlantic to posts on the upper Great Lakes. With the exception of Quebec, none of the towns in Canada was properly fortified and most of the so-called frontier "forts" were small posts that functioned more as supply depots than as military defence works. Everything – soldiers, money, provisions, weapons – was in short supply and Prevost could not count on much assistance from a Britain preoccupied with the war against Napoleon.[12]

Prevost's plan was to abandon no part of Canada but to defend vigorously only the most important points. Certain that the war would be brought to a diplomatic end before there was heavy fighting, he adopted a defensive strategy of "wary measures and occasional daring enterprises" that suited his essentially cautious nature.[13] Halifax and Quebec were vital parts of his sea link to Britain, but as Halifax was protected by the Royal Navy, he regarded the security of Quebec as his primary objective. The best overland route for an invader trying to approach Quebec was by way of Montreal, either along the shore of the St. Lawrence from Lake Ontario or by the Hudson-Lake

Lieutenant General Sir George Prevost, British Army (1767-1816)
The governor general and commander-in-chief of British North America during the war, Prevost was cool, controlled and cautious. An excellent administrator, he was a somewhat nervous field commander and his erratic performances at Sackets Harbor in 1813 and Plattsburgh in 1814 blighted what was otherwise a long and productive career. (Courtesy, Chateau Ramezay Museum, Montreal)

Champlain-Richelieu corridor that debouched into the St. Lawrence valley southeast of Montreal. Prevost therefore placed the bulk of his regular forces around that city and stationed only a small part of his strength in Upper Canada. If pressed, he was prepared to abandon that province and fall back on Montreal until reinforcements reached him from Britain.

The American campaign of 1812 bogged down from the outset. Major General Henry Dearborn concentrated his forces near Albany but found they consisted of raw levies that first had to be trained. It was not until November, too late in the season, that Dearborn moved north against Montreal. Transport difficulties and the refusal of Dearborn's militia, which made up much of his strength, to cross the border caused him to withdraw after a brief demonstration. The diversionary attacks against Kingston and the Niagara never took place because the militia generals in command realized their forces were inadequate for such operations.

In the west Brigadier General William Hull, responsible for the attack across the Detroit river, only reached the area in early July. He made a brief foray into Upper Canada but, worried about his long and tenuous supply line, withdrew to the village of Detroit on 11 August. Five days later Major General Isaac Brock, the British commander in Upper Canada, moved on Detroit with a much smaller force of regulars, militia and Indians. In a colossal bluff he urged Hull to surrender, explaining that, once fighting commenced, he would be unable to control his Indians and a massacre might result. His nerve gone, Hull surrendered his entire army without a fight.

This victory had an electric effect on the people of Upper Canada. There was reason for optimism as it appeared that the war, barely begun, might soon end, but on 13 October 1812 an American force under the command of New York Colonel Solomon Van Rensselaer crossed the Niagara and occupied the heights overlooking the village of Queenston. Brock, at nearby Fort George, gathered up what troops he could and attacked the American position but was killed in the fighting. The American force, however, was cut off from the river and forced to surrender after fierce fighting. All was then quiet on the Niagara until 28 November when Van Rensselaer's successor, Brigadier General Alexander Smyth, made an abortive attempt to land near Fort Erie. Winter then brought a halt to military operations.

By the close of 1812 it was obvious to Madison and his cabinet that the conquest of Canada would require more than "marching." Changes of command were necessary and in January 1813 Eustis was replaced as secretary of war by John Armstrong, Continental Army veteran and amateur strategist. Armstrong took firm control of the War Department, brought order to the administrative chaos left by Eustis and replaced many of the aged, incompetent generals with younger, more capable men.

The events of the first abortive campaign had demonstrated to the United States the importance of gaining naval superiority on the lakes. In November 1812 Captain Isaac Chauncey, USN, was dispatched, with an army of workmen, to construct warships on the lakes. He established his main base at Sackets Harbor, New York, the best anchorage on the American side of Lake Ontario, and created satellite shipyards at Plattsburgh, New York, on Lake Champlain and Presque Isle, Pennsylvania, on Lake Erie. In response, the British Admiralty sent Captain Sir James Lucas Yeo, RN, to take over the Provincial Marine and initiate naval construction at Kingston while Captain Robert Barclay, RN, did the same at Amherstburg on Lake Erie. Throughout the war, both navies engaged in a shipbuilding race on the lakes that would give first one, then the other, temporary superiority.

As spring approached, Madison and Armstrong turned their attention toward operations for 1813. The secretary decided to attack Kingston, the British naval base on Lake Ontario. If Kingston fell, Upper Canada would be cut off and the British territory to the west could be rolled up at leisure. Chauncey expected to have naval superiority on Lake Ontario when the campaign season opened in April so Armstrong ordered Dearborn to move his army from the Lake Champlain area to Sackets Harbor and co-operate with the navy in an attack on Kingston.

This plan immediately began to go awry. Dearborn and Chauncey convinced themselves that Kingston was too strong and decided instead to attack the subsidiary objective of York. Surprisingly, Armstrong agreed to the change and on 27 April 1813 Dearborn's troops landed at York (present-day Toronto), the capital of Upper Canada, which they captured after a brief fight. Dearborn then sailed for Fort Niagara where he waited until 27 May before making a successful attack against Fort George on the opposite bank of the Niagara River. This proved to be the high point of Dearborn's campaign as a probe toward the British base at Burlington Bay (present-day Hamilton) was stopped by a confusing night action at Stoney Creek on 6 June and another American force was forced to surrender at Beaver Dams on 24 June. Suffering from illness, Dearborn turned over command to Brigadier General John Boyd, who kept his army within the immediate vicinity of Fort George. Here they spent a long, hot and sickly summer in a loose state of siege from a numerically-inferior British force.

In September 1813 Armstrong came north to try to put some momentum back into his campaign. Again he let himself be again dissuaded from an attack on Kingston by Dearborn's successor, Major General James Wilkinson, in favour of a two-pronged offensive against Montreal. One force under Wilkinson's personal command would move by boat down the St. Lawrence while another, under Major General Wade Hampton, would march overland from the Lake Champlain area.

Accordingly the bulk of the regular troops were shifted from Fort George to Sackets Harbor and by late October all was ready. Wilkinson's army, four thousand strong, embarked in an armada of small boats and rowed for the St. Lawrence. However, Wilkinson's resolve, never strong, disappeared after a detachment of his army (which included Jarvis Hanks) was beaten by a smaller British force at John Crysler's Farm on 11 November in the engagement recounted in the prologue to this book. When he learned that Hampton had retreated after suffering a similar defeat in a brisk little action at Chateauguay on 26 October, Wilkinson cancelled the offensive against Montreal and went into winter quarters at French Mills, New York, across the St. Lawrence from Cornwall. His men were condemned to spend a miserable time shivering through a northern winter in a hastily-prepared and inadequate camp.

Defeats in the east were balanced by victories in the west. Major General William Henry Harrison successfully defended his base at Fort Meigs on the Maumee River near Lake Erie against two attacks by British Brigadier General Henry Procter and the Indian leader Tecumseh in May and July 1813. A disaster followed when Barclay, Procter's naval counterpart, was defeated by an American naval squadron at Put-In Bay on 10 September with the loss of all the British ships. Harrison then went on the offensive and by early October had retaken Detroit and was hot on the heels of Procter, who attempted to retreat to the safety of Burlington Bay. Catching up with the British general at the Thames River on 5 October, Harrison reduced his tired and dispirited army to a rabble – Procter escaped but Tecumseh was killed in the rout. Harrison continued on to Fort George where he found militia Brigadier General George McClure with twelve hundred New Yorkers. Ordered to Sackets Harbor, Harrison boarded Chauncey's ships and on 16 November sailed for that place.

McClure was a nervous man. His militia were beginning to disappear as their terms of enlistment expired and, feeling increasingly isolated, he decided to withdraw across the river to the more easily defended Fort Niagara. McClure had instructions from Armstrong to burn Newark if it was necessary to the defence of Fort George, but on 10 December he ordered the destruction of the village even though he abandoned the fort. When British troops arrived the next morning, they viewed "a ruin, nothing to be seen but brick chimneys standing, what the fire could not destroy, of the once beautiful town of Newark."[14]

The British commander in Upper Canada, Lieutenant General Gordon Drummond, immediately demanded to know whether the destruction of Newark "had been committed by the authority of the American government, or is the unauthorized act of any Individual."[15] McClure made no reply but an angry Armstrong ordered Wilkinson to formally disavow the action on the part of the United States. Unmollified, Drummond coldly decided that "retributive justice demanded of me a speedy retaliation on the opposite shore of America."[16]

In the early hours of 19 December 1813, a British and Canadian force crossed the river and moved on Fort Niagara. They were able to gain entrance, and after a short and vicious fight the fort was in British hands.[17] In the days that followed, Drummond's subordinate, Major General Phineas Riall (pronounced "rile"), scoured the American side of the Niagara, destroying supply depots and barracks at Lewiston and Schlosser, burning the little village of Buffalo to the ground and razing every building between that place and Lewiston, a distance of some twenty-five miles. The American side of the Niagara became a wasteland and it was with no little satisfaction that Drummond reported to Prevost the "infliction of a severe retaliation for the burning of the town of Newark."[18]

After eighteen months of war, the United States was staring defeat in the face. The war in Europe was winding down and Britain would soon be in a position to send massive reinforcements to North America, reinforcements that would not only be able to defend Canada but also to launch a major invasion of the United States. Unnerved by the failure of the recent campaign, Madison agreed to a British offer to hold peace talks, but it would be some time before negotiations could commence. Meanwhile, New York Governor Daniel D. Tompkins was pressing for action to protect his state's defenceless Niagara frontier. To placate him, Armstrong ordered Colonel Winfield Scott, one of the most promising officers in the army, to Albany with orders to organize a force to serve on the Niagara. At the same time the secretary directed Wilkinson to break up his camp at French Mills and march the greater part of his army to Plattsburgh. The other part was ordered to Sackets Harbor under the command of Major General Jacob Brown.[19]

On 13 February 1814, Brown set out for the Harbor with two thousand men, among them Drummer Hanks, now a seasoned veteran with a campaign behind him. Brown arrived at the Harbor three days later to find an order appointing him commander of the Left Division of Military District Nine. This district, which included Vermont and the northern part of New York, was divided into two subordinate commands – Major General George Izard, with headquarters at Plattsburgh, commanded the Right Division with responsibility for the Champlain area and the St. Lawrence, while Brown, with headquarters at Sackets Harbor, was to be responsible for the New York frontier west to the Pennsylvania border.[20]

Jacob Jennings Brown was thirty-nine when he assumed command at Sackets Harbor. His appointment was something of a gamble on Armstrong's part, for Brown was not a professional soldier although he had a reputation as a fighter. He had first attracted attention as a New York militia general when he had repulsed a British raid on Ogdensburg in October 1812. That, and his prominent role during the British attack on Sackets Harbor in May 1813, had led to a commission as a brigadier general in the regular army. He had served with distinction during the ill-fated St. Lawrence expedition of the previous autumn, fighting two small but successful actions, and had gained promotion to major general.

Of Pennsylvania Quaker origins, Brown was a somewhat unlikely candidate for a general. He had received a good education and worked as a schoolmaster and surveyor before coming to the attention of Alexander Hamilton, who was raising an army for the threatened war with France. Hamilton had appointed him his secretary and Brown served in this capacity until the crisis subsided. In 1799 he left for a large tract of wilderness he had purchased with his father and brothers in the Black River country of northern New York, and for the next thirteen years worked hard to develop the little community of Brownville, building roads, mills and dams and acting as land agent, surveyor and magistrate.[21]

His local prominence led to him being commissioned in the state militia, and by 1812 he had reached the rank of brigadier general. In his own words, Brown "was not one of those who believe a war with Great Britain is the best thing that can happen to my country" but when war came, he per-

Major General Jacob Brown, U.S. Army (1775-1822)
Almost forgotten today, Jacob Brown fought and won more pitched battles against British regular troops than any other American general in history. A militia officer with a reputation as a fighter, he was brought into the regular army and given command of the Left Division early in 1814. During the following summer, he demonstrated that, properly led and trained, American troops were capable of beating the British regular in open battle. (Portrait by James Herring after an original by John Wesley Jarvis. Courtesy of the New York Historical Society, Neg. 6384.)

formed his duty without hesitation.[22] Described as above average height, with good features, Brown's outward demeanour reflected his Quaker up-bringing – calm, practical, orderly and considerate. These were qualities that appealed to the militia, who had little respect or liking for military pomp and circumstance, and Brown was able to get more out of these citizen soldiers than any other American general of the war. He displayed a resourcefulness derived from an active, seeking intellect unafraid to try novel or untried means to solve problems. He also possessed great determination and was straightforward in his dealings with superiors, peers and subordinates.

But Brown did have weaknesses. He was not always able to control a quick temper and his determination could turn into an obstinacy that would not let him withdraw from a course of action even if events proved that course to be wrong. Compared to some of his predecessors in the northern army, however, this obstinacy appeared almost as a virtue.

Having got a fighting general into the most important command on the frontier, Armstrong resolved to carry his long-cherished goal: an attack on the British naval base at Kingston. On 9 March 1814, Brown received a puzzling communication from the secretary. Stating that the British intended to attack Detroit and would probably take troops from Kingston, Armstrong urged Brown to make a surprise attack on that place if certain conditions were met: the Kingston garrison was actually weakened, the roads and weather were favourable and Chauncey agreed to co-operate. To cover his intentions, Armstrong directed Brown to "use the enclosed letter to mask your object, and let no one into your secret but Chauncey."[23] This second letter stated that Scott had been ordered to take a train of heavy artillery to attack Fort Niagara and directed Brown, if he thought Sackets Harbor secure, to march west to join him.

It is not clear how the secretary of war expected Brown to use this second and false letter and his overly-clever ruse proved too much for Brown's straightforward disposition. Concluding that an attack on Kingston was impossible because a recent thaw had made the ice unsafe, Brown decided to follow the instructions in the second letter. He therefore set out in mid-March 1814 for the Niagara with a brigade of infantry and some field artillery. These troops were the nucleus of a field formation that was sometimes called either the First Division of the Ninth Military District or the Army of the Niagara. Brown always called it the Left Division in his official correspondence and that term will be used to identify his army in this book.[24]

The misunderstandings produced by Armstrong's confusing instructions led to considerable marching and counter-marching on the part of Left Division while Brown tried to comprehend his orders. Finally, at Batavia, N.Y., he received a communication from the secretary. Armstrong, who had learned of the westward move, chided Brown for mistaking his meaning, concluding with the admonition that "if you hazard anything by this mistake, correct it promptly by returning to your post," but if "you left the Harbor with a competent force for its defence, go on and prosper" as "good consequences are sometimes the result of mistakes."[25] The secretary's tacit approval of Brown's error shifted American operational emphasis from the Montreal-Kingston corridor. In doing so, Armstrong was in some measure responding to Tompkins's demands for action on the Niagara and, the same day he penned his comforting words to Brown, the secretary ordered Scott to join him.[26]

Quick off the mark, Scott had actually caught up with Brown at Batavia on 7 April, a full day before Brown received Armstrong's approval of his westward march. The two men knew each other, having served together in Wilkinson's army during the campaign of the previous autumn. Brown then moved west again, intending to concentrate his forces at Buffalo, "with a view to passing into the enemies country."[27] As they neared their destination, his men were angered by the destruction caused by the British campaign of fire and sword of the previous December. In the village of Buffalo itself the only brick building standing was a tavern and most of the inhabitants were "living in sheds of frame lined with rough boards."[28] Jarvis Hanks recalled that the sight "gave us feelings of deep sympathy for the desolate and plundered inhabitants; and sharpened up our courage to prepare for effectual retaliation."[29]

While Scott laid out a camp site near the village, Brown tried to make some sense out of his situation. His perceived objective was the recapture of Fort Niagara, but beyond Armstrong's confusing second (and false) letter, Brown had no definite orders to attack that place. In any case, he decided that such an attack was unfeasible given the state of the roads which would not bear heavy artillery (a conclusion that was hardly relevant since he had left all his heavy guns behind at the Harbor). Considering other options, he proposed to Armstrong that his division cross Lake Erie and, joining with troops from Detroit, move on the main British depot at Burlington Bay. With the aid of Chauncey and his ships, they would then attack the forts at the mouth of the Niagara River. As Brown saw it, such an operation would make effective use of American naval superiority on Lake Erie and create a maximum amount of return with a minimum number of troops.[30]

Before Armstrong could reply, Brown received a panicky communication from Brigadier General Edmund P. Gaines, whom he had left in command at the Harbor, reporting that it was under threat of imminent attack. Concerned about the safety of the major American naval base on Lake Ontario and confident that "Scott can do all that is necessary," Brown turned over command of the troops at Buffalo to that officer and returned to the Harbor on 20 April.[31]

In Washington, meanwhile, Madison and his cabinet had been pondering their next move throughout the spring. There was a sense of urgency, if not quite desperation, in the air – Napoleon's abdication in April had ended the war in Europe and it would not be long before Prevost received reinforcements. The British and American peace commissioners had not yet commenced discussions and successful offensive action was needed to give the American delegates a stronger hand in the negotiations to come. To be successful, the United States had to achieve local superiority somewhere on the northern frontier and, as the bulk of the British army was positioned around Montreal, the cabinet began to favour the western theatre. Unable to decide, however, they vacillated and valuable days of campaigning went to waste.[32]

Finally, on 7 June, Madison called an extraordinary session to establish the military priorities for 1814. The resulting plan underscored the government's strategic confusion. The most vulnerable point in the British defence, Kingston, was ignored in favour of a demonstration by Izard's Right Division against Montreal. The real emphasis was to be in the west: part of the Lake Erie squadron would transport a landing force to Mackinac at the mouth of Lake Michigan while the other part would land Brown's Left Division on the north shore of Lake Erie. Brown's initial objective was to be Burlington and later, with the co-operation of Chauncey, York and Kingston. The cabinet noted that Brown's success would "depend on Commodore Chauncey getting control of the lake [Ontario], without which supplies could not be received, and with which these might be conveyed safely by water from depots on the south side of Lake Ontario."[33]

In transmitting the cabinet's decision to Brown on 10 June, Armstrong, noting that all military operations "begin with the belly," cast doubt on whether Brown possessed the land transport to mount such a prolonged operation. Even if Brown took Burlington, the secretary reasoned, he could do nothing until Chauncey was out on Lake Ontario and Armstrong did not think that this would be before the end of June at the earliest. Thus, the secretary concluded, "though the operation be approved, its execution must be suspended till Chauncey shall have gained command of the Lake." In a fateful phrase, however, Armstrong suggested that, to "give immediate occupation to your troops and to prevent their blood from stagnating ... why not take Fort Erie" and "push forward a Corps to seize the bridge of the Chippeway and be governed by circumstances either in stopping there or going further." If attacked, Brown should not "decline a contest" as a victory would enable him to avail himself "in the most direct way of Commodore Chauncey's aid, (should he beat Yeo)," to capture Forts George and Niagara.[34] This seeming afterthought by Armstrong was the genesis of the Niagara campaign of 1814.

This letter took over two weeks to reach Brown at Buffalo where he had returned in early June. Brown decided to follow the Armstrong's advice and

Major General George Izard, U.S. Army (1776-1828)
The commander of the American Right Division, Izard was a well-qualified officer educated in European military schools. In late September 1814, he assumed command in the Niagara but unable to make any progress, withdrew his troops to the United States in November bringing the 1814 Niagara campaign to a close. (From Benson Lossing, *Pictorial Field Book of the War of 1812* (New York, 1869))

mount a limited campaign. Choosing to cross the Niagara directly from Buffalo, he ordered his quartermaster to have enough boats ready by 1 July to
transport the bulk of his division. He then requested Chauncey to state exactly when he would take the squadron out on Lake Ontario and whether
Brown could expect to meet him at Fort George by 15 July.[35]

Dated 25 June 1814, Chauncey's reply was equivocal. He expected to be
ready by the first week in July but his actions would be governed by the British. If Yeo, the British naval commander on Lake Ontario, accepted a battle, Chauncey would either go to Kingston or "be at leisure to co-operate
with you in any Enterprise against the money" but, if the British naval commander refused action, Chauncey would stay with him and would only sail
to the Niagara if the enemy did.[36] In a short note written the same day
Chauncey added that "I shall sail on or about the 10th [of July] but I shall
not leave this vicinity unless the Enemy's fleet leads me up the Lake."[37]

Although the American naval commander made it quite clear that his
movements would depend on those of the British fleet, not the American
army, Brown appears to have read what he wanted to read in these words.
He construed Chauncey's words to mean that the commodore would meet
him on the shore of Lake Ontario on or about the 10th of July – an error
that was to colour the forthcoming campaign. Brown needed Chauncey's
ships to transport the heavy artillery from Sackets Harbor necessary for an
attack on the forts at the mouth of the Niagara River and he also needed
the American squadron for logistical purposes. Operating on the Canadian
side of the Niagara without the fleet, Brown's overland line of communications back to Buffalo would be threatened to the east by the British-held
Fort Niagara and vulnerable on the west to attack from Burlington Bay. If
Chauncey did not appear after the Left Division moved into Canada, it
might be cut off and crushed between superior forces.

Worried that "Sir James [Yeo] will not meet Chauncey and Chauncey
will not meet me," Brown discussed the problem with his two senior subordinates, Brigadier Generals Winfield Scott and Eleazar W. Ripley.[38] Ripley
favoured delaying a crossing until Chauncey was on the lake but the aggressive Scott was anxious to cross immediately. Turning it over in his mind,
Brown decided to go ahead because an invasion of Upper Canada would "at
least ... restore the tarnished military character" of the United States, "an
object worth the sacrifice of the whole force he commanded."[39] Brown was
confident because he knew his Left Division was the best-trained fighting
force in the American army.[40]

Major General Jacob Brown's Left Division, United States Army

Brave Brown and Scott next taught the foe,
And taught 'em mighty quick, sirs,
That we had still kept up the breed
Of our old Seventy-Sixers!

(Chorus)
Yankee Doodle is the tune,
It comes so 'nation handy,
And nothing makes a Briton run
Like Yankee Doodle Dandy!

SONG, "THE NEW YANKEE DOODLE DANDY," 1814

The Left Division's high state of preparation was the work of Winfield Scott. Six feet, five inches tall, broad-shouldered, full-chested, handsome and stern, Scott looked the perfect "God of War."[1] A Virginian, he had read the law before obtaining a captain's commission in the artillery in 1808. He had served in Louisiana, where he ran afoul of Wilkinson with the result that he was suspended from duty for a year. He put this time to good purpose studying military texts. When war broke out, Scott received a double promotion to lieutenant colonel and command of a battalion of the Second Artillery Regiment. "At the age of 26, with a hot war before me," he later recalled, "there was nothing to be desired but the continued favor of Providence."[2]

Scott's war record was impressive. He had commanded at Queenston Heights during the latter part of the battle and spent some time as a prisoner before being paroled. He rejoined the northern army in May 1813 as colonel of the Second Artillery and, acting as chief of staff to Dearborn, planned and led the successful assault on Fort George that same month.

Three months later he led an amphibious raid on York. With Brown, he had been one of the few senior officers to distinguish himself during the abortive 1813 offensive against Montreal, winning a minor action at Hoople's (or Uphold's) Creek while the main force was being defeated at Crysler's Farm. In the spring of 1814 the twenty-eight-year-old Scott was rewarded by being promoted the youngest general officer in the army.

Large in frame and reputation, Scott was a natural leader. He possessed an extensive knowledge of the theoretical aspects of his profession which he expanded constantly by means of a personal reference library. He was aggressive in the extreme, always seeking opportunities for offensive action and, once committed, persisting until his objective was achieved. But his weaknesses were also writ large. He was impetuous to the point of rashness and his strong will and great resolve bordered on inflexibility – Scott could be plain pig-headed. His personal ambition was boundless and it was coupled with a touchy vanity that would explode if he felt his deeds were not properly recognized. This ambitious side of his nature did not pass unnoticed. Major Jacob Hindman of the artillery, who served with him throughout the war, regarded Scott "as a great intriguer" who "was never my friend, he is professionally so from motives."[3]

When he turned over command at Buffalo to Scott in April 1814, Brown directed him to "attend particularly" to the infantry of the Left Division and "cause them to be placed in that high State of discipline which such excellent material warrants."[4] Scott had the advantage of working with veteran troops as the four regiments under his command – the Ninth, Eleventh, Twenty-First and Twenty-Fifth Infantry – were experienced units which, as Brown remarked, "I shall be willing to trust myself with in any situation."[5] The artillery was drawn from Scott's old regiment, the Second, which he himself had trained, and led by capable officers. The men in these units were far from being raw recruits – even one of their most humble members, Drummer Hanks, had seen combat – and Scott was happy to find that his command was "composed of regiments with whose high Character for discipline – patience under fatigues and conduct in view of danger, he [was] well acquainted."[6] To a friend, he boasted that, if "of such materials, I do not make the best army now in service by the 1st June, I will agree to be dismissed [from] the service."[7]

It was not training that was lacking in the American army, it was effective training, and this deficiency had been exacerbated by other problems. The army had been saddled with a succession of aged and incompetent sen-

**General Winfield Scott, U.S. Army
(1786-1866)**
Tall, stern and imposing, 28-year-old
Winfield Scott was a highly professional officer who put the Left Division through a rigorous training
camp at Buffalo in the spring of
1814. He was badly wounded at
Lundy's Lane but survived to become
one of the dominant figures in the
19th-century U.S. army. (Courtesy,
National Portrait Gallery, Smithsonian
Institution, Neg. 07910)

MAJOR GEN.ᴸ WINFIELD SCOTT,
Of the United States army.

ior officers who enjoyed neither the respect nor the trust of their men.
Many of the junior officers, commissioned directly from civilian life, were
"swaggerers, dependants, [and] decayed gentlemen ... utterly unfit for military service."[8] Weak leadership caused low morale and created other difficulties that dogged an army campaigning in a remote theatre: poor health,
inadequate rations, shortages of uniforms and equipment, overdue pay and
a general lack of discipline. The result was a desertion rate that, by the
spring of 1814, was nearing disastrous proportions.[9]

Scott could not do much about the personnel of the officer corps, nor did
he really have to, as the relentless process of elimination that is war had
begun to solve the problem. The average age of an American general officer
was now thirty-four, down from fifty-five at the outbreak of the war, and the
1814 generals were men like Brown, Scott and Ripley who had proven
themselves in combat. Improvement at the top was mirrored at the lower
levels. The dilettante "butterflies" of the early war years – officers who
served in the summer but who "at the first appearance of winter fled their
commands to bask in the sunshine of court influence" – were replaced by
tough and competent veterans.[10]

One by one, Scott tackled the other problems. He had seen at first hand
the disastrous effect a poorly administered camp could have on the health
of soldiers, having been present at the notorious Terre-aux-Boeufs camp in
Louisiana in 1809-1810 where approximately one thousand men (a fifth of
the enlisted strength of the army) had been lost through sickness. He had
also served at Fort George in 1813 when sickness hospitalized seven hun-

dred men, one third of the garrison, with only three surgeons to attend to their needs. He knew that the Niagara area with its heavy precipitation and long, humid summers was unhealthy and took pains to select the best available camp site and maintain the highest standards of sanitation. The location he chose, Flint Hill, was on commanding ground west of Buffalo and enjoyed fresh water, good drainage and cooling breezes off Lake Erie.[11]

"Discipline is but the second object," Scott informed his officers, "the first is the health of the troops," and from the outset he followed this credo.[12] He ordered his men to bathe three times a week in the lake under the supervision of an officer who was to ensure that they were to "wash themselves from head to foot, but not to remain immersed in the water more than five minutes."[13] Unusual for the time, this insistence on hygiene paid dividends – from April to the beginning of July, only two men died of sickness at Flint Hill and, to the amazement of medical personnel, "even the demon diarrhoea appeared to have been exorcised by the mystical power of strict discipline and rigid police!"[14] Thereafter, reinforcements who came from less sanitary camps brought disease with them and by 23 June one of eight men in camp was sick. Given the sanitary standards of 1814, this was not unusual; Brown himself believed that even a healthy army could expect to have at least one-ninth of its strength on the sick list.[15]

Scott managed to obtain equipment and better rations for his men and he got a paymaster with funds to come to Buffalo and pay them. His biggest headache was a shortage of uniforms, something that Jarvis Hanks with his homemade blanket trousers could attest to, and Scott estimated that ten to fifteen men of every infantry company lacked proper uniforms and were "in other respects untidily clad."[16] He made the proper requisitions but discovered that the clothing set aside for his regiments had been taken by Wilkinson to clothe the troops at Plattsburgh. Annoyed, he complained directly to Armstrong, who intervened, but it required a lengthy correspondence before the badly needed uniforms were received. When they arrived, Scott found that, instead of the regulation blue infantry coatee, he had been issued grey wool "roundabouts," or jackets, usually worn as a fatigue dress or as an undergarment in winter. But Scott did not care what his men wore so long as they were adequately and uniformly clothed. All camp stocks of blue coatees were given to the Twenty-First Infantry and the other regiments were issued the grey jackets.[17]

Scott believed that troops who were properly fed, clothed, equipped and kept busy would stay out of trouble and, for a time, he was not disappointed.

In early May the *Buffalo Gazette* reported that the troops at Flint Hill "are generally in good health, in excellent discipline, and behave remarkably well to the inhabitants."[18] On 4 May Scott boasted to Brown that he had no need of a provost guard, or military police, because his men were in order. That same day he informed Armstrong that the regiments in camp were "broken into habits of subordination."[19] Unfortunately this idyll came to end when the men received their overdue pay. Drunken soldiers appeared on the streets of the village, gambling became widespread and, inevitably, there were cases of a "worthless miscreant" deserting by using "the bounty of his Country as the means by which to effect his escape from the service he had sworn to perform."[20]

Angered, Scott cracked down. Camp discipline was tightened and a general court martial was convened to try the worst offenders. Ten were found guilty, six of the crime of desertion and four of lesser offences such as sleeping on guard, unsoldierlike conduct and drunkenness. The minor offenders were punished by being "picketed" – forced to stand on one foot with the other foot bared and resting on a sharp stake for a certain period each day.[21] The deserters fared worse. Desertion was the blight of the army – twice during the war, the government had issued blanket pardons to stem the exodus of trained soldiers. In the early war years recaptured men stood a good chance of being let off lightly but by 1814 attitudes had changed. So it was at Buffalo: one of the deserters was "fortunate," being sentenced to "have his head half shaved, to have his ears cropped, to be branded with the letter D on one cheek and to be Drummed out of the Service."[22] The remaining five were sentenced to death and the troops were ordered "to witness the awful execution" on 4 June 1814.[23]

Jarvis Hanks well remembered that scene. The five condemned, dressed in white robes with red targets fastened over their hearts and white caps pulled over their eyes, knelt in front of their freshly dug graves while firing squads lined up in front of each man. The volleys rang out and five figures fell. A few seconds later, one of the men struggled upright and moaned, "By G__, I thought I was dead." This soldier, Private William Fairfield of the Eleventh Infantry, had been reprieved because of his youth but, to drive the lesson home, Scott had not communicated this fact to him but had instead issued blank cartridges to the men assigned to Fairfield's execution.[24]

Scott was as strict with officers as with enlisted men. Observing a captain fail to return a sentry's salute one day, he immediately informed the officer that "if he did not repass the sentinel and 'reform the fault' within twenty minutes, he would be tried before a court-martial."[25] When Captain George Bender of the Ninth Infantry struck a soldier, he was suspended from the service for six months and Bender was by no means the only officer in Scott's bad books. Of the fifty-four soldiers under arrest at Flint Hill on 23 June 1814, ten held commissions.[26]

All of Scott's activities paled beside the effort he put into making the Left Division ready for battle. Crysler's Farm had demonstrated that valour alone was not enough to defeat British regulars and, from the day he assumed command, Scott prepared the division to meet and beat the best-trained infantry in the world. In North America, even more so than in Europe, infantry were the most important military arm as the heavily wooded terrain and primitive road system limited the mobility and utility of cavalry and artillery. Only infantry could take and hold ground and the tactics of land warfare in 1814 were based on the capabilities of the infantry's weapon – the smooth-bore, flintlock musket.

The standard U.S. musket was the Model 1795, a copy of the French military muskets supplied to Washington's army during the Revolutionary war. Five feet long, it weighed about 11 pounds with its 15-inch bayonet fixed, and fired a .65 calibre soft lead ball weighing just under an ounce from its .69 calibre bore. The American musket ball was smaller and lighter than its British counterpart, which was .71 calibre and weighed just over an ounce. As a result the American projectile had longer range but less hitting power.[27]

Firing a musket was a complicated process that required at least twenty separate motions. On his right hip, the soldier carried a leather box filled with cartridges – tubes of strong, greased paper, sealed by pack thread and containing a powder charge at one end and a ball at the other. To load, the infantryman held his musket horizontally in his left hand and, removing a cartridge from his box with his right, bit off the end containing the powder, shook a small amount onto the pan of the musket and closed the frizzen (the hinged cover that fitted over the pan). Grounding the butt, he next inserted the remainder of the charge, the ball and the cartridge paper, in that order, into the muzzle. Drawing his ramrod from the underside of the stock of his weapon, he rammed them home to the bottom of the bore. Replacing the ramrod, he then brought the butt to his shoulder and brought the hammer, with its flint securely fastened between its screw-tightened jaws, back to full cock. To fire, the soldier pulled the trigger, bringing hammer and flint down on the frizzen, forcing it open and striking sparks that ignited the priming charge in the pan and, through the touch-hole, the main charge. Far from the enemy, a trained man might load and fire in fifteen seconds but he was much slower in action – two to three rounds per minute was the average.[28]

The musket was a difficult and dangerous weapon to fire. The flint often failed to strike sparks or might be knocked out of the jaws of the hammer and, in any case, had to be frequently replaced. The priming might not fire or might "flash in the pan" without igniting the main charge. The ramrod easily dropped from the stiff fingers of tense men or was sometimes forgotten in the barrel and fired off with the ball. Due to these inherent problems it was calculated that fifteen per cent of the times its trigger was pulled, the musket did not fire. There were other problems. In hot, dry conditions, the sparks discharged with each round could set fire to the surrounding grass. Wet weather made the powder difficult to ignite. Even if the weapon discharged, the combustion built up a residue of "fouling" in the barrel that blocked the touch-hole and had to be cleaned out with the small brush and pricker that every soldier carried attached to his cross belt. Finally, each discharge produced a cloud of dense, acrid smoke that half-choked the firer and, unless there was a stiff breeze, nearly blinded him.[29]

Even when the weapon fired without incident its smooth bore, lacking rifling to impart a stabilizing spin to the projectile, provided a highly irregular trajectory. The musket had a tendency to fire high so that aim had to be taken at least a foot below the target at close range. The weapon's theoretical maximum range was about two hundred and fifty yards but, while a volley might have some effect at one hundred and fifty yards, a single marksman might have difficult hitting an individual target at one hundred yards. One modern commentator has calculated that only 2 to 5 per cent of the musket rounds fired actually hit their target. Period authors were even more sceptical of the musket's capability, estimating that only between .3 and 1 per cent of the rounds fired were effective. A significant declaration on the weapon's lack of accuracy is contained in the statement made by the head of the British ammunition column at the battle of Vittoria in 1813, who calculated that the British and allied infantry fired 3,675,000 rounds at very close ranges to inflict only 8,000 casualties of all types on their French opponents, or one hit for every 458 rounds expended.[30]

To fire this clumsy weapon, soldiers were drilled until they could function like automatons. The emphasis was on speed, not marksmanship, and most armies did not even issue ammunition for practice as their men were not expected to aim, but simply to present their weapons at the enemy and

U.S. Model 1795 Musket, .69 calibre
The smooth-bore, flintlock musket was the main infantry weapon of the period and Napo-
leonic tactics featured the conflict of formations of men armed with such crank weapons.
Although it was difficult to fire, the musket could be lethal if used in large numbers. The
enlargement shows details of the flintlock ignition system. (Photograph, courtesy of Parks
Canada)

fire. The British army did put some emphasis on accuracy, however, and
each British infantryman was supposed to receive an annual issue of thirty
ball (live) and sixty blank rounds, and three flints, for target practice. The
American army also stressed accuracy and Scott instituted musketry practice at Flint Hill, ordering each soldier to fire at least twenty blank rounds
each week, and holding regular regimental and brigade firing exercises that
sometimes lasted four hours.[31]

Used properly, the musket could achieve deadly results. It has been calculated that twenty effective volleys fired by British infantry at the battle of
Talavera in 1809 inflicted some 1,250 to 1,300 French casualties. Musket
balls that hit human targets produced a horrendous effect. At a range of
thirty yards, British balls could penetrate sheet iron three-eighths of an inch
thick or nearly five inches of oak and were capable of breaking large limb
bones and destroying major joints. At medium ranges, the soft lead round,
when striking human flesh, flattened and disintegrated into fragments that
caused a massive conical-shaped wound. At ranges over two hundred yards,

the velocity of the ball diminished drastically – one of the reasons there are so many accounts from the Napoleonic wars of multiple but minor wounds and of miraculous "saves" occasioned by the lucky placement of bibles, watches, love letters or the odd crust of bread.[32]

To have any chance of being effective, the musket had to be used in mass, and the employment of formations of musket-armed infantry against similar formations was the foundation of tactics in 1814. The main infantry combat unit was termed the battalion in the British army and the regiment in the U.S. army. Every British battalion of "foot" or American regiment of infantry had, in theory, ten companies, each consisting of about one hundred men at full strength, but units were rarely at full strength. British battalions in Canada averaged four hundred and fifty men while the regiments of the Left Division mustered many less. A British battalion had eight centre companies and two "flank" or elite companies – the grenadier company, theoretically composed of the most experienced and steadiest men, and the light company, supposedly recruited from the most agile and intelligent soldiers in the battalion. American infantry regiments were authorized two flank companies of either grenadiers or light infantry but, although some companies in the Left Division came to specialize in skirmishing, most American regiments in 1814 do not seem to have had designated flank companies.[33]

The manuals used by both armies laid great stress on the formation of the battalion or regiment in battle. These same manuals stipulated that units were to form in a line of three ranks (a rank is series of men ranged alongside each other) but both armies favoured the line of two ranks in action. Theoretically, a British battalion in line consisted of ten companies with the light company on the left flank and the grenadier company on the right. Drawn up for battle, each company was further organized into one or two platoons, a term that was used differently in 1814 than it is today. At that time, it meant an *ad hoc* formation organized for fire and movement purposes. Company officers and sergeants took position three paces behind the rear rank as "file closers" – as casualties were taken, they would move the files (a file is a series of men positioned one behind each other) of the first two ranks into the centre. The battalion commander, usually a lieutenant-colonel, took position on his horse in the centre of the battalion. To his left and right were stationed the two majors, also mounted, each commanding a "wing" or half the battalion. The drummers and fifers took post in line behind their respective companies and three paces to the rear of the rank of file closers.[34]

An American infantry regiment formed only slightly differently – a regiment of ten companies at full strength was divided, for fire purposes, into twenty platoons. The commanding officer, company officers and sergeants were positioned as were the British except that the platoon commanders stood in front and to the right of the foremost rank of their platoons, dropping back just before firing commenced, while the musicians took position in the centre of the regiment. In both armies, each battalion or regiment had a pair of flags or "colours" that were positioned in the centre of its line, in front of the commanding officer. These were more than ornamental or symbolic devices, they served as a guide upon which the dressing or alignment of the ranks could be maintained while moving and they also marked the location of the commanding officer. Messengers looking for such officers made for the regimental colours, which were usually distinguishable above the smoke of battle.[35]

The purpose of this complicated battalion and regimental battle organization was to permit controlled firing by platoon sub-units and to equalize the strength of these sub-units as casualties were taken. Using this organization, musketry could be delivered by as few men as a single file up to both ranks of the entire battalion or regiment. When firing by platoons, a three-second delay was allowed between each unit for the noise of the previous unit's firing to die away before the officer commanding the next platoon gave the order to fire. It was American practice for a platoon commander not to give the order to fire until he saw that some of the previous sub-units had completed their loading procedure. In theory, firing orders were elaborate: in the U.S. Army they consisted of the unit command, e.g. "Platoon!"; the cautionary command, "Ready!"; the operative commands, "Aim!" and "Fire!"; and the preparative "Prime and Load!" In practice, these commands were probably shortened to one word – "Fire!" – loading being automatic afterward.[36]

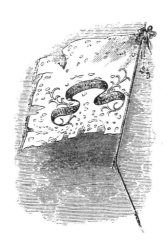

Regimental Colour of the Twenty-Fifth Infantry
One of a pair of colours carried into action by each American infantry regiment, this colour, with a broken staff and numerous perforations made by bullets, demonstrates the ferocity of the fighting at Lundy's Lane. (From Benson Lossing, *Pictorial Field Book of the War of 1812*, New York, 1869)

Properly trained, infantry battalions or regiments constituted potent weapons in the hands of commanders who could deliver that degree of fire they deemed most appropriate on the target they deemed most suitable. The sub-unit organization also helped to overcome the inefficiency of the single musket – the battalion or regiment became the weapon, not the individual soldier. The first volley was the most important – it was loaded out of the heat of battle, there was no smoke from a previous discharge to obscure vision and it inflicted the heaviest casualties. Commanders hoarded their first volley and usually fired it by entire ranks or wings to achieve maximum effect. Thereafter, because of smoke and the lengthy loading time, they usually preferred to fire by sub-units so that there were always loaded muskets ready for any tactical emergency.

The two-rank line was the ideal fire formation as it brought the maximum number of muskets to bear on a broad front. But it was awkward for movement and it took well-trained troops to manoeuvre in line. Only the British army was partial to the line for movement, the U.S. and most European armies favouring the more flexible column. Column formations were of two types: the column of march, which was the normal formation for movement, and the attack column, which resembled a thickened line. The attack column allowed commanders to concentrate a heavy mass of men at a chosen point on the enemy's line. Scott favoured an attack column with a two-company front and a five-company depth which he felt could be easily combined with similar formations for a major attack and was easier to deploy into line. The attack column was less useful for fire action as only the first few ranks could fire their muskets. Although the British army favoured the line for movement while the U.S. army favoured the column, the infantry of both armies were capable of adopting either formation as circumstances dictated.[37]

Generally, the intention of the commander of an attack column was to deploy into line and close with the enemy, a tricky operation under fire. Period doctrine held that, on occasion, the column's impetus in the attack might carry it through an enemy line without it having to deploy. Veteran commanders defending against attack columns screened the front of their line with skirmishers whose fire would force the columns to deploy to return the fire or lose their nerve and become susceptible to counterattack. Experience showed that once an attacking formation halted to fire it rarely moved forward again as "the soldiers of themselves, taking out a sort of carte blanche, blazed away, in the most independent manner, in all directions ... to little purpose, beyond that of raising noise and smoke."[38] Even in columns, infantry moved slowly in battle – manoeuvring in 1814 was a fairly stately business and could afford to be, given the poor effectiveness and low rate of fire of the weaponry. The most difficult manoeuvres to perform and the most dangerous to attempt under fire were "deployment" from column to line and "ployment" from line to column, as infantry were at their most vulnerable while performing these manoeuvres.[39]

The infantryman's second weapon was his bayonet. Measuring between fifteen and seventeen inches, this was an elongated metal spike with a triangular cross-section and a socket that locked onto the muzzle of the musket with an L-shaped mortice. Soldiers often fired with their bayonets fixed – yet another negative factor on the musket's lamentable accuracy as the added weight of the bayonet made it difficult to hold the weapon steady. Bayonet fighting was rare and, in the meantime, infantrymen found other uses for their edged weapons; they were useful for digging potatoes and, inserted into the ground, made excellent candle holders.

It was the perceived threat of the bayonet, not its actual use, that made it effective. As one American officer remarked, the bayonet "is a potent weapon, on the side of high discipline and strong nerves" but "the charge of the bayonet is not often used."[40] A British surgeon who saw considerable combat in Spain at this time agreed with this assessment. According to G.J. Guthrie, "opposing regiments when formed in line and charging with fixed bayonets, *never* meet and struggle hand to hand and foot to foot; and this for the best possible reason, that one side turns and runs away as soon as the other comes close enough to do mischief."[41] Fighting with the bayonet usually only occurred in confined areas such as farm houses, field fortifications or when two opponents accidentally encountered each other. It was much less common on the open battlefield.[42]

Period armies also included a proportion of "light infantry," who formed the advance guard on the march and the rearguard when retreating. In battle, they covered and protected the line infantry by providing skirmishers that hung on the flanks and front of an attacking formation and annoyed it with individual aimed musketry. Light infantrymen usually fought in pairs, one man always keeping his musket loaded to cover his partner and, although they moved more quickly than ordinary infantry, they maintained a loose but controlled formation. In North America, where the heavily-wooded terrain made cavalry of less use than in Europe, light infantry performed many of the reconnaissance aspects of that arm. Each British battalion included a company of light infantry and the British army in Canada possessed an entire unit of this type, the Glengarry Light Infantry Fencibles. Although up to two light infantry companies were authorized for each American regiment, there appears to have been no formal organization for such companies in the Left Division. This is not surprising as the manuals on which the division trained were based on a French original that made little mention of such troops. Both armies tried to use militia and Indians in the light infantry role – with varied success, as good light troops had to be highly trained and disciplined and the militia and warriors of neither country possessed these qualities.

The second arm of the Left Division was its artillery. There were two main types of field artillery weapons in 1814 – guns and howitzers. Guns, often incorrectly called "cannon," fired their projectiles on a fairly flat trajectory out to long ranges. Howitzers were designed to throw shells, explosive projectiles, on a curved trajectory at shorter ranges and were shorter and stubbier in appearance than guns. The calibres of guns were denominated by the weight of roundshot they fired, howitzers by their bore diameter. The carriages for both weapons were simple in design and sturdy in construction but their weight was considerable. The 6-pdr. gun, the standard field piece used by both armies during the war, weighed about fifteen hundred pounds on its carriage and required four to six horses to pull it.[43]

Smooth-bore artillery fired three main types of projectiles – roundshot from guns, shells from howitzers and canister from both weapons. Roundshot, the proverbial "cannon ball," was a solid iron sphere used to destroy structures, men and horses. Shells were hollow iron spheres filled with powder and exploded by a fuse at a predetermined time. Canister, as its name implies, was simply a tin container filled with small lead bullets used as an anti-personnel round against mass formations. A fourth type of projectile, employed only by the British Royal Artillery in 1814, was shrapnel – a shell loaded with lead bullets as well as powder and fired from both guns and howitzers. At long ranges, guns fired shot and howitzers shell; at close ranges, both types switched to canister.

Throughout the War of 1812, artillery generally performed better in the defence than it did in the offence because, unlike in Europe, not enough guns were deployed in the field to create the massed batteries that could destroy opposing formations of infantry. In addition, the primitive roads in North America hindered the mobility of artillery. During the war, therefore, the primary function of field artillery was to support friendly infantry. As artillery fire in 1814 was direct fire only: gun positions had to be carefully chosen to achieve concentration of fire and so that the enemy could be kept in view as

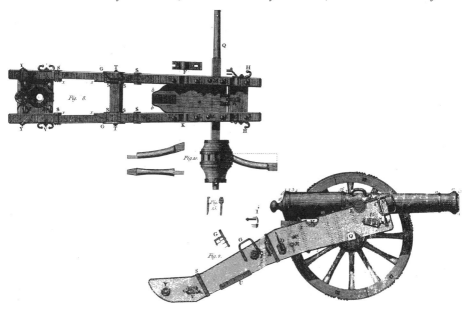

Plan of an American 12-pdr. field gun and carriage
Firing an iron round shot weighing 12 lb., pieces similar to this one were brought into action at Lundy's Lane by the U.S. artillery. (From Louis de Tousard, *American Artillerist's Companion*, Philadelphia, 1812)

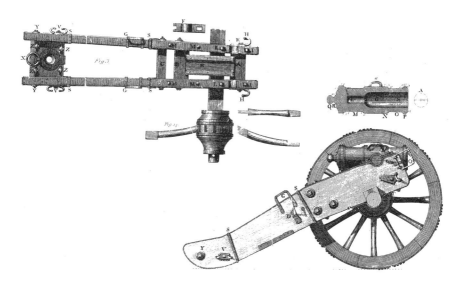

Plan of an American field howitzer of the War of 1812
Both the American and British artillery at Lundy's Lane were equipped with field howitzers with 5 ½-inch bores that fired explosive shells. They were useful if somewhat erratic weapons. (From Louis de Tousard, *American Artillerist's Companion*, Philadelphia, 1812)

long as possible. The best positions were those that would subject the ground over which an enemy must advance to enfilade or oblique fire and, hopefully, a cross fire from two or more artillery positions. The heavier calibres were placed so that they could observe great distances to allow their superior range to have effect for a longer period. Elevation was desirable but had to be chosen carefully lest it interfere with the relatively flat projectile trajectories of smooth-bore guns. The artillery had to be positioned so that it could support friendly infantry without inconveniencing both arms, and for this reason gun positions in front of or between infantry formations were frowned on.

Battles of the Napoleonic period were concentrated in both time and space. They rarely lasted more than a day and the onset of darkness or any kind of wet weather usually brought the fighting to a halt. The tactical formations used and the short ranges of the weaponry allowed the generals of 1814 to compress their forces to a degree that is almost inconceivable to the modern soldier. Although they tended to be short, early 19th century battles were extremely bloody and the infantry, then as now, took the heaviest casualties. Drawn up in ranks a few feet apart and packed so close that each man could feel his neighbour's elbows, they stood and watched as the enemy approached or as roundshot came bouncing toward them. Not that there was much to see from the rear ranks as their view was obscured by the men in front. Even those in front could see little after they fired their first volley and became enveloped in smoke. This smoke would hang over the ranks and, as volley followed volley, completely obscure any object, including the enemy, more than a few yards away. To men who lived in a quieter pre-industrial age, the noise of battle, with the thunder of artillery and the discharge of muskets a few inches from their ears, must have been a terrifying experience.

This was the type of warfare for which Winfield Scott prepared the Left Division in the spring of 1814. Before commencing he had to solve a problem that had plagued the army for much of the war – the lack of a standard infantry drill manual. This problem originated in a War Department decision to replace Steuben's 1779 *Blue Book* with an abridgement by Alexander Smyth of the current French manual, the *Règlement* of 1791. Smyth's manual was officially adopted in 1812 but it came under fire from William Duane, a newspaper editor with good political connections, who had prepared his own abridgement of the *Règlement*, which he termed the *Handbook for Infantry*. In February 1813 Armstrong appointed Duane adjutant general of the army and directed that his manual replace Smyth's work.

Most of the regimental commanders in the northern army refused to accept this change because they regarded Duane's *Handbook* as inadequate for training purposes. Instead, they either continued with Smyth, reverted to Steuben's *Blue Book*, compiled their own drill treatises or, in the case of the Twenty-First Infantry, used the current British manual. The result was that units trained on different manuals could not manoeuvre together. Refusing to be "idle for want of a *prescribed guide*," Scott opted for Smyth.[44] On 22 April he directed that at Flint Hill the "French regulations or the system of discipline laid down by Smyth (which are the same) will govern the infantry."[45]

That same day, with snow still on the ground, the infantry at Buffalo began intensive training. Scott ordered company drill in the morning followed by two to three hours of regimental drill under his personal supervision in the afternoon. A week later he reported to Brown that the division was drilling seven hours a day, and by early May there were four hours of company drill in the morning which all officers (including quartermasters and paymasters) were required to attend. Weekly inspections were held and the acting inspector-general, Second Lieutenant Edward Randolph from Virginia, was quick to note any deficiencies or backwardness in manoeuvre. As the days became longer, company exercises began at reveille and lasted until breakfast before being resumed for two more hours. They were followed in the afternoon by regimental instruction for three to four hours. Scott often participated in a very vocal fashion. "General Scott drills & damns, drills & damns, and drills again," wrote Captain John Murdock of the Twenty-Fifth Infantry. "I hope he will drive something into the noddles of his Yankee Brigade."[46]

When the troops were proficient in their regimental drill, Scott turned over supervision of this work to Colonel Charles K. Gardner, the divisional adjutant general. He now began to manoeuvre the regiments together as a single formation to the "great delight" of the men, "who began to perceive why they had been made to fag so long."[47] But the work went on. Major Thomas S. Jesup of the Twenty-Fifth Infantry recorded that by the end of June 1814 his men were at it seven to ten hours daily while Captain Joseph Henderson of the Twenty-Second recalled his company often drilled late into the night. Young Jarvis Hanks, resplendent in a new uniform, worked as hard as his older comrades but did not complain as he knew the toil made "us well acquainted with our business as soldiers and fit us for the contests which were expected during the summer in the enemy's camp."[48]

Scott did not neglect his other responsibilities. Brown had directed him by all the means in his power to possess himself "of information relative to the enemy's force and movements."[49] To gather intelligence Scott employed members of the Canadian Volunteers, a corps of renegades serving with the Left Division, who, with the co-operation of Lieutenant Andrew Sinclair, the American naval commander on Lake Erie, were landed clandestinely in Upper Canada. Using these spies, Scott "gained considerable information as to the numbers, situation and movements of the enemy in the upper province" while Sinclair became familiar with the north shore of the lake.[50]

Sinclair's ships also brought in reinforcements, including a force of regulars from the Seventeenth, Nineteenth and Twenty-Second Infantry commanded by Lieutenant Colonel John B. Campbell and a regiment of Pennsylvania Volunteers under Colonel James Fenton which had been stationed at Erie, Pennsylvania. Both officers had reported to Scott for orders and he summoned them to Buffalo, although in Campbell's case he had no authority to issue such an order. Sinclair, seeing an opportunity, proposed to Campbell that they raid the Long Point area of Upper Canada which Sinclair believed produced half the breadstuffs for the British army in the province. Campbell enthusiastically agreed as he had been contemplating just such an operation and, on 14 May, the navy landed a force of regulars, seamen and Volunteers under Campbell's command near the little Canadian village of Dover[51].

The next morning Campbell moved into the village. Urged on by members of the Canadian Volunteers who told him that it was "inhabited mostly by revolutionary tories and half pay officers noted for the suppression of those who were suspected of being friendly to the success of our arms," he put it to the torch.[52] A local girl, Amelia Ryerse, hearing the family dogs bark, looked out to see "the hillside and fields as far as the eye could reach

Colonel Charles K. Gardner, U.S. Army (1787-1869)
The adjutant general of the Left Division, Gardner functioned as Brown's chief of staff throughout the 1814 campaign. He was ill on the day of Lundy's Lane but rose from his sick bed to advise his commander and assist in the transmission of orders. (From Benson Lossing, *Pictorial Field Book of the War of 1812*, New York, 1869)

Major Thomas S. Jesup, U.S. Army (1788-1860)
Jesup commanded the Twenty-Fifth Infantry at Lundy's Lane and fought an independent action in the early stages of the action. Seemingly indestructible, he was wounded four times but was still on his feet when the fighting ceased. Jesup served in the regular army until his death in 1860. (Used with permission of the Washington National Cathedral)

covered with American soldiers." They spared her widowed mother's house but burned the other farm buildings, so that "what at early morn had been a prosperous homestead, at noon remained only smouldering ruins."[53] Although Sinclair protested at the destruction of civilian property, Campbell continued his work for two days, burning and looting public and private property indiscriminately. When the squadron sailed on 16 May, his own men were "generally disgusted with Campbell's conduct."[54]

Senior officers of both sides were appalled by this event which presaged a return to the medieval "slash and burn" tactics of the previous winter. When the local British commander, Major General Phineas Riall, asked whether the destruction was authorized by the American government, Campbell replied that: "What was done ... proceeded from my orders, the whole business was planned by myself & executed upon my own responsibility."[55] On the orders of the secretary of war, Campbell was suspended from duty pending the result of a court of inquiry into his actions. The verdict was that he did right to destroy public property as it was a war asset but had erred in destroying private property. Following this slap on the wrist, Campbell was promoted colonel and given command of the Eleventh Infantry; the United States would have reason to rue his actions.[56]

By mid-May enough reinforcements of regular infantry had arrived at Flint Hill for Brown to form the troops there into two brigades. Scott was given command of the First Brigade while the Second went to the newly-promoted Brigadier General Eleazar W. Ripley. Cool and reserved, the thirty-two-year-

Brigadier General Eleazar W. Ripley, U.S. Army (1782-1839) Cool and controlled, Ripley commanded the Second Brigade of Brown's Left Division during the battle and was the senior unwounded American officer at the end of the fighting. His decision not to return to the battlefield the following day but to withdraw to Fort Erie earned him the censure of Brown, who prepared court martial charges against him. (Courtesy, Hood Museum of Art, Dartmouth College, N.H.)

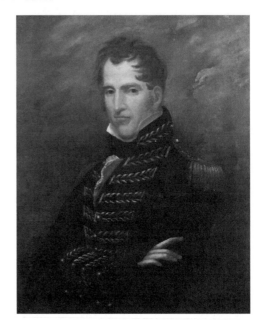

old Ripley was a study in contrast to the outgoing, aggressive Scott and he did not inspire the same admiration among his subordinates. His aide de camp, Captain William McDonald, thought that "tho' he is a brave man, yet he is too much of a Yankee [too cold] for me."[57] A graduate of Dartmouth College, Ripley had pursued a legal and political career in Massachusetts becoming speaker of the state house of representatives in 1810. In contrast to the general sentiment in New England, Ripley supported the war and was rewarded with a lieutenant-colonel's commission in the Twenty-First Infantry, which he turned into a good unit that had fought well during the campaigns of 1813. Retaining his politician's instincts, Ripley was never backward in bringing his deeds and those of his regiment before the public and this angered fellow commanders who felt that their men were being slighted. On the strength of his combat record and possibly because of his political connections, Ripley was promoted brigadier general in April 1814. Although Brown thought him an "excellent selection" for general officer, the New Englander was not his first choice as a brigade commander in Brown's own division.[58]

Also under orders to proceed to Buffalo was a force of New York Volunteers from the northern part of the state. This force had originated in an offer from Governor Tompkins to Armstrong in January to raise state troops to supplement any regular troops sent against Fort Niagara. These men, volunteers in federal service, were paid, equipped and armed by the War

Department. Despite Tompkins's offer, it was not until mid-March that a call was issued for one thousand men to serve for six months under the command of New York militia Brigadier General Peter B. Porter.[59]

The thirty-eight-year-old Porter was an ideal choice. A graduate of Yale College who had moved to the Niagara area, he was by 1812 a wealthy landowner and businessman active in both state and federal politics. A friend and associate of Tompkins, Porter was an excellent public speaker with a born politician's easygoing manner that won him many friends. He was a prominent member of the "war hawk" faction and chairman of the House Committee on Foreign Relations, which had done much to impel the United States into war. He had seen action as a militia commander in the fighting around Fort George in 1813 and was regarded as a competent soldier.[60]

Porter was optimistic that the New York Volunteers could be raised without too much difficulty. He assured Armstrong that his men would "not be controlled by *constitutional* scruples" – that is, they would not refuse to cross the international border as state militia had done in the past.[61] He also suggested to the secretary that Indian warriors from the American side of the Niagara who were "exasperated by the late barbarities of the enemy" be invited to participate in the forthcoming campaign.[62] When Armstrong agreed, Porter met with the Seneca chief Red Jacket in early April and obtained the promise of a force of five hundred warriors to join him at Buffalo.[63]

Brigadier General Peter B. Porter, N.Y. Militia (1773-1844)
Amiable and intelligent, Porter was a prewar politician who supported a declaration of war. Unlike most politicians, however, he practised what he preached and served as a militia general in 1813 and 1814. Porter was lightly wounded while commanding the Third Brigade of the Left Division at Lundy's Lane. (Courtesy, Buffalo and Erie County Historical Society, C-19269)

Red Jacket (c. 1750-1830)
Red Jacket, a Seneca war chief, was one of the leaders of the contingent of native warriors that formed part of Porter's Third Brigade during the early part of the 1814 campaign. (From Benson Lossing, *Pictorial Field Book of the War of 1812*, New York, 1869)

It proved more difficult to raise the New York Volunteers. Porter had planned to be ready by 1 May 1814 but when the federal government failed to provide the promised arms and equipment in time, he was forced to postpone the assembly of his force. He was still not ready by mid-June and Brown, concerned that the New Yorkers would not be able to join the division before he entered Canada, suggested to Armstrong that, if Porter "cannot get out his volunteers in time, he can FOLLOW."[64] That is exactly what happened. Porter's New York units were just starting to straggle into camp at Buffalo when the Left Division crossed the Niagara.[65]

A militia general in a division composed largely of regulars, Porter was in an awkward position. He had hoped to command on the Niagara frontier himself and disliked being junior to "two young brigadiers," particularly Scott. He complained to Tompkins that had he "forseen the situation in which I was to be thrown, nothing would have induced me to have undertaken the task I did."[66] But he was wise enough not to "take exception to the preference given to a man of more military acquirements than I can pretend to."[67] For his part, Scott was aware of Porter's feelings and was conciliatory toward him in public. In private, he expressed his fear that "we shall be disgraced if we admit a militia force either into our camp or order of battle".[68] As for serving under Porter or any other amateur who "styles himself a general," Scott refused to "submit to the orders of a militiaman," and was "prepared to leave the service on this point."[69]

When the Pennsylvania and New York Volunteers marched into camp, they encountered the imposing figure of Winfield Scott and immediately began to drill. Private Alexander McMullen from Franklin County, Pennsylvania, remembered that "Regulations new to us and very strict were now adopted."[70] Another Volunteer recorded that "we live very well here, but eat no idle bread, for drilling and parading occupies our attention."[71] The citizen soldiers were awed by Scott, "the universal favourite," who liked to "career" through the camp with his aides in a "dashing style".[72] "This day I got [to] See General Brown and Brigadeader Wingfield Scott," recorded Corporal John Witherow of Fannetsburg, Pennsylvania, on 25 June with more enthusiasm than literacy.[73] The Volunteers were also impressed by the regular troops – "the best in appearance ever in the service of the United States, greatly improving in discipline and very healthy."[74] Scott was justifiably proud. "I have a handsome little army," he wrote to a friend. "The men are healthy, sober, cheerful and docile" while "the field officers highly respectable and many of the platoon officers are decent and emulous of improvement."[75]

What kind of men were the soldiers of the Left Division in 1814? They were mostly young, the average age being between twenty-one and twenty-four. Their average height was five feet, eight inches and they were inured to hard physical labour. Two of every five had been farmers while most of the remainder had been either skilled or unskilled labourers. The great majority, eighty-six per cent, were native-born Americans and well over half those of foreign birth were of Irish origin. The dragoons and gunners were recruited throughout the United States but the infantry regiments were largely raised in specific states and had a regional affiliation that promoted group cohesion. Thus, the Ninth and Twenty-First Infantry were Massachusetts units, the Eleventh was from Vermont, the Twenty-Second from Pennsylvania, the Twenty-Third from New York and the Twenty-Fifth from Connecticut. The Left Division was truly a Yankee division.[76]

At Flint Hill camp every detail of the soldier's daily life was closely regulated. They were awakened at daybreak (defined as being enough light to distinguish objects at fifty feet) by the drummers beating "reveille." In late June in Buffalo this was around 4:30 A.M. Roll was called and the men drilled until the breakfast call, "peas on a trencher," was beat. Drill or fatigues followed until noon when the traditional "roast beef" call summoned the men to their dinner. Regimental or brigade drill then followed and so it went throughout the day. The last call was "tattoo," the signal for the men to snuff their candles and remain in their tents until next morning. This was the soldier's day and varied only on Sundays when church parade was followed by the weekly inspection.[77]

They considered themselves well fed. Each soldier received daily a quarter pound of beef or three quarters of a pound of pork and eighteen ounces of bread. The men eked out this diet with what they could scrounge or, if they had money, purchase from the sutler, the travelling shopkeeper authorized to sell to the troops. Usually they didn't have money, as privates received only eight dollars per month and sergeants eleven, and their pay was almost always in arrears. Each man also received a daily ration of one gill (four ounces) of whisky, rum or brandy, and again the sutler would sell him more if he had the coin. The issue and sale of alcohol was deplored by senior officers but it provided one of the few escapes from what was a hard and often miserable existence.[78]

The regulars wore a smart but highly impractical uniform. The worst item was the tall black leather shako with its "tombstone" front decorated with a white pompom and cord and an oblong pewter plate stamped with the American eagle and regimental number. This clumsy headgear was easily knocked off by tree branches or jarred loose when its wearer had to run. The infantry of Scott's brigade were clothed in a single-breasted grey wool jacket with a high collar reaching to the ears, white cotton trousers, black cloth ankle gaiters and stout, laced boots. The men of Ripley's brigade and Hindman's gunners were similarly dressed except they substituted a blue wool coatee with short tails for the grey jacket.

The infantryman's fighting equipment consisted of two buff or black leather belts that went over his shoulders and overlapped on his chest to produce a "cross belt" effect. These belts held the black leather cartridge box on his right hip containing 38-40 rounds of ball cartridge and the bayonet scabbard on his left. Over these belts went the harness for his knapsack of blue-painted canvas and the belts of his canteen and ration haversack which hung from his left hip. Scott was strict about what his men put in their knapsacks; they were to have only "one shirt, one pair Summer pantaloons, one pair shoes, one pair socks (or stockings), one fatigue frock, one pair trousers and one blanket" although they could add "a brush and pocket handkerchief ... but *nothing else*."[79] Fully accoutred, the American infantryman hoisted a load of forty to fifty pounds. To this he added the tools of his trade: his .69 calibre Springfield musket and his fifteen-inch bayonet with its triangular blade.[80]

On 6 June 1814, when Brown returned to Buffalo from Sackets Harbor, his "handsome little army" was taking its final form. Scott's First Brigade included Major Henry Leavenworth's Ninth Infantry, Colonel John B. Campbell's Eleventh, Major Ralph Marlin's Twenty-Second and Major Thomas

Colonel Henry Leavenworth, U.S. Army (1783-1834).
Shown in a postwar portrait c. 1830, Leavenworth was a skilled tactician with a reputation for coolness under fire. He needed these qualities at Lundy's Lane where he fought continuously for almost five hours and ended up commanding the First Brigade. Courtesy, Frontier Army Museum, Fort Leavenworth, Kansas)

S. Jesup's Twenty-Fifth Infantry. Ripley's Second Brigade was composed of Major Joseph Grafton's Twenty-First Infantry, Major Daniel McFarland's Twenty-Third and two "orphan" companies of the Seventeenth and Nineteenth attached to the Twenty-First.

Artillery and cavalry rounded out the regular component of the division. Marylander Major Jacob Hindman's artillery battalion had four companies equipped with different types of ordnance. The company of Captain Nathan Towson, also a Maryland native, was armed with 6-pdr. guns as was that of Virginian Captain John Ritchie. Philadelphian Captain Thomas Biddle's company had 12-pdrs. while the company of Captain Alexander Williams, another Pennsylvanian, had 18-pdr. guns. There was also a reserve park of heavy artillery comprising 18-pdr. guns and some howitzers. Like the infantry, the gunners had worked hard during the last two months as Hindman, "one of the best drill masters in the service," had been relentless in training them.[81] Finally, there was Captain Samuel D. Harris's troop of regular light dragoons.[82]

Not all of the regulars had been trained by Scott. The Seventeenth, Nineteenth and Twenty-Second Infantry did not arrive in camp until mid-June, the Twenty-Third marched in on the 26th of that month and Harris's dragoons only arrived on the day the division crossed into Canada. The recipients of Scott's instruction, however, set the tone for the rest of the division and they formed the professional cadre that was its foundation.[83]

The regular units were badly under strength. A general judged his strength by the numbers of his infantry and an American infantry regiment in 1814 was authorized a total of about one thousand officers and men. Since the Left Division possessed six such regiments, its authorized infantry strength was six thousand, but on 1 July 1814 it mustered only 2311 men fit for duty – 1319 in the First Brigade and 992 in the Second – 38.5% of its authorized strength. Reinforcements were on the way but these would only replace the casualties Brown could expect to lose in battle and they would not be of the same calibre as the men trained by Scott. The Left Division was a very potent but a very fragile instrument.[84]

Still forming was Porter's Third, or Light, Brigade. This brigade would consist of Fenton's Pennsylvania Volunteers, 728 strong, and the New York Volunteers under militia Brigadier General John Swift consisting of a regiment of infantry under Lieutenant Colonel Philetus Swift, 320 strong, and a detached battalion of 120 men under Lieutenant Colonel Isaac Stone comprising a company of dragoons under Captain Claudius V. Boughton and a light infantry company under Captain Hope Dewey. Rounding out the brigade were the Canadian Volunteers, fifty-six strong, under of the command of forty-one-year-old Lieutenant Colonel Joseph Willcocks, former elected member of the Legislative Assembly of Upper Canada. Also attached to Porter's command was an Indian contingent composed mainly of Senecas but including contingents from the Tuscarora, Onondaga and Oneida nations under the command of their war chiefs, Red Jacket, Cornplanter and Farmer's Brother. When all its units joined, the Third Brigade would bring the fighting strength of the division to about five thousand regulars and non-regulars and five to six hundred Indians.[85]

The divisional staff consisted of Brown's two aides, Captains Ambrose Spencer from New York and Loring Austin from Massachusetts, and six other officers. Colonel Charles K. Gardner, another New Yorker and adjutant general, functioned much as a modern chief of staff, ensuring the divisional headquarters ran smoothly, leaving Brown free to command in the field. Gardner was assisted by Major Roger Jones, a native of Virginia and an ex-marine who had transferred to the army at the outbreak of war. Brown could also call on the expertise of Lieutenant Colonel William McRee, the divisional engineer, and his assistant, Major Eleazar D. Wood. The twenty-six-year-old McRee from North Carolina, an early graduate from the infant military academy at West Point, had served in the corps of engineers since 1805. Wood, a New Yorker, had studied medicine before entering West Point and, after gradua-

New York Militia captain, c. 1813
Both armies at Lundy's Lane incorporated numbers of non-regular troops. Porter's Third Brigade of the Left Division was composed of New York and Pennsylvania troops drafted from their respective state militias who performed creditably in a bloody battle. Militia officers purchased their own uniforms and were usually better dressed than the men they led. (Painting by H.C. McBarron, courtesy Parks Canada)

U.S. Light Dragoon, 1814
Although they wore splendid and striking uniforms, the regular cavalry of both armies played a very minor role during the battle because Canada was not good horse country and the action at Lundy's Lane offered few opportunities for cavalry action. This American light dragoon wears a dark blue jacket trimmed with silver braid, white breeches and a leather cap with a white horsehair fall. (Painting by H.C. McBarron, courtesy Parks Canada)

American infantry, Scott's First Brigade, 1814
These two soldiers wear the grey jacket which Scott issued to his brigade at Williamsville in the spring of 1814. The men of the First Brigade would make this simple garment, normally worn as fatigue dress, famous on the field of battle in July. (Drawing by R.J. Marrion, author's collection)

tion in 1808, had joined the corps of engineers. He had gained a brevet promotion to major for his services at the siege of Fort Meigs in 1813. These two intelligent and capable officers would play a major role in the forthcoming months. Finally there were two more Virginians: Captain John Camp, the divisional quartermaster, a former navy midshipman, and Second Lieutenant Edward B. Randolph, acting divisional inspector-general. Brown expected much from his military "family" and they did not disappoint him.[86]

As June turned to July, the Left Division, weary of incessant drill, was spoiling for a fight. One regular officer remembered that "every one was anxious of an opportunity to remove the disgrace which former disasters and defeats had attached to our arms, and to our military character."[87] When small groups of Indian warriors began to arrive at Flint Hill, the men guessed they would soon be going into action. The Indians proved to be a popular attraction, "trading moccasins, trinkets, &c. and some times running races, shooting with the bow and arrow, throwing the tomahawk, and shewing the war dance, at all of which diversions they are very expert."[88] Scott was always highly visible. Surgeon William Horner remembered him making a flying visit to the camp hospital and remarking, "Well Doctor, but little work as yet." "No General," responded Horner, "we are looking for some." "You will get it before long," was the quick reply.[89]

On the morning of 2 July 1814, the anxiously-awaited order was finally issued. Brown informed the Left Division that it would be "put in motion against the enemy" that night.[90] The troops had been expecting to enjoy the traditional 4th of July holiday and some had planned a special meal for the occasion but all hopes of a celebration were dashed as the day passed in a frenzy of last minute preparations. The final arrangements for the crossing of the Niagara were decided in a morning conference between Brown, Scott, Ripley, McRee and Wood. All available boats would be divided between the two regular brigades who would land at locations reconnoitred by the two engineers – Scott below and Ripley above Fort Erie. As evening came on, Ripley displayed for the first time the behaviour that would mar his conduct in the weeks ahead. He sought Brown out and informed him that he was dissatisfied with the transport arrangements and feared his brigade would come to disaster because of possible strong British defences at its landing site. Brown was surprised but declined to change the plan, and when Ripley tendered his resignation, refused to accept it. Chastened, Ripley left headquarters. "We go," said Brown to Major Thomas Jesup, "and nothing but the elements shall stop us."[91]

CHAPTER 3

The Defenders of Upper Canada

Eyes right, my jolly field boys,
Who British bayonets bear,
To teach your foes to yield, boys,
When British steel they dare!
Now fill the glass, for the toast of toasts
Shall be drunk with the cheer of cheers,
Hurrah, hurrah, hurrah, hurrah!
For the British Bayoneteers.
SONG, "THE BRITISH BAYONETEERS," 1814

Lieutenant General Gordon Drummond, the British commander in Upper Canada, had been expecting an attack for some time. During the first six months of 1814, while trying to put the province in the best possible state of defence, Drummond had closely watched American movements and had noted the concentration of troops at Buffalo. By the end of June, he was certain that an American offensive was imminent in the Niagara area.

Gordon Drummond had been a professional soldier for nearly a quarter of a century. Born at Quebec in 1772, he was the third son of Colin Drummond, laird of Megginch in Perthshire, Scotland and deputy paymaster general of the British forces in Canada. In September 1789, at the age of seventeen, Drummond entered the British army as an ensign in the 1st Regiment of Foot but stayed with that regiment only seven months before commencing a rapid rise made possible by the purchase system. By February 1794, having served in three regiments in less than five years, he was a twenty-one-year-old lieutenant colonel in the 8th Foot and saw his first action in 1794-1795 when he commanded his regiment in Flanders and Holland. That ill-fated campaign, which revealed serious flaws in the British army, was, one participant later recalled, a good learning experience. As the future Duke of Wellington, Lieutenant Colonel Arthur Wesley of the 33rd Foot, remarked, the campaign taught him "what one ought not to do, and that is always something."[1]

In 1799 Drummond went to the Mediterranean with the 8th where he remained three years, participating in the Egyptian campaign of 1801. In 1804 he was promoted brigadier general, and the following year major general. He then served in a series of senior North American staff appointments – two years as second-in-command of Jamaica, 1805–1807, were followed by three years, 1808–1811, as second-in-command of Canada. In 1811 he was promoted lieutenant general and given a military district in Ireland. He had never held an important command in the field and it now appeared as if Drummond's career had reached its zenith. His appointment, on the basis of his considerable North American experience, to the post of Upper Canada must have come as a welcome opportunity to achieve further distinction.

A handsome man, somewhat above average in height, with stern, even features, Drummond had married in 1807 and was devoted to his wife and their three children. The most capable British general to serve in Canada since Brock, Drummond did not possess that officer's charisma nor did he inspire the same fierce loyalty among his subordinates. He was, however, a good administrator whose appetite for staff work meshed with that of his superior, Sir George Prevost. Outwardly Drummond was cool and controlled – traits that led one Upper Canadian to remark that, although the British general was "a very superior private character," he appeared to lack the "military fire and vigour of decision which the principal commander of this country must possess in order to preserve it."[2]

To assist him, Drummond had Major General Phineas Riall, with headquarters at Fort George, commanding the Right Division which included all troops west of Kingston, while Major General Richard Stovin at Kingston commanded the Centre Division responsible for that place and the St. Lawrence. Although Drummond was superior in rank to Stovin, he had his powers curtailed by Prevost, who would not let him move troops away from the St. Lawrence without his prior consent.[3]

In January 1814 Drummond assessed the major threat to Upper Canada as coming from the American forces in the Detroit area. He decided that his first priority was to restore his open right flank by making an attack against the American Lake Erie squadron frozen in the ice at Put-In Bay at the mouth of the Detroit River. The capture or destruction of these vessels would at one blow reverse Barclay's defeat, divest the United States of con-

Lieutenant General Gordon Drummond, British Army (1771-1854)
The British commander in Upper Canada, Drummond was a brave and resourceful leader but he had not seen much action in the decade preceding the War of 1812. At Lundy's Lane, he underestimated the quality of his opponents but by the end of the campaign he had come to have a healthy respect for the American regular. (McCord Museum of Canadian History, Montreal, M400)

trol of Lake Erie and strengthen the province's western flank. In February Drummond travelled as far as Moraviantown on a tour of inspection but the unseasonably warm weather convinced him that an attack over the ice was impossible. He therefore contented himself with ordering Riall to supply ammunition to the western Indians and post detachments at Long Point and along the Thames. As American intentions were at this time unclear, Drummond decided to wait and watch.[4]

Other problems demanded his attention. There had been numerous acts of treason in Upper Canada since the war had begun and Drummond wanted to set a firm example for the future. At the urging of the provincial attorney-general, John Beverley Robinson, he brought the matter before the session of the Legislative Assembly that met at York in February. Assuming his civil function as president of the Assembly, Drummond reminded its elected members in his opening address that two of their number, Joseph Willcocks and Abraham Markle, were serving in the ranks of the American army, and expressed his confidence that he could rely on the assembly's "good sense" to "strengthen the hands of Government as to obviate all apprehension of the recurrence of a similar problem."[5]

This not so subtle warning had effect. At Drummond's request the Assembly passed a series of acts providing for the more effective trial of traitors, the confiscation of the estates of those suspected of treason or designated as aliens, and the partial suspension of *habeus corpus* so that persons suspected of treasonable acts could be detained. Commissioners were appointed to report on disloyal citizens and supervise the abandoned or confiscated property of these persons. Next, the full measure of the law was brought to bear on those guilty of disloyalty. At the Ancaster "bloody Assize" of May and June 1814, a special court heard charges of treason laid against fifty citizens, including Joseph Willcocks, the commanding officer of the Canadian Volunteers serving in Brown's army, and his two principal subordinates, Markle and Benajah Mallory. Only nineteen of those charged were actually in custody and the judges found fifteen of them guilty of high treason. Eight were sentenced to suffer the extreme penalty for this crime – hanging followed by beheading – and this sentence was duly carried out at Burlington Bay on 20 July. By these stern measures, Drummond served notice that acts of disaffection would no longer be tolerated by the Crown.[6]

He had less success with his other major problem – a critical shortage of provisions. The 1813 harvest had been the worst in years and there were not enough foodstuffs to feed the seven thousand people on the Crown's ration list for a prolonged period. His predecessor, Major General Francis De Rottenburg, had tackled the food problem by declaring martial law in the eastern district of the province, whose farmers were required to sell their produce to the army at a fair price set by local magistrates. This measure had caused great dissatisfaction and Drummond had revoked it shortly after he had arrived in the province. He tried other solutions: prohibiting the distillation of grain into spirits, sending all military dependents to Lower Canada and forbidding the export of meat and wheat. He also considered reducing the rations given to the Indians but was forced to relent after they protested they would be unable to feed their families as military service prevented them from farming or hunting. All these measures had some effect but food stocks were still too low. Frustrated, Drummond replaced his principal commissary officer, but inevitably he was forced to follow De Rottenburg's precedent: in April 1814 he declared martial law regarding the purchase of food stocks. This brought limited relief but the supply shortage was to remain critical throughout the remainder of the war.[7]

In the spring of 1814 a wave of optimism swept through Upper Canada as news of the abdication of Napoleon reached the province. Many Canadians believed that the United States would now seek a quick peace before massive British reinforcements were sent to North America. "I am much of the opinion that the rapid decline of their ally, Boney, will make them *sing small*," one wrote of the Americans, "and of course a peace must take place, but God forbid that any peace should be granted them until they are completely humbled."[8] For the moment there was little sign of that.

By late April both Drummond and Yeo thought it imperative to take some sort of action on Lake Ontario. The ice had broken up at Kingston on the 10th of that month and shortly afterward Yeo launched two new warships, the *Prince Regent* and *Princess Charlotte*, which gave him naval superiority. He now believed he could beat Chauncey or at least "dance with him" until he could be beaten.[9] To Drummond, still worried about the supply shortage – his commissary was issuing two thousand barrels of foodstuffs a month and twelve hundred of them were going to the Indians – it did not appear that Upper Canada would be able to withstand a prolonged campaign. As its safety largely depended on British control of Lake Ontario, the two commanders reasoned their most effective course would be a pre-emptive strike against the American naval base at Sackets Harbor.[10]

Drummond calculated that such an attack would require at least four thousand troops but he could provide only thirty-two hundred, including militia and Indians, from his own resources. He asked Prevost for the balance but the commander-in-chief was cool, feeling he was not in a position to justify "exposing too much at one stake," and refused to supply the needed men.[11] Thwarted, Drummond and Yeo instead raided the American depot at Oswego in early May and Yeo then mounted a blockade of the Harbor. Unable to make an assault, he planned to bombard the place with Congreve rockets fired from his ships' boats. Unfortunately most of these craft were lost on 27 May when one of Yeo's subordinates was ambushed and forced to surrender after following an American small boat convoy up the Sandy Creek near the Harbor.[12]

On 3 June, Yeo sailed away from Sackets Harbor and stationed his squadron midway between that place and Kingston. This move caught Drummond by surprise as he was depending on Yeo's blockade of that place to "distress the enemy and to retard the armament and equipment of his new ships."[13] Nevertheless, he agreed that Yeo should remain on the defensive until his powerful new ship of the line, the 104-gun *St. Lawrence*, was ready to take the lake.

In the meantime it was becoming clear that the initiative had passed to the Americans and Drummond suspected that they would attack in the Niagara peninsula. He expressed his fears to Prevost that Riall's Right Division, responsible for the defense of the area "would not be able to hold its ground" but was unable to make his superior perceive the danger.[14] For his part, Prevost was certain that Montreal would be the objective of any major American offensive and smugly assured Drummond that his strength in Upper Canada was sufficient to enable him "to meet and completely frustrate the meditated designs of the enemy."[15]

As June wore on, Drummond became impatient with Prevost's inability to comprehend what to him was a clear danger. When he remonstrated that a major attack across the Niagara was "imminent" while any American move against Montreal would probably be a feint to prevent reinforcements being sent to Upper Canada, Prevost noted that this belief was "not founded on fact." Drummond realized that he could not expect further assistance and the defence of Canada was now, in a large measure, in the hands of Riall and his Right Division.[16]

Thirty-eight years old in the spring of 1814, Major General Phineas Riall was the younger son an Anglo-Irish banking family in Clonmel, County Tipperary. He had entered the army in March 1794 at the age of eighteen as an ensign and, like Drummond, had risen swiftly through the purchase system. By December of 1794, Riall was a major in the 128th Foot but went on half pay when his unit was disbanded in 1798. Riall saw his first active service during the Irish "troubles" of 1798–1799 but his most extensive field experience had come in the West Indies, where he had been posted as a major in the 15th Foot in 1803. He commanded a brigade for a brief period during the attacks on Martinique, the Saintes and Guadaloupe in 1809 and 1810. He was promoted colonel on his return to the United Kingdom in 1810 and two years later was made a major general.[17]

In August 1813, Riall, termed "an active and intelligent young man," was sent to Canada, arriving in time to command the Right Division during Drummond's campaign of retribution on the Niagara that December.[18] A subordinate who came to know him well described him as "very brave, near sighted, rather short, but stout" and a man "thought by some rather rash, which, by the by, is a good fault in a General officer."[19] A period portrait shows a dark-haired, thick-set man with strong, even features.

From the outset Riall was certain a major American offensive would come in the Niagara and worried about the ability of his division to meet it. Unlike Brown's Left Division which was a field formation, Riall's Right Division was a geographic and administrative entity – basically a collection of infantry battalions and other units not formed into permanent brigades.

Major General Phineas Riall, British Army
The British commander in the Niagara at the beginning of the 1814 campaign, Riall was a brave and aggressive officer who had beaten American troops in a number of small actions the previous winter. At Chippawa on 5 July 1814, he encountered Brown's Left Division for the first time and the result was something very different. Riall was wounded and captured at Lundy's Lane. (Courtesy Riall Family)

Although nominally Riall commanded all troops west of Kingston, in practice Drummond only allowed him control of those in the Niagara peninsula and the area west of it. It was a difficult assignment – his main line of defence along the Niagara River was open to attacks from all directions. In March Riall concluded that he was overextended and his best course was to withdraw the bulk of his units back from the line of the Niagara to a central position from which he could move to any threatened point. He proposed this disposition to Drummond with the warning that unless he received more troops his situation would become "extremely critical."[20]

Despite the fact that he himself had somewhat similar problems with Prevost, Drummond was unsympathetic. Admitting that "a Military man unacquainted with the character of the Enemy he has to contend with, or with the events of the last two Campaigns," would have agreed with Riall's proposal, he would not permit any withdrawal from the Niagara line. He gave Riall instructions to withdraw only if a major attack came from Detroit in which case, after leaving adequate garrisons in Forts George and Niagara, he could retreat to Burlington Bay. But if the enemy crossed the Niagara, Riall was to stay put and try to prevent the Americans from possessing both its banks. As Drummond explained to his subordinate, premature abandonment of this line might "expose the whole frontier to outrages" and he assured Riall that he should not fear an attack across the river because a large part of any attacking force would necessarily be occupied in screening or besieging Fort Niagara.[21]

Drummond recognized the strategic importance of the Niagara peninsula, one of the most fertile and heavily settled areas of Upper Canada. A
rectangular block of land about thirty miles wide and fifty miles long jutting
out between the western end of Lake Ontario and the eastern end of Lake
Erie, and bounded on the east by the Niagara River, the peninsula was a
major transportation route. Dominating it was the great natural wonder of
the falls of Niagara with its towering cloud of spray that on clear days could
be seen fifty miles away. The falls and the eight-mile gorge below it rendered that part of the Niagara River impassable and made the construction
of a portage road necessary along the Canadian side of the river. This busy
artery provided additional wealth to the local settlers, who had been attracted to the area by its rich soil and luxuriant forests. Blessed with a mild
winter and a relatively long summer, the Niagara possessed impressive
stands of oak, maple, walnut and chestnut as well as the more prosaic soft
pine, cedar and fir. Apples, peaches and cherries grew wild after a first plant-
ing. The first settlers were quick to take advantage of these natural assets
and by the time of the war the Canadian side of the Niagara was a patch-
work of small farms interspersed with wood lots so advanced in development that visitors remarked on the "English appearance" of its tidy fields
and neatly-kept white frame houses.[22]

Ordered to stay put and defend this valuable agricultural area, Riall made
the best of it. The northern part of the Niagara line was anchored by three
fortifications that formed a mutually-supporting defence system: Fort
Niagara on the American side commanded the river mouth and was in turn
commanded by Forts Mississauga and George on the Canadian side. Seven
miles to the south, fieldworks covered the village of Queenston, an ideal
crossing point. The next eight miles of river formed the impassable gorge of
the falls and required no defence works. Three miles above the falls was the
village of Chippawa at the junction of the Chippawa and Niagara rivers.
Here, fieldworks were sited to protect both the village and the vital bridge
over the Chippawa. It was the next sixteen miles that worried Riall. The
Niagara could be easily crossed anywhere between Chippawa and Fort Erie,
and he did not have enough troops to adequately defend or even patrol this
section. That left the southern anchor of his line, the small stone Fort Erie
across from Buffalo, isolated and vulnerable.[23]

West of Fort Erie, the peninsula was open to invasion anywhere along
the north shore of Lake Erie but Riall could spare only small detachments
to guard it. By April even those had been withdrawn and there had been no

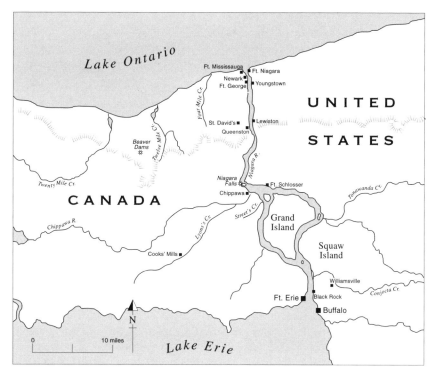

The Niagara frontier

regulars to oppose Campbell's raid on Long Point the following month. Riall also fretted about the safety of his main depot at Burlington Bay which was vulnerable to attack either from Lake Ontario or from the Detroit area. Knowing that "he who would defend everything, defends nothing," Riall decided that he had to shorten his line at some point.[24]

The logical place was Fort Niagara. Its defences were in poor condition and it required a large garrison, which because of the cramped conditions within the fort suffered from low morale despite the extra food and alcohol rations they received in compensation. In March the state of the garrison, the 8th Foot, became so poor that its commanding officer begged Riall "in the name of God remove us as unworthy of retaining the Post of Honour."[25] Referring to that "cursed fort," Riall requested Drummond's permission to compress its defences and remove most of the garrison. Even this mild suggestion was rejected and he was forced to replace the 8th with the 100th Foot, one of his best units.[26]

By May 1814, convinced from the American activity at Buffalo that the southern part of his line was threatened, Riall made plans to withdraw the

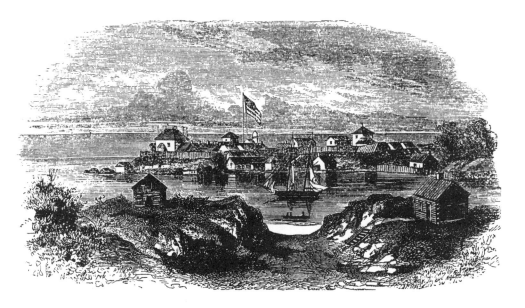

Fort Niagara from Fort George, c. 1860
Located on Lake Ontario, Fort Niagara was a strategically-located position that dominated the mouth of the Niagara River. Its loss to the British in December 1814 was a major setback to American arms and, indirectly, triggered the bloody Niagara campaign of 1814. (From Benson Lossing, *Pictorial Field Book of the War of 1812*, New York, 1869)

garrison of Fort George and use it to defend the river bank south of Chippawa. He also tried to bring forward some of the troops stationed at Burlington, replacing them with part of the garrison from York. Drummond vetoed these arrangements, however, and also turned down Riall's requests for reinforcements. He had none to give and no shipping to move them. Even worse, Drummond ordered Riall to contribute part of his field artillery and his Indian force to the expedition planned against Sackets Harbor.[27]

A few weeks later, Riall concluded that his situation was untenable. The final straw was a medical report that informed him that two of his regular battalions, the 1st and 8th, were riddled with sickness and the 8th would have to be removed from the peninsula. In desperation, he appealed for more troops, plaintively asking Drummond why, if "an American Army is able to march from Sackett's Harbor to Buffalo ... a British regiment may not march from Kingston to York?"[28] He urged Drummond to give "this representation ... your most serious consideration [and] adopt such measures as you may conceive most proper to have Reinforcements forwarded to this Div[ision] before it is too late."[29]

These were strong words. It is not known whether Drummond forwarded this letter to Prevost but, in bolstering his own requests for reinforcements, he had been transmitting many of the Right Division commander's concerns to his superior. What is certain is that Prevost was beginning to have doubts about Riall and had decided to replace him.

Drummond was appalled when the commander-in-chief suggested that Riall be removed and defended his subordinate in a strongly worded letter dated 2 July 1814. Subtly chiding Prevost for a lack of knowledge of local conditions, he praised Riall for trying to overcome almost insurmountable problems. As for Riall's repeated warnings about the state of things in the Niagara, Drummond continued, it was that officer's duty to transmit all the "information he could procure, and every opinion he formed in consequence." There should be no concern about Riall's steadiness – Drummond had personally witnessed "his zeal, energy, and intrepidity ... in action with the Enemy, and in no instance whatever can I tax my recollection with the most trifling want of ability in that officer." To remove him at this time,

Fort George from Fort Niagara
Constructed in the 1790s, Fort George dominated Fort Niagara across the Niagara River. Along with the British-held Fort Niagara and Fort Mississaga, it constituted part of a self-supporting defensive position that controlled the mouth of the Niagara River in July 1814. (Painting by Edward Walsh, National Archives of Canada, C-000026)

Drummond concluded, "would not strictly accord with that delicacy of proceedings, which Major General Riall's rank demands" especially "when an opportunity may soon offer of distinguishing himself, and of rewarding himself thereby for his labour in his Country's cause."[30] This strong endorsement had effect and Riall retained his command.

By this time Riall was daily expecting an attack. To meet it, he had about thirty-four hundred men spread along the thirty-mile length of the Niagara River with his main strength in three regular infantry battalions, the 1st, 41st and 100th Foot, stationed in the three forts at the mouth of the river and at Fort Erie. In support were the 103rd Foot at Burlington Bay and the Incorporated Militia Battalion at York. In addition, he shortly expected to be reinforced by three more units: the 8th Foot, on its way back from a rest at York, and the 89th and Glengarry Light Infantry from Kingston.[31]

These battalions were the heart of the Right Division. Of the eight that Riall had under command or expected to receive, six were regular units – the 1st, 8th, 41st, 89th, 100th and 103rd Foot – and five of them veteran battalions which had seen considerable service and were inured to North American campaigning. The 103rd Foot was a different matter. Although it had been in Canada since 1812, the 103rd had not seen much active service possibly because it was composed largely of very young recruits and had instead spent much time working on labour details. It was not a well-disciplined unit; its men committed numerous crimes and it suffered from a high rate of desertion. The root of the 103rd's problems may have been its shortage of officers or the fact that its commander, Colonel Hercules Scott, a competent soldier, was absent from it for long periods on staff duties.[32]

The men of these battalions were infantry of the line, the famous "red coats." They formed the backbone of an army that had seen victory in a dozen recent battles against the French and they had rarely been beaten by the Americans. The red coats were tough men who lived a hard life. They were somewhat smaller than their American counterparts, the average height of an infantryman in the Right Division being a little over five feet, six inches. They were also somewhat older, most being between twenty-five and thirty-five years of age. They came from every county in the United Kingdom but a high proportion were Irishmen. This was true not only of the 100th Foot, whose official title was The Prince Regent's County of Dublin Regiment, or the 89th, recruited in Ireland, but of every battalion in the division. Even the august 1st Foot, The Royal Scots and the senior infantry regiment of the army, had a surprising number of Donagheys, Flahertys,

Kellys and Kennedys recruited from such hamlets as Baleron, Calgraney, Clonfickle and Dunamore.[33]

The vast majority of enlisted men in the Right Division had signed on for "life" (usually about twenty-one years) and had an average of five years with the colours. Most had been forced into the army by economic misery. Others had been lured by a misguided sense of adventure, by the glowing promises of a recruiting sergeant, a desire to get away from bad debts or bad marriages and in some cases as the better of a hard choice between the army or transportation to Australia. There were even a number (and they were not few) who had enlisted out of patriotism. British recruiting sergeants were quick to take advantage of all these reasons and, by 1812, had raised the process of personnel acquisition to an art form. In the words of one,

> ... it was never much trouble getting them to enlist. The best way was to make up to the man you had in your eye and ask him what sort of web he was in. You might be sure it was a bad one ...
>
> Ploughboys had to be hooked in a different way. Tell your man how many recruits had been made sergeants, how many were now officers. If you see an officer pass tell him he was only a recruit a year ago, but now he's so proud, he won't speak to you ...
>
> To be sure, some of your sentimental chaps might despise all of this; but they were the easiest caught after all. You had only to get into heroics and spout about glory ... deathless fame ... and all that and you had him safe as a mouse in a trap![34]

The regular British soldier lived under draconian discipline. The gulf between officer and enlisted man was immense and was widened still further by the power of corporal punishment officers had over their men. Regulations allowed a regimental commander to punish a soldier with up to three hundred lashes if he thought it necessary and some battalions, notably the 8th Foot, were "hard punishment" units. In 1814 the spectacle of a British infantry battalion formed in a hollow square to watch one of its number being flogged was not uncommon. But the army was changing – Drummond disliked flogging, urging commanders to use milder forms of punishment, and his opinion was shared by many other officers. One colonel told his men that "if he could not stand fire better than witness flogging, he would be the worst soldier in the Army.[35] Lieutenant John Le Couteur of the 104th Foot fainted while witnessing his first punishment parade. His fellow officers teased him unmercifully but his men, noting their officer's dislike of corporal punishment, reacted favourably when he tried to maintain discipline without the lash.[36]

Regimental life for the private soldier was a combination of endless drill and fatigues occasionally broken by active service. The pay was no compensation; private soldiers received a shilling a day but, with deductions for rations, sundry equipment, medical treatment and other charges, were lucky if they received a penny of it. Meal times certainly were not the high point of the soldier's day – one man recalled that the rations were "miserable stuff," the bread "being composed of the coarsest materials, and such was its adhesive qualities, that if a piece was thrown against the wall, there it would remain."[37] For many, the only relief from the drudgery and boredom was oblivion through alcohol and drunkenness was the curse of the army. The combination of harsh discipline, monotony and low pay led many to desert and the nearby United States provided a ready haven. Between January and June 1814, the six regular battalions of the Right Division lost two hundred and eleven men through desertion.[38]

The regular infantryman wore a uniform similar to that of his American opponent but of a different colour. The war in Europe had delayed the issue of new clothing and equipment in Canada and by 1814 some units were becoming quite ragged. Only officers, non-commissioned officers and drummers wore uniforms of the expensive scarlet cloth, the rank and file being issued coatees of a brick red colour that soon faded to a liverish, greyish pink and were disfigured by multi-coloured patches and crookedly-resown seams. There were more patches on the grey, wool trousers worn over gaiters that covered the soldier's stout boots and the high, black felt shakos were faded by the sun and melted by the rain into a fantastic variety of shapes. Like his American counterpart, the British infantryman had to suffer the wretched indignity of a leather neck stock that forced him to hold his head in an upright position. His fighting and personal equipment – cartridge box, scabbard, haversack, canteen and all their attendant belts – were similar but his knapsack was different being black-painted canvas stretched over a wooden frame that cut into his back when he marched long distances. Into this went the soldier's "necessaries," his issue clothing and items and his few personal possessions. The British infantryman's total load in 1814 was close to sixty pounds, causing one to complain that the Crown should "issue us with new backbones to bear the weight."[39] Added to this was the soldier's nine-and-a-half-pound India Pattern musket, the "Brown Bess" of legend.

Private soldier, Glengarry Light Infantry
The Glengarry Light Infantry was a fencible regiment, a regiment of regulars raised in Canada. Wearing green uniforms rather than the more familiar red, they were light infantry specialists and experienced skirmishers. During the early stages of the battle, they proved very effective in harassing the left flank of Scott's First Brigade. (Painting by G.A. Embleton, courtesy Parks Canada)

Private, 1st Regiment of Foot, British Army, c. 1812
The 1st Foot, the Royal Scots, played a major role in the Battle of Lundy's Lane. This private wears a brick-red, wool coatee, or short-tailed jacket, and a black felt shako. Well-trained, well-led and incredibly obstinate in the defence, the British regular infantryman was a dangerous opponent who had seen victory on dozens of North American and European battlefields. (Painting by G.A. Embleton, courtesy Parks Canada)

The field grade and junior officers of these battalions tended to be seasoned professionals and not the aristocratic fops of mythology. Most had entered service after the Duke of York's reforms of the 1790s had corrected the flagrant abuses of the purchase system. By 1814, only twenty per cent of the officers in the army had purchased their first commission and the great majority of promotions were gained either by merit or seniority. York's re-

British ensign and colour sergeant, c. 1814
Each British battalion of infantry possessed two colours, the King's Colour and the Regimental Colour. Visible above the smoke of battle, these colours were useful for aligning the ranks in action. They were traditionally carried by the most junior officers and it was post both of great honour and great danger. The colour sergeant who protected the ensign in battle can be identified by his rank badge, a single chevron below a stylized coat of arms. (Illustration courtesy Parks Canada)

forms ensured that officers had to serve a certain amount of time in each grade before being promoted and, as promotion within a regiment went by regimental, not army, seniority, officers tended to stay with their units for long periods and they became closely knit families. William Dunlop of the 89th Foot recalled of his comrades that "a more honest-hearted set of fellows never sat around a mess table."[40]

Many of these officers had considerable experience – the captains of the 89th Foot, as an example, possessed an average of twelve years in the army and the lieutenants about six. The battalion commanders were men like thirty-nine-year-old Hercules Scott of the 103rd who had fought in India

Sergeant and gunner, Royal Artillery, c. 1812
The Royal Artillery was the most professional arm in the British army. During the early stages of the battle of Lundy's Lane, British gunners inflicted heavy casualties on Scott's First Brigade. Dressed in blue uniforms with red trim, these two men are shown positioned near a heavy iron gun mounted on a garrison carriage as would be found in permanent fortifications. (Courtesy Parks Canada)

with Wellington; thirty-one-year-old Joseph Wanton Morrison of the 89th, the victor of Crysler's Farm; George Hay of the 100th, the Marquis of Tweeddale, only twenty-seven years of age but a wounded veteran of ten years service and six of those with Wellington; and thirty-seven-year-old Thomas Evans of the 8th who had fought at Detroit and Queenston. Among them, these four officers represented seventy-three years of military service and, as individuals, possessed more combat experience than either Drummond or Riall. They could be depended upon to provide competent leadership at the unit level.[41]

Two of Riall's infantry units were Canadian. The Glengarry Light Infantry Fencibles had been recruited from "none but British subjects of unsuspected loyalty" who were "chiefly Scotch and their descendants" throughout the Canadas.[42] As a fencible regiment, the Glengarries were not required to serve outside North America but in all other respects – discipline, training and equipment – they were like the regulars. A light infantry corps, the Glengarries wore a green uniform similar to that of British rifle regiments and had fought as skirmishers in numerous actions along the border in the past two years.

The other Canadian unit was the Incorporated Militia Battalion of Upper Canada. Recruited from militiamen who had volunteered for active service for the duration of the war, it was commanded by a British officer, Captain William Robinson of the 8th Foot with the local rank of lieutenant colonel. The Incorporated Militia was uniformed, armed, drilled and equipped as regular British infantry but its men were not subject to the punishment of flogging. The choice of Robinson, a thirty-two-year-old Irishman with an irrepressible sense of humour, as their commander was an inspired one on the part of the authorities. Possessed of "military talents" and "invincible good temper," he had in a few months "rendered a body of raw lads from the ploughtail as efficient a corps as any in the field."[43]

Cavalry and artillery completed the fighting strength of the Right Division. Riall had two small cavalry units: Major Robert Lisle's squadron of the regular 19th Light Dragoons and Canadian Captain W. Hamilton Merritt's troop of militia cavalry. Both were posted in small detachments along the entire Niagara line. Captain James Maclachlan commanded the company of Royal Artillery that provided the division's field artillery and manned the guns of Fort Erie and the fieldworks at Queenston and Chippawa. This company was fresh from England but Maclachlan, with nineteen years service, was an experienced officer as was his second captain, James

Mackonochie, with fourteen years. Also under Maclachlan were detachments of Royal Marine and militia artillery stationed in the forts at the river mouth while Mackonochie commanded that part of the company that had been organized into a field brigade (battery) with one 5½-inch howitzer and six 6-pdr. guns. The divisional field artillery also included two 24-pdr. brass guns which had been cast as experimental pieces in the mid-18th century and, weighing 2050 pounds each without their carriages, were the heaviest field pieces used in battle by either side during the war. These two guns usually operated independently under the command of a lieutenant from Mackonochie's brigade. Finally, there was a section of Royal Marine Artillery equipped with the British army's secret weapon, the Congreve rocket.[44]

Riall could also call on the services of between two thousand and three thousand sedentary militia. This was basically every able-bodied male from the ages of sixteen to sixty, organized into regiments by county and companies by neighbourhood and equipped with a variety of weaponry, most of it bad. The militia of Upper Canada possessed a variable combat record, performing well in some actions but not as well in many others. Some units, such as the 1st and 2nd Lincoln Regiments from the Niagara area, had been called out so often for duty that they had become fairly experienced soldiers – the lst Lincoln, in particular, had a good reputation as skirmishers – but they were an exception. By 1814 the more daring souls in the sedentary organization had found their way into the ranks of the Canadian fencible units or the long-service militia corps such as the Incorporated Battalion and Merritt's dragoons; the rest were essentially very cautious civilians. Although the militia was a military organization, there was a reluctance on the part of British commanders to call these men away from their farms as it

The Congreve rocket in action
Britain's "secret weapon" of the Napoleonic wars, the Congreve rocket was a military adaptation of the civilian sky rocket. A detachment of the Royal Marine Artillery used 12-pdr. Congreve rockets, similar to those shown here, at Lundy's Lane. They were dramatic but very inaccurate weapons. (Courtesy Museum Restoration Service, Bloomfield, Ont.)

Vedette, 19th Light Dragoons, British Army, 1814
The 19th Regiment of Light Dragoons were the only British regular army cavalry to fight in Canada during the War of 1812. Their magnificent uniforms belied their effectivness, as mounted troops could only play a minor role in the closely-wooded terrain. (Drawing by A. Robinson-Sager, courtesy Parks Canada)

British brass field artillery and limbers
The British artillery which fought at Lundy's Lane were equipped with brass (actually bronze) field pieces similar to those shown here. They were the most lethal weapons in use during the early (daylight) stages of the Battle of Lundy's Lane. (Photograph, reproduction artillery at Fort George National Historic Site, courtesy of the Friends of Fort George)

interfered with the harvest. The sedentary militia constituted a reserve for Riall but it was a last and limited reserve.[45]

Finally Riall had a large force of Indian warriors. These were drawn from the Five Nations settled along the Grand River and the western nations who had followed Tecumseh's brother, Tenskawatawa, or the Prophet, to Burlington after the debacle at the Thames the previous autumn. The western contingent was split into two factions: one group, 479 strong, was at Fort George under the command of Colonel William Caldwell and Captain William Kerr of the British Indian Department while another group was at the Grand River under Tenskawatawa. The Five Nations could field between four and five hundred warriors who were usually led by their war chief, John Norton. The son of a Scots mother and a Cherokee father, Norton was a veteran of almost every major action fought in Upper Canada in the last two years. He was highly regarded and had been given a captain's commission but was disliked by the white officers of the Indian Department, who resented both his popularity with the warriors and his independence of attitude.[46]

There was a strained and precarious relationship between the British soldiers and the "Nitchies," as the regulars called their native auxiliaries.[47] The warriors were good scouts and skirmishers but their insistence on fighting when, where and how they wished was frustrating to the British military mind and led to complaints that they were unreliable. In addition, their excesses in battle made their white allies uneasy. Very few British regulars understood the Indians like Lieutenant Colonel William Drummond of the 104th Foot, an officer popular not only with regulars and militia but also with the Indians, including Norton. As a sign of his sympathy and respect for the native peoples, Drummond wore strings of Indian beads around his neck, even in uniform. But he was an exception. Most of the regulars shared the feelings of Sergeant James Commins of the 8th Foot who branded them "the most cowardly despicable characters I ever saw ... their cruelty exceeds everything I have ever seen among enemies."[48] His comments were echoed by a British officer who thought them "cunning, cowardly and revengeful in the highest degree, *brave* only when their enemy is Broken or flying and then the tomahawk and scalping knife are liberally made use of."[49] Yet these "cowardly, despicable characters" rendered invaluable service during the war and their presence was a powerful psychological weapon. If nothing else, it was better to have them as friends than as enemies.[50]

From the Indians' point of view, though the British often broke the promises they made, an alliance with the British was preferable to fighting unaided against the expansionist tendencies of the United States. The western nations from the Detroit area had been steadily resisting the Americans since the 1790s, with or without British help. Their lands were now occupied and laid waste and, for this reason, they were the most ferocious of the many warriors that were to fight alongside the British in the summer of 1814. The Grand River nations, having family connections with their counterparts in New York state and seeing little advantage in becoming involved in the white man's war, were not quite as aggressive. Many of their young warriors, however, were prepared to follow Norton, who enjoyed an immense personal reputation. Of all the protagonists who fought in the war, the Indians paid the highest price as the conflict totally disrupted their way of life and reduced them to supplicants for the Crown's not very generous welfare.

It was to Norton that Riall turned at the beginning of July to get information about the enemy force massing at Buffalo. Learning that the Americans were breaking up their camp at Flint Hill, he ordered a reconnaissance sent out from Fort Niagara, but when they reported nothing unusual Riall requested the Indian leader, camped at the falls of Niagara, to cross into the United States and ascertain the whereabouts of the Left Division. On 3 July Norton was preparing to undertake this mission when word came that the Americans had crossed the river during the previous night and invested Fort Erie. The Niagara campaign of 1814 had begun.[51]

Captain John Norton, or the Snipe
The son of a Cherokee father and a Scots mother, Norton was a resourceful and intelligent leader of the warriors who fought alongside the British army throughout the war. After Tecumseh, he was the most successful native leader of the War of 1812. (Oil portrait by Thomas Philips, R.A., c. 1818, Syon House, Brantford, U.K. Reproduced by gracious permission of the Duke of Northumberland)

PART II

The Invasion
of Canada,
3 July–24 July 1814

Chippawa Village and the King's bridge, c. 1807
This watercolour looks east down the Chippawa River toward its junction with the Niagara
River. On the left is the north bank which, in July 1814, was protected by British
fieldworks and artillery positions. The Chippawa represented the best defensive position
for the British between Fort Erie and Lake Ontario. (Watercolour by George Heriot. courtesy National Archives of Canada, C-12768)

CHAPTER 4

Opening Moves and Battle at Chippawa

*The British swear, by St. George and the Virgin Mary,
they never yet met such a d____d bloody minded set of
rascals as those Yankees are – they march up against
double their number of His Majesties best troops as at
their exercise and then all of a sudden open such a hell
of a fire upon them, with ball and buckshot, they are
cut down by scores.*
CAPTAIN GEORGE HOWARD, TWENTY-FIFTH INFANTRY, JULY, 1814

*A red coat is a famous mark and so well do this Ameri-
can banditti understand their business, that they select
officers and sergeants in preference to privates.*
LETTER IN THE *London Star*, 21 JULY, 1814

Determined to be the first man of the Left Division to step on Canadian soil, Winfield Scott nearly became its first casualty. He was in the bow
of one of the lead boats of his brigade as it headed through heavy fog for the
Canadian side of the Niagara at about 2:00 A.M. in the morning of 3 July
1814. As the craft neared the shore below Fort Erie, he tested the water
with his sword and, thinking it only knee deep, plunged in – to discover
that he had made a mistake and "had to swim for his life ... encumbered
with sword, epaulets, cloak and high boots."[1] Scott splashed ashore with
only his ardour undampened and, in a few minutes, the lead elements of his
brigade had cleared the bank of British sentries, who withdrew into the
darkness.

Ripley did not have such an easy time above the fort. There were not
enough boats to transport his entire brigade, so part marched to Scott's
embarkation point at Black Rock and crossed below the fort. The remain-

der embarked in all available craft and three small USN schooners but lost their course in the dense fog and landed several hours late.[2]

When Brown stepped ashore at dawn, he found Scott's brigade formed up and ready to move on Fort Erie. Jesup and his Twenty-Fifth Infantry were ordered to approach the fort from the north, to meet Ripley moving up from the south and prevent the escape of the garrison. As the Twenty-Fifth neared the fort they came under artillery fire and Jesup could see that the Second Brigade was not yet in position. He informed Brown, who detached his adjutant general, Gardner, to complete the investment with that portion of the Second Brigade that had crossed with Scott. At the same time, McRee and Wood began to site battery positions on the high ground north of the fort; the army then waited for Hindman to bring over his guns to begin the attack.[3]

Major Thomas Buck, the British commandant of Fort Erie, was well aware that his garrison of a single infantry company and a dozen gunners had no chance against the enemy he could see moving outside his walls. As soon as he learned of the landing, Buck had sent off a messenger to Chippawa with the news and, as the Americans neared the fort, had fired off his three small guns at them. But Buck knew the outcome was inevitable. A "mild, honorable, and pleasant" officer of thirty-four, he wanted to avoid "a useless sacrifice of men's lives" and decided to capitulate although most of his officers wanted to fight "to the last extremity."[4] At midday, Buck sent out a flag of truce and, four hours later, surrendered the one hundred and thirty-seven men of the garrison – in Porter's words, "rather too soon perhaps to satisfy the claims of military etiquette."[5] A few minutes after, the British marched out to the tune of "Yankee Doodle," rendered by the fifes and drums of Brown's infantry, and were replaced by a detachment of United States artillery under the command of Lieutenant Patrick McDonough. An American flag, donated by Towson's gunners, was run up over Fort Erie.[6]

Throughout the day of 3 July, boats shifted the division's artillery, ammunition and supply wagons to the Canadian shore. They also brought over some of Porter's New York Volunteers and Indians and Captain Samuel Harris's troop of regular light dragoons. Harris, the scion of a prominent Boston family, had arrived the previous night after riding two hundred and fifty miles in five days to reach Buffalo in time to cross with the division. By nightfall, the greater part of the two regular brigades camped near the ferry station across the river from Black Rock. It rained heavily during the night but their rest was otherwise undisturbed.[7]

When Buck's messenger arrived at Chippawa, Lieutenant Colonel Thomas Pearson, the British commander at that place, relayed the news to Riall at Fort George and then marched south with the flank companies of the 100th Foot and a party of Indian warriors led by Norton. Reaching Black Creek, Pearson saw the Americans in strength near the ferry station; he also heard rumours from local inhabitants that another American force had landed at Point Abino on Lake Erie and were pushing on to Chippawa from the west, while still more Americans were planning to cross from Grand Island and land in his rear. Pearson was not greatly perturbed by these rumours but, seeing that he could accomplish nothing with his small force, posted pickets and returned to Chippawa where Riall joined him late in the day. The British general had received word of the landing at 8:00 A.M. that morning and had quickly ordered five companies of the 1st Foot forward from Fort George to reinforce Chippawa. Hoping to catch Brown with parts of his force on each side of the river, Riall wanted to attack immediately. He delayed because, unaware that Buck had surrendered, he was confident that Fort Erie would hold up the Americans long enough for the 8th Foot, on its way from York, to join him.[8]

The next day, 4 July, Brown ordered Scott north to Chippawa, to "be governed by circumstances," but cautioned him "to secure a good military position for the night."[9] Following a general salute fired by the whole division in celebration both of the taking of Fort Erie and the national holiday, Scott marched at noon with his own brigade, Harris's dragoons and Captains Nathan Towson and Thomas Biddle's companies of artillery. He had only progressed a few miles north on the road that ran along the Canadian bank of the Niagara when he encountered a British force drawn up behind Putnam's Creek.[10]

These troops, commanded by Pearson, consisted of the flank companies of the 100th Foot, the light company of the 1st, a detachment of the 19th Light Dragoons and two 24-pdr. brass field guns. Pearson, a veteran light infantry officer with sixteen years service who had been badly wounded in the Peninsula, was experienced at rearguard actions and had chosen his position well. Swollen by rain, Putnam's Creek was virtually impassable near its junction with the Niagara, where the road crossed it on a small bridge. As the American column, with Harris and Towson in the van, came into view, Pearson's men tore up the planks of the bridge and formed in line along the north bank of the creek while the light dragoons took position upstream to discourage flanking movements.[11]

Seeing the British drawn up for a fight, Scott deployed from column of march into line and unlimbered his guns in preparation, whereupon Pearson's men loosed off a couple of rounds and disappeared north, their withdrawal covered by the dragoons. Before resuming his march, Scott had to replace the planks of the bridge. And so it went, creek after creek – Putnam's, Frenchman's, Winterhoot's, Halfway and Black's – for nearly seven hours.[12]

At one of these creeks, Towson almost met his end. Riding ahead of the column, he approached too close to the British rearguard and received a volley of musketry. Unharmed, the gunner officer wheeled his horse and galloped to safety. He later discovered that a musket ball had penetrated between the strap and the padding of his epaulette.[13]

As the day wore on, Scott began to gain on the British. At Street's Creek, a little over a mile south of the Chippawa, Captain Turner Crooker's company of the Ninth Infantry, leading the brigade, was some distance ahead of the column and was able to ford the creek upstream just as the main body approached the bridge, which was as usual missing its planks. But Crooker had overstepped himself. In front of the horrified eyes of Scott, who was unable to help him, his small company was enveloped by British dragoons. Crooker, however, kept his head and conducted a fighting withdrawal into a nearby farmhouse from which his men put the British to flight.[14]

The American advance took Riall somewhat by surprise. He was still waiting for the 8th Foot and, reluctant to attack without this reinforcement, decided to stand on the north side of the Chippawa. It was a strong position – the village of Chippawa was divided by the river which was about two hundred and fifty feet wide in 1814 and about twenty feet deep near its junction with the Niagara. It was crossed by a high, narrow, wooden bridge protected on the northern bank by a line of entrenchments and a redoubt, and anchored on the southern bank by a *tête du pont*, or fortified bridgehead. To deny the Americans cover, Riall ordered that part of the village south of the river set on fire, and after Pearson's weary men had crossed over to the north bank, his engineers dropped the centre of the bridge, rendering it unusable.[15]

It was almost sunset when Scott's column came up to the Chippawa. His men, marching in "heat and dust" that was "scarcely bearable," were tired after skirmishing continuously for nearly seventeen miles.[16] The bridge was shrouded in smoke from the burning buildings, and as the lead American elements approached, they were met by a "masterly fire of grape and canister" from the British guns on the north bank.[17] Deciding that he had accomplished enough, Scott withdrew south a few miles to the farm of Samuel Street, called the Pine Grove, and set up camp under a heavy downpour of rain. Around midnight, he was joined by Brown with the Second Brigade, the remainder of the artillery and the supply train. They spent a miserable night trying to sleep on the ground "which was covered with water owing to the Clayey surface."[18]

The American camp was south of Street's Creek, a small stream running into the Niagara parallel to the Chippawa. Rain had flooded it and it was about twenty yards wide at its mouth, where the river road crossed it on a small wooden bridge. The creek was fordable higher up and the thick bushes and vegetation that lined its banks screened the American camp. To the west and northwest of the camp were swampy, dense pine woods, obstructed with fallen timber, that connected to a strip of woodland near the Chippawa, a quarter of a mile in depth, stretching almost to the Niagara. This belt of standing timber effectively masked the positions of the two armies from each other's observation. Between it and Street's Creek was a flat, open area (called a "plain" in most accounts) that was between a half and three quarters of a mile in breadth and sparsely covered with meadow grass about three feet high. Dotted throughout the area were a number of frame farm buildings surrounded by split rail fences.[19]

Throughout the night Riall pondered his next move. He had assembled the better part of the 1st and 100th Foot, his field artillery brigade, Lisle's squadron of the 19th Light Dragoons, the 1st and 2nd Lincoln Militia regiments, a considerable force of Indian warriors and he expected the 8th Foot at any minute. There was no thought of withdrawal as the Chippawa offered one of the best defensive position on the Canadian side of the Niagara between Lakes Erie and Ontario – the decision facing Riall was whether to remain in his fieldworks and defend, or cross the river and attack. He was concerned about the threat of a second American landing in his rear, on the Lake Ontario shore, and early in the morning sent the 1st Lincoln militia, "the best flankers in the country," back to Fort George.[20] At the same time, he ordered Norton to scout the American camp "without giving any alarm" and issued similar orders to other detachments of Indians and militia.[21]

Shortly before dawn on 5 July, scouting parties slipped across the Chippawa. Moving cautiously and quietly through the woods and along the Niagara River bank they approached the pickets surrounding Brown's camp. When day came – a bright sunny day – they could hear the drums beating "reveille" and see men moving in the American tent lines. The target was too tempting – although Norton and his men obeyed their orders and did not reveal their presence, the less-disciplined began to snipe at the American pickets. Once started, the firing between the pickets and the British scouts continued in a desultory fashion throughout the morning.[22]

Captain Joseph Henderson of the Twenty-Second Infantry, commanding the picket posted north of the junction of Street's Creek and the Niagara, recalled that this firing began at dawn. Several of his men were wounded and Henderson himself had a close call when a "ball entered a Knapsack upon which I was seated and another entered the Supplies against which I was leaning close to my head."[23]

At 8:00 A.M. Henderson was relieved by Captain Benjamin Ropes's company of the Twenty-First Infantry, and to provide cover for his men Ropes positioned them in a nearby building and tore down the wall facing north. The heaviest firing took place to the west of the camp where the British could utilize the woods to get in close to the American pickets. Captain Joseph Treat's picket of the Twenty-First Infantry was in the process of being relieved when it came under a heavy fire that wounded several men. Hard pressed, Treat had to temporarily leave one of his wounded on the ground but returned for him later. Unfortunately Brown witnessed this incident and, deciding that Treat had abandoned a casualty, immediately dismissed the unfortunate New Englander from his division.[24]

Riall received a steady stream of information from his scouts but, not completely satisfied with its veracity, made a personal reconnaissance with Pearson and Norton late in the morning. Still unaware that Fort Erie had surrendered, he was convinced that the greater part of Brown's army was engaged in besieging it and as a result estimated that there were no more than two thousand Americans in front of him. The 8th Foot had finally arrived and Riall now had about thirteen hundred and fifty regular infantry, two hundred militia and three hundred and fifty Indians. Having seen Americans run away from British regulars the previous December, he had a low opinion of his opponents and was confident that he could defeat Brown and push south to relieve Fort Erie. Before he could attack, however, his engineers had to repair the Chippawa bridge so that it could bear the weight of artillery. He set them to work and instructed his units to be ready to cross the river at 3:00 P.M. that afternoon.[25]

While the Right Division waited for the engineers to finish their hammering, Brown was planning his own attack. Annoyed by the harassing fire of the British scouting parties, he wanted to clear them out of the woods around the camp. Such an operation required bush fighting skills and Brown decided to use Porter's Volunteers and Indians. Porter, who had crossed the Niagara that morning with Fenton's Pennsylvanians and a strong force of Indians, was just approaching the camp in the early afternoon when Brown rode up. Assuring him that the enemy were not in strength south of the Chippawa, and that he would be supported by Scott's brigade which would be ordered to move out onto the plain north of Street's creek, Brown directed him to scour the surrounding area.[26]

Porter's men had eaten little that day and were tired after the long march from the crossing point, but when he called for volunteers he had no problem mustering a force of about five hundred Pennsylvanians and Indians. To avoid risking his Volunteers being mistaken for Canadian militia, Porter ordered them to leave their hats behind. For the same reason he ordered his warriors to tie strips of white cloth around their heads as a recognition symbol. The Volunteers were eager to see action; the officers gave up their swords and borrowed muskets or rifles which were more useful for bush fighting. Captain Samuel White from Adams County, Pennsylvania, watched as the warriors "painted their faces, making red streaks above their eyes and foreheads," then, using charcoal, "drew their fingers down their cheeks leaving large black streaks – after this preparation they were ready for the action."[27] When all was ready, Porter formed his command into a single line at right angles to the Niagara and, with the Indians in front, marched into the woods half a mile south of the camp. The time was just after 3:00 P.M..[28]

When the Indians were swallowed up by the brush and the rear of the line, composed of the Volunteers, was still in the clear area of field along the Niagara, Porter halted and faced to the right. His command now formed a continuous skirmish line half a mile in length and Porter gave the order to advance north with caution and drive the enemy before them.

As they moved north past the camp, the Americans flushed their quarry out of the thick bushes along the upper reaches of Street's Creek. The British-allied Indians and Canadian militia opened fire, the Americans returned it, and a sharp little action commenced. It did not last long. Overwhelmed by American numbers and threatened with encirclement, the scouting parties pulled back, with the Americans hard on their heels. The withdrawal became a rout and in a few minutes Porter's men, sensing victory, were in hot pursuit.[29]

When the Americans neared the edge of the woods overlooking the cleared fields on the south bank of the Chippawa, resistance began to stiffen measurably and the advance began to slow. Suddenly they were met with volley after volley of disciplined musketry that brought them to a halt. Moving forward to the edge of the woods, Porter found himself "within a few yards of the British army formed in line of battle."[30] He tried to steady and reform his men but it was hopeless. Seeing the British moving forward, he ordered a retreat and the situation reversed itself as the Volunteers and American Indians ran through the woods with the Canadian militia and Indians close on their heels.[31]

What Porter had encountered was the right flank of Riall's main force, which had crossed the Chippawa about 3:30 P.M. and had begun to deploy behind the cover of the strip of woods that screened the village from American view. Riall had detached Colonel Thomas Dickson's 2nd Lincoln Militia and a body of western Indians about three hundred strong with orders to move through the woods and attack the American camp from the west. At the same time he had ordered Norton, with a smaller body of warriors, to try to encircle the American camp.[32]

As the Lincolns and Indians moved into the woods in a skirmish line, they collided with the remnants of the British scouting parties in full retreat, and Porter's men in full pursuit. A confusing skirmish resulted, made all the more bewildering by the fact that both the Volunteers and the Canadians lacked uniforms and spoke the same language. Despite the fact that the Volunteers had purposely gone into action hatless as a means of identification, mistakes occurred. One Canadian remembered encountering a group of American Indians but "not having a red coat [they] mistook me as much as I did them for they could not have missed me if they had directed a shot at me."[33]

The opponents sorted themselves out and in the ensuing vicious fight Dickson of the 2nd Lincolns, a prominent merchant from Queenston down the river, was hit in the chest by a musket ball that deflected off the spectacles he had placed in his breast pocket and did not kill him. Dickson went down, as did four of the five Lincoln officers, but the Canadians were rallied by Major David Secord from St. David's. The British-allied Indians also took casualties and both detachments recoiled onto Riall's right flank, composed of the light companies of the 1st and 100th under Pearson. Pearson ordered his regulars to open fire and it was their volleys that had turned the Americans back.[34]

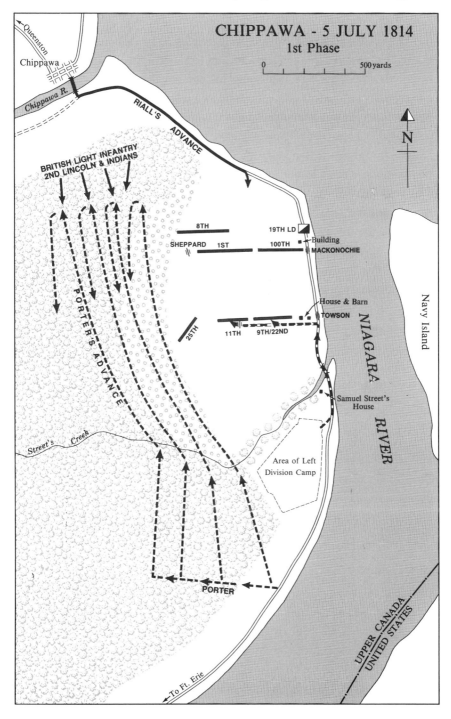

Porter's attack delayed Riall's deployment but as soon as the Volunteers had been pushed back he ordered his three regular battalions to move along the river road and deploy in the open fields north of Street's creek. Captain James Mackonochie, RA, positioned his artillery to support this advance – two 24-pdr. guns under the command of Lieutenant Richard Armstrong, RA, unlimbered on the river road along with a 5½-inch howitzer under the command of Lieutenant Thomas Jack of the Royal Artillery Drivers, while Lieutenant Edmund Sheppard, RA, brought three 6-pdr. guns into action to the west of the road. Major Robert Lisle's troop of the 19th Light Dragoons took position on the road behind Mackonochie's gunners. At about 4:30 P.M., the 1st, 8th and 100th Foot began moving toward the American camp.[35]

Brown was one of the first soldiers in the Left Division to realize that a major British movement was under way. Accompanied by Gardner, he had ridden north of Street's Creek to observe Porter's progress. The steady volleys of musketry and clouds of dust created by the advancing British regulars provided a warning that more than a skirmish was about to begin. Brown immediately sent Gardner to Scott with orders to form his brigade and "advance to meet the enemy."[36]

Galloping to the First Brigade's lines, Gardner found it in the process of assembling for drill. The men were in a good mood, having earlier "despatched" a special dinner that Scott had procured to celebrate the 4th of July. Scott heard Gardner out with annoyance – the bushes along Street's Creek concealed the plain from his view and he was certain there were not more than three hundred British south of the Chippawa. He disliked being called out to support Porter's hapless Volunteers who had got themselves into trouble. Nonetheless, as he had intended to drill on the plain that afternoon anyway, he formed his brigade in column and led it north along the river road.[37]

As it neared the bridge over Street's Creek, Brown rode up and shouted: "You will have a battle!"[38] Not convinced, Scott repeated his sentiments about the uselessness of non-regular troops but the words were hardly out of his mouth when his men came under artillery fire. Spurring his horse, Brown rode on to the camp to alert Ripley while Scott hurried his men over the bridge.[39]

The fire came from Armstrong's guns and Jack's howitzer, which were shooting straight down the river road. Riall and his staff, observing from the north end of the plain, could see the American column approaching, but noting their grey jackets, decided they were only militia wearing the home-

Major John McNeil, U.S. Army (1784-1859)
The commander of the Eleventh U.S. Infantry, McNeil had made his mark at Chippawa on 5 July 1815 but was badly wounded during the early stages of the fighting at Lundy's Lane three weeks later. (From Benson Lossing, *Pictorial Field Book of the War of 1812*, New York, 1869)

spun wool common to farmers in both Canada and the United States. Experience had taught Riall that such men would not stand before British regulars and he deployed his three infantry battalions for an attack. Lieutenant Colonel the Marquis of Tweeddale's 100th Foot and Lieutenant Colonel John Gordon's 1st Foot were formed in line, with the 100th on the left near the Niagara, while Major Thomas Evans's 8th Foot remained in reserve in the right rear. At the same time, Sheppard's three guns took position on Gordon's right flank and opened fire. At this point, the British line was about eight hundred yards from Street's Creek, which to Tweeddale appeared as a wooded "bank about five foot high in a straight line."[40]

Forced to remain in close column in order to cross the bridge over Street's Creek, Scott's brigade presented a good target and the British gunners brought it under heavy fire. Henderson had his second close call of the day when his hat was knocked off his head by a shell fragment. An obliging soldier returned it to him with the homily that "an inch is as good as a mile."[41] Jesup of the Twenty-Fifth had his horse killed and Captain Thomas Harrison of the Ninth lost part of his leg to a roundshot. Refusing help, he lay on the ground and urged his men forward. Drummer Hanks was intrigued to see the British roundshot that missed the column strike "a bend of the [Niagara] river where they glanced along for some distance upon its surface" like the stones he and the other boys of the army skipped on the water for amusement.[42]

Stepping over their dead and wounded, the First Brigade crossed the bridge in quick time. As his units reached the other side, Scott deployed them on the plain to the left of some farm buildings located a few hundred feet north of the creek. Leavenworth's Ninth Infantry, with the Twenty-Second attached, formed in line west of the river road and parallel to the British line on the north end of the "plain." Ropes hauled his picket out of the barn in which they had been sheltering and formed on Leavenworth's left flank while Campbell placed his Eleventh Infantry in line with Leavenworth but some distance to the left. Campbell was wounded almost immediately and Major John McNeil assumed command of the regiment. Jesup began to form his Twenty-Fifth on the left of the Eleventh but Scott, seeing that the British light infantry in the woods to the west threatened his flank, ordered him to the extreme left, there "to be governed by circumstances."[43]

While moving into position, the brigade continued to suffer from artillery fire, particularly from the two 24-pdr. guns which Armstrong had advanced to within four hundred yards of the American line. Mackonochie later remarked that at Chippawa artillery never had "a fairer opportunity of doing execution among the Enemy's ranks."[44] Scott, always keen when it came to professional matters, recorded that the "enemy's batteries were admirably served."[45] Towson, who had followed the brigade over the bridge, went into action on the right of Scott's line with two 6-pdr. guns and a 5½-inch howitzer. Almost immediately the howitzer was disabled by a 24-pdr. shot, but before it went out of action one of its shells exploded a British ammunition limber. This, and the steady fire of Towson's two 6-pdr. guns, slowed the British rate of fire and provided the First Brigade with some breathing space.[46]

Watching the grey-uniformed Americans manoeuvre under heavy fire without faltering, Riall realized he was facing more than militia – "Why, these are regulars!" he is said to have exclaimed.[47] Confident in the quality of his own infantry, however, he did not hesitate to order the 1st and 100th Foot to close with the American line and push home with the bayonet. At the same time he ordered Evans to move his battalion in line to counter Jesup's Twenty-Fifth Infantry, which he could see moving in column towards the right. Gordon and Tweeddale gave their orders, the company commanders repeated them, and the 1st and 100th, about nine hundred men deployed in a line of two ranks, advanced toward Scott's brigade.[48]

As the ominous red line moved slowly forward, Scott made his preparations. To fill the space left by Jesup's Twenty-Fifth, he had extended the interval between the Eleventh and Ninth/Twenty-Second to four times the normal distance so that his front was now wider than that of the approaching British formation. Riding to McNeil, he ordered him to throw forward his left so that the Eleventh would be able to fire into the flank of the British line. On his way back, he rode along the front of his brigade and, a firm believer in "a little arrogance near the enemy, when an officer is ready to suit the action to the word," reminded his men that they had just celebrated their national holiday and exhorted them to "make a new anniversary." His final stop was Towson's artillery on the right flank who were carrying on a private war with the British gunners. Pointing out the advancing British infantry, Scott requested Towson to change targets. By this time, the two opposing lines were not more than one hundred yards apart and Scott ordered the First Brigade to open fire.[49]

The entire front of the Ninth and the Eleventh was immediately shrouded in a pall of smoke as the first, properly-loaded and most lethal volley of musketry rang out. Volley followed volley in quick succession. The British line faltered for a minute as men fell, singly from musket balls, in clumps of two or three from artillery fire, but the company officers and sergeants steadied the survivors and closed them in to the centre. The two British battalions "came to a standstill and began firing," and a vicious firefight ensued.[50] The British had the worst of it but both sides took casualties.[51]

The long hours of drill at Flint Hill began to pay off as Scott's infantry fired, loaded and fired. The first rounds startled McNeil's horse, which began to prance excitedly. Unable to control him, McNeil dismounted, slapped his rump and sent him galloping to the rear. It was at this point that Henderson had his third close call of the day when a large man in front of him was killed by shell fragments and, falling backward, knocked him flat. Unharmed, the Pennsylvanian wiggled out from under the weight and resumed his place. Though half-choked by the thick, acrid powder smoke, the men in the ranks continued to fire without pause. Jarvis Hanks slung his drum over his shoulder and held his sergeant's ramrod in between rounds, allowing him to load faster as volley followed upon volley.[52]

While the Ninth and Eleventh were engaged with the main British force, Jesup and the Twenty-Fifth were fighting their own little battle. Jesup had advanced in column to the edge of the wood and then deployed into line. He was immediately assailed by musketry from Canadian militia and British-allied Indians on his left, the British light companies posted behind a rail fence to his front, and artillery fire from Sheppard's three 6-pdr. guns off to his right. The Twenty-Fifth lost nearly fifty men in ten minutes, but did not waver. Jesup returned the fire but, realizing that it was ineffectual against a concealed enemy, soon ordered his men to stop. As a withdrawal would open up the flank of Scott's line, Jesup decided to advance against the British light infantry. It all happened so quickly – Captain George Howard from Connecticut, commanding the right flank company of the Twenty-Fifth, remembered that this movement "brought us within *grinning* distance!" Then followed the commands: "Halt! Ready! Fire! ... Charge!" and "when the smoke cleared – the enemy were in full run and we in pursuit."[53]

Ordering Captain Daniel Ketchum to pursue the enemy with his company, Jesup promptly changed front to the north. He then moved forward in line to take the 8th Foot in the flank but Evans, a twenty-year veteran, withdrew his regiment in good order. Again, Jesup advanced, outflanking the 8th and forcing it back. Then he was forced to halt in order to support Ketchum who had become involved with three times his numbers in the woods.[54]

While the First Brigade was hotly engaged, the remainder of the Left Division had not been idle. As soon as he had left Scott, Brown ordered Ripley to take his best unit, the Twenty-First Infantry, skirt the woods to the west and fall on the British rear. Ripley moved off, accompanied by Gardner, but his progress was impeded by the swampy ground. In the ranks of the Twenty-First, fighting as a volunteer private, was the same Joseph Treat who had been dismissed from the division that morning by Brown. Porter, meanwhile, was regaining control of his brigade. Most of his men had streamed, hatless, out of the woods where Harris's light dragoons managed to slow them long enough for Porter, mounted on a fine horse he had found riderless in the camp, to get a grip on them. His Indians had managed to regroup near the camp and were holding off the Lincolns and the British-allied Indians.[55]

The divisional artillery commander, Hindman, seeing Jesup's perilous position, ordered Captain John Ritchie's company of artillery, with two 6-pdr. guns and a howitzer and Lieutenant James Hall from Biddle's company with a 12-pdr. gun forward to support the Twenty-Fifth. He then requested permission to bring up the remainder of his field pieces but Brown held him back until the battle between the First Brigade and the British was resolved.[56]

Despite all their efforts, Tweeddale and Gordon could not get their men to advance the last few yards and close with the bayonet. Tweeddale rode to his elite grenadier company and ordered its captain to lead a charge but that officer almost immediately went down, as did his lieutenant and then his second lieutenant. At this range, the Americans could use aimed fire and their targets were the officers they could see urging their opponents onward. The result was appalling casualties among the officers of the two battalions: of the fourteen officers in the 100th Foot, only three remained unwounded. Tweeddale and Gordon, both mounted, made good targets and inevitably they were hit. Gordon took a musket ball in the mouth and, unable to give orders, had to leave the field. He was soon followed by Tweeddale, who, already lame in one leg, had the achilles tendon of his good leg severed.[57]

The American musketry and artillery was relentless. Lieutenant John Stevenson of the 100th remembered the "dreadful and destructive fire" that caused men to fall "like hail."[58] His regiment was particularly hard hit – Captain William Sleigh went down with a musket ball in the groin, Captain Thomas Sherrard was hit in four places while Lieutenant George Lyon, commanding the left flank company near the Niagara, was knocked over by a bullet through his right thigh a few inches above the knee. When Ritchie and Hall's guns came into action they added to the carnage by firing canister that opened windrows through the British ranks. Watching the effect, Scott thought that "the enemy could not long withstand this accumulation of fire."[59]

It was more than even British infantry could take. First the flanks "mouldered away like a rope of sand," and then, as the delighted Americans watched through the smoke of the incessant discharges, the two British battalions recoiled slowly backward without breaking.[60] With the action clearly lost, Riall ordered a withdrawal and the 1st and 100th fell back by stages, covered by Pearson's light infantry and Evans's 8th Foot. Lisle's dragoons helped to get the artillery away and the entire force made it safely across the Chippawa, where the engineers dropped the centre portion of the bridge behind them. The last men over the river were John Norton and his party, who had spent a frustrating time trying to get past Porter's Indians close to the American camp. Hearing the British bugles blowing the retreat, Norton pulled back only to find that the bridge was no longer usable, but enough of its pilings remained in place for his agile, lightly-equipped Indians to cross to safety.[61]

The Left Division was hard on their heels. To keep the pressure on, Scott had ordered an advance and, led by Harris's dragoons, the First Brigade crossed a plain now "strewed" with "Red Coated Gentry" and approached the bridge.[62] The British artillery on the north bank of the Chippawa brought them under fire and Scott ordered his men to form line on the opposite bank and lie down with their heads toward the enemy. Porter came up a few minutes later and took position on Scott's left, where for the first time his Volunteers experienced artillery fire, which one thought "a new but not a very pleasant sight."[63] McNeil took the opportunity to reclaim his horse from Porter while Hindman brought his artillery forward and prepared to batter the British earthworks in preparation for an attack. But as there were only a few hours of daylight left and being satisfied with the day's work, Brown ordered the division back to its camp.[64]

Nearly seven hundred men lay dead and wounded in the fields and woods around Samuel Street's farm. Riall recorded 456 casualties, about twenty-five per cent of his attacking force. The 1st and 100th Foot, with 228 and 204 casualties respectively, had lost nearly half the men they had taken into action. Lieutenant George Lyon's company of the 100th was particularly hard hit, losing twenty-nine dead and wounded from the thirty-five officers and men it had mustered that morning.[65]

Brown reported 295 casualties: 60 dead, 210 wounded and 50 missing. Fenton's Pennsylvanians had suffered, losing their second-in-command, senior major and ten other casualties. But it was Scott's brigade that paid the heaviest price – 41 dead and 219 wounded. Some of his companies had been particularly hard hit – that of Captain George Howard of the Twenty-Fifth lost 11 killed and 13 wounded, over a third of its strength. This slaughter was the outcome of an engagement that had lasted about ninety minutes, while the losses suffered by the 1st and 100th Foot and Scott's brigade resulted from an action that lasted not more than thirty minutes.[66]

As the Americans were in possession of the ground at the end of the battle, the task of clearing away the debris of war fell to them. It was late in the evening before most of the wounded could be gathered and there were so many that Ropes of the Twenty-First (whose strong suits were not spelling or grammar) remembered that many "died that Night & the groans of the livining was Shocking." He had occasion to go into one of the farm houses "ware they ware Dressing [the wounded], ther was not a room in the house but what they had a man on the Table amphetating."[67]

The surgeons were overwhelmed by the number of casualties and Henderson, who had been trained as a doctor, was forced to personally treat the casualties of his own company. Not all the wounded received proper care. Porter was horrified to discover that his warriors had slit the throats of three wounded British Indians they had discovered in the woods. He remonstrated with them only to receive the honest reply that it was "hard to put these men to death, but we hope you will consider that these are very bad times."[68]

British morale was naturally low. Norton remembered that the "Loss of our friends gave us all a gloomy appearance" and all the houses were filled with the wounded.[69] Captain Hamilton Merritt, who arrived with his troop of cavalry after the battle, spent a "very unpleasant night" among "many officers ... lying wounded, groaning with pain."[70] The next morning, Riall sent a flag of truce to Brown with a request to recover the bodies of his men, particularly those of the Canadian militia whose families wished to inter them properly.

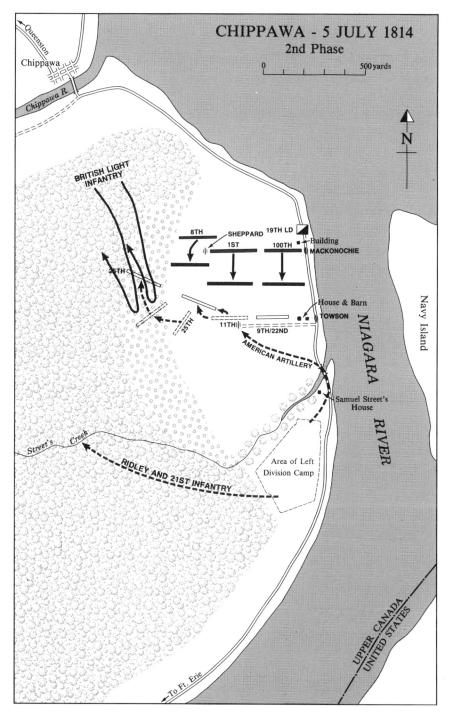

This request was refused and word spread around the British camp that Brown had "replied that he was able to bury all the men he could kill."[71] No one in the British lines had any doubts about the outcome of the battle; as Merritt stated, "we candidly confessed we were beaten." The opinion in the ranks was that Riall had "acted hastily," since he did not "employ all the means in his power and should have waited for more reinforcements before attacking."[72]

In his official report to Drummond, Riall made no excuses for an "affair [that] was not attended with the success which I had hoped for" but praised the gallantry of his troops and noted that the Americans had "deployed with the greatest regularity" under fire.[73] Reporting to Prevost, Drummond attributed the defeat to superior American numbers but also picked up the theme of the fighting qualities of the Left Division, which "withstood our attacks with the greatest steadiness."[74] Publicly, Prevost agreed that the action "terminated less successfully then we have been accustomed to" because of "the improvement in discipline and the increased experience of the Enemy," who "evinced judgement in the position selected and ... had confidence in their numbers for its defence."[75] Privately, he was unhappy with Riall and expressed the opinion that "in the Sortie at Chippawa, neither the Union of Science, organization or force will give the affair any éclat."[76] One outcome of the battle of Chippawa was clear to all three British generals – Brown's army was an enemy that would have to be treated with respect.

The Left Division rejoiced but their jubilation was tempered by the long casualty list for the trained troops who had fallen could not readily be replaced. But they were justifiably proud. For the first time during the war, American infantry had met and defeated British infantry in open battle. As Brown exalted to Armstrong, the victory at Chippawa was "gained over the enemy *on a plain*."[77] The stain of Crysler's Farm and so many other defeats of the past two years had been erased by the division's performance in an equal contest. "No battle could have been better arranged to test the superiority" of the respective armies, felt Henderson, as there "was no advantage on either side from numbers or position."[78] A fellow officer agreed that the action had been "a fair trial of nerve and discipline ... on plain ground; without any local advantage or any adventitious circumstance ... and the result was the entire *repulse*, to use no harsher phrase" of the enemy.[79] Even captured British officers were unsparing in their praise. "We had never seen those grey-jackets before," one commented, and "supposed it was only a line of Militia-men" but "it became clear enough we had something besides Militia-men to deal with."[80]

CHAPTER 5

Move and Counter Move,
6 July–24 July 1814

We are now halted here by two things – the removal of either of which would enable us to go on – the possession of the forts down at the corner, or Chauncey's operation. The latter we are not to have. It would be as mortifying to him to have the army proceed down the lake – before his capturing Yeo – as it would be to have Yeo captured without his being present.
COLONEL CHARLES K. GARDNER TO DANIEL PARKER, 17 JULY 1814

For two days following the battle, an uneasy calm prevailed between the two armies. Shaken by his defeat, Riall contemplated retreat and on 7 July 1814 made some initial preparations. The 100th Foot was marched back to a position near the falls of Niagara, useless or damaged supplies and ordnance were dumped in the river and the baggage was sent to the rear. These actions did not escape the notice of Riall's Indian allies, who had been augmented after the battle by a large contingent led by Tenskawatawa, and almost all of the warriors disappeared from camp in the space of a few hours. Riall sent Norton to bring them back but even that able leader could only gather fifty of the more aggressive. At the same time, the 2nd Lincolns, their morale sapped by the heavy casualties they had suffered on 5 July and worried about the safety of their families, began to drift away. Riall was now unwilling "to hazard another action with so superior a force without the support of light troops" – his Canadian and Indian skirmishers.[1] But he was also reluctant to abandon his strong defensive position along the Chippawa.[2]

Brown relieved him of his dilemma. The American commander was anxious to get over the Chippawa and reach Lake Ontario by 10 July, the date on which he expected to meet Chauncey. On the evening of 6 July, Brown got lucky when a local inhabitant told him of a disused logging road that led from Street's farm to the junction of Lyon's Creek and the Chippawa, upstream from Riall's position at the mouth of the river. The following morning, Brown, with Wood and McRee, explored this road. They found a rough trail about four miles in length blocked by fallen trees and brush, and decided that with some work it could be made passable for artillery by nightfall. Brown therefore resolved to attempt to bridge the Chippawa upstream of the British position and the two engineer officers supervised the repair of the road and the collection of bridging materials.[3]

Early in the morning of 8 July, Ripley, with his own and Porter's brigade under command and Biddle's and Williams's companies of artillery, moved along the trail. Progress was slow as it took time to get the guns and the bridging materials (lumber torn from local barns, with small boats for makeshift pontoons) over the rough path. Brown became impatient at the delay and assumed command of the operation. When the column reached the Chippawa, the men fanned out to cut trees for the bridge. By early afternoon all was ready and, under the protection of the artillery, the regulars and Volunteers began to construct a pontoon bridge over the Chippawa.[4]

The noise of falling timber alerted a vedette of the 19th Light Dragoons posted on the opposite bank to protect against just such an eventuality. A witness in the main British position remembered a dragoon "coming down the Chippawa at full speed ... under whip and spur" and "in a few minutes the camp was all abustle."[5] Riall sent Pearson with the flank companies of the 1st Foot and three 6-pdr. guns to delay the crossing and formed his remaining troops for action. Pearson did his best but he was outgunned by the massed firepower of the American artillery and had to watch as the bridge extended into the river. He appealed to Riall for assistance but before the British commander could move, he was pinned in his defences by a strong demonstration made across from the village of Chippawa by Scott's brigade and the remainder of the Left Division's artillery. When a false report reached him that the Americans had already crossed further upstream, Riall concluded he was outflanked and ordered a general withdrawal. Before the astonished eyes of the bridge builders, who had got their somewhat shaky structure about halfway across the river, the British disappeared from the opposite bank.[6]

As Riall's troops moved north at a quick pace in the late afternoon of 8 July, an American prisoner watched the large iron camp kettles "dropping along the roads, one here, one there, shaken from the wagons by the unusually rapid motion."[7] Near the falls of Niagara the column encountered the Incorporated Militia Battalion of Upper Canada, just arrived from York and under orders to proceed to Chippawa. The Militia moved aside to let it pass and twenty-year-old Ensign John Kilborn from Leeds County was startled to see that behind the troops were many of the local populace, who had abandoned their farms to follow the British army to safety. He watched with amazement as "hundreds of women and children, besides men on foot and in vehicles" passed in front of him.[8] With Merritt and Lisle's dragoons forming the rearguard, Riall's troops and the refugees reached the safety of Fort George late that night.[9]

After the British withdrawal, Brown abandoned the bridging attempt and moved downstream opposite Chippawa. The bridge over the river had been totally destroyed and there was some suspicion that the British were still in the neighbourhood but this was dispelled when Harris and some of his dragoons swam their horses over and found the village empty. Brown crossed his regular infantry and artillery in boats that night but there was no chance of catching Riall. On the following day he pushed north to Queenston with the two regular brigades, leaving Porter behind to repair the bridge. Porter had finally managed to get his entire brigade assembled, Swift's New York regiment, Stone's detached New York battalion and Willcocks's Canadian renegades having arrived from Buffalo. Even so, it took them two days to put the bridge into a usable state before they marched to catch up with the regulars.[10]

Queenston was a "delightful place."[11] The small, pretty village of a few dozen houses was nestled at the foot of the Niagara escarpment. The regulars camped in and about the hamlet while Porter's brigade tented near an abandoned fieldwork on the heights from which they could clearly see Fort George and Lake Ontario seven miles away. Here Brown waited, "with the hope of hearing from Com[o]d[ore] Chauncey" – but the white sails of American warships did not appear on the lake.[12] Scott put the time to good use tightening up discipline in his brigade and a busy round of drills and inspections commenced for his men. But it was not all work: Jarvis Hanks and his friends found time to swim each day in the Niagara and Hanks became quite proficient at diving out the second storey of an abandoned warehouse overlooking the river.[13]

During their stay at Queenston, reinforcements began to reach the division. A large detachment of the Twenty-Second Infantry came in and was combined with the companies serving with the Ninth to form an independent unit under the command of Colonel Hugh Brady. McFarland's Twenty-Third Infantry was increased by another detachment of the same regiment under the veteran Major George Brooke, while Colonel James Miller, another experienced officer, arrived to take command of the Twenty-First Infantry from Major Joseph Grafton. On 10 July a company of bombardiers, sappers and miners (engineer troops) arrived from the military academy at West Point (where they had been serving as a demonstration unit) and were attached to Hindman's artillery battalion as gunners.[14]

The commander of this company, Lieutenant David B. Douglass, newly commissioned and on his first campaign, left a charming word portrait of the Left Division as he first saw it at Queenston in July 1814:

> Beneath our feet were a small village and a broad expanse of open plain, adjoining, literally whitened with tents. Long lines of troops were under arms; columns in motion; guards coming in and going out; Divisions of artillery at drill; videttes of Cavalry at speed; and Aides and Staff- officers, here and there, in earnest movement. There was no display of gaudy plumes or rich trappings; but, in their stead, grey-jackets – close-buttoned – plain white belts, steel hilts, and brown muskets; but there were bayonets fixed, and a glance of the eye would show that those boxes were filled with ball-cartridges. There was an earnestness, and with good reason, for, yonder, in plain sight, are the colors of the enemy waving proudly over the ramparts of Fort Niagara and Fort George; and a straggling ray, now and then reflected, tells of bayonets fixed, there too. This, then, was no mere parade – no stage play, for effect – it was simple and sublime reality – IT WAS WAR.[15]

Behind this stirring façade there were tensions between the senior officers of the division. Brown was growing increasingly disenchanted with Ripley's lack of enthusiasm and his perpetual tardiness. He also had problems with Scott arising from the action at Chippawa. On the day after the battle, Brown had issued a general order praising the First Brigade but mentioning only Scott by name. Scott's officers felt slighted, and when the *Buffalo Gazette* published letters from the officers of the other brigades describing the deeds of their units during the battle and downplaying the role of the First Brigade, they became angry. Jesup, who had not been mentioned in the general order or in any other publication about the battle, was disgusted and became "anxious to leave the army."[16] Scott went further. On 10 July he complained in a letter to Brown that the lack of official recognition accorded to his officers had "repressed" his zeal and asked his superior to "accept the tender I now make of my commission in the Army of the U.

States."[17] Brown replied in writing that same day, smoothing his temperamental subordinate's feathers and promising to include the names of worthy officers in the lengthier official report which he had not yet written. His pride salved, Scott promptly withdrew his resignation.[18]

To secure information and prevent surprises, Brown initiated a policy of aggressive patrolling. Porter's brigade, Boughton and Harris's dragoons, and the Indians, guided by members of the Canadian Volunteers who knew the area, were usually detailed for this work. In contrast to the previous year, however, when much of the local population had been neutral during the American occupation, Canadian attitudes had shifted and the sight of Willcocks and his renegades, responsible for much distress in the Niagara in 1813, guiding American patrols only reinforced these feelings. Although Brown had issued an order forbidding the destruction or plundering of private property on pain of death, inevitably some of the patrols looted and the worst culprits seem to have been the Volunteers and Indians. On 12 July Brown reissued his order but the misdeeds of his men caused increasing local resentment and it was not long before patrols were being ambushed, sentries were disappearing and no American was safe outside the perimeter of the camp.[19]

As the Left Division drilled or patrolled, Brown watched for Chauncey. He felt that he was "in no condition to invest Fort George and Niagara without the aid of Com[o]d[ore] Chauncey and my battering guns that I expect him to bring from the harbor."[20] He also needed the squadron to open a supply line to the depots at Genessee and Sodus on the south shore of Lake Ontario. His supplies now could only be brought by water as far as Schlosser on the American side of the Niagara River or Chippawa on the Canadian side. From these points they had to travel by wagon around the obstacle of the falls. From Schlosser to Lewiston, on the American bank, the road was poor and supplies still had to be ferried across the river to Queenston, while Lewiston itself was open to attack from the British-held Fort Niagara seven miles away. On the Canadian side there was a fine road from Chippawa to Queenston but it was vulnerable to ambush. Brown favoured the American route and stationed a force drawn from the Pennsylvania and New York Volunteers at Lewiston under the command of Volunteer Lieutenant Colonel Philetus Swift to defend it.[21]

Brown waited but there was no sign of Chauncey. By 13 July, three days after what Brown thought was the appointed time for the commodore's appearance, he grew impatient and wrote to Chauncey. Pleading "For God's sake let me see you," he assured the naval commander that "we have between us the command of sufficient means to conquer Upper Canada within two months if there is prompt and zealous co-operation, and a vigorous application of these means."[22] In the meantime, uncertain what to do, he called a council of his senior officers but their deliberations were interrupted by the news that Riall had moved out from the forts at the mouth of the river.[23]

When Brown halted at Queenston, Riall correctly concluded that his opponent was waiting for the arrival of the American squadron. Not wanting the only British field force in Upper Canada to be trapped between Brown's army and Chauncey's fleet, he decided to withdraw and take up a position where he could better await events. On the night of 12 July he sent Evans of the 8th Foot to reconnoitre a route from Newark to the west. Evans encountered a force of Volunteers under New York Brigadier General John Swift of Palmyra, N.Y., and in the resulting skirmish Swift was killed and his men hastily withdrew. Satisfied that the Americans were not in a position to interfere with his movements, Riall left the 41st and 100th Foot and a strong detachment of gunners in the forts and marched out on the night of 13 July with the 1st, 8th, Incorporated Militia and his field artillery. He reached the Twenty-Mile creek the next day, where he was joined by Colonel Hercules Scott and the 103rd Foot from Burlington Bay.[24]

When he learned of it, Drummond approved of this movement. The British commander had been following the campaign closely from his headquarters at Kingston and had pushed forward all the reinforcements he could spare to the Niagara area. The Glengarry Light Infantry were ordered into the peninsula from York, the 89th Foot and the flank companies of the 104th Foot were alerted to follow them and the sedentary militia were ordered to muster at Burlington Bay. The problem was how to feed these men. Drummond possessed a fleet of small boats and had obtained the services of two brigs from Yeo to carry provisions but he was concerned that, if Chauncey emerged on the lake, Riall's lines of communication would be cut. He reasoned that if an attack were to be made on the Americans, it would have to be made while the Royal Navy had control of the lake and that would have to be soon. Drummond decided to assume command in the Niagara himself.[25]

At the Twenty-Mile, Riall re-organized his troops for field service. Colonel Hercules Scott was given command of the 1st Brigade with the 8th and his own 103rd Foot while Pearson took over the 2nd, or light brigade, with the Glengarry Light Infantry and the Incorporated Militia. Lisle's squadron of the 19th Light Dragoons and Mackonochie's field artillery were split between the two while Gordon, still recovering from the wound he had received at Chippawa, commanded the reserve, which consisted of his own 1st Foot.[26]

Drummond's order for the sedentary militia to muster at Burlington had met with an enthusiastic response. Riall reported that "almost the whole body of militia is in arms, and seem actuated by the most determined spirit of hostility to the enemy."[27] He formed them into two brigades under the command of British regular officers.[28]

He was less fortunate with his native auxiliaries. After the warriors had left the army at Chippawa, Riall had sent Norton and the Indian Department officers to get them back. Largely on the basis of his personal reputation, Norton had been able to assemble nearly five hundred Grand River warriors at Burlington Bay and the departmental officers were able to bring nearly as many from the western nations. Norton was preparing to move the whole force forward to the Twenty-Mile when two emissaries arrived from the American Indian contingent serving with Brown bearing a proposal that the warriors on both sides declare a truce in this white man's war that was no concern of their people. The departmental officers wanted to arrest the two men but Norton, insisting that they had come under a flag of truce, allowed them to address the Grand River warriors. Their proposal was rejected but it caused considerable unrest and adversely affected morale – many of the Grand River Indians went home and those that remained displayed so much less enthusiasm that they were regarded with suspicion by their more aggressive comrades from the western nations.[29]

To cover his position at the Twenty-Mile, Riall established a screening force of militia around the American camp at Queenston. Drawn mainly from the 1st and 2nd Lincoln Regiments, the 2nd York and Merritt's dragoons, they were soon "daily skirmishing and driving in States' parties, who were plundering every house they could get at."[30] The local population eagerly provided information about American troop movements and no patrol could leave Queenston without it soon being known to Canadian scouting parties. The assistance rendered by the inhabitants negated the usefulness of Willcocks and his Canadian Volunteers and indeed Willcocks and his men became prime targets. On 17 July "King Joe" was nearly captured while leading an American detachment near the little village of St. David's a few miles west of Queenston. One of his senior officers, Major Benajah Mallory, narrowly escaped from another ambush.[31]

Porter, whose brigade fought most of these actions and suffered most of the casualties, complained bitterly to Brown that his losses were "the vic-

Right
Mohawk Warrior, Grand River Nations
Painted in 1804, this warrior has covered his face with red, black and yellow colours. The native warriors were useful and effective auxiliaries to the British army in Canada but played a lesser role at Lundy's Lane, a bloody engagement fought largely by regulars on both sides. (Watercolour by Sempronius Stretton, courtesy National Archives of Canada, C-14827)

Tenskawatawa, or the Prophet
Half brother of the great Tecumseh, Tenskawatawa led a large force of warriors from the western nations which fought along side the regular British army throughout the 1814 Niagara campaign. (From Benson Lossing, *Pictorial Field Book of the War of 1812*, New York, 1869)

tims of your own generous policy of suffering the inhabitants, who profess neutrality, to remain unmolested," and requested that civilians be kept away from the camp, even those who claimed to be friends of the United States.[32] "The whole population is against us," wrote McFarland of the Twenty-Third Infantry. "Not a foraging party but is fired on, and not infrequently returns with missing numbers."[33]

Inevitably, these attacks led to retaliation. Porter's men began to burn farmhouses near ambush sites and on 18 July, following a particularly vicious encounter near St. David's, Lieutenant Colonel Isaac Stone's New York Volunteer battalion entered the hamlet with the "avowed intention to burn, plunder and destroy that Tory village."[34] This they proceeded to do, egged on by informants (probably Willcocks's Canadians) who told them that St. David's had been "the headquarters of the British army." "My God, what a service!" commented McFarland, whose regulars arrived after the village was in flames. "I never witnessed such a scene."[35]

Brown was outraged when he learned of this misdeed. Although Stone denied having ordered the destruction, the American general, holding that the "accountability" for an act that "was directly contrary to the orders of the Government and those of the Commanding officer" had to "rest with the senior officer," immediately dismissed Stone from the army.[36]

Riall's withdrawal from the forts placed Brown in a quandary – should he move against Fort George or against the British general? His senior officers were themselves divided. Scott and Gardner favoured investing the fort until the heavy guns arrived from Sackets Harbor but Ripley, Porter, McRee and Wood felt that Riall's army should be the main object. According to Jesup, Brown, "contrary to his usual habit of relying on his own sound judgement, was, it is thought, overruled by the zeal and importunities of General Scott" and decided to invest the fort.[37] Brown had no fear about fighting a major engagement against Riall, and if nothing else a move forward might provoke the British into such an action. But first he needed to find out more about Fort George's defences. On 15 July Ripley was ordered to make a demonstration along the river road while Porter took a long, roundabout route to come in behind the fort. Porter had a sharp skirmish with a detachment from the garrison which sortied out but he was able to get near enough to let Willcocks guide McRee and Wood in close to make a detailed examination of the defences.[38]

Brown decided to move forward to Fort George if for no other reason than it might bring on a general action. Hoping that Chauncey would appear, he delayed another five days but on the morning of 20 July the Left Division blew up the fieldworks on Queenston Heights and marched north. The Indian contingent did not accompany the division. Telling Brown that he had nothing more to fear from their British cousins who were sure to accept their truce proposal, the warriors crossed over to Lewiston and dispersed before either he or Porter could stop them.[39]

For two days, the Left Division hung about Fort George trying in vain to provoke either the British garrison or Riall at the Twenty-Mile into battle. The British defenders were active and there was a constant exchange of artillery fire. Howard of the Twenty-Fifth remembered "our first look [at the fort] was within range of Congreve rockets, bombshells and large shot, all seasoned with a sprinkling of grape and canister."[40] During one of these demonstrations Drummer Hanks witnessed Winfield Scott survive a close call. It was about noon, "the soldiers lazily reclining on their arms, some preparing and some eating their dinner," when a shell was fired from the fort:

> In a moment we all saw it, and heard it buzzing through the air and were all upon the look out to ascertain where it was going to fall. Gen[era]l Scott threw up his sword, in such a manner as to take sight across it, at the bomb, and found that it would fall upon him and his charger, unless he made his escape instanter. He wheeled his spirited animal to the left, and buried his spurs in his sides. The whole army was gazing on the scene ... when the shell actually dropped upon the very spot he had a moment before occupied.[41]

On 22 July, concluding that there was no chance against the fort without heavy artillery, and frustrated in his attempt to draw the British into open battle, Brown ordered the division to retrace its steps to Queenston. As the advance guard neared the village, it discovered that in their absence the Canadian militia had somewhat cheekily occupied the Heights. Porter, Willcocks and Harris went forward to evict them and in a running fight that lasted most of the day drove the Canadians some miles into the woods and captured several prisoners – sweet revenge for Porter's brigade, who had been suffering at their hands for nearly two weeks. Merritt, who was present, escaped but Willcocks trapped a group of Canadians in a farm house. Knowing "King Joe's" reputation only too well, they refused to surrender until Harris rode up with his light dragoons. Even then, despite the presence of the American regulars, the Canadians "were abused and insulted, in a most barbarous" manner by Willcocks's men.[42]

One of the prisoners taken this day was Captain William Kerr of the British Indian Department, who had been prominent in the fighting around Fort George in 1813. When news of Kerr's capture spread through the camp, Leavenworth of the Ninth Infantry and Howard of the Twenty-Fifth waited on Brown and "asked permission to *blow out Kerr's brains* (a very civil request truly) he having been the means of many murders during our previous campaign in that vicinity."[43] To their disappointment, Brown refused and, in Howard's words, "Justice had to sleep!"[44]

Brown's advance had caused Riall some anxious moments. On 16 July he had moved from the Twenty-Mile to the Twelve-Mile creek and his light troops were as far forward as the Four-Mile stream. Riall could hear the firing from the direction of Fort George but was uncertain what action he should take. His defeat at Chippawa appears to have shaken Riall's confidence and he began to exhibit signs of indecision. On 20 July he explained to Drummond that, although it "will be expected that I should do something to relieve Fort George which I have every inclination to do," he was reluctant to advance because Brown might move on Burlington; and besides, "should any reverse occur, I look upon it as fraught with the greatest danger to the province."[45] This statement overlooks the fact that Riall was between Brown and Burlington. Two days later, Riall confessed himself "most anxious" for Drummond's arrival – in the meantime, he had decided to undertake no major movement until he received clear directions from Drummond "as the attempt may involve the safety of the whole of the troops as well in the field as in the garrisons."[46] Not knowing what to do, Riall did nothing.[47]

He was, accordingly, puzzled by Brown's withdrawal to Queenston but did not press hard on the American general's heels. Riall continued to worry about the security of Fort George and when he received information that Brown was constructing batteries at Youngstown, across the river from the fort, he expressed the fear that the fort would suffer from heavy artillery fire. This information was false. Brown had given no orders to construct batteries on the American side of the Niagara although he had occasionally ordered a demonstration made from Lewiston toward Fort Niagara to keep the British garrison at that place occupied. The American commander at Lewiston, Philetus Swift, may have started reconstructing an old battery dating back to 1812 but he had no heavy guns to place in it. False or not, however, this information was the catalyst that spurred Drummond into action.[48]

On the evening of the 22 July the British commander arrived at York from Kingston. There he received Riall's dispatch informing him of the construction of the batteries at Youngstown and resolved to attack them. He decided to use fresh troops for this operation – the two flank companies of the 104th, which had left York for the Niagara in small boats, and the 89th Foot, which he had brought with him from Kingston. As Yeo still had control of the lake, he intended to send the 89th across to Fort Niagara by ship on the evening of the 23rd and go himself the following day. Then, on the morning of 25 July, these troops, under Drummond's eyes, would attack the batteries. If the attack went well, he planned to assemble every available man, including the garrisons of the three forts, and drive Brown out of Canada before the American fleet emerged on Lake Ontario.[49]

To distract Brown and prevent him from reinforcing Youngstown,

Drummond ordered Riall to demonstrate against Queenston. He was not to attack but, should "the enemy by pressing suddenly and boldly ... make an action unavoidable," Drummond, perhaps with the results of Chippawa in mind, issued his subordinate clear instructions on the tactical arrangements he was to make. If attacked, Riall was to withdraw, "until you reach an open space in which, keeping your guns in your centre and your force concentrated, your flanks secured by light troops, militia and Indians, you must depend upon the superior discipline of the troops under your command for success over an undisciplined though confident and numerous enemy."[50]

Drummond's plan was a good one, but for it to work the American army had to remain at Queenston and Brown had other ideas. Discouraged by Chauncey's failure to appear and frustrated by Riall's refusal to be drawn into battle, he had decided to pull back to Chippawa. This decision was triggered by a letter he received from Gaines at Sackets Harbor dated 20 July informing him that Chauncey was prostrate with fever but refused to let the squadron be taken out on the lake by a subordinate. At Brown's request, Gaines had tried to send him five heavy 18-pdr. guns in a strongly guarded convoy of small boats but they were blockaded by alert British warships. Disgusted, Brown explained to Secretary of War Armstrong that he "thought it proper to change my position with a view to other objects."[51] He later wrote that the foremost of these "objects" was the British depot at Burlington Bay but at the time stated only that he intended "to march into the interior of the country as far as I can carry or find subsistence in hopes of finding Riall and forcing him to action."[52]

To have any chance of success, the Left Division would have to travel as lightly as possible and Brown therefore sent his sick, camp followers and all excess baggage across to Lewiston. As he eventually intended to leave his line of communication along the Niagara River, he would need to re-supply the division and the best place to do this was Chippawa, a short boat journey from his main depot at Buffalo. Brown decided to fall back on Chippawa, draw supplies, and from there "be governed by circumstances" in going after Riall or moving on Burlington Bay.[53]

In the late morning of 24 July 1814 the Left Division broke camp and marched south down the Portage road for Chippawa. It was a fine day, bright but not too hot. As the column approached the billowing cloud of spray that marked the falls of Niagara, they passed through a small hamlet of houses and farms clustered around the junction of the Portage road and a tree-shrouded country route known as Lundy's Lane.[54]

PART III

The Battle of Lundy's Lane

Country lane near the Niagara River
This 1838 watercolour shows a typical country lane as it would have appeared at the time
of the battle. Note the Crown road allowance which is wider than the actual lane itself
and the split-rail snake fences that border it. Similar fences cut across the battlefield itself. (Watercolour by James Estcourt, 1838, courtesy, National Archives of Canada, C-93975)

CHAPTER 6

Advance to Contact, 24–25 July 1814

All the mysteries of manoeuvres and combats is in the legs.
MARSHAL SAXE, *Mes Rêveries*

Brown's withdrawal from Queenston was discovered by Norton. Scouting near St. David's in the afternoon of 24 July, the Indian leader apprehended an American deserter who informed him that the Left Division, five thousand strong, had moved south and planned to camp that night near the falls. Norton immediately sent a mounted messenger with this information to Riall at the Twelve-Mile Creek and then pressed forward hoping to harass the Americans on the march.[1]

For Riall, with his forces scattered over a wide area, it was imperative that he maintain contact with the enemy to avoid unpleasant surprises. He therefore ordered Pearson to take his brigade and Lieutenant Colonel Love Parry's 1st Militia Brigade forward from the Twelve-Mile to shadow the retreating Americans. Pearson's men had been on the alert for forty-eight hours and, with two days cooked rations in their haversacks, were ready to move. The buglers of the Glengarry Light Infantry blew the assembly and at 10:00 P.M. the brigade marched out of camp and took the road for St. David's.[2]

Under his command Pearson had a detachment of cavalry consisting of a squadron of the 19th Light Dragoons and Hamilton Merritt's militia dragoons, his own brigade with the Glengarry Light Infantry and the Incorporated Militia Battalion and Parry's 1st Militia Brigade with detachments from the 1st, 2nd, 4th and 5th Lincolns and the 2nd York. Bringing up the rear were two brass 6-pdr. guns and one 5½-inch howitzer. Pearson's total strength was between eleven and twelve hundred men. The remainder of the Right Division – Hercules Scott's brigade, the 2nd Militia brigade and the reserve under Lieutenant Colonel John Gordon – remained in position near the Ten and Twelve-Mile creeks.[3]

Pushing hard, Pearson arrived at the charred ruins of St. David's just as dawn broke on 25 July. Here he rested before continuing on to the Portage Road. His cavalry, riding ahead, had reached the junction of that road and Lundy's Lane about two hours earlier. By 7:00 A.M. Pearson and the two in-fantry regiments had come up and shortly afterward he was joined by Norton and his party, who had spent a comfortable night in a convenient barn after a futile pursuit of the Americans the previous day.[4]

Although now less than a mile from the falls of Niagara where, accord-ing to his information, Brown's army was camped, Pearson had not yet en-countered any Americans. He therefore dispatched Norton and Merritt with a small force of militia and Indians toward the falls. They found no enemy near the cataract but, moving further south, observed an American picket just north of Chippawa. They assumed correctly that this was an out-post of the American camp but could see nothing of that camp, which was hidden from view by the village and a belt of trees along the Chippawa. Having located the enemy, Norton and Merritt returned to Pearson about 9:00 A.M. after exchanging a few shots with the picket.[5]

Satisfied that the Americans posed no immediate threat, Pearson posted a dragoon vedette[6] at Willson's Tavern, midway between the two forces, and deployed two companies of Glengarries around the tavern. He stationed his remaining troops in the woods, fields and orchards near the junction of the Portage Road and Lundy's Lane and settled down to wait. It was a fine morning with a "beautiful sky" and the spray from the nearby falls rolled up to vast heights while hummingbirds and insects busied themselves in the surrounding trees and bushes. When the artillery and a large force of Indians arrived, they took position with the other troops along the lane. Riall arrived late in the afternoon and, after hearing Pearson's report, rode north to Fort George to confer with Drummond, who was expected that day from York.[7]

Drummond had embarked on the schooner *Netley* the previous evening and arrived off the mouth of the Niagara at daybreak. Lieutenant Colonel John Tucker, the commandant of Fort Niagara, informed him of Brown's withdrawal from Queenston. Realizing that this movement made it easier for the attack he planned on the batteries at Youngstown, Drummond or-dered Tucker to take five hundred infantry from the garrisons of the forts together with a body of western Indians and move on Youngstown. He also directed Lieutenant Colonel Joseph Morrison to take his 89th Foot (which had landed from York the previous day) and other detachments from the garrisons of Forts George and Mississauga and move south up the Canadian side of the river. Preparations took time to execute and it was not until mid-morning that Tucker advanced along the American side while Morrison, joined by Drummond, paralleled his movement on the Canadian shore. The two columns were accompanied on the river by a number of boats manned by armed seamen and commanded by Captain Alexander Dobbs, RN.[8]

Hampered by trees and bushes laid across the road and forced to extend skirmishers on either side of it to guard against ambush, Tucker's progress was slow. He evicted a force of New York Volunteers from Youngstown, two miles from Fort Niagara, and then continued on to Lewiston, five miles distant, taking the batteries that had threatened Fort George in the process. About noon, as Tucker's men approached Lewiston, the detachment of Volunteers posted there by Brown took to their heels, leaving a partially cooked meal, a quantity of supplies, much of the Left Division's baggage and one hundred tents. Tucker pursued them but, as they showed no sign of making a stand, brought his men back to Lewiston.[9]

In the meantime Drummond and Morrison, keeping pace on the Canadian side of the Niagara, had reached Queenston, directly across the river. His objectives on the American shore achieved, Drummond ordered Tucker to return to Fort Niagara with part of his force; the remainder, including the Indians, crossed over to Queenston in Dobbs's boats, a process that took considerable time and was not completed until about 3:00 P.M. The troops were then permitted to cook and eat their dinner.[10]

Riall arrived at Queenston early in the afternoon and the two British generals discussed their next move. There had been no signs of American activity on the Canadian side of the Niagara and, as the day was getting on, Drummond resolved to assemble all his forces at the forward position along Lundy's Lane. He ordered Riall to bring up Hercules Scott's brigade, the 2nd Militia brigade and the reserve from the Ten and Twelve-Mile creeks, and Riall dispatched a courier for this purpose before riding back to Pearson.[11]

Up to this point the day had gone well for Drummond. Brown appeared to be in retreat and no longer threatened the forts at the river mouth, the batteries at Youngstown had been neutralized, and the eastern bank of the Niagara had been cleared of enemy troops as far as Lewiston. It remained only to assemble his scattered forces in strength enough to fight a decisive engagement with some chance of success. If Brown refused battle, the position at Lundy's Lane would still protect the forts and allow Drummond to move west if necessary to counter an American probe against Burlington Bay. Ultimately he could either shepherd Brown out of Canada or bring on the major action that he was confident would end in a British victory. In any case, it had been a good day's work and, as the day was drawing to a close the main thing was to concentrate the Right Division.

Late in the afternoon, having fed and rested his men, Drummond ordered Morrison to continue on to Lundy's Lane. Morrison's force now comprised about eight hundred regulars consisting of the 89th Foot, three companies of the 1st Foot, the light companies of the 8th and 41st Foot, an artillery detachment under Captain James Maclachlan, RA, with two 24-pdr. brass field guns and a Royal Marine Artillery rocket section armed with Congreve rockets, as well as a large force of Indians.[12]

At about the same time, Riall's messenger reached Hercules Scott at the Twelve-Mile Creek. Having expected to move forward that morning as part of the demonstration planned by Drummond against Queenston, Scott had turned out his men, ready to march, at 3:00 A.M.; but when no orders came he sent them to breakfast. Late in the morning he began to consolidate the scattered units under his command at the Twelve-Mile and, as soon as Riall's messenger arrived, set out for Lundy's Lane. With him were Lieutenant Colonel John Gordon and seven weak companies of the 1st Foot, five companies of the 8th under Major Thomas Evans, seven companies of Scott's own regiment, the 103rd Foot, commanded by Major William Smelt, the two flank companies of the 104th Foot under Captain Richard Leonard and a detachment of artillery under Captain James Mackonochie, RA, with three 6-pdr. brass guns. Also with Scott was Lieutenant Colonel Christopher Hamilton's 2nd militia brigade with detachments from the 1st and 2nd Norfolk Regiments, 1st Essex, 1st Middlesex and the Western Rangers. His total strength was nearly fifteen hundred regulars infantry and about two hundred and fifty militia.[13]

By the time these two columns had set out the day had grown quite warm and the troops kicked up clouds of dust on the dry roads as they marched toward Lundy's Lane. A few miles to the south of that place another force was assembling in the American camp at Chippawa.[14]

Monday, 25 July 1814, was a "fine" day "not excessively hot" and the men of the Left Division were thankful for the rest period Brown had granted them to bathe, wash their clothes and clean their weapons.[15] The division was camped on both sides of the muddy Chippawa near its mouth. The Second and Third Brigades were along the Niagara while the First Brigade – except for the Ninth Infantry which was on the north side – occupied the south bank of the Chippawa. To protect the camp, pickets were posted around its perimeter. Picket No. 1, commanded by Captain Azariah W. Odell of the Twenty-Third Infantry, was situated about a quarter mile north of the camp on the Portage Road.[16]

Odell was the first soldier in the division to become aware that the British were much closer than anyone in Chippawa realized that bright and peaceful morning. Between 8:00 and 9:00 A.M., he observed British troops at Willson's Tavern, some two miles north of his position. He immediately reported this to the field officer of the day, Major Henry Leavenworth, who informed Brown. The commanding general was somewhat sceptical that the enemy could be in strength so close to his camp, but to make sure he dispatched a fighting patrol of about one hundred men of the Nineteenth Infantry under Pennsylvanian Lieutenant David Riddle with orders to "take off" the enemy picket at Willson's. Some time before noon, Riddle marched over the Chippawa bridge and began a long and circuitous approach toward the tavern.[17]

Not long after this patrol marched out, Brown received a message from Lieutenant Colonel Philetus Swift of the New York Volunteers at Lewiston stating that the British were in force at Queenston and that four British ships were lying off Fort Niagara while boats were moving up the river. Within minutes, a second message arrived from a Captain Denman, another Volunteer officer at the same place, with the information that enemy were advancing on Lewiston and that the division's supplies at that place, at Schlosser, and on the road in between, were in danger of capture.[18]

Schlosser was Brown's major supply depot and he was sensitive about it. He knew that his withdrawal from Queenston had "left much at hazard on our [American] side of the Niagara," and it now appeared that "the enemy was about to avail himself of it."[19] There was not much he could do to counter this threat – he had neither boats enough to transport troops over the river to defend Schlosser nor to remove its supplies to a place of safety. He discussed the problem with Colonel Charles Gardner, his adjutant general, who, although weak from illness, was gamely trying to do his duty. Gardner was certain that the British move on Lewiston was a feint and that their main strength was probably on the Canadian side of the Niagara around the falls. Concluding that he needed more reliable information than that provided by non-regular officers such as Swift, who might easily be panicked, Brown ordered Second Lieutenant Edward Randolph of the divisional staff to proceed "with all dispatch" to Lewiston, assess the situation and report back.[20]

Brown's concerns were not shared by his soldiers who went about their appointed chores while messengers came and went from the headquarters tent. Lieutenant Colonel Hugh Dobbin, commanding the New York Volunteer regiment, had been suffering from dysentery for some time and decided "to take the fresh air to improve my health."[21] He went for a morning ride along the Niagara and, returning to Chippawa, he was looking forward to an evening meal of fresh green peas picked from a large patch that the divisional forage masters had located near the camp. Dobbin wasn't alone in this thought. Captain Benjamin Ropes of the Twenty-First Infantry was also anticipating tasting "the first New Vegetable" he had seen in weeks and throughout the day his appetite was whetted by the sight of his men "picking & Shelling" shakos full of peas.[22]

Others were not so fortunate. The grumbling men of Scott's brigade, for instance, were conscientiously cleaning their arms and uniforms. A few days earlier, Scott had admonished his officers for not paying "sufficient attention to the cleanliness & military appearance of their men" and had warned in daily orders that if they did not "apply the proper remedy" he would take "the subject into his own hands by beginning with the highest authority."[23] Soldiers of the First Brigade were expected to have their arms in order, their uniforms neat, their faces shaved, and "where necessary the hair cropped."[24] Besides, the brigade was scheduled for drill that afternoon and in Scott's brigade drill was often followed by a rigorous inspection. As if this wasn't enough, Scott had ordered his men to cook in advance enough provisions to fill their haversacks.[25]

Drill was also on the mind of Second Lieutenant David Douglass of the U.S. Engineers, who commanded the company of bombardiers, sappers and miners attached to the artillery. The twenty-five-year-old Douglass, commissioned in the army only nine months before on his graduation from Yale College, was proud of his first command and the two iron 18-pdr. guns assigned to it. He decided to exercise his company at their weapons that afternoon.[26]

Azariah Odell of the Twenty-Third had more pressing problems than appearance, supper or drill. All morning he had watched small parties of British moving in his front and was able to identify two companies of infantry and a troop of cavalry. Between noon and 1:00 P.M., British skirmishers approached Odell's picket and shots were exchanged. He again reported the presence of the enemy to Leavenworth but received the reply that Brown ridiculed the idea that the British were close in strength.

At 2:00 P.M. Leavenworth and Odell were joined on the picket by Jesup. After observing the enemy at Willson's by telescope, Jesup and Leavenworth agreed that the British would not risk placing a picket so close to the camp unless a stronger force was within supporting distance. Leavenworth went to report to the commanding general but Brown by this time had concluded that the British objective was Schlosser and dismissed the enemy observed by the picket as only a screen of light troops pushed forward to distract the Americans from a major movement on the other side of the river. Having considered his options, Brown then decided that "the most effectual method" of defending Schlosser was to make a corresponding movement down the Canadian side of the river to threaten Fort George. He sent for Winfield Scott.[27]

That tall fire-breather, "ever ambitious to distinguish himself and his command," was chafing at the bit when he arrived.[28] The evening before he had requested permission to take his brigade alone to attack Burlington Bay but Brown had refused, not wanting to divide his force. Scott had repeated the request in writing that morning and was pleased when Brown told him to take his brigade, a company of artillery and some cavalry north to Queenston. He instructed Scott to report if the enemy appeared and to call, if necessary, for assistance. To Scott this translated into a command "to find the enemy and to beat him."[29]

Scott received his orders about 3:00 P.M. just as Riddle's patrol was cautiously approaching Willson's. While moving through the woods toward the tavern, Riddle suddenly caught sight of the British along Lundy's Lane. Realizing that an attack in the face of this superior force was out of the question, the Pennsylvanian turned and began a long and roundabout march back to Chippawa.[30]

In a few minutes, Scott had his brigaded paraded in light marching order. Under his command were four infantry regiments: Leavenworth's Ninth, McNeil's Eleventh, Brady's Twenty-Second and Jesup's Twenty-Fifth. Towson's company of artillery and Harris's dragoons completed the force. The infantry regiments could only muster about eleven hundred men in total, while Towson had about seventy gunners and Harris the same number of dragoons. Three officers of the divisional staff – Major Roger Jones, the assistant adjutant general, Wood, the divisional engineer, and Hindman, the divisional artillery commander – received permission to join the march.[31]

Although he assembled quickly, Scott did not immediately leave Chippawa. He may have been held back by Brown in hopes that Riddle would return with information – but there was no sign of Riddle. It was not until after 5:00 P.M. that the First Brigade headed for the bridge over the Chippawa. They were watched by the men in camp who, in Scott's words, were "unbuttoned and relaxed."[32] Most of the onlookers thought the brigade was going out for one its incessant drills. Moving through the camp, Wood spotted Douglass and riding over, mentioned that there might be a chance to "feel the pulse" of the enemy.[33] Anxious to see some action, Douglass asked for and received permission to join the expedition. Between 5:00 and 6:00 P.M. the First Brigade, "in Excellent order," with the tall figure of their general prominent in the van, tramped across the Chippawa bridge and then, under "the influence of fine martial music" from the fifes and drums of the infantry regiments, took the road north.[34]

As they marched, the men could hear the roar of the falls but there was no opportunity to stop and view the great spectacle. Nevertheless there was almost a holiday atmosphere for it was a pleasant march through scenic country on a fine road shaded by tall, leafy trees. The rumour in the ranks was that they had been called out to disperse some Canadian militia and Indians who had been annoying the pickets. Certainly no one expected serious fighting. As the column moved north, however, the leading elements began to see small groups of the enemy forming and slowly retiring as the brigade neared them. Scott decided to take some precautions and, halting the brigade, ordered Leavenworth's Ninth Infantry into the woods and fields on the left of the road as a flank guard. This done, the column resumed its march at the slower pace dictated by the Ninth's awkward off-road movement.[35]

Scott, his aides and accompanying officers were with the advance guard, which consisted of Harris's dragoons and Captain John Pentland's company of the Twenty-Second Infantry. As they rounded a bend in the Portage Road just north of the Bridgewater Mills, Willson's Tavern came in sight. Standing in the courtyard were a number of saddled horses attended by enemy dragoons. Several British officers suddenly rushed from the tavern and mounted; some rode away briskly but three or four observed the Americans as they approached. Douglass remembered that one of the enemy "waived [sic], with his hand, a military salute, which was promptly returned by us" then "they all wheeled and rode swiftly away."[36] At the same time bugle calls began to issue back and forth in the woods to the north. It was becoming obvious that more than an enemy picket lay ahead.[37]

Willson's Tavern was located near the Table Rock, a favourite place to view the falls. It had been dispensing hospitality since at least 1795 when its location appeared on a map of the area published in London with the derogatory comment, "a bad tavern."[38] Despite the adverse publicity, this establishment, also known as the "Falls House," became a popular stopping place and is mentioned in many travellers' accounts of the time. The tavern remained in business throughout the war, its amiable hostess, the widow Deborah Willson, dispensing food, drink, hospitality and information to both sides with equanimity. The wartime popularity of Willson's may have

View of the falls of Niagara from the Canadian bank, 1805
As Scott's First Brigade marched north from Chippawa in the late afternoon of 25 July 1814 to their appointment with destiny, the men in the ranks could hear the roar of the great falls of Niagara. This 1805 watercolour shows the falls and the surrounding area as it would have appeared at the time of the battle. Willson's Tavern was behind the trees on the high ground to the left. The buildings in the foreground are the little hamlet of Bridgewater Mills, which was burned to the ground by the Left Division on 26 July 1814. (Watercolour by George Heriot, courtesy National Archives of Canada, C-12797)

had been due less to its proximity to the falls, or that it was regarded as neutral by its military clientele, than to the fact that widow Willson had two attractive daughters, Harriet and Statira. The latter lady so impressed one young British officer that he termed her the "Naiad of the Falls."[39]

Dismounting, Scott and his entourage entered the tavern and questioned the proprietress about the enemy officers who had just exited. The complacent widow, an American by birth, cheerfully informed them that General Riall was nearby with eight hundred regulars, three hundred Canadian militia and two guns – dead accurate information. Scott asked more questions but the proprietress had nothing to add. Looking up, his eye fell on Douglass and he posed the question: "Would you be willing to return to camp, Sir?"[40] Douglass, who had never been introduced to Scott, was somewhat flustered by the attention paid to him, a very junior officer, and decided Scott was testing his mettle. He therefore said nothing. An embarrassing moment of silence followed before Wood, divining Scott's meaning, introduced Douglass to Scott and assured him that, yes, the young officer would, indeed, be happy to take a message back to Chippawa. Scott ordered Douglass to inform Brown that he had met a detachment of the enemy in the strength described by Mrs. Willson and would engage it in battle. Mounting his horse, Douglass galloped south down the Portage Road.

Scott was sceptical that the British in front of him were in force. At most he thought he faced "a small body, detached from a inferior army that had committed the folly of sending at least half of its number to the opposite side of the river."[41] Rather than wait for a reply to his message, or for orders or reinforcements, he decided to continue his advance. Moments later, as his advance guard approached a chestnut wood north of the tavern, Indian war calls echoed through the trees. Shots rang out and a dragoon was wounded. Pentland cleared the skirt of the wood with his infantry while Harris took his dragoons straight up the road through the wood into open fields beyond. Coming out of the trees, the Bostonian saw a British force positioned on a low, flat hill about seven hundred and fifty yards to the north. He halted and sent word back to Scott.[42]

The firing in the woods and "the savage yell of the British Indians" was heard in the ranks of the brigade, which stopped short of the chestnut wood. A wide-eyed Jarvis Hanks watched as a dragoon trumpeter "with the blood streaming profusely down his temples & cheeks," rode furiously back to the rear. Also a musician, young Hanks became "alarmed for my own safety, not knowing but I should be in as bad or worse situation in a few minutes."[43]

Scott now directed Major Roger Jones to ride to Brown and tell him that the British were in strength to his front and that he intended to advance. He then informed his regimental commanders of his intentions and made his dispositions. Jesup was ordered to take the Twenty-Fifth to the right and "occupy the wood extending to the river Niagara."[44] Leavenworth's Ninth was brought back into the column and the Ninth, Twenty-Second and Eleventh Infantry, in that order, were directed to move through the woods past the advance guard and deploy in the open area beyond. Towson was to act in concert with the infantry.[45]

As the officers received their orders, the brigade made ready. The colour sergeants uncased the regimental colours. Each regiment had two silk colours: a dark blue national standard, six feet in the hoist by seven and a half in the fly, embellished with an eagle surrounded by a galaxy of stars, and a somewhat smaller buff regimental colour with the unit designation embroidered in gold letters on a scroll. The infantrymen looked to their weapons – checking priming, cleaning vents, testing the condition and fit of their flints, loosening bayonets in scabbards and adjusting their cartridge boxes on their hips, stomach or back according to personal preference. If they had not already done so, they now loaded the first crucial round into their muskets. Towson's gunners went through a similar process with their larger weapons, removing the lead shields over the vents and the wood tompions from the muzzles. The competent Towson probably ordered his two 6-pdr. guns loaded with roundshot, the charge fixed by a brass priming wire stuck down the vent and the shot secured by a wad. This would allow him to open fire a precious second or two faster.[46]

It was about 7:15 P.M. when the First Brigade, with Scott at its head, debouched from the chestnut wood. With colours flying, drums beating and fifes playing a lively air (probably the traditional "Yankee Doodle"), the grey-uniformed column moved from the shade of the trees into an open, sunlit area. As they emerged, they came into "full view, and in easy range of a line of battle drawn up in Lundy's Lane, more extensive than that defeated at Chippawa." Writing nearly fifty years later, with the "aches in broken bones" prompting his recollection, Scott remembered the anger he felt at that moment over the "blundering, stupid" report made that morning by a nervous Volunteer officer at Lewiston that had brought his brigade to this spot.[47] For it was obvious as he stared at the enemy in front of him that the main strength of the British was on this side of the Niagara and not moving on Schlosser as Brown believed. His brigade was now in contact with a well-

placed and apparently stronger enemy force, too far from Chippawa to receive immediate assistance.[48]

Watching from the high ground to the north as the Americans emerged
from the woods were Drummond and Riall. They had not been there long;
shortly before Scott's appearance a nervous Riall had ordered a withdrawal
from the position along Lundy's Lane.

Word of the American advance had reached Riall from Indians scouting
the enemy camp and confirmation was brought in by the pickets posted
along the Portage Road. Ensign John Kilborn of the Incorporated Militia
remembered that "our dragoons, posted about a mile in front, came hurridly
back with the intelligence that the whole American army were marching
down upon us."[49] Riall sent a messenger with the news to Drummond to
inform him that the enemy were advancing in "great force" and then took
stock of his situation. Chippawa had made him wary of this new breed of
American soldier who fought like a rock-steady professional, and as reports
of the enemy's progress continued to come in, he concluded that Brown's
entire army, reputed to be five thousand strong, was bearing down on his
eleven hundred to twelve hundred regulars and militia. This was a worri-
some prospect and Riall decided to withdraw to Queenston, where, joined
by Drummond, Morrison and Hercules Scott, he could give battle on more
even terms. Accordingly, he ordered Pearson to withdraw from the lane and
sent a messenger to Hercules Scott with orders to march to Queenston.[50]

Pearson quickly pulled his units out – the sedentary militia, Indians and
wagons first, next the Incorporated Militia and artillery and, finally, the
Glengarry Light Infantry, who formed the rear guard. So swift was the withdrawal that Norton and Lieutenant Colonel William Drummond of the
104th, who had gone forward for a few minutes to examine the American
column, returned to find the former position almost deserted. But even as
they were informed of the retreat, the two men saw dust clouds approaching from the north – British troops were returning to Lundy's Lane.[51]

Drummond and his staff were the first to arrive. The British commander
had been riding at the rear of Morrison's column when he received Riall's
report that the enemy were advancing in force. Spurring his horse, he galloped past Morrison's troops and encountered Pearson's brigade retreating
in what he thought was considerable confusion. About two miles from the
lane, near the Muddy Run Creek, he met the more orderly column of the
Incorporated Militia Battalion, whom he promptly halted, and then Riall.

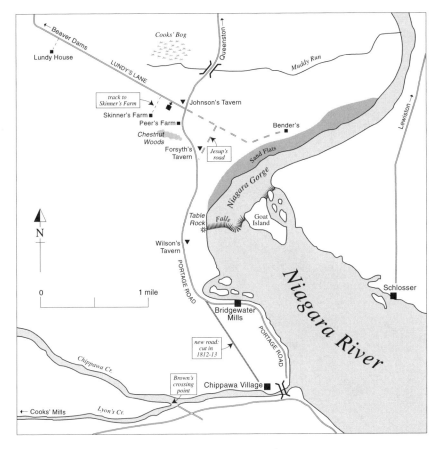

The environs of the battlefield of Lundy's Lane, 25 July 1814

There is no record of what was said between the two generals but shortly afterward they rode onto the hill that dominated the junction of Lundy's Lane and the Portage Road. The time was close to 7:00 P.M.[52]

This hill was a sandy ridge running from east to west nearly a mile long and less than half a mile wide. About fifty feet above the surrounding country at its highest point, it sloped gently to the south and west but more steeply to the north and east. It was traversed along its length by Lundy's Lane, a sunken road shaded by peach, apple and cherry trees that projected their boughs over the rail fences that lined it. Bounded on its eastern flank by the Portage Road and cut on its western by a track that ran south to Haggai Skinner's farm a mile distant, the ridge commanded a cleared area of farm fields, ripe with buckwheat and corn, crossed by fences that ex-tended to a belt of chestnut trees some seven hundred and fifty yards to the south. East of the Portage Road were more cleared fields, interspersed with dense pine woods extending down to the Niagara gorge about one mile away. The same mixture of fields interspersed with small woods lay to the north and west although the slopes of the hill were largely clear of trees.[53]

About two hundred and fifty yards west of the Portage Road a low, log meeting house, often described as a "church" but actually used as a place of worship by a number of denominations, crowned the hill. Adjoining it was a half-acre cemetery plot with rough wooden or stone grave markers enclosed by a split-rail fence overgrown with bushes and shrubs. Below the cemetery on the southeast slope of the hill was a young orchard surrounding the Peer family farmhouse, a white frame structure called the "white house" in many accounts of the battle. Running beside the orchard, about three hundred yards in front of the hill, was a track that connected the Portage Road with the track to Skinner's farm. It was a well-settled area and numerous farms and buildings were dotted around the hill – as early as 1797, a traveller had described the junction of the Portage Road and Lundy's Lane as "a small village, consisting of about half a dozen straggling houses."[54]

This was Loyalist country. William Lundy was a former Pennsylvanian who had come to Canada in 1786 with his wife and five sons to take up land lying a mile and a half along an Indian trail running west from the falls. Charles Green, a New Jersey Loyalist who owned the land over which the trail ran, donated it as a public road and it became known as Lundy's Lane in honour of the prominent farmer whose property bordered it. South of the ridge, on both sides of the Portage Road, lay the property of James Forsyth who owned a tavern and livery stable midway between Willson's Tavern and the junction of Lundy's Lane with the Portage Road. Forsyth's daughter Sarah had married Christopher Buchner, formerly of New Jersey. Buchner had obtained from Forsyth, either by purchase or gift, most of the ridge south of the Lane and had built a house on the southwest slope of the hill. West and south of Forsyth were the farms of Benjamin and Haggai Skinner, members of a large Loyalist clan from Delaware. Haggai's daughter Lydia had married a recent American immigrant, Stephen Peer, and the couple resided at the southeast foot of the hill.[55]

Drummond saw at a glance that the ground would make a good defensive position. The gentle southern slope of the hill would allow his artillery to transform the cleared fields in front into what a later generation of soldiers would call a "killing ground." The Americans would have to advance over these fields to close with his main line, which he could shelter, if need be, on the reverse slope. The enemy would take heavy casualties to reach that line, and as they neared, his infantry would move forward to the crest, pour in several quick volleys of musketry and then push their enemies back with the bayonet. The terrain would allow Drummond to fight the kind of defensive action at which the British army excelled and he was quick to appreciate its merits.[56]

Certain that Brown would not attack with only part of his force, Drummond was convinced that, with a total of twenty-two hundred men at best, he faced the entire Left Division with an estimated strength of four to five thousand. Retreat was out of the question – there was no better defensive position between Chippawa and the mouth of the Niagara River. But with the advantage of the terrain, Drummond, confident in the quality of his regular troops, would have a good chance of gaining a victory. He issued orders to bring Pearson and Morrison's troops up to the lane at the "double quick," and sent a messenger to Hercules Scott countermanding Riall's instructions and urging him to bring on his column with all possible speed – Drummond was going to give battle at Lundy's Lane.[57]

As his troops came pounding up, Drummond deployed them along the ridge. The two 24-pdr. guns and the rocket detachment were stationed with the two 6-pdrs. and the 5½-inch howitzer of Pearson's brigade near the cemetery to the west of the meeting house. Under the overall command of Captain James Maclachlan, RA, they occupied a position that gave them a clear field of fire south and east. Behind the guns, Drummond placed his regular infantry in line with their left flank on the Portage Road. The centre of this line was composed of his best unit, Morrison's 89th Foot, while the right was formed by three companies of the 1st under Captain William Brereton and the left by Captain Joseph Glew's light company of the 41st. To hold the wooded far left flank, between the Portage Road and the Niagara River gorge, Drummond ordered Captain Francis Campbell's light company of the 8th Foot and Lieutenant Colonel William Robinson's Incorporated Militia to take up positions along a trail that formed an extension of the lane to the east of the Portage Road. Drummond's right flank was held by the Glengarry Light Infantry who took post west of the track to Skinner's farm while Major Robert Lisle's troop of the 19th Light Dragoons halted at the junction of the Portage Road and Lundy's Lane. Viewed from the axis of the American advance from the south, the British line was a concave curve with the hill at its centre and its flanks advanced.

The sun was dipping low as the troops were directed to their proper places by shouting officers. First into position were the Glengarries, the last unit to leave the field, their dark green uniforms, which had earned them the name of the "black stumps," blending into the lengthening shadows in the fields to the west of the hill.[58] They were joined there by the more daring members of the sedentary militia and Norton's Indian party.[59]

In the cemetery, Maclachlan's gunners, their blue coats stained with sweat and covered with the dust of the road, unlimbered their guns and manhandled them into place among the grave markers. The limbers, horse teams and ammunition wagons were removed to the rear and the guns readied for action. Maclachlan, estimating the range to the chestnut wood, probably chose roundshot or shrapnel as the first projectile to be loaded, holding his canister in reserve until the range came down. Nearby, Sergeant Austin and his marine rocket gunners had an easier task to make ready their 12-pdr. Congreve rockets. The flimsy firing tripod was carried by one man who, on order, spread the three legs and emplaced it. The apparatus was then pointed in the direction of the enemy, the correct elevation estimated, and the first 12-pdr. rocket laid in the cradle ready for firing. Weapons ready and portfires lit, the gunners on the hill may have had a few minutes to gaze around and perhaps comment on the roar and clouds of spray from the falls of Niagara, a mile away.

At the same time the regular infantry, many tired after a fifteen-mile march from the mouth of the Niagara but moving with the easy gait of trained soldiers, came into position. Harried and chivvied by sergeants, they formed a two-rank line, each man occupying, according to regulations, twenty-two inches of space with two paces separating the ranks. If the dust of a day-long march had not obscured them, the trained eye could distinguish the different regiments by the colour of the facings or trim on their collars and cuffs – the dark blue of the 1st and 8th, the red of the 41st and the black of the 89th.[60]

There was little talking in their ranks. Standing orders in the Right Division forbade "Noise or inattention to the Word of Command," which "tend to produce Confusion" and "reduce us to the level of our opponents."[61] Orders were backed up by keen eared sergeants and the men were quiet as they formed in the shadows of early evening and prepared for action in a fashion similar to their American opponents – checking flint, priming, loading a round and perhaps easing the straps of their load-carrying equipment to a marginally less stiff muscle. Some, like Private Shadrach Byfield of the 41st, received the traditional tot of rum before battle but most had to be content with a swig of warm, fetid water from their canteens. Until Chippawa, these men had thought little of taking on "Cousin Jonathan" or "Jonathan Yankee" and beating him. But Chippawa had changed all that and the men in the ranks guessed they were in for a stiff fight.[62]

On the Portage Road to the left of the infantry and watching the American cavalry directly in front of them was Major Robert Lisle's squadron of the 19th Light Dragoons. As their mounts pawed, snorted and whisked their tails to clear away the flies, which were always bad around the lane in July, the dragoons sat resplendent in their dark blue coats with brass buttons and yellow collars, cuffs and plastrons. The troop's effectiveness did not equal its colourful appearance as Canada was not cavalry country and there were few opportunities to engage in the charge, the British cavalryman's favourite tactic. For the time being, Lisle's main duty, assumed if unspoken, was to keep an eye on the infantry and intercept any man who left his place for the rear.[63]

Still arriving were the units on the left flank, the light company of the 8th Foot and the Incorporated Militia. Meanwhile the Indians and sedentary militia took position west of the hill to the rear and right of the line of regular infantry. Drummond's Indian force, which may have been five hundred strong, was composed of warriors from several different nations with no overall leader. The man who could best fill that role, John Norton, intended to place them in the most suitable position, east of the Portage Road, but for the time being he was preoccupied with the right flank. None of the senior British officers knew how to lead these mercurial auxiliaries and, uncertain how to deal with them, Drummond left them to their own devices.[64]

The Canadian militia forming west of the regular infantry consisted of detachments from the 1st, 2nd, 4th and 5th Lincoln and 2nd York Regiments. It was the 2nd Lincolns who had the greatest personal stake in the coming fight for it was over their land that the contending armies were about to fight. The 2nd had fought hard at Chippawa and lost sixteen dead and thirteen wounded, the heaviest losses incurred in a single engagement by a Canadian militia unit during the war. Chippawa had created ten new widows in the regiment's area, including Hannah Forsyth, the wife of the man who owned much of the property to the immediate south of the Lane, and Lydia Peer, who lived in the white house at the foot of the hill. Lydia's husband, Stephen, killed by Porter's men on 5 July in the woods west of Samuel Street's farm, never saw the son his wife would bear him in a few days.[65]

There were many local men in the ranks of the 2nd Lincolns that summer evening. Lieutenant Christopher Buchner was standing with his son, John, a few hundred yards from his own house. In the same company were Charles and Henry Green, offspring of the man who had donated the land over which Lundy's Lane ran and Sergeant James Lundy, son of the man after whom it was named. Also present was thirty-eight-year-old William Biggar who farmed up the lane and whose wife and children were sheltering at the Lundy house less than a mile away. Finally, there were John Bender, whose father owned considerable property between the road junction and the Niagara, and Gideon and Noah Skinner, sons of the Loyalists who farmed to the south of the hill. Neighbours and friends who had known each other since birth and who had worshipped in the meeting house visible from their ranks, it would have given these men no pleasure to watch the destruction of years of labour as the troops knocked down fences, trampled crops and despoiled orchards.[66]

Some of the British and Canadians coming into position around the hill could see American cavalry stationary on the Portage Road and skirmishers moving in the chestnut woods. Before the last units had got into place, "enemy colours showed themselves coming out of the wood" and a column of grey-clad American infantry followed by artillery advanced up the road and began to deploy in the cleared fields south of the hill.[67] The order was given, Maclachlan's guns opened fire and the battle began.[68]

CHAPTER 7

The First Brigade Stands and Dies

Usually when people discuss generals they consider only courage. Courage is but one of many qualities of generalship. Now a courageous man is certain to engage recklessly and without knowing the advantages. This will not do.

Wu Ch'i, "Art of War," c. 380 b.c.

After recovering from his initial shock at seeing the British arrayed in front of him, Winfield Scott considered retreating. He decided to remain on the ground as by "standing fast, the salutary impression was made upon the enemy that the whole American reserve was at hand and would soon assault his flanks."[1] Moreover, a withdrawal might cause confusion among his troops and result in disaster. It might also create panic in the other two brigades which Scott expected to march to his relief, "for an extravagant opinion generally prevailed throughout the army in respect to the prowess – nay, invincibility of Scott's brigade."[2] Scott therefore resolved to engage the enemy with the eleven to twelve hundred men under his command and began forming for battle while Hindman rode back to camp to bring up more guns to support him.[3]

It was about 7:15 P.M., thirty minutes before sunset, and long shadows were reaching out across the fields as the First Brigade deployed. Towson moved past Harris's dragoons and unlimbered his two 6-pdr. guns and one 5½-inch howitzer near the Portage Road. He was immediately fired upon by the British artillery. Scott ordered the three infantry regiments that followed to "form line to the front."[4] Major Henry Leavenworth, commanding the lead Ninth Infantry, turned his regiment off the road into the field on the left.

This movement was not executed smoothly, as the Ninth had to cross a split rail fence which, like all the fences in Stamford Township, the area of the battle, was required by law to be at least five feet high with four "rails or logs sufficiently well made."⁵ These obstacles cut across the entire cleared area of the battlefield and rendered the movement of formed troops difficult. But Leavenworth's men kicked the rails down or climbed over them and then formed in line to the left of Towson's artillery. Pentland's company of the Twenty-Second, which had been covering the Ninth's advance, then formed on Leavenworth's right between the Ninth and the guns. Colonel Hugh Brady's Twenty-Second and Major John McNeil's Eleventh Infantry followed. As the brigade moved into the field, "the enemy [artillery] commenced firing upon us."⁶ Jarvis Hanks, sitting on top of the fence and about to jump down on the other side, was horrified as the balls of a shrapnel round "rattled around me" cutting "the branches of trees over my head, and on my right hand and on my left, also splintered the rails, on either side and under my feet."⁷ Unharmed and thankful for a "most wonderful Providential preservation from instant death," the fourteen-year-old scrambled to take up his position in the ranks.

The Eleventh and Twenty-Second next moved in two parallel columns behind the Ninth until they had cleared it and then, the Twenty-Second preceding, began to deploy into line on Leavenworth's left. As the last company of the Twenty-Second was coming into line, it was hit particularly hard by artillery and its commander, Captain Willis Foulk, wounded. His men broke and ran to the rear, rushing in their panic through the Eleventh, moving behind them. Part of that unit also broke and in a moment the left flank of the brigade dissolved into a mob running for the cover of the chestnut woods in the rear. While his senior captain, John Bliss, steadied the remainder of the regiment and kept it in place, the Eleventh's commander, McNeil, and officers and N.C.O.'s of both regiments chased after the running men. Most were stopped and reformed – others kept going. Disgusted, McNeil ordered First Lieutenant Henry Blake of the Eleventh to go "to Chippewa, or to Hell if necessary but to find the fugitives and bring them back."⁸

This crisis over, the three regiments formed a line of two ranks and opened a fire of musketry on the British line. Scott could see the British artillery on the hill and, in front and to the west of the guns, a line of enemy infantry stationed obliquely to the American left. This was Brereton's three companies of the 1st Foot; the remainder of the British infantry were behind the guns. Scott may have thought that Drummond was in greater strength than was the actual case and would move to the attack. He therefore did not advance but maintained his ground and waited for reinforce-ments. It soon became apparent, however, that his regiments were placed "too far from the enemy to act with decisive effect" as the British were out of range of musketry.[9] But the First Brigade was within range of the British gunners who took full advantage of such a tempting target. Seeing the in-fantry's plight, Towson tried to neutralize the enemy artillery.[10]

Thirty years old, Nathan Towson was a peacetime militia officer from Maryland with a fondness for poetry. He had served in Scott's former regi-ment, the Second Artillery, and had fought in most of the major actions on the northern frontier. His commander thought well of him, and when Scott was promoted brigadier general in the spring of 1814, he specifically re-quested that Towson's company be attached to his brigade. Scott's trust was not misplaced; at Chippawa Towson had rendered the First Brigade excel-lent support engaging in a duel with the British artillery before using canis-ter with great effect to break up the attack of the enemy infantry.[11]

Towson could see that he was outgunned but he was not a man to shrink from a difficult task. He opened a brisk counter-battery fire on the British artillery but soon realized that he had a particular problem; the British guns were within range but their position was much higher than that of his pieces. To hit his target with roundshot, Towson had to elevate his muzzles as much as possible, resulting in his shot descending on the target at a steep angle and reducing the ricochet effect that made roundshot so destructive. At best, his fire was having only a nuisance effect and, although Leavenworth thought that Towson's "incessant discharges highly animated the spirits of the troops," they did little else.[12] Realizing that his efforts were ineffective, Towson ceased fire and began to shift his guns from place to place trying to find a position high enough to hit the British guns without having to use extreme elevation.[13]

In contrast, there was nothing wrong with the position of Captain James Maclachlan, RA. His two 24-pdr. guns and two 6-pdr. guns benefited from the additional range provided by the elevation of the hill but were still low enough so that their shot had a fairly flat trajectory and could make maxi-mum use of ricochet. Maclachlan had a clear field of fire, there was no ef-fective counter-battery fire and, best of all, his target was a line of infantry standing stationary at between five and six hundred yards distance – outside canister range but a good middle distance for roundshot and shrapnel. These were ideal conditions and the experienced Maclachlan was quick to take advantage of them.[14]

Maclachlan and the other Royal Artillery officers present that night were determined to prove their worth to the two British generals on the hill, particularly Riall. Three weeks before, they had done their utmost to support that officer's ill-fated attack at Chippawa, advancing their guns to within a dangerous distance of the American infantry, but Riall had given the gunners scant mention and little praise in his official dispatch and, even worse, had arrogated to himself the credit for placing the guns during the battle. As if this was not insult enough to a proud and "Distinct Corps ... mentioned as such in all Dispatches from the Duke of Wellington," Riall told one of the artillery officers who had fought at Chippawa that "he was not worth the salt of his Ration."[15] Ultimately Riall's poor treatment of his gunners would result in an acrimonious correspondence that reached Prevost's desk. For now they were content to display their professional skill before Drummond, Riall's superior and Winfield Scott had provided them with an excellent opportunity.[16]

Maclachlan maintained a steady rate of fire, probably one round every two minutes for each of the two 24-pdr. guns and one round per minute from his 6-pdr. pieces and the 5½-inch howitzer. He likely used roundshot in preference to shrapnel because there was a shortage of the latter projectile in Upper Canada. The gunners could have fired faster but a slow, steady rate was preferred because it conserved ammunition, prevented loading accidents and allowed the thick, choking cloud of smoke created by each discharge to disperse before the gun was fired again. To reduce the amount of smoke, the guns were fired in turn, one after another, rather than in unison. Firing by rotation also meant that the target could be kept constantly under fire and there would always be a loaded piece to take advantage of opportunities.[17]

The British gunners could see the blue and buff colours marking the positions of the three American infantry regiments above the smoke created by their musketry and concentrated their fire on these useful aiming points. As regimental commanders usually positioned themselves near the colours so that they could be easily located in action, this concentration had an immediate effect. Almost as soon as his regiment had formed, Major John McNeil of the Eleventh was hit above the knee by a shell fragment which broke his thigh bone. The thirty-year-old McNeil, six feet, two inches tall and described as "one of the finest...men and soldiers ever looked upon," tried to stay with his men but, faint with pain and the loss of blood, was forced to ride to the rear leaning on the neck of his horse.[18] Shortly afterward Hugh Brady of the Twenty-Second Infantry was wounded in the hip and side. At forty-four the oldest of Scott's regimental commanders, Brady continued in action although he had to be continually helped "off and on his horse during the engagement, when he was like to faint from loss of blood."[19]

Leavenworth was now the only unwounded regimental commander in the American line. A peacetime lawyer and militia officer from Delhi, New York, Leavenworth had been commissioned as a captain at the outbreak of war and had achieved promotion both by his bravery as a soldier and his skilful use of influence with the secretary of war. He was a good officer and Scott regarded the thirty-one-year-old Leavenworth and his fellow commander, Jesup of the Twenty-Fifth, as "elegant tacticians of the French school."[20] Leavenworth had a reputation for steadiness under fire – in his report of the battle of Chippawa, Scott had singled out his behaviour when the British "cannonade ... did not prevent [him] from preserving his corps in the most excellent order, at all times prepared to advance or fire, to give or to receive the charge."[21] In the hours ahead, Leavenworth would live up to that reputation.[22]

The British artillery fire was relentless and the American colour parties suffered severely. One of the colour bearers of the Ninth Infantry was cut down, as was one of the Eleventh – the first of nine men who would be killed or wounded carrying that regiment's standard during the battle. Behind the colours were the regimental musicians – a position of "equal danger with any other portion of the army," as Jarvis Hanks proudly recorded later.[23]

Scott's three regiments kept up their ineffective fire of musketry but the range was far too great and only the occasional round took effect. In return, the British gunners subjected the brigade to a "warm and destructive fire."[24] Although Maclachlan was probably firing at a conservative rate, several of the Americans likened it to a "hailstorm" of shot and shell.[25] The casualties were constant: Captain John Bliss who succeeded McNeil in command of the Eleventh, fell with a leg wound; his successor, Captain Valentine Goodrich, was killed shortly thereafter and a lieutenant assumed command of the regiment. The other regiments fared no better. Second Lieutenant Adolphus Burghardt of the Ninth was hit in the side but continued in action. "We were completely cut up," remembered Lieutenant Samuel Brady of the Twenty-Second, "more than half the officers and men being wounded."[26]

But they did not waver. As roundshot came bouncing across the field and then scythed through them, or shells exploded overhead, the men of the First Brigade, formed in two ranks standing close enough that each man could touch his neighbours' elbows, returned the fire. The regiments fired by platoons, the small battlefield fire-and-manoeuvre units normally organized in each infantry company just prior to action so that officers could more easily control their men's musketry. There were two platoons per company and about fifteen files, or thirty men, in each platoon. The strength of the platoons was kept as constant as possible; if casualties became heavy, a company would be reformed into one platoon, and if more men were hit, two companies would be combined into a single platoon.[27]

The men loaded and fired on order as casualties were dragged out of the ranks and the survivors were shifted in toward the colours by the file closers. Choked by the bitter from the cartridges they tore open with their teeth, blinded by the dense clouds of smoke from each volley, deafened by the successive discharges and their uniforms scorched or even set on fire by the muzzle blasts of the weapons around them, the men of Scott's brigade fired, loaded, closed in toward the centre and held their ground.

Brereton's companies of the 1st Foot returned the American musketry but it was Maclachlan's sweating gunners that were doing the most harm to Scott's brigade. As each round was fired, the gun detachments, moving with an ease borne of long practice, loaded the next and ran the gun back up to its firing position. This was no simple task as the lightest gun on the hill weighed nearly a ton with its carriage – one of the reasons why recruits for the Royal Artillery had to be a minimum of one hundred and eighty-two pounds. Maclachlan's men had an advantage, however, in that the position of their guns meant that they recoiled up a slope and were easier to return to their firing positions.[28]

The gun being loaded, the gun commander, usually a sergeant, would "lay" or aim the gun at the chosen target. Gunlaying in 1814 was a combination of art and science that required a well-trained and experienced gun commander. While laying the piece, he instinctively took into account and made allowances for such factors as wind force and direction, air temperature, humidity and the age of the gun (older weapons with worn bores had less muzzle velocity and therefore needed an additional bit of elevation.) Following Royal Artillery practice, the weapon would be aimed to fire obliquely through the American ranks and care would be taken "to fire so as to do execution, for a shot flying over the enemy's heads only hardens them and discourages your own troops."[29] After the gun was laid, the commander would step back and give the word "Fire!" Each round was accompanied by a billowing cloud of thick, acrid smoke and a shower of sparks as the projectile left the muzzle and thousands of pounds of wood and metal recoiled six to eight feet. When the weapon had stopped moving, the whole procedure was repeated on the command "Load!"

Sergeant Austin's Royal Marine Artillery rocket detachment had much lighter work as the 12-pdr. Congreve rockets with their solid shot, shell or shrapnel warheads were easily lifted onto the firing apparatus. The problem came after the rocket was ignited when the "fidgety missile begins to sputter out sparks and wriggle its tail for a second or so ... then darts forth."[30] If the marines did not get clear of the after-blast, they "exhibited a strange appearance" as the "practice of discharging the Rocket ... proved a great injury to the men, burning their hands and faces. Some had no hair on their heads and their hands and shoulder severely scorched."[31]

Firing rockets was dangerous enough but their accuracy was entirely another matter – a witness who watched a rocket troop in action noted that, although the gunners "kept shooting off rockets, none ... ever followed the course of the first; most of them, on arriving about the middle of the ascent, took a vertical direction."[32] The fiery rocket contrails shooting through the dark sky were long remembered by many of those who fought at Lundy's Lane, but there is little evidence that these dramatic projectiles caused much damage.

Behind the gun line, Maclachlan and his officers supervised the supply of ammunition to the guns from the caissons parked safely in the rear, pointed out targets, observed the fall of shot and either gave orders to the gun commanders or made the necessary corrections to the guns themselves. They were careful to appear calm and composed in action for, as one period manual advised, artillery officers had to "preserve, even in the most trying moments, an air of coolness both by word and deed, to encourage the timid, and to repress the ardor of the violent."[33] Their studied behaviour was imitated by their subordinates and the five gun detachments loaded and fired with a steady efficiency that was murderous to their opponents.[34]

Following standard practice, Maclachlan concentrated his fire against the American infantry but occasionally spared a few rounds for the artillery. Towson's gunners were hit several times and his two subordinate officers, Second Lieutenants Henry Campbell and Jacob Schmuck, were wounded. Schmuck was sent to the rear but Campbell elected to stay with guns and continue the fight. Unable to find a position that would enable him to effectively engage the British guns, Towson finally ceased fire to conserve ammunition. On the road behind, Harris's dragoons also suffered from the "particular notice of ... Artillery & Congreves" and lost a number of men and horses.[35] Finding his men "uselessly exposed," Harris retired them behind the cover of the woods and returned alone to the field to offer his services to Leavenworth.[36]

As his brigade was slowly decimated, Scott rode up and down the line with his aide, Lieutenant William Worth, encouraging his men. Anxious for reinforcements from Chippawa, he sent Major Eleazar Wood back to camp to hasten the arrival of Brown and the rest of the division. Scott was convinced that he was badly outnumbered and felt he could not attack with any chance of success nor could he retreat – the brigade had to maintain its position until Brown arrived with reinforcements. This was galling to an officer whose hallmark was offensive action. A British officer present later recalled that the "Enemy remained firm in the position which he had at first assumed" as "Dread seemed to forbid his advance, and Shame to restrain his flight."[37]

After enduring about forty-five minutes of artillery fire, Scott decided that he had to do something and ordered the brigade "to advance upon the enemy with a view to charge him."[38] The three regiments ceased firing and moved forward but had only gone about one hundred yards when the order was countermanded and they halted. The brigade was now about four hundred and fifty yards from the British guns and their front paralleled the farm track that ran west from the Portage Road.[39]

Lieutenant Colonel Love Parry, commanding the 1st Militia Brigade, and Lieutenant Colonel Francis Battersby, commanding the Glengarry Light Infantry posted in the fields to the northwest of Scott's line, noted that the American advance had brought the Scott's flank out from the cover of a skirt of the chestnut wood. Seeing an opportunity, the Anglo-Irish Battersby, from County Meath, moved the Glengarries forward and Parry ordered the militia to support them together with some of Norton's Indian party. The Glengarries formed a skirmish line behind the trees and bushes along the track leading to Skinner's farm, kicked flat the rail fence bordering the track and advanced toward the American flank.[40]

The 2nd York Regiment was one of the regiments taking part in this attack. Raised in the Burlington Bay area, the 2nd, with other militia units, had contested Queenston Heights in a day-long battle with Porter's brigade three days before. One of the better sedentary units, it was commanded by Colonel Richard Beasley but he proved unworthy of the men he led. After Parry ordered the regiment to open fire, Beasley contradicted the order, enraging his second-in-command, Major Titus Geer Simons, who shouted

Major Titus Geer Simons, Upper Canada Militia
Simons took over the 2nd York Regiment during the battle when its colonel proved unfit for command. He was badly wounded while leading his men in an attack on Scott's brigade but survived due to the personal nursing care of his devoted wife. (From Transactions of the Wentworth County Historical Society)

that "I will cut down" the "first man that ceases firing."[41] When the regiment advanced, Beasley lagged behind, giving up his musket to one of his officers before retiring behind a nearby shed to "observe the action" with the belief that "if the fire recedes we are gaining, if advancing we are losing."[42]

Simons led the regiment and Simons, like the artillery officers on the hill, had reason to prove himself in battle. Less than a month before, he had been a major in the Incorporated Militia but an altercation in the officers' mess had blighted his career and forced him to resign his appointment. The son of a prominent Loyalist family from Connecticut, Simons now served with the 2nd York, a good unit but not as good as the Incorporated Battalion.[43]

Observing Parry and Battersby's advance, Drummond ordered Brereton's three companies of the 1st Foot to move to the farm lane in front of the hill in support them. Brereton was another officer anxious for the attention and approval of his superiors. Three weeks earlier at the battle of Chippawa, he had fallen behind his company when it went into action. The twenty-seven-year-old Brereton had pleaded exhaustion but his brother officers suspected cowardice and were murmuring against him – he desperately needed to recover his reputation and playing a prominent role in battle was the best method. He moved forward with alacrity and opened a steady fire against the Americans.[44]

To Leavenworth in the American line, it appeared that the British "were pressing very hard upon our left."[45] Seeing the danger, Scott ordered the Eleventh Infantry on his left flank to wheel back facing the Canadians. The Eleventh returned the skirmishers' fire with volleys of musketry that had little effect as the Canadians and Indians "were scattered according to the practice of irregular Warfare, taking ev'ry advantage of which the open na-

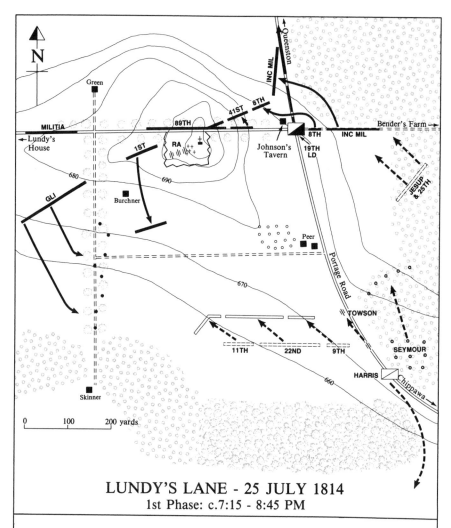

LUNDY'S LANE - 25 JULY 1814
1st Phase: c.7:15 - 8:45 PM

1. Drummond deploys along Lundy's Lane with his artillery positioned on the hill near the meeting house and cemetery (building with a cross and group of crosses). Scott's brigade forms west of the Portage Road while Towson's gunners unlimber on the road itself.

2. Coming under heavy fire, Scott orders an advance on the hill but countermands the order after his brigade has moved only a short distance. The Glengarry Light Infantry move forward in skirmish line to attack his flank and are supported by the 1st Foot.

3. Jesup, having left Seymour's company to hold his front, moves his Twenty-Fifth Infantry north and caves in the British Left flank. The 8th Foot and Incorporated Militia take up a new position west of the Portage Road.

ture of the ground would admit."[46] The exception was Simons, who did not dismount when he led his men forward. Struck by three musket balls that penetrated his upraised sword arm and lodged in his chest, he fell unconscious to the ground. The two sides continued to exchange musketry at a distance but neither moved to the attack.[47]

As Scott's brigade never came within decent musket range of the main British position, it is incomprehensible why he ordered their futile firing to continue for so long. As it was, the continuous musketry had a predictable result: soon after they took up their new position, the three regiments began to run short of ammunition. According to standing orders, each soldier in the First Brigade was to have forty rounds at all times in his cartridge box; a further twenty rounds per man were carried in the brigade's ammunition carts. It was the responsibility of Scott and his regimental commanders to ensure that, when required, an adequate supply of ammunition reached the men in the ranks from the transport. Either the ammunition re-supply arrangements broke down or, more likely, the First Brigade fired off its entire supply of sixty rounds per man – in any case, first the Eleventh, then the Twenty-Second and, finally, the Ninth ceased firing.[48]

It was at this point that Lieutenant Henry Blake of the Eleventh Infantry reappeared with a flock of fifty to sixty stragglers that he had collected on McNeil's orders. After assembling this group, Blake had embarked on a curious little odyssey that saw him move north to Towson's caissons parked on the Portage Road and halt for some time before moving into a field to the east in order to avoid the round shot that occasionally came bouncing down the road. He had remained there until Joseph Willcocks rode up and ordered him to return to the battle, when he marched across the road and found Scott who directed him to form on the right of the brigade and, despite the general shortage of ammunition, to open fire. Twilight was now turning to dusk; the American line had ceased fire although the British guns were still active. For the next half hour, Blake carried on an independent firefight with the British artillery – an extremely one-sided contest.[49]

Scott's First Brigade was now in desperate shape. Of the three regiments that had marched on to the field nearly an hour before, nothing but remnants remained and only darkness saved them from total destruction. After the American line ceased firing, however, there were no muzzle flashes to give away their position and Maclachlan's gunners began to fire wildly, their rounds often passing clean over the infantry and hitting the woods behind or bouncing down the Portage Road. The gunners concentrated their fire on the most visible target, Blake's party, and in the thirty minutes that Blake was in action before running out of ammunition, killed or wounded half of his men. The rest of the brigade suffered occasional casualties. Scott's personal aide, Worth, was hit in the thigh and, thought to be mortally wounded, carried to the rear. He was soon followed by the brigade major, New Yorker Captain Gerard D. Smith. By this time the Eleventh, which had entered the field about one hundred and fifty men strong, was reduced to about sixty able-bodied men commanded by a lieutenant. They lost another colour bearer and their standard was now carried by a soldier of the Ninth Infantry.[50]

Leavenworth began to waver as he watched his regiment disintegrate around him. He sent Harris to inform Scott that the "rule for retreating was fulfilled."[51] This was a reference to one of Scott's personal maxims that a military force could retire with honour only if "every third or fourth man is killed or wounded" and the First Brigade had certainly met that condition.[52] In reply, Scott rode over to tell Leavenworth to hold on, as Brown was marching to their support with Ripley and Porter's brigades. While he was giving this encouragement, artillery fire killed Scott's horse.[53]

In his report of the action, Drummond stated that the "Field Artillery, so long as there was light, was well served," and that was the simple truth.[54] For over an hour, Maclachlan had pounded the American troops, firing at least sixty rounds of 24-pdr. and one hundred and twenty rounds of 6-pdr. ammunition of all types, as well as howitzer shells. The result was horrific – the First Brigade was "literally cut to pieces."[55] The Ninth, Eleventh and Twenty-Second had begun the action with a combined strength of between seven hundred and seven hundred and fifty men – when the British artillery had ceased firing there were perhaps two hundred and fifty of them left in line, a casualty rate of over sixty per cent. For every round they fired, the British gunners had inflicted about two American casualties – the standard rate of lethality for artillery of this period given the range and duration of the bombardment.[56]

During this time, Scott's three regiments never approached closer than four hundred yards to the top of the hill but Drummond, whose regular infantry outnumbered them, did not attack. As darkness covered the survivors of the First Brigade, reduced to a remnant out of ammunition and with no reinforcement in sight, American officers expected that the British would move forward. They were puzzled when this did not occur, one later noting that the British general, in being "unwilling to leave Lundy's height, because it afforded a strong position" and attack, "committed a great military error."[57] If Drummond had made a "bold and gallant forward movement at once with his whole force and the bayonet" it "would have settled, in fifteen minutes, the fate of that portion of the American army." The British commander did not attack because he was still convinced that he was facing Brown's entire division, which he believed to be at least four thousand strong, nearly twice the size of his own force.[58]

Drummond had also been distracted by the operations of Major Thomas S. Jesup's Twenty-Fifth Infantry on his left flank. Before he deployed in front of the hill, Scott had ordered Jesup to occupy the woods between the road and the Niagara River gorge to cover the American right flank. It was a wise choice of man and unit. Thomas Sidney Jesup had entered the army as a second lieutenant of infantry in 1808 (the same day that Winfield Scott had been commissioned as a captain of light artillery) and had quickly demonstrated a talent for military administration. After service on the staff of Hull's army at Detroit and Harrison's army in the northwest, Jesup had been promoted major and given command of the Twenty-Fifth in April 1814. He had been one of the stalwarts of Scott's training camp at Flint Hill and had turned his unit, mainly recruited in Connecticut, into a well disciplined regiment. At Chippawa, Jesup and the Twenty-Fifth had been detached from the rest of the First Brigade and the twenty-five-year-old Kentuckian had performed brilliantly, making a major contribution to the American victory. As events would demonstrate, the intelligent, aggressive and conscientious Jesup was well suited for independent command.[59]

Moving to the right of the Portage Road, Jesup discovered "a small road ... which had been neglected by the Enemy" but was wide enough for him to march his regiment with ease.[60] This country trail probably followed the course of the present Allen Avenue, running between Main and Ferry Streets in the modern city of Niagara Falls, Canada and may have been used as a route to the ferry station established near Bender's farm below the falls. Realizing that he might be able to "operate with considerable effect" on the British flank, Jesup left his assigned position and led the Twenty-Fifth forward.[61] He placed one company under First Lieutenant Thomas S. Seymour in extended order to cover his front and moved with the remaining five companies north down the road. His advance was screened from observation by the woods and brush to the east of the road, and in any case British attention was focused on Scott's brigade in the open fields before the hill.

Unnoticed, Jesup reached a position directly east of the hill where he could see the British left flank. It was now twilight and Jesup formed the Twenty-Fifth in line at the edge of the tree line and prepared to attack.[62]

The British left flank, composed of Lieutenant Colonel William Robinson's Incorporated Militia Battalion and Captain Francis Campbell's light company of the 8th Foot, was stationed along a trail that formed an extension of Lundy's Lane east of the Portage Road. The Incorporated Militia was one of the last units to return to the field after Riall's retreat and they were still getting into position when Jesup approached. On coming into line, their attention was directed to a force of American "Riflemen" ahead of them.[63] These riflemen, at whom the Canadians were "blazing away like the devil," were actually Seymour's company of the Twenty-Fifth which had advanced north through the fields east of the road keeping pace with Jesup's movement through the wood.[64] It was "Sharp firing, hot work," according to Ensign Andrew Warffe of the Militia, and only at the last moment did the Canadians notice Jesup's Twenty-Fifth, partially hidden by the shadows of the tree line and a rail fence, to their left front.[65]

Firing a volley, the Twenty-Fifth advanced and overran the Incorporated Militia's easternmost companies commanded by Captains Daniel Washburn and Archibald Maclean. Some of the Canadians got off a scattered volley in return but in a matter of seconds the two companies disintegrated – Washburn was hit, Lieutenant Daniel McDougall went down with seven different wounds and both captains and many officers and men were captured.[66]

Robinson tried to rally his regiment but was struck by a musket ball that hit him in the forehead and exited behind his ear. The Militia began to crumble and the Twenty-Fifth took more prisoners, including the regimental quartermaster, George Thrower, with the battalion's ammunition cart. Assuming command, Major James Kerby, a peacetime merchant from Queenston, steadied the crumbling unit and withdrew it. While men fell fast, the Incorporated Militia and Campbell's company of the 8th Foot fired and retired by companies to a new position west of the Portage Road. Through the efforts of Kerby and others, the Incorporated Militia managed to extricate itself from a perilous situation but lost nearly a third of its strength doing so. As the survivors formed in line west of the road, the wounded Robinson was carried to the rear in a blanket. The thirty-two-year-old Irishman, a noted wit, asked his bearers to stop while he spoke to his men. He is said to have advised them that "a stump or a log will stand a

**Major James Kerby, Upper Canadian Militia
(1785-1854)**
A major in the Incorporated Militia Battalion,
Kerby took over command of the unit at Lundy's
Lane when its commander was wounded. He managed to get his men out of a very tight situation
by leading a very creditable fighting withdrawal to
a better position. Kerby was badly wounded at the
siege of Fort Erie. (Courtesy, National Archives of
Canada, C-130537)

leaden bullet better than the best of yees, and therefore give them the honour to be your front rank men."[67]

Drummond's left flank was now in the air and he changed his dispositions. The 89th faced half left and formed on Campbell's company and the
Incorporated Militia along the west side of the Portage Road. The new British line ran along the lane and behind Johnson's Tavern, located on the
northwest corner of the junction of Lundy's Lane and the Portage Road,
over to the west side of the road. The 19th Light Dragoons, who had been
posted in the road junction, were now exposed and they retired north to the
Muddy Run Creek.[68]

As the British retired, Jesup advanced west across the fields to the Portage Road. His brief but successful action had not been without cost; the
Twenty-Fifth had suffered casualties and Jesup himself had received a musket ball through the shoulder. Twilight was turning to dusk and visibility
was fast fading but Jesup could see Lisle's dragoons at the junction and prepared to attack them. To his disappointment – as stationary cavalry would
have been very vulnerable to a bayonet charge – the British horsemen withdrew. Jesup would have been even more disappointed if he had known that
one of the dragoons riding away that night was Lieutenant William Arnold,
the twenty-year-old son of Benedict Arnold.[69]

Arriving at the Portage Road, Jesup formed the Twenty-Fifth at right
angles to Lundy's Lane behind the cover of a rail fence. From this point, he
could see the muzzle flashes of the British artillery firing and decided to attack the British guns from the rear. As a first step, he detached Captain
Daniel Ketchum and his company to secure the road junction and reconnoitre. The selection of Ketchum, described by Jesup as "a very good man

for the service on which I sent him," and his men for this task was no accident.[70] The previous spring, Ketchum had recruited his company in Connecticut and, with special permission, had "particularly dressed ... equipped, and drilled, them as light infantry."[71] He had trained them well; at Chippawa, Ketchum had held off three times his number before being supported by the remainder of the regiment. Now on an independent mission again, Ketchum moved into the Portage Road and began to intercept and capture individuals and small groups of British and Canadians moving through the road junction in the near dark. In a few minutes, he returned to Jesup with a number of prisoners, including a most valuable prize – Major General Phineas Riall.[72]

Riall had been hit in the right arm, most likely by a stray musket ball, and was riding slowly to the rear with his orderly dragoon when he was caught in Ketchum's trap. A few minutes later, Captain Robert Loring, one of Drummond's aides, attempting to ride through the junction with orders to Lisle to bring back his dragoons, was pulled off his horse and put in the bag. Next came Canadian Hamilton Merritt on his way to report to Drummond about the situation of his left flank. When Merritt did not return in due time, a personal friend, Captain John Clark, the adjutant of the Lincoln Militia, was sent to deliver the same message and also fell into the American trap. On seeing Clark, Merritt asked what had brought him there only to receive the somewhat dim reply that Clark had been sent to find Merritt. After taking more prisoners, the aptly named Ketchum rejoined Jesup and the main body of the Twenty-Fifth.[73]

Jesup was now in a quandary; he had captured almost a dozen officers and over a hundred soldiers, more than he could spare men to guard if he was going to attack the British guns. The thought crossed the Kentuckian's mind that he would be justified "under the stern rules of war" in executing his prisoners, but he banished it.[74] Riall asked to be paroled so that he could return to the British lines and have his wounds dressed by his own surgeon but Jesup replied that he had no power to grant such a parole and that in any case the British general would get medical treatment from the Americans sooner than he could from his own side. While talking to Riall, Jesup was horrified to see that some of his men appeared to be using their knives on the prisoners and immediately ordered them to stop. His men replied that they were only cutting their captives' suspenders, forcing them to hold their pants up with their hands and making it difficult for them to run. At that moment a British officer rode out of the darkness and, drawing up beside Riall, managed to say, "General Drummond is impatient for information" before being made prisoner.[75] This was the first knowledge that anyone in the Left Division had of Drummond's presence in the Niagara.[76]

Jesup ordered Ketchum and his company to escort the prisoners to the rear. It was now completely dark and only the British artillery on the hill was firing. Having no muzzle flashes from the American line to orient himself, Ketchum blundered into a British unit which opened fire on both prisoners and escorts, who scattered for cover. He managed to retain Riall, Loring and Merritt and the captured officers but most of the other prisoners escaped although they had lost their arms and equipment. Ketchum subsequently deposited the remainder of his charges with another guard in the rear of the American line and returned to the battle.[77]

Shortly after sending Ketchum, Jesup received word that the rest of the brigade had been cut to pieces and that there was no hope of reinforcement from the remainder of the division. Concluding the battle was lost and his primary duty was to save his own unit, Jesup moved toward the American rear. It was now quite dark and the guns were silent. As the Twenty-Fifth filed quietly back to their own lines, using the cover of the split rail fences that bordered the road, they could hear the steady roar of Niagara Falls. They were about half way near the Peer farmhouse, when they heard the rumble of artillery wheels and saw troops moving toward them on the Portage Road. Some brave soul hailed the approaching figures and Jesup was soon conversing with Captain Thomas Biddle of the U.S. Artillery who informed him that Major General Jacob Brown had arrived with reinforcements and was about to renew the battle.[78]

CHAPTER 8

"I'll Try, Sir!":
Brown Renews the Battle

*No engagement is decided in a single moment, although
in each there are crucial moments which are primarily
responsible for the outcome.*
CLAUSEWITZ, On War

It was about 7:30 P.M. and in the camp at Chippawa the drummers were
beating the signal for "Retreat," the final parade of the military day. Lieutenant Colonel Hugh Dobbin, who had excused himself from attending
because of illness, was still waiting for his fresh green peas. As the drums
rolled and the soldiers began to fall in, the sound of firing was heard. At his
picket, Odell of the Twenty-Third could clearly make out the crackle of
musketry and when Captain Ambrose Spencer, Brown's personal aide, rode
up to ascertain the location of the firing, Odell informed him that it came
from the north, up the Portage Road. Douglass, carrying Scott's first message to Brown, heard the firing as he spurred his "wearied and foaming"
horse across the bridge over Chippawa Creek.[1] Riding straight to Brown's
tent, Douglass found the commanding general and McRee, the army's chief
engineer, listening to the gunfire with rapt attention.[2]

"Well, Sire?" inquired Brown and the young officer reported that he had
left General Scott at Willson's Tavern and that Scott "desired me to say that
he has met with a detachment of the enemy, under General Riall, number-
ing eight hundred Regulars, three hundred militia and Indians, and two
pieces of artillery."[3] Brown then asked about the firing and Douglass replied
that Scott had said that he would attack the enemy. By this time artillery
could be heard and it was obvious that Scott was heavily engaged.

Brown immediately put the troops in camp into motion. Ripley was directed to take his brigade and Hindman's remaining artillery as rapidly as possible to Scott's support while Porter was ordered to leave two companies to guard the camp and assemble the remainder of his brigade on the northern bank of the Chippawa to await further orders. These instructions given, Brown left Gardner to see that they were carried out and, accompanied by McRee, Wood and his aides, rode north "with all speed, towards the scene of action."[4]

The camp was a flurry of activity as men ran to get arms and equipment, form their companies and march. Hugh Dobbin forgot his peas as he led the New York Volunteers across the Chippawa Bridge to take up their position. Brown was soon followed out of camp by most of the division. Hindman got his gunners on the move first, Captains Thomas Biddle and John Ritchie's companies of artillery preceding Ripley up the road. The two regiments of the Second Brigade, Miller's Twenty-First and McFarland's Twenty-Third Infantry, had been assembling for "Retreat" when Ripley received his orders and marched without taking time to call in their men who were serving on various guards, details and pickets. Moving at a near trot to keep up with their general's horse, the brigade crossed over the bridge and followed Hindman north. In front of both Hindman and Ripley was Odell, who had been given permission to march with his picket, and Lieutenant David Riddle's company of the Nineteenth Infantry. The Pennsylvanian Riddle had just been returning to the camp from his lengthy and, it would appear, rather leisurely reconnaissance when he heard the firing. He immediately turned about and marched toward the sound of the guns.[5]

Some distance behind came Lieutenant Colonel Robert C. Nicholas and the First Infantry Regiment, which had just joined the Left Division after a long spell of garrison duty on the western frontier. In the course of the afternoon three companies of the unit had crossed the Niagara from Schlosser and had waited a number of hours on the river bank for the fourth and last company. It was nearly sunset when Nicholas learned that this company would not be coming over that day; he had then marched for the camp but just as he was approaching it he heard gunfire. Without waiting for orders, Nicholson marched through Chippawa and followed the other units up the road. Including Porter's brigade, these units amounted to some sixteen hundred combat effectives.[6]

As he rode, Brown could hear the loud and continuous noise of artillery and musketry resounding through the woods. The sound of the battle was audible as far as Buffalo some twenty miles away, where Captain George Howard had just "spent a pleasant evening with some old friends and was snugly seated at the Hotel, when the thunder of Artillery came booming across the Niagara and told that the foe was in Motion."[7] A Buffalo resident later remembered how, as a boy, he listened to the "firing of small arms in the direction of Niagara Falls ... very soon cannon began to roar, and fired so fast as to all most drown the report of the muskets."[8] About a mile from the camp Brown encountered Scott's second messenger, Major Roger Jones, with the now-redundant information that Scott had engaged the enemy. Brown sent Jones to order Porter to march his brigade to the scene of the action and then rode on. A little later, Brown met Scott's third messenger, Wood, who (stating that the fighting was "close and desperate") urged him to bring up the reinforcements as fast as possible.[9] As this was being done, Brown continued on, past Willson's Tavern, "which was brilliantly lighted up for the accommodation of wounded men," through the chestnut woods and onto the battlefield.[10]

A few miles to the north the British and Canadians in Hercules Scott's column could also hear "the roar of Artillery and Musketry pealing in Our front, sometimes rattling in heavy surges – sometimes scant, as if troops pressed were retiring."[11] These men had left their position at the Twelve-Mile creek late that afternoon to march by way of the Beaver Dams and Lundy's Lane to join Riall. They were at a point on the lane only three miles from the Portage Road when a messenger from Riall reached Scott with orders directing him to retire on Queenston. Rather than proceed to Queenston by way of the Portage Road, however, Hercules Scott opted to retrace his route to pick up the Beechwoods Road which ran along the es-carpment to Queenston. He had moved about four miles west when another messenger rode up with orders from Drummond to come forward to the junction of Lundy's Lane and the Portage Road as fast as possible.[12]

His men had marched over twelve miles in a few hours and were hot, tired and dusty. However, they dutifully turned in their tracks again and moved east. They were urged on by the sounds of gunfire and soon the men "were not marching but running up, for our anxiety to aid our hard pressed comrades."[13] As the column neared the battlefield, nineteen-year-old Lieutenant John Le Couteur of the 104th Foot made his "usual prayers to God to grant me his protection and my life, ready though I was to lay that down for my country, at his pleasure, but hoping that no worse than a wound might befall me - nor a fall into the hands of the Savages - death we thought preferable."[14]

Although he was probably anxious for Hercules Scott's force to arrive, Drummond had reason to be satisfied with his situation. With a maximum of about sixteen hundred infantry, he had maintained his ground for well over an hour against what he believed to be Brown's entire army. The American force in his front had been hammered by Maclachlan's gunners and harassed by Brereton's companies of the 1st Foot, Battersby's Glengarries, militia and Indians. It was obvious that the enemy had suffered heavy casualties. The potentially serious situation on his left flank had been stabilized. That flank had been forced back but not broken. It was now reformed along the west side of the Portage Road and the Americans seemed to have disappeared from the road junction. Finally, all his units with the exception of Hercules Scott's column were on the field and in position. With some justification Drummond might feel that victory was his.

But the British commander was taking no chances in the face of what he believed to be an enemy far superior in numbers, and as the American infantry ceased firing, he began to re-align his force. The Glengarries and their accompanying militia and Indians were pulled back from the left flank of the American line to their original position in the fields on the western side of the track running south from Lundy's Lane to Skinner's farm. Brereton's companies of the 1st were withdrawn from their position on the track in front of the hill and placed to the right of the artillery. As the British and Canadians moved back, they ceased firing and soon only Maclachlan's gunners were carrying on the fight.[15]

Drummond's re-alignment meant that contact with the Americans was broken as the new British infantry line ran beside and behind the artillery. There were now no friendly troops between Maclachlan's gunners and the Americans some distance to their front. In such a situation the standard procedure was to post a skirmish line in front of the guns to give warning of an enemy advance. Drummond did not post such a line and his failure to do so is all the more puzzling because he had under his command at this time the four light infantry companies of the 1st, 8th, 41st and 89th Foot as well as the Glengarry Fencibles, nearly six hundred trained and experienced skirmishers.

Brown had less reason to feel satisfied when he reached the field at about 8:30 P.M.. It was nearly dark and "altho there was a moon, the smoke and surrounding woods cast a shade over the fields ... that rendered it very difficult to distinguish at any considerable distance, the Hostile columns or Lines."[16] With the exception of Blake's party, the American infantry had stopped firing but the British guns were still active. Winfield Scott, who had found a new horse, rode up and reported on the events of the action and the present dispositions of both friendly and enemy troops. He also told

Brown that, according to information obtained from prisoners, the British were shortly expecting reinforcements to arrive. Scott's Brigade had, in Brown's words, "suffered severely"; over one half of the Ninth, Eleventh and Twenty-Second Infantry were casualties and the whereabouts of Jesup's Twenty-Fifth was at this time unknown.[17] Seeing the condition of Scott's men, Brown resolved to "form a new line with the troops advancing to the front so as to disengage Genl Scotts command and hold it in reserve."[18] As the two officers conferred, Biddle and Ritchie's companies of artillery came up and halted on the Portage Road. Knowing that the Second Brigade would not be far behind, Brown dispatched his aide, Captain Ambrose Spencer, to find Ripley and guide him into position on the field.[19]

Both McRee and Wood were with Brown when he arrived on the battle-field. Throughout the action, McRee would function as Brown's chief of staff in place of Gardner, who was incapable of performing this duty. As soon as they arrived on the field, the two engineers made separate reconnaissances of the enemy position. Douglass, who had accompanied Brown's party back to the action, remembered riding with McRee in the dark to the base of the hill, where they halted for some time, ignoring the artillery firing over their heads. Pointing with his hand, the engineer told Douglass that the British battery was the key to the enemy's line and must be captured.[20]

Spencer, meanwhile, did not have far to go to find the Second Brigade – Ripley had covered the nearly four miles from the camp at Chippawa to the battlefield in about forty minutes. He overtook Riddle's company of the Nineteenth Infantry which had preceded him on the road and, as Riddle was attached to one of his regiments, Ripley took him under command and ordered him into the woods west of the road as a flank guard. Moving north, the column began to encounter men from Scott's brigade who had left the fighting and were trying to return to camp. Passing Willson's Tavern, Ripley sent his aide, Captain William McDonald, to ride forward to find out from Brown where he should place his brigade. McDonald had gone only a few yards when he encountered Spencer riding back with Brown's instructions.[21]

As the Second Brigade marched through the chestnut woods to emerge on the field of battle, roundshot was knocking down the branches overhead and bouncing down the Portage Road. To McDonald, riding at the head of the column, "the fire of the enemy was very heavy, and their shot and shells fell about us in great quantities, but was more particularly directed at General Scott's brigade on the left."[22] The Second Brigade did attract some fire; two shrapnel shells exploded in the ranks of the Twenty-Third Infantry, killing or wounding twenty-four soldiers. Although they had been listening to the sounds of the fighting throughout their march from camp, the noise of the battle was loud to the new arrivals as they came on to the field. One officer had "never heard anything equal to it, a continual roar of cannon, bursting of bombs, sky rockets & musketry and a shout on one side or the other."[23] When Ripley's men passed Scott's position, the survivors of the First Brigade "gave a general hurrah that cheered the whole Army."[24] It also drew a shrapnel round from the Royal Artillery that knocked down four men and an officer near Scott. Immediately afterward, the British guns ceased firing.[25]

For over an hour, one imaginative participant later recorded, the artillery had "roared, *hoarse, loud* and *strong,* volleys of musketry vomited out death and destruction ... I became dizzy and confused by the multiplication of increased sounds. The air appeared to lose its elasticity by counter percussions – echoes and re-echoes reverberating from every side."[26] Lieutenant Joseph Baker of the Canadian Volunteers was only slightly more restrained, writing that "the musketry exceeded anything ever heard on the Continent."[27] As the firing ceased, men began gradually to make out the low roar of the falls. In the British and Canadian ranks the officers put this interlude of calm to good use and dealt out ammunition to their men. There was a shortage of ammunition and Parry's militia brigade, which had seen little fighting, was stripped of its cartridges to supply the regular troops. As they received their ammunition, the men could hear the sound of American troops manoeuvring in the darkness and "every order given."[28] Many assumed that the battle was over and the Americans were retreating.[29]

Hercules Scott's force arrived in Drummond's lines about this time. Having covered nearly twenty miles that day and the last few in double time, the sweating men and lathered horses were "a good deal blown."[30] As they came up Lundy's Lane, the British and Canadians already on the field gave them a cheer which one American later remarked "went down us like rain."[31] The three 6-pdr. guns under the command of Captain James Mackonochie, RA, were sent ahead to join Maclachlan on top of the hill. Hercules Scott's reinforcements amounted to some eighteen hundred men, all of them weary; Drummond now had nearly thirty-seven hundred men under his command and eight pieces of artillery but between five and six hundred were poorly-armed sedentary militia who would be of limited use in hard fighting.[32]

The American troops that the British could hear manoeuvring were from the Second Brigade. Brown had ordered Ripley "to pass [Winfield] Scott's line and display his Columns in front," but when he reached this position and began to deploy Ripley became dissatisfied because his brigade would have difficulty advancing in line through the brush on the east of the Portage Road.[33] He therefore reformed into column of march and continued north to the farm track at the base of the hill. Here he ordered Miller to position the Twenty-First in line along the track and McFarland to form his Twenty-Third in line to the east of the Portage Road, "extending their right into the thickets."[34] Ripley too realized that the hill was the key to the British position and that "our only means of safety was to advance upon the Heights & carry the enemy's Artillery."[35]

Brown had come to the same conclusion. Seeing Drummond's advanced units pulling back, he assumed the British were retreating. Leaving Scott, the American commander rode closer to the hill, where he was joined by McRee and Wood, who had completed their reconnaissances. Brown listened to their reports and questioned them extensively about the British dispositions. McRee explained that the British had taken up a new position to the rear of the crest and summed up the tactical situation succinctly – "the Enemy held the Key of the position with their Artillery - to secure the Victory, their Artillery, with the height on which it rested, must be carried."[36] Brown's division was not in good case: the First Brigade had been shattered and one of its regiments was missing while his other two brigades amounted to only about fifteen hundred effectives. The choice was simple – he couldn't just maintain his ground – he had to either attack or retreat. Brown decided to attack. He directed McRee to ride to Ripley and order him to prepare Miller's Twenty-First Infantry for an assault on the hill.[37]

The American commander then rode with his staff along the track toward the British right flank. Straining his eyes in the dark, he saw a line of British infantry posted along the crest of the hill to the west of the enemy guns. As these troops (probably Brereton's 1st Foot) were in a position to hit Miller from the flank, it was imperative that something be done about them. But Brown was running out of men: the First Brigade was exhausted, the Second was fully occupied and Porter's had not yet arrived. Then Brown remembered Nicholas's First Infantry and sent Wood to find them and conduct them a point where they could form "a line facing the Enemy at the height with the view of drawing his fire and attracting his attention, while Col. Miller advanced with the Bayonet ... to carry his Artillery."[38] He waited until Wood returned with the First and then, becoming impatient for Miller's attack to start, rode over to Ripley's brigade, where he asked that officer about his dispositions for the attack. Ripley replied that he had given orders to Miller "to advance directly forward in line and gain the height" while he had formed the Twenty-Third into column on the road, intending to lead it personally in a flank attack up Lundy's Lane onto the hill.[39]

Brown expressed his satisfaction and left Ripley for Miller's Twenty-First. He found them in line along the track running west from the Peer house, where, under the eye of their tall commander, they had just knocked down the rail fence bordering the track in preparation for their advance against the British guns.[40]

James Miller was a thirty-eight-year-old native of New Hampshire described as "a rare union of personal excellency of character with a strength and firmness of mind and body."[41] Miller's strength of will was probably shaped by his early years – the product of a rural background, he had spent nine years alternately working and studying to acquire a college education. In 1803 Miller was called to the bar but, having a life-long enthusiasm for military affairs, accepted a major's commission in the regular army in 1809. By the outbreak of war, he was a lieutenant colonel serving with Hull's army on the Detroit frontier, where on 9 August 1812 he gained the first notable American success of the war and a brevet colonelcy by defeating a force of British and Indians at Maguaga. After a period of frustration during the ill-fated St. Lawrence campaign of 1813, Miller had been appointed commander of the Twenty-First Infantry, Ripley's old regiment, in March 1814. A large, physically imposing man with a modest manner, Miller was a competent, single-minded and aggressive soldier and a good choice to lead the crucial attack.[42]

Drawing up beside him, Brown said, "Col. Miller, take your Reg[imen]t. and storm that work and take it."[43] The tall, taciturn officer "raised his herculean form and fixed his eye, for an instant, intently upon the battery; then turning his bit of tobacco," gave a reply that was to become the stuff of American schoolboy legend – "I'll try, Sir!"[44] Before Miller could move, however, the First Infantry attacked the hill.

Although the First was the senior infantry regiment of the American army, it had not seen much action during the war but had remained dispersed in small frontier posts in the western territories. In the early summer of 1814 its widely-scattered companies had been consolidated and it was ordered to join the Left Division. The regiment was pitifully under strength. In his own words, Nicholas brought only a "detachment" of three companies totalling one hundred and fifty men into action. To march such a small unit into the middle of a hard-fought and confusing night action might have daunted a lesser man but the Virginian Nicholas was a strong-minded

James Miller, U.S. Army (1776-1851)
Shown here in the uniform of a brigadier general, Miller was the modest but effective colonel commanding the Twenty-First Infantry during the battle. His famous reply, "I'll try, sir," to Brown's order to capture the British artillery at Lundy's Lane became the stuff of legend. (Courtesy, Essex Institute, Salem, Massachusetts, Neg. 150222)

individual "who always inspires his troops with heroic ardor and who dares without *fear* of slander to use caution where *he thinks* caution adviseable."[45]

Following Ripley from camp, the First had cleared the chestnut woods and halted on the Portage Road while Nicholas, who knew none of the senior officers present, tried to get some orders. The British guns had ceased firing but he was told to get his men off the road because their presence would draw artillery fire. Nicholas moved into the fields west of the road, where he met Winfield Scott, who pointed out to him the location of the enemy artillery and the necessity of attacking it. Wood then rode up and conducted him to a point west of the orchard behind the Peer house. McRee arrived next and informed Nicholas that the Twenty-First, on his right, were about to attack the British battery and that he was to move "to the left and form a line facing the enemy on the heights with a view to drawing off his force and attracting his attention."[46] As his company formed up, thirty-four-year-old Captain John Symmes from the Michigan Territory, concerned that his green soldiers would prove unequal to the task ahead, scrutinized their faces closely while giving them "a few exciting words" and was reassured by the resolve he saw reflected there.[47]

Although Brown's intention had only been for Nicholas to mount a demonstration, his order must have been garbled in transmission because the Virginian led his regiment straight at the British artillery. From their position on the hill, Maclachlan's gunners could see little of the southern slope and the fields in front. The smoke of battle had cleared and the moon was low in the southwest sky, but it did not illuminate the lower slopes of the hill, which were shrouded in darkness. The gunners could, however,

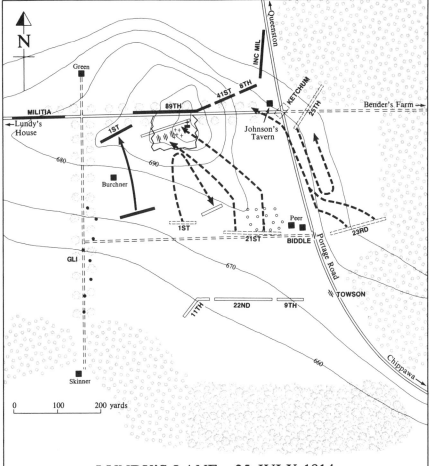

LUNDY'S LANE - 25 JULY 1814
2nd Phase: c. 8:45 - 9:45 PM

1. Ketchum's company scoops up prisoners in the road junction before Jesup withdraws only to later return after encountering U.S. reinforcements.

2. Ripley's brigade forms in front of the hill and to the east of the Portage Road. On Brown's orders, the First Infantry mount a demonstration. The Twenty-First Infantry then attacks and takes the British guns, while the Twenty-Third Infantry under Ripley's command also moves forward.

3. Using the 1st, 41st and 89th Foot, Drummond mounts several unsuccessful local counterattacks to recapture his guns from the Twenty-First Infantry.

clearly hear the shout of orders and the sounds of marching troops as Ripley's brigade deployed and occasionally they would fire a round to keep the Americans on the *qui vive*. When Scott ordered his men to give "three cheers" at the news of Riall's capture, it attracted a shrapnel shell that "exploded in the column of artillery ... and blew up a caisson of ammunition belonging to Captain Ritchie's company."[48] Aware that something was happening to their front but uncertain what it was, Maclachlan and his men loaded their guns and waited.[49]

As the First Infantry advanced in line out of the darkness in front of the British guns, Maclachlan opened a furious fire with canister and round shot. Fortunately for the Americans, the British gunners' elevation was too high and most of the rounds passed harmlessly overhead. With Nicholas and his adjutant, Lieutenant John A. Shaw, both mounted and urging them on, the First moved closer to the British guns. The gunners corrected their aim and now the Americans began to take casualties; Lieutenant Lewis Bissell, the regimental quartermaster, was hit in the leg by one canister bullet while his watch stopped another. Bissell attempted to stay with the regiment but was finally forced to go to the rear. As the fire intensified, Nicholas realized that it would be suicidal for his tiny unit to attack straight into the muzzles of the British guns. Concluding that there "was no possibility of my annoying the enemy and a certainty of his destroying my men," the Virginian ordered the First Infantry to "right about face" and march back down the hill.[50] Ignoring a staff officer who shouted, "Where are you going?" Nicholas then re-formed his regiment in line at the base of the hill.[51]

His abortive attack had not been in vain; it had drawn the attention of Maclachlan's gunners, and in the noise and confusion of the First Infantry's advance and retreat, they failed to hear or see the approach of Miller's Twenty-First Infantry up the southeast slope of the hill. The Twenty-First was a wartime regiment, recruited in Massachusetts and New Hampshire, and had campaigned on the northern frontier under Ripley since the autumn of 1812. Noted for its discipline and smartness of dress, the Twenty-First had a good fighting record. Ripley had proved an excellent commander and had brought the regiment's drill up to a high standard even before it joined the camp at Flint Hill in April 1814. Miller had continued to provide strong leadership and the Twenty-First was possibly the best regiment in the Left Division. When he ordered it to attack the British artillery Ripley had no doubts that it would succeed, as he "felt confident of extraordinary efforts from the veterans ... under the Conduct of the gallant Miller, whose Courage had been repeat-edly tried."[52] His confidence was not misplaced; as the men advanced, some of them "called out to play up 'Yankee Doodle'"[53]

It was about 9:15 P.M. when the Twenty-First moved quietly up the hill, in a line of two ranks, with their "bayonets at a charge."[54] The muzzle flashes of the British guns firing at the First Infantry illuminated the faces of the advancing men and one later admitted that as he climbed he felt "d____d bashful."[55] For much of their progress up the steeper southeast slope of the hill, the Twenty-First were moving in "dead" ground and invisible to the British gunners and the infantry behind them. There were no enemy skirmishers to impede or warn of their advance and in a few moments they had reached the old rail fence overgrown with shrubbery that surrounded the cemetery and the meeting house. They were now about a hundred feet from the muzzles of the guns and could see the gunners' "port fires and slow matches burning and ready."[56] Miller "very cautiously" ordered his men "to rest [their muskets] across the fence, take good aim, fire & rush."[57]

Maclachlan had ceased firing at the First Infantry, who had disappeared into the blackness at the bottom of the hill. His subordinate, Mackonochie, had just arrived from the Twelve-Mile Creek bringing three 6-pdr. guns and the two gunners were probably too involved in the process of positioning these pieces, while the gun detachments were intently watching where the First Infantry had disappeared, to notice the quiet movement of the Twenty-First to the cemetery fence. The American were spotted at the last moment – Norton was conversing with two officers when one of them "enquired what Body of men it might be that were approaching."[58] Going towards them, Norton "observed the Moon glimmer faintly on the plates of their Caps, the form of which denounced them to be our Enemies, – before I could speak, they fired."[59]

The well-directed American volley cut down Maclachlan's startled gunners so that "not one man at the cannons was left to put fire to them."[60] Maclachlan was wounded and nearly twenty of his men became casualties. Before the dazed survivors could react, the Twenty-First, with Miller and their colours in the lead, pushed the rail fence flat, charged and were in among the gun detachments with their bayonets. The "fight was but for a moment" and most of the British gunners either fled or surrendered.[61]

The American assault took Lieutenant Colonel Joseph Morrison by surprise. Morrison's 89th Foot was formed in line north of the lane behind the artillery position. Before he could recover, some of the artillery horse teams parked in the lane, frightened by the noise of the attack, stampeded his ranks causing great confusion. While shouting officers struggled to regain control, Drummond, who was close by with his adjutant-general, Lieutenant Colonel John Harvey, ordered Morrison to wheel his left wing "so as to take in flank that Body of the Enemy which advanced to the Guns," then to open fire and charge.[62] A veteran of service in Spain and the Mediterranean, Morrison immediately complied, and Miller remembered that as soon as the Twenty-First "got into the centre" of the gun position the "British line ... opened a most destructive flank fire on us, killed a great many and attempted to charge with their bayonets."[63] At his command, the Twenty-First formed in line and "warmly" returned the fire.[64]

As the 89th advanced across the lane and into the cemetery, their progress was hindered by the guns, limbers, wagons, trees, fences and grave markers around which they had to move. Moving awkwardly, they were subjected to volleys of musketry from the Twenty-First which brought them to a halt. The two regiments began to exchange fire at a range "so close that the [muzzle] blase of our guns crossed each other."[65] The struggle was relentless – one American remembered that first "my cartouch[e] box was shot away, which deprived me of all my ammunition," then "my hat was shot off – next my companion ... on my right, had his head shot ... which almost blinded me with blood and brains."[66]

The 89th Foot and the Twenty-First Infantry had last met eight months before on John Crysler's muddy fields. Then the Twenty-First had retired, this time it was the turn of the 89th who withdrew in good order across the lane. A few minutes later, with Drummond and Harvey cheering them on, they returned to the attack with the light company of the 41st Foot on their left and Brereton's companies of the 1st on their right.[67]

Another firefight ensued and again casualties were heavy. Morrison was wounded and Major Miller Clifford assumed command of the 89th; Brereton of the 1st was wounded and his successor, Lieutenant William Hemphill, was killed. A member of Drummond's staff, Lieutenant Henry Moorsom, fell while cheering on the Royal Scots, the fifth of five brothers to die in the service of the Crown. Both Drummond and Harvey had their horses shot from under them. The 89th momentarily faltered when Morrison was wounded but Drummond and Clifford steadied them and, as the casualties mounted, the various detachments in the British line formed on the 89th and closed in toward their colours.[68]

A few hundred yards away, Le Couteur of the 104th experienced none of the ferocity of this fighting. The two companies of his regiment, which had arrived with Hercules Scott's column, were positioned to the rear of the

89th on the north slope of the hill. Sheltered behind a split rail fence and "ordered to lie down till we were wanted," the 104th found it "funny and very satisfactory too to hear the balls rattling against the rails just over our heads, without hitting any of us." From their position, the men could see their regimental commander, thirty-four-year-old Lieutenant Colonel William Drummond of Keltie in Perthshire, "seated on his war horse like a knightly man of valour ... exposed to a ragged fire from hundreds of brave Yankees who were pressing our brave 89th."

Suddenly a private of the 104th stood bolt upright. Le Couteur brusquely ordered him down and the soldier obeyed but soon again got to his feet. This sequence happened several times until, exasperated, the young Channel islander – his family came from Jersey – admonished the man for disobedience in the middle of a hot action – "no place for finding fault with a good Soldier!" The culprit, a Scot, replied: "Wall Sir, de ye no see Col. Drummond sitting on that great horse, up there amongst all the balls – and sale I be laying down, sneaking whan he's exposed – Noe I wunt!" Le Couteur, who "could not but admire the fellow's generous heroism," thereafter left him alone.[69]

William Drummond led a charmed life that night. But then luck had always been with this charismatic Scotsman, one of the most popular officers in Canada and a survivor of fourteen years duty in the graveyard of the West Indies. That evening he was to have two horses killed under him and his double-barrelled shotgun, which he habitually carried in action, shot to pieces in his hands, though he suffered no wounds. Others were not so lucky and both sides lost heavily in the exchange of fire. But the Twenty-First Infantry maintained its ground and the British line once more retired.[70]

They returned a third time. Again, there was a deadly exchange of volleys at close range. British casualties were lessened by the fact that their ranks were ordered to drop to one knee. In one of these exchanges General Gordon Drummond was wounded by a musket ball that entered under his right ear and lodged in the back of his neck. He lost a great deal of blood but, tying some handkerchiefs around his neck, continued in action. The two opposing lines fought across Mackonochie's guns from the Twelve-Mile Creek, which were standing, still limbered, in the lane. For a brief moment, they were in the possession of Captain Joseph Glew's light company of the 41st Foot, but Glew was unable to get them away because their horse teams had either been killed or run off and, in the end, the British line once more stepped back into the night. This time they did not return.[71]

The struggle for possession of the guns was a confused affair that, as one participant remarked, "was so rapid that he hardly had time for a distinct idea, until it was over."[72] Miller himself was unsure how many attacks the British had made but he was certain that it was at least two, if not more. When the fighting was over, however, he was in undisputed possession of Drummond's artillery, consisting of "ammunition wagons and all amounting to seven pieces of elegant brass cannon one of which was a 24-pounder with eight horses and harness, though some of the horses were killed."[73] He also had thirty or forty prisoners, including Mackonochie, whom he imprisoned in the meeting house under guard. He then positioned the Twenty-First in line facing the lane with their right in front of the meeting house, and he dispatched his adjutant, Second Lieutenant John W. Holding, "with a party of men, to roll the captured cannon down the hill toward our friends."[74] The British guns secured and his regiment in position, Miller waited for the rest of the Second Brigade.[75]

When the Twenty-First had commenced its attack against the British guns, the Twenty-Third Infantry was formed in column on the Portage Road. Unlike the elite Twenty-First, the Twenty-Third was a hard luck unit. Recruited largely in New York and Vermont, it had spent most of the war dispersed in small detachments along the border and had suffered de-

The Battle of Lundy's Lane
This 1815 engraving by William Strickland shows the high point of the battle – the capture of the British artillery by the Twenty-First U.S. Infantry. Although somewhat stylized, the essential details are correct: the moon, smoke, the bare, low, flat hill and the distance between the British fieldpieces. (Engraving by William Strickland, first published in the *Portfolio*. Courtesy of the National Archives of Canada, C-4071)

feat in three of the four major actions it had fought. As the regiment's colonel and lieutenant-colonel were absent, it was commanded by Major Daniel McFarland, a native of Washington County, Pennsylvania, with a dry and ironic sense of humour, who once summed up military training with the statement: "We drill every Day and are making such progress that we shall Die with some grace."[76] McFarland's detachment of the Twenty-Third had only joined the Left Division five days before it crossed into Canada and did not have the full benefit of Winfield Scott's camp of instruction. Another detachment of the unit, under the command of Virginian Major George Brooke, joined at Queenston on 14 July. Knowing that the unit was green, Ripley had decided to accompany it because he "felt apprehensive that it would fall into confusion from the destructive fire of the enemy."[77]

After Miller had advanced on the hill, Ripley marched the Twenty-Third in column north up the Portage Road until they had cleared the Peer house and were in position to attack in line directly west against the British artillery. As the regiment came into this position, Ripley ordered them to deploy from column into line facing the hill but at that moment they were fired on. "With one accord, the Column fired without orders – immediately broke & sought refuge behind a house."[78] Eighteen-year-old Private Amasiah Ford from Saratoga, New York, was in the lead platoon of the Twenty-Third, and recalled that "a party of the enemy which lay in ambush rose & fired upon us ... out of 32 in the first platoon, only eight of us escaped the desperate slaughter."[79] McFarland was killed instantly.[80]

With the help of Brooke and the other officers of the Twenty-Third, Ripley struggled to get control of the milling mass of frightened men and to form them into a semblance of organization. As Ford sheltered with his comrades behind the Peer house, his company commander, Captain Azariah Odell, who had been absent on picket, caught up with his men. He found them "all broke up," and "exclaimed with a loud & desperate voice amidst the roar of cannon & musketry & the groans of the dying, 'Is this my company in this situation, form my good fellows' & at that instant almost every man of his company who was not shot down formed by his side."[81] Under Ripley's direct command, the regiment finally ascended the hill.[82]

The American assault on the guns, an "act of bravery ... never excelled since time began" in the eyes of Captain Richard Goodell of the Twenty-Third Infantry, was over.[83] Ripley's brigade had captured Drummond's artillery and fought off at least three determined local counterattacks. The scales were now tilting in favour of the Left Division.

CHAPTER 9

Both Armies Make Ready

Night operations are not merely risky;
they are also difficult to execute.
CLAUSEWITZ, *On War*

When the British disappeared into the darkness north of the hill, contact between the two armies was broken. As the smoke from the last volleys dissipated, Miller's men could make out the debris from the fight for the guns – clusters of dead and wounded men and horses, gun carriages, limbers and ammunition wagons, lines of rails showing where the fences had stood, and overturned grave markers. A new moon had risen but it gave little light and the night remained quite dark. The time was about 9:30 P.M. and Miller anxiously awaited reinforcements from the remainder of the Left Division.[1]

The first unit to arrive was Nicholas's First Infantry. Miller, unaware that Nicholas and his regiment had even joined the division, was pleased to see the Virginian and the First formed on the left of the Twenty-First. They were followed by Ripley and the Twenty-Third, which formed on Miller's right between the meeting house and Lundy's Lane. On his way up the hill, Ripley encountered Second Lieutenant John Holding, whom Miller had directed to roll the captured British artillery down the hill. Holding was preparing to do this when Ripley ordered him to stop. Arriving on the crest, he conferred with Miller and then sent his aide, Captain William McDonald, to find Hindman and ask him to bring up his guns to support the Second Brigade.[2]

Hindman was expecting this request. Within a few minutes, Towson and Ritchie's companies, each equipped with two 6-pdr guns and one 5½-inch howitzer, moved up to reinforce Ripley. Towson placed his pieces on the lane in front of the meeting house and to the right of the Twenty-Third

Infantry, while Ritchie positioned his somewhat in front of the First Infantry. Hindman's remaining company, commanded by Captain Thomas Biddle, with three 12-pdr. guns, which had been firing from a position near the Peer farmhouse, now moved up to the junction of Lundy's lane and the Portage Road. Satisfied the position was in a good state of defence, Ripley sent McDonald to find Brown and get permission to remove the captured artillery.[3]

Riding down Lundy's Lane, McDonald met Brown and his staff coming up. After having given Miller the order to attack the guns, Brown had ridden north with Wood and Spencer along the Portage Road. The three officers were approaching the road junction when the firing and cheers from the hill signalled the Twenty-First Infantry's success but they drew to a halt when they heard a shout: "they are the Yankees!" Peering into the gloom, Brown made out a line of infantry drawn up west of the Portage Road with its right flank resting on Lundy's Lane. A few seconds later, a volley of musketry blazed forth from another line of infantry positioned behind a fence about sixty feet away across the Portage Road. More volleys followed and "the slaughter," Brown later wrote, "was dreadful." The firing ceased when the troops on the west side of the road withdrew into the darkness. Brown rode forward to the other force and found Jesup and his Twenty-Fifth Infantry.[4]

When he had learned that Brown was coming to Scott's assistance, Jesup had decided to resume his position on the British left flank. Moving under the cover of the rail fences east of the Portage Road, he had encountered a British force north of the lane and Brown had just witnessed the result. After listening to his report, Brown ordered Jesup to join Ripley on the hill.[5]

Brown appeared "highly elated" when McDonald encountered him. The aide transmitted Ripley's request for permission to remove the captured guns but Brown stated that there were more important matters to attend to and accompanied McDonald to Ripley. Seeing Miller, Brown told him that he had just immortalized himself but added that "my heart ached for you when I gave you the order" to attack.[6] By the time Brown arrived at the British guns, a number of officers had gathered to examine the captured artillery, young David Douglass particularly enjoying "the satisfaction of seeing and handling [these] brass guns of the most beautiful model, of different calibres, from six to twenty-four pounders."[7] Brown joined the group and after a brief inspection observed to Towson that the captured ordnance "together with our artillery will make a formidable battery, should the enemy attack us in our present position."[8] From this Towson inferred that the British guns were to be left on the hill.[9]

Brown and Ripley then assessed the situation. Ripley was certain that the British were preparing a counterattack; but Brown, convinced that his division had won a resounding victory, doubted Drummond would return. Ripley insisted that the enemy were not far away as he could hear commands being issued and troops moving in the darkness north of the hill. Deciding to see for himself, Brown rode with his staff in front of the American line.[10]

Moving west along the lane, Brown's party were able to make out "a more extended line than he had seen during the engagement ... near and advancing upon us."[11] The question was whether they were British or American? Without hesitation, Brown's aide, Captain Ambrose Spencer, spurred his horse forward to the oncoming line shouting "What Regiment is that?" only to receive the prompt reply, "The Royal Scots, sir." "Stand you fast, Scotch Royals" shot back the quick-witted Spencer before wheeling and returning to his general.[12] It was clear that the British were advancing and Brown wasted little time in finding the protection of the nearest friendly unit – Porter's Volunteers just coming into position on the left of Ripley's brigade.[13]

When Brown and Ripley had left Chippawa to march to Scott's assistance, Porter had been ordered to assemble his brigade at the north end of the Chippawa bridge and await further instructions. A short time later, Major Roger Jones had galloped up with orders to come on as fast as possible. Porter's brigade was the division's "maid of all work" and detachments had already been made from it to garrison Buffalo, Lewiston, Schlosser and Fort Erie. Two companies were now left behind to guard the camp and, when the brigade reached the field, more men were detailed to guard prisoners. As a result Porter brought only about three hundred men into position on the left of the First Infantry where he formed with his left flank angled back down the hill toward the Buchner farmhouse. The New York Volunteers under Dobbin were on the left of the brigade, the Pennsylvania Volunteers under Major Thomas Wood of Newville, Franklin County, in the centre, and Willcocks's Canadians on the right. As they came into position, the Volunteers heard the news that the British artillery had been captured and Riall taken prisoner, which gave one of them "incuragement that the battle was nearly over."[14]

Riding up, Brown ordered Porter to wheel his left flank back into line and then departed to warn Ripley of the British advance. As the brigade moved into this new position, the Volunteer officers could hear orders being shouted "some distance to our left in front."[15] As far as Porter knew, there were no troops in that direction and, puzzled, he ordered his brigade major, Major John Stanton, to reconnoitre. He then followed Stanton into the darkness but was called back by Dobbin, who, certain that there were British about, asked for permission to wheel the brigade back so that its flank would not be exposed. Porter was reluctant to disobey Brown's direct order but, pressed by Dobbin, gave him permission to return the brigade to their first position, and then disappeared into the night. He was fortunate that Dobbin had delayed him as Stanton, riding ahead shouting "Where are they?" was almost immediately captured by the British.[16] Coming behind, Porter saw his plight and, galloping back to Dobbin, ordered the brigade to move sixty feet to the left, open its ranks "to arms distance," and prepare for imminent attack.[17]

As soon as he had withdrawn from the hill, Drummond knew that he would have to counterattack. More than honour was at stake – the Right Division had lost its field artillery and, without these weapons, Drummond would be unable to fight in open battle against the Americans. An attack to recapture these guns was absolutely necessary, but first Drummond had to reform his command, which had become disorganized by the recent fighting. Many officers had been killed or wounded, units had become jumbled together by the confusion of the combat or the darkness and there was a general shortage of ammunition. Worse still, the 103rd Foot and Hamilton's militia brigade, which had come up with Hercules Scott, had marched straight into the melee on the hill and broken in confusion. As soon as the firing died down, Drummond began sorting out his units and forming them for a counterattack.[18]

The fighting had turned his front and the British line now ran from southwest to northeast. Although the evidence is very imprecise, Drummond appears to have formed his troops in one line divided into two wings by a gap near the junction of Lundy's Lane and the track to Skinner's farm. His left flank rested at the bottom of the slope of the hill, due north of the meeting house, while his right flank was located a few hundred yards to the west of the track to Skinner's farm, about parallel with the Peer house. On the far left of the eastern wing were three companies of the Incorporated Militia commanded by Captains Rapelje, Kerr and Walker, Brereton's companies of the 1st and Campbell's light company of the 8th Foot. The centre of this wing was composed of the 89th Foot, while Glew's light company of the 41st Foot, McDonnell's company of the Incorporated Militia and about half of the 103rd Foot formed the right.[19]

Near the junction of the lane and the track to Skinner's came a gap of approximately fifty yards and then the western wing of the line formed by the other half of the 103rd Foot and seven companies of the 1st Foot. On the far right of this wing, Drummond placed the flank companies of the 104th and the grenadier company of the 103rd. Battersby's Glengarries, Norton's Indians and some of Parry's militia remained in their advance positions, near the track to Skinner's, while five companies of the 8th Foot and the remaining Sedentary Militia and Indians were in reserve further west along Lundy's Lane. Exclusive of the Sedentary Militia and Indians, who would play little part in the forthcoming fight, but counting the five companies of the 8th Foot, Drummond now disposed of around three thousand infantry. Although his numbers compared favourably to the strength of Brown's army, many of Drummond's men were exhausted after a gruelling march and the remainder had been fighting hard for well over two hours.[20]

The darkness made the process of forming up difficult – and it also made it dangerous. The two armies spoke the same language and wore a similar uniform with an identical silhouette and this led to many cases of mistaken identification. Captain John Symmes of the First Infantry recalled that his regiment's "white pantaloons made the enemy mistake us for a Reg[imen]t. of their own and led to our taking prisoners."[21] "The confusion of columns reconoitering in the dark," recorded Lieutenant Colonel William Drummond of the 104th Foot,

> ... and the ridiculous mistakes which could only occur fighting an army speaking the same language were laughable though serious – Who goes there? – A friend. – To whom? – To King George. If the appellants, as you would call them, were of that persuasion, all was well, but when a friend to Madison, then there was a difference of opinion.[22]

Sometimes these mistakes verged on the comic. Shortly after the capture of the guns, Douglass was approached by a British N.C.O. who ran up, saluted and transmitted a message. When Douglass seized the man's musket and drew it over his horse's neck, the uncomprehending soldier protested: "And what have I done Sir? I'm no deserter. God Save the King, and dom the Yankees."²³

At other times, such mistakes provided windfalls. One of Harris's dragoons took a British officer and four enlisted men prisoner after their wagon, loaded with some of Riall's official correspondence, wandered into the American lines. The Philadelphian Thomas Biddle was astounded when another wagon drew up to his gun position on the Portage Road and its British escort proceeded to transfer its load of ammunition into his keeping. The escort's confusion is understandable as both British and American gunners wore blue uniforms of similar cut.²⁴

Mistakes in identification also had tragic results. Just after the flank companies of the 104th Foot got into position on the extreme right flank, they saw a "black line rising ... in our front." Ordered to open fire, the 104th and the units in line with them "raffled away" at the enemy – actually the Glengarry Light Infantry pulling in from their advanced position to re-ammunition. Battersby, the Glengarries' commander, galloped up to the firing troops "in the most daring manner" and shouted that his men were British. Le Couteur of the 104th remembered that his unit immediately ceased firing in "consternation"; but "the 103rd fired another volley not knowing it so soon." Fortunately, owing to the darkness of the night, there were few casualties.²⁵

Under these circumstances it took Drummond and his officers nearly thirty minutes to prepare for a counterattack. During this time, "the night," remarked Norton, "resumed its natural tranquility [sic]" and the low roar of the falls could again be heard.²⁶ That sound must have been sweet torture to men with throats parched by the bitterness of black powder, exertion and tension. But, other than those fortunate few who still had refreshment in their canteens, there was no relief as the closest water was the Niagara River a mile away and men could not leave the ranks.

Even worse was the plight of the wounded lying in the darkness – groaning with pain, pleading for help and begging for water. The regulars had more pressing tasks at hand, so the Canadian militia were ordered to gather in the wounded and carry them to the Lundy and other nearby farmhouses which had been turned into emergency dressing stations. Some of the militiamen, such as Daniel Field of Merritt's Canadian Dragoons, spent the entire night on this mission of mercy.²⁷

These same militia were given other non-combat duties to perform – guarding prisoners, transporting ammunition and tearing down the split rail fences that lined Lundy's Lane and the adjacent farm roads so that the regulars could manoeuvre. Because they were poorly armed, equipped and trained, most of their ammunition was taken from them and distributed among the regular infantry. This must have been galling to men like Captain Daniel Springer of the 1st Middlesex, who had been arrested in his home by American raiders for his Loyalist sympathies the previous February and had spent four months in captivity before being released. But it was just as well – this was no battle for untrained amateurs and the militia knew it. Colonel Andrew Bradt, commanding the 5th Lincoln, later reported that he was nearly killed by the one volley fired by his regiment and that four of his officers disappeared when the fighting started and did not reappear until after it had ended.[28]

Some men in the British and Canadian ranks that night were willing to fight harder and take more risks than their duty demanded because they hoped to salvage reputations or careers that were in jeopardy. Two such, already noted, were Simons of the 2nd York and Brereton of the 1st Foot. Another was Captain James Basden, commanding the light company of the 89th Foot, who, under the influence of a "blind infatuation," had disobeyed general orders and had taken a woman on campaign.[29] This misdemeanour might have been overlooked if Basden had not neglected his company, which got out of hand and looted civilians. The twenty-nine-year-old Isle of Wight native's career barely survived this incident and was further set back in the spring of 1814 when his men behaved like a "plundering banditti" toward the local farmers, when stationed at Turkey Point on Lake Erie.[30]

An act of temper had cut short the career of nineteen-year-old John Winslow, standing that night in the ranks of the 104th Foot. The scion of a New Brunswick Loyalist clan, Winslow had been serving as a lieutenant with the 41st Foot at Fort George in March 1812 when he became involved in a fight with a fellow officer in the mess. On learning of this incident, Major General Isaac Brock told both officers to submit their resignations. Winslow was still at Fort George when war broke out in July 1812, but Brock refused all his requests to serve in the ranks of the 41st. When the regiment marched out to fight at Queenston Heights, Winslow grabbed a musket and fell in with his old company. Brock was killed during that action and his successor, Major General Roger Sheaffe, impressed by the young man's bravery, tried to salvage Winslow's career. His efforts were in vain and in May 1813 Winslow had lost his commission. Determined to regain his name, he enlisted in the 104th Foot and had fought in their ranks as a gentleman volunteer ever since.[31]

Heroes or cowards, reckless or reluctant, the British and Canadians formed in their companies. Cursing N.C.O.s herded the regular infantry into positions indicated by mounted members of the staff, where they dressed their ranks with the aid of lanterns and prepared for action. Officers and drummers, their hats full of cartridges held in front of them, walked down the ranks and the men filled their pouches. Each made use of the combination pricker and brush that he carried to clean the vent of his musket, replaced his flint and loaded a careful round. Knowing the quality of their American opponent might require the use of the bayonet, many tied the sockets of their triangular blades tightly on to the muzzles of their muskets with string. There wasn't time for much else, perhaps a quick prayer, perhaps a whisper with the man to either side about who had been killed or wounded, or about incidents in the fighting. Conversation froze at the approach of an officer or the rebuke of an N.C.O. and all too soon the cautionary command "Company!" was successively passed down the line, followed in a few seconds by "The Battalion will advance!" and, finally, "March!"[32]

CHAPTER 10

A Conflict Obstinate
Beyond Description

Nothing could stop that astonishing infantry. No sudden burst of undisciplined valour, no nervous enthusiasms weakened the stability of their order, … their measured tread shook the ground, their dreadful volleys swept away the head of every formation.
NAPIER'S DESCRIPTION OF BRITISH INFANTRY
AT THE BATTLE OF ALBUERA, 1811, FROM
*History of the War in the Peninsula
and the South of France,* 1852.

Nothing could resist the obstinate desperation of the Yankees; every charge with the bayonet … proved how idle and how vain the boasting of the British infantry is when opposed to full blooded eaters of the pumpkin.
CAPTAIN JOHN W. WEEKS, ELEVENTH INFANTRY,
1 AUGUST, 1814

The attack in line, described in its manual as "the most important and most difficult" of military movements, was the standard offensive formation of the British army in 1814.[1] It had served that army well in Europe and had been used with success the previous autumn against the Americans at Crysler's Farm. The procedure was straightforward: the line, formed in two ranks, marching slowly to preserve its alignment and disregarding casualties, advanced until within musket range of the enemy. It halted, fired a concentrated volley and followed it up with a short, vicious bayonet charge. The enemy was often so unnerved by the approach of that silent, imperturbable and unwavering line that they were put to flight by the volley, rendering the use of the bayonet unnecessary. The decision of just when to stop advancing and open fire required careful timing, however, and it was a tricky enough matter in daylight when the enemy's position was readily apparent. At night, when that position was concealed by darkness, it was extremely difficult.

There were many advantages to the line formation. It did not require any complicated preliminary movements because it was also the standard defensive formation. As it lacked depth, troops in line did not suffer as heavily from artillery fire and its breadth would allow it to outflank an enemy position. The use of the line also allowed Drummond to bring more muskets to bear and thus give, as he stated, "the farest Scope to the discipline of the Troops – by allowing their fire to its full Effect."[2] Discipline was the key word for, in Drummond's opinion "Charges in Mass or rather in Mob never produce any brilliant or successful Effect," especially against "lines of unbroken Infantry"; and such movements should only be undertaken by "Troops in the most correct State of formation and Capable of reforming after being unavoidably thrown in some degree of disorder by their own Charge."[3]

It is not difficult to comprehend why Drummond chose the line formation for his counterattack. What is puzzling is the fact that he put such a formation in motion toward the hill without covering its advance with skirmishers drawn from his British light infantry companies or the Glengarry Fencibles. Supporting an advancing line was a normal role for the light infantry and any of the six light companies Drummond now commanded was capable of performing this task. Skirmishers would have located the American line in the dark, harassed, it, unsettled it and protected the British line from similar harassment during its advance.

Drummond did initiate a reconnaissance toward the hill but the soldiers involved had not returned by the time he launched his attack. The British general's earlier failure to make proper use of his light infantry had cost him his guns and he now compounded this error by failing to use them for his counterattack. Drummond may have been affected by the loss of blood caused by his wound and may not have been reasoning clearly. But this omission may also have been the result of Drummond's inexperience – this was the first action in which he commanded as a general against a tough, well-trained and determined opponent.[4]

The order was given and, at about 10:00 P.M., the British and Canadians moved forward. They marched "with profound silence," since their commander disapproved of "Screams and Shouts" because "British discipline and intrepidity do not require such paltry aid."[5] The left flank of the advancing line was composed of two companies of the Incorporated Militia and the light company of the 8th Foot while the 89th and 1st Foot were in the centre and the light company of the 41st Foot with two companies of the Incorporated Militia formed the right flank. Most of these units were drawn from Drummond's eastern wing. His western wing does not appear to have participated in this attack and it is not known why, to make this important assault, he chose units that had been fighting since the beginning of the action in preference to those from Hercules Scott's force, which formed most of the western wing and had not seen much fighting or suffered heavy casualties. Nevertheless, moving slowly to clear obstacles and halting at frequent intervals to "dress," the British and Canadians climbed the hill.[6]

The Left Division was waiting for them. The last unit to come into place, Jesup's Twenty-Fifth, had just formed to the right of the meeting house, with its left resting on Towson's artillery and its right thrown forward "so as to flank the enemy."[7] Hindman would not be able to use the captured artillery to defend the hill because most of the gun implements were missing. His men therefore loaded their own weapons with canister, devastating at short range, and waited. As the British approached, Hindman was assisting Captain John Ritchie to bring one of his 6-pdrs., posted too far forward, back into line. Ritchie, who had been wounded earlier in the action but had refused to leave his company, was having difficulty with the horses of the gun team, which were balking.[8]

Like Drummond, both Brown and Ripley had neglected to post skirmishers in front to give warning of an attack. It was the noise of the British advance that alerted the American line as by "degrees ... low commands ... often repeated, became more and more audible" until "a dark line could be seen at a distance of perhaps sixty paces."[9]

Musket locks were pulled back to full cock as Ripley, riding up and down behind his men, ordered them to let the British fire first so that their muzzle flashes could be used as an aiming point. "Perfect silence was observed throughout both armies" as the British moved up the hill and then halted.[10] The opposing lines were not exactly parallel; witnesses estimated the distance separating them varying between thirty and ninety feet. The word of command was given in the British ranks and, starting on their left, a rolling volley shattered the stillness. On command, the Left Division returned fire and "the action then became general."[11]

The first British volley inflicted heavy casualties on the American gunners posted in front of the infantry line. Ritchie was cut down – the Virgin-

ian's body was found the next day on the field with thirty-six wounds in it –
and the working party with him were all killed or wounded. Hindman's
horse was hit and collapsed, pinning its rider under it, and he was forced to
lie still beside his captain's lifeless body while the two sides exchanged musketry over his head. Lieutenant Edward Randolph, who had returned from
his reconnaissance to Lewiston to take command of one of Towson's 6-pdr.
guns, remembered that "as the match was lighted ready to be applied, the
enemy gave a raking fire which cleared the gun of every man tending it."[12]
Randolph gathered up the "fragments" of his gun detachment and withdrew
to the shelter of the infantry in the rear. The American gunners were out of
the action and the fight now became one of infantry against infantry.[13]

A number of Canadians from the Incorporated Militia who had gone forward at Drummond's request to establish the exact location of the American line were caught between the two armies when they opened fire.
Twenty-two-year-old Lieutenant Henry Ruttan had taken a corporal and
"quietly advanced under cover of a fence and by trees" until he was close
enough to identify details of American uniforms especially "long tailed
coats turned up with white" which convinced him that "those in front of us
were enemies."[14] The native of Northumberland County, Upper Canada,
had just begun to retrace his steps when "firing at once became general."
Ensign John Lampman, a peacetime farmer from the Twenty-Mile Creek
area, was returning from a similar mission when a "furious and sustained
fire" broke out that made him increase his speed.[15] Lampman was showered
by musket balls in the act of jumping a fence and had his epaulette shot off
and his trouser knee shot through but, otherwise unharmed, rejoined his
comrades.

The Americans were not shaken by the first British volley. Therefore,
instead of rushing in with the bayonet, the British continued to fire. Volley
followed volley at close range as the two armies, unwilling to retreat, "engaged in a conflict, obstinate beyond description."[16] The men in Ripley's
line soon realized that they had an advantage: the British, firing from lower
on the hill, were overcompensating and much of their fire was too high.
Porter's brigade on the far left of the American position, stationed on the
slope of the hill, noted a somewhat similar phenomenon: the British, who
were above them, were firing over their heads. The American fire was in
turn rendered less effective because Drummond had again ordered his men
down on one knee. But casualties were taken – Ruttan, for instance, shot
through the right collar bone, "scarcely felt the shock, but was conscious

that something unusual was the matter, as I was involuntarily brought upon both feet ... and turned quite round."[17] Captain Thomas Fraser of the same regiment also went down, hit in the arm.[18]

The musketry continued "from both sides with great spirit."[19] One participant observed that although it appeared to be "the intention ... of both parties to have charged ... both lines were so soon cut to pieces that neither could effect a charge."[20] Participants were impressed with the ferocity of the fighting and thought it "was the most desperate battle for the numbers engaged that they had ever witnessed."[21] The steadiness of the Americans led one British officer to remark that "the Yankees behaved noble."[22] The veteran Sergeant James Commins of the 8th Foot, while admitting that the action "was the most obstinate that I ever was in," was less generous, attributing the gallantry of the Americans to the fact that they were "well fortified with whiskey" which "made them stand longer than they ever had."[23]

Both sides fired "with as much deliberation as if it had been a sham fight."[24] In places, the British were so close that, despite the darkness and the smoke, the "continual blaze of light" from the musketry allowed the Americans "distinctly to see their buttons."[25] An American officer noted that the muzzle blaze from the muskets of the two opposing lines blended. A better soldier than a speller or grammarian, Ropes of the Twenty-First remembered that "Our Min fought like bull dogs so close did they charge that the fire from their Discharges would seem to strike our faces."[26] "The opposing lines were so near each other," recorded another American, that "at the flash of the enemy's guns, as they fired volley after volley," his comrades could,

> ... through the darkness, by the lurid glare of the flash and the blaze, see the faces and even mark the countenances of their adversaries ... the darkness and smoke combined with the fitful light made the faces of those in the opposing ranks wear a blue sulphurous hue, and the men at each flash had the appearance of laughing.[27]

Brown watched the attack with his staff but was content to let Ripley, whose brigade formed the centre of the American line, fight the actual battle. Riding up and down ten or twelve paces behind his troops, Ripley shouted orders, gave encouragement and ignored the pleas of his aide, McDonald, to take cover. His horse was wounded and his hat and clothing pierced by musket balls but this cool "Yankee" general from Massachusetts, often derided for his caution, seems to have found his element in this set-piece defensive fighting. McDonald "never knew him more collected" as he "gave his orders with perfect coolness and deliberation, and attended, as far as possible, to their proper execution."[28]

Drummond had a different command style. Shouting "stick to them, my fine fellows!" he ranged the length of his line, urging his men on.[29] Lieutenant Duncan Clark of the Incorporated Militia remembered him, "notwithstanding the presence of his wound, ... galloping from one Reg[imen]t to the next, encouraging the troops and exciting them by his presence and example."[30] Watching the British commander ride up to a neighbouring unit, Le Couteur received "a lesson in war." Drummond shouted "My lads, *will you* charge the Americans?" As the young Jerseyman dryly noted, "He *put a question* instead of *giving the order* – they fired instead of charging."[31]

The British line outflanked the American position on both the left and right. On the right, however, Jesup's Twenty-Fifth was protected by the steeper slope to their front and the British could not close, while on the left Porter's brigade, sheltered from the worst of the British musketry by the slope of the hill, maintained their position. The centre, composed of the Twenty-Third, Twenty-First, Chunn's company of the Seventeenth, and the First Infantry, also stood its ground. Seeing that the Americans remained unshaken, Drummond gave the command and the British line slowly withdrew, in good order, back down the hill. From the time the first shot was fired until the last British soldiers disappeared into the darkness between twenty and twenty-five minutes had elapsed.[32]

Ripley was certain they would be back and made his preparations. As the American units dressed their lines and closed in to their centres, gaps appeared between the regiments and it was obvious to Ripley that he could not cover the same extent of ground he had previously held. He ordered Porter's brigade wheeled up into line to extend his front on the left. When the volunteers moved up, they "passed over the dead and dying, who were literally in heaps, especially where the British had stood during the battle."[33] Three of Hindman's artillery companies were now in action but someone remembered Douglass's company of sappers and bombardiers with their two 18-pdr. guns back at Chippawa and Douglass was ordered to return to camp and get them ready should they be needed. Before he left, the young New Jersey native made a final fond inspection of the captured British guns.[34]

Ammunition was taken from the cartridge boxes of the dead and wounded and distributed among the survivors. Expenditure had been heavy – Private Alexander McMullen of the Pennsylvania Volunteers calculated that he fired off nineteen rounds during the attack. By this time Gardner had risen from his sick bed to take control of the American rear area. Wagons had been brought up from the camp at Chippawa to carry the wounded; Harris's regular and Boughton's New York dragoons were busy collecting them and distributing ammunition. The prisoners were marched off under guard but there were now no prisoners left in the meeting house on the hill. During the heat of the attack they had taken the opportunity of their guards' distraction to slip out a window and escape to their own lines.[35]

These essential "chores" taken care of, the men of the Left Division, faces blackened by powder, shoulders numb from recoil and "almost choked from thirst," checked flint and priming and then leaned on their muskets to wait.[36] The sound of marching to his front alerted Ripley that the British were forming up again. Worried that his weakened forces could not hold, he observed to Brown that "now was the critical moment, as the Enemy was advancing in great force," and requested that Winfield Scott's brigade be brought up to reinforce him.[37] Brown hesitated; he had decided to remain on the ground "knowing it to be the best in the vicinity," and to keep up the fight "until day should dawn and be governed by circumstances."[38] He also knew that Scott "had suffered much" and he wanted to hold the First Brigade "in reserve to give the finishing blow to the Enemy at some favourable moment, when we could more distinctly see our way."[39] Apparently Brown never considered removing the captured artillery, the object of Drummond's attacks, to a place of safety. Perhaps he forgot about it in the heat of the action. In any case, Brown was still turning Ripley's request over in his mind when Leavenworth arrived to report that the First Brigade was ready and waiting for orders. Brown rode back with him to see Scott.[40]

For more than an hour, Scott's brigade had been resting in the fields south of the hill while the other brigades had been carrying on the fight. His three regiments were in very bad case and he had ordered them consolidated into a single formation. While he rode up and down shouting orders, the survivors were organized into eight platoons or half companies, about two hundred and forty men, and put under the command of Brady, the senior regimental commander. This re-organization was done in a hurried and confusing fashion – there were more officers than positions available for them and the residue had to serve as file closers. Nor were all the men in the brigade eager to rejoin the fighting. Lieutenant Henry Blake, by now the senior officer of the Eleventh, did not assume his proper station but instead helped a wounded fellow officer to a dressing station set up in one of the nearby farmhouses. He then disappeared into the night.[41]

The re-organization was not quite complete when Scott ordered the consolidated *ad hoc* battalion formed into column and marched west, near the track to Skinner's farm, where it halted and received ammunition. Riddle's company of the Nineteenth, which, emerging from the chestnut woods with Ripley, had joined the brigade toward the close of the first part of the action, was detached "to the left, to a fence by the side of a wood, to watch some Indians who were yelling in that quarter."[42]

Having no command in the reformed battalion, Leavenworth volunteered his services as Scott's aide and was sent to find Brown and get orders. While he was absent on this mission, Ripley's brigade fought off Drummond's first counterattack. Leavenworth returned with Brown and the two generals discussed the situation; it was decided that Scott would take position in rear of the Second Brigade. As Brady was weak from loss of blood, Scott ordered Leavenworth to assume command of the composite formation. Brady, however, refused to leave the field but followed the remnants of the brigade at a distance when it marched onto the hill. Here Leavenworth formed in line with his right on Lundy's Lane and his left in the rear of the captured British artillery.[43]

At about 10:45 P.M., just as Leavenworth was getting into position, Drummond "showed himself again, ... apparently undismayed and in good order."[44] His second attack was a duplicate of his first: in McDonald's words, the British advanced "nearly in the same manner, attacked precisely in the same point, but did not approach so near."[45] Participants estimated the distance between the two lines at about ninety feet. Once again, Ripley ordered the American line to let the British fire first and in a moment there was a "sheet of fire from both armies" as another firefight commenced.[46]

Hindman's artillery were unable to give the American infantry the support they needed because of the darkness, the proximity of the opposing lines and the fact that the British were lower on the slope of the hill. Hindman had another problem. Ammunition scales for the U.S. Artillery in 1814 provided about thirty rounds of canister per gun for ready use, carried on the gun carriage or in the ammunition wagon or caisson that accompanied it. A further supply was transported in the reserve caissons but a number of these had earlier been destroyed by British artillery fire.

Hindman's gun detachments were coming to the end of their canister without hope of replacement while his gunners suffered heavy casualties from the British musketry. According to Hindman, "Every moment deprived us of some brave soldier and rendered our fire less effective."[47]

The second musketry duel was "more severe, and ... longer continued than the last" and, although the Americans grimly returned the British fire, some of Brown's units began to waver.[48] Porter's brigade had become somewhat disordered when they moved forward and were still dressing their ranks when the British approached and halted to fire a volley. "A death-like silence for a few moments prevailed and both armies stood still" – then a voice yelled from the British line asking if the Americans had surrendered.[49] When there was no reply, the question was repeated. A New York officer shouted back that "we never would surrender." The tension was too much for Willcocks's Canadian renegades, who, if captured, faced charges of high treason and the business end of a hemp rope, and they began to move back down the hill. The rest of Porter's brigade fired an irregular volley and followed them, "the British complimenting us with a shower of musket balls."[50] After the Volunteers had retreated about a hundred yards, their officers caught up and began to re-establish control. On Porter's right, Nicholas of the First Infantry, seeing the peril, wheeled his flank to the left and poured several rapid volleys into the British to discourage them from advancing further.[51]

There were also problems in the centre. Part of the Twenty-Third Infantry ceased firing and edged backward, oblivious to the commands and entreaties of their officers and N.C.O.s. Some of the adjoining platoons of the Twenty-First joined this rearward drift and for a few moments matters looked serious. Ripley personally rallied the frightened men and led them back to their place in line.[52]

On the right Jesup maintained firm control of the Twenty-Fifth which came under a heavy fire that gave him his second wound, a graze on the neck. A few minutes later he received a third and more serious wound when a musket ball shattered the hilt of his sword, driving its fragments into Jesup's right hand, causing him "excruciating pain." But Jesup remained on his feet and continued in action.[53]

Winfield Scott now rejoined the fight. Watching the British approach, he "resolved to try an experiment" by attacking in column through Drummond's line.[54] Shouting to Leavenworth "in a loud and animated voice," he asked, "are those troops prepared for the charge?"[55] Before Leavenworth could reply, Scott added, "I know they are prepared for anything" and ordered him to form his brigade in close column. It took some time to complete this formation, but when it was ready, Scott shouted, "Forward and charge my brave fellows," and rode for the British line.[56]

The First Brigade obeyed and marched straight into disaster. Writing six months later, Leavenworth recalled that they passed between the pieces of artillery and came into contact with the British line "which immediately gave way" but, "owing to the darkness of the night, our column had become in some degree irregular," and so the brigade formed on the extreme left of Porter's brigade.[57] Leavenworth was not telling the whole truth; to get to Porter's left, the First Brigade had to move west along Lundy's Lane *between the two armies* and thus risk being caught in a crossfire. Scott later insisted that he had "explained his intentions and forcibly cautioned his own brigade and Ripley's ... not to fire."[58] Someone did not get the message and the Second Brigade opened fire on the First, as it moved in front of them, while at the same time the British fired at it from the opposite direction. Captain John Pentland of the Twenty-Second Infantry, commanding the rear platoon in Scott's column remembered that "the Enemy opened a most destructive fire upon us, which was followed by a fire in a different direction nearly as I thought at right angles, which cut us up most dreadfully."[59] Burghardt of the Ninth, already wounded, was killed by a ball through the chest and both Scott and Leavenworth had their horses shot from under them. Second Lieutenant Samuel Brady of the Twenty-Second held up his hands and implored the Second Brigade to cease firing. A platoon of the First Infantry realizing what was happening, grounded their muskets, and informed their officers that the men in front were American. But the crossfire was too much; in Pentland's words, "it cannot be expected that men engaged as long as we were, and so much exhausted could withstand a fire of that kind without breaking, which we did."[60] The survivors fled west to the shelter of the fences bordering the track to Skinner's farm where they were brought under control and formed again in column.[61]

The musketry duel continued but, as before, the British and Canadian line did not press home with the bayonet. Gradually the firing died down and again Drummond withdrew north of the hill. He had inflicted heavy casualties on the Americans but he was no closer to reclaiming his artillery.[62]

Both armies had fought themselves to a standstill and there was now a longer interval, "not to exceed three quarters of an hour," before the fighting resumed.[63] The Right Division was tired. Some of Drummond's units, such as the 89th Foot, had been marching or fighting for well over twelve hours and could not give much more. "Affairs just then looked very gloomy on our side," remembered Le Couteur.[64] But Drummond may have reasoned that, if his units were in such poor shape, the enemy was as badly off and another attempt might just succeed. He therefore ordered a third attack.

The Americans were in a bad state. "They had neither water nor whiskey to refresh themselves, after the fatigues they had endured," recorded McDonald.[65] There was also some despondency in the Left Division's ranks: Randolph (curiously enough using the same adjective as Le Couteur) remembered that "the condition of things around us was gloomy ... exhaustion throughout the ranks was unsurpassed."[66] These feelings were not helped by the wounded lying near the American position, and "it was a scene of distress in the extreme to behold the dead on our side and hear the agonies & groans of the dying on the other & the lamentations of the wounded."[67]

Brown was running out of troops. It is doubtful that more than twenty-eight hundred men from the division had participated in the action; there were about eight hundred still in the ranks. So many officers had become casualties that it was difficult to keep the men at their posts and some began to slip away in the darkness. "We maintained the ground until companies were commanded by corporals, and all nearly fainting for [lack of] water," remembered an officer of the Second Brigade.[68] Scott's brigade was in worse shape: Lieutenant Frederick Sawyer of the Eleventh Infantry reported that, towards "the close of the action, as there was hardly a company remaining of our regiment and but one man in my platoon, I volunteered [to serve] in the 9th [Infantry]."[69] The Twenty-Fifth Infantry had taken so many casualties in the second British attack that, to cover his ground, Jesup was forced to form his regiment into one rank instead of the more normal two or three and insert his file closers into this single rank. Brown's army was tottering and one good, hard shove would push it over.[70]

Shortly before 11:30 P.M., a weary but determined line of British and Canadians advanced for the third time. Although he had superior numbers of regular infantry – a fact that allowed him some flexibility in his choice of dispositions and tactics – Drummond apparently did not consider any other possibility than an attack in line directly against the hill. In the darkness, there was no easy way for him to ascertain the number and position of Brown's forces – he may still have been convinced that he was outnumbered and that his best course was to concentrate his attacks on his main objective. In any case, Drummond seems to have learned nothing from the fail-

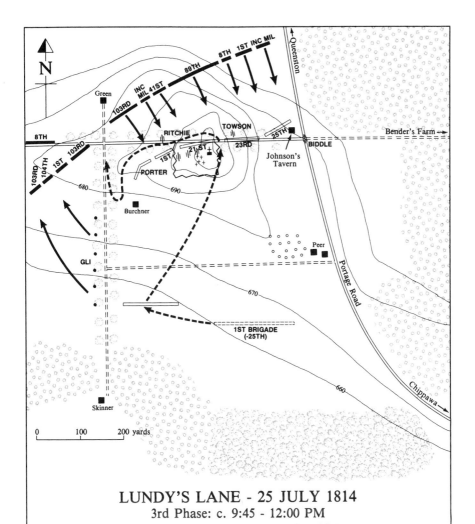

LUNDY'S LANE - 25 JULY 1814
3rd Phase: c. 9:45 - 12:00 PM

1. Drummond reforms his troops, including Hercules Scott's reinforcements, into a single line divided into section by Lundy's Lane. As they withdraw to re-ammunition, the Glengarry Light Infantry are fired on by their own troops.

2. Porter's brigade takes position on the left of the American line while the remainder of the Second Brigade form along Lundy's Lane. Ritchie, Towson and Biddle's companies of artillery take position to support the infantry.

3. Drummond mounts a series of attacks to recapture his artillery. In the middle of the fighting, Scott's brigade re-enters the battle and moves west along Lundy's Lane but, fired upon by both armies, breaks in confusion but then reforms in the farm lane west of Porter's position.

ure of his two previous attacks and, instead of probing around Brown's flanks for weak spots, went straight for the centre of the American line.

As the British commenced their attack, Brown was with Porter's brigade, where he had ridden after conferring with Winfield Scott. With the assistance of Wood, Porter and his officers had brought the Volunteers under control and moved them back up to the left flank of Ripley's line although, as McMullen remarked, many were still "contending for places in the rear."[71] Here, Porter was joined by Riddle and his company of the Nineteenth Infantry, which Scott had forgotten when he marched onto the hill, and who now formed on Porter's left flank.[72]

Scott now made his last attack. After hours of fighting under this rashly aggressive officer, there were some in the First Brigade who were beginning to doubt his generalship. One of them was Brady, badly wounded, but still gamely following the brigade in its travels. He remarked to Captain John Pentland of his regiment that Scott "lost himself" when he had tried to attack the British line in column formation.[73] But Scott still had fight left in him. His horse having been killed in the previous attack, he led his brigade on foot north toward Lundy's Lane to try to turn what he thought was the British flank. Brown reported that the "last I saw of him on the field, was marching near the head of Column in a direction that would have placed him in the rear of the Enemy's right flank."[74]

This attack was even more disastrous than Scott's previous effort. Leavenworth cryptically stated that "finding that flank supported by a heavy second line his [Scott's] charge was withdrawn."[75] Again, Leavenworth was not telling the whole story. What happened was that, as the First Brigade moved north in column, it passed in front of the western wing of Drummond's line, which opened fire. Le Couteur of the 104th remembered a column crossing "our front" into "which we poured volleys till they retreated."[76] Pentland, who was at the head of the column, later stated that "we had not moved ten paces until we were discovered and [a] destructive fire opened [that] compelled Genl. Scott to draw off his men."[77] Captain Abraham Hull, commanding the Ninth Infantry, fell wounded, Lieutenant David Perry of the same regiment was captured and Pentland himself went down, shot through both legs. The remnants of the brigade fell back behind the American line where, under Brown's eyes, Leavenworth reformed them yet again although he later admitted that his exertions were somewhat "feeble."[78]

Of the eight hundred to nine hundred men in the three regiments (the Ninth, Eleventh and Twenty-Second Infantry) that Scott had brought onto the field nearly five hours before, about one hundred were still in formation. One of them was Vermonter Sergeant Festus Thompson of the Eleventh Infantry, the tenth soldier of the regiment to carry its colour that terrible night. Although wounded in the hip, Thompson proudly waved the Eleventh's bullet-holed flag, its shaft reduced to a stump, over his head to rally his comrades.[79]

Brown was hit just as Scott made his final attack. A musket ball, possibly from the British volleys fired at the First Brigade, passed through his right inner thigh "very high up" carrying in a piece of the general's woollen pants.[80] A few minutes later his aide, nineteen-year-old Captain Ambrose Spencer, was struck by two musket balls and slid, mortally wounded, from his horse but, hanging onto the bridle, was able to stand upright for a few seconds before crumpling to the ground.[81]

Brown did not dismount but rode forward as the British advanced. Suddenly he received "a violent blow from a ball of some kind on his left side" that "nearly unhorsed him."[82] Weak from loss of blood, he began to doubt his ability to "sit on his horse" and, seeing Wood, informed him of his condition. "Never mind my dear General," replied the imperturbable engineer, "you are gaining the greatest Victory that has ever been gained by your Country." Still in pain but perhaps somewhat mollified, Brown rode with Wood to watch the fighting from behind Porter's brigade.[83]

For the third time the British line closed on the Americans. It was McDonald's impression that they seemed to be in greater force and Drummond may well have thrown every man he had into this effort. As before, the British halted within range and opened fire by volleys, which Ripley returned. Under the eyes of Brown, Porter's volunteers stood their ground although their officers suffered heavily from the British fire. Major James Wood, commanding the Pennsylvania Volunteers, was shot twice and nearly crushed when his horse fell on him. Adjutant Thomas Poe of the same regiment was mortally wounded and Quartermaster John McClay was left a speechless idiot by a musket ball in the forehead. Captain William Hooper of the New York Volunteers was killed while Dobbin, commanding the regiment, was slightly wounded. Porter had his arm grazed by a ball that penetrated his sleeve. Only the Canadian Volunteers got off lightly, Willcocks having his horse shot out from under him but suffering no injuries.[84]

The British fire was heavy but they appeared reluctant to close with the bayonet. Seeing that the enemy unit opposite was not going to advance, Porter decided to attack. With engineer Wood's assistance, he led his small brigade against the enemy line, which gave way before him, and took a number of prisoners. Nicholas moved the First Infantry forward in conjunction and briefly crossed bayonets with the British before pushing them back.[85]

Things also went well on the right flank where the British had approached very close to the Twenty-Fifth Infantry's single rank before opening fire and inflicting heavy casualties. Both Captain Joseph Kinney, who was hit in the chest by a ball, and Ensign William Hunter, promoted from sergeant only three weeks before, were killed while the regimental adjutant, First Lieutenant Ephraim Shaylor, and Lieutenants George McChain and Henry De Witt were wounded. Jesup remembered that the "contest was now more obstinate than in any of the previous attacks of the enemy; for half an hour the blaze from the muskets of the two lines mingled, but our fire was so well directed and so destructive that the enemy was again compelled to retire."[86] Jesup's biggest problems were the pain from his right hand and a shortage of ammunition; his men were running low and he was proud to see wounded men lying on the ground offer up their cartridge boxes to those still on their feet.[87]

As if Jesup did not have worries enough, Scott suddenly appeared in the Twenty-Fifth's position. While talking with Jesup, he was knocked unconscious by a musket ball through the left shoulder joint and Jesup had him carried to the shelter of a nearby tree. A few minutes later, Jesup received his fourth wound, "a violent contusion in the breast by a piece of shell or perhaps the stick of a rocket" that knocked him senseless to the ground but, in a few minutes, this seemingly indestructible Kentuckian was back on his feet directing his regiment's fire.[88]

But the battle would be decided in the centre of the American position around the meeting house and the captured artillery. Here, the British and Canadian attack seemed to meet with success. According to Ripley, "the last charge compelled the whole line to recoil, and it was with unexampled difficulty that it was rallied."[89] As the centre of the British line, probably formed by the 1st and 89th Foot, approached, Hindman's artillery was silent: they had used up all their ammunition. The two veteran British units – one the senior infantry battalion of the British army and the other "a fine jovial unsophisticated set of 'wild tremendous Irishmen'" – were facing the First Infantry, the senior regiment of the American army, and the Twenty-First led by the redoubtable Miller.[90]

Under the command of thirty-four-year-old Major Miller Clifford, a vet-

W. Hamilton Merritt, Upper Canada Militia (1793-1862)
A dashing young Canadian cavalry officer, Merritt participated in almost every major action fought in the Niagara during the war but his military career ended at Lundy's Lane when he was captured. Merritt went on to postwar fame as the builder of the first Welland Canal linking lakes Ontario and Erie. He is shown here in old age. (National Archives of Canada, C-29891)

Captain Alexander Roxburgh, Glengarry Light Infantry (1774-1856)
Roxburgh commanded a company of the Glengarries during the battle and experienced hard fighting on the British right flank. This portrait, painted about 1830, shows him in the uniform of a Glengarry officer. Note the whistle on his belt, used to control his men in skirmish actions. (Courtesy, National Archives of Canada, C-18010)

eran of campaigns in the West Indies, Holland and the Peninsula, the 89th got in among the captured guns. A vicious struggle followed on, over, and around the gun carriages, wagons and limbers. Frantic men shot, stabbed and clubbed at each other, neither side able to gain the advantage nor willing to withdraw. For a brief moment, the battle hung in the balance; and then, as the British and Canadians on the flanks pulled back, the centre followed and the guns remained in American hands. Drummond's final attack had failed.[91]

When "the enemy's bugle sounded the retreat for the last time," an American officer recorded, "our troops were left in undisturbed possession of the heights."[92] There was distant, scattered firing in the woods but gradually it faded away and quiet descended. It was about midnight. After five hours of fighting, Major General Jacob Brown and the Left Division of United States Army had prevailed in the bloodiest battle of the War of 1812.[93]

CHAPTER 11

Disengagement, 26 July 1814

*This memorable battle closed, by apparent consent, and desire of both
armies. They retreated from the scene at the same time, weary and exhausted.*
DRUMMER JARVIS HANKS, 11TH INFANTRY

As the last firing died away, McRee and Wood were confident that
the British would not attack again and urged Brown to withdraw to
Chippawa so that his exhausted men could get some food and water. Brown
agreed after some discussion and, deciding to turn command over to
Winfield Scott, rode slowly from Porter's position with his staff east along
the hill to find the tall Virginian. The moon was hidden by "fleecy clouds"
and a breeze had sprung up that dispelled the powder smoke; but the darkness, the debris from the fighting, the cries of the wounded and the confusion and fatigue of officers and men made it difficult to transmit orders.[1]

Brown and his entourage encountered Leavenworth and the remains of
the First Brigade, which, reformed yet again, had marched back onto the hill.
Leavenworth reported that Scott had left the field in a litter. Before he had
done so, that indomitable soldier, conscious again, had advised Leavenworth,
"in case the enemy should again return to the contest, to seek an opportunity
to charge, and drive them from the field with the bayonet."[2] Brown replied
that he was also returning to camp and directed Leavenworth to look to
Ripley for orders as command now "devolved on him."[3] He then entered the
position of the Twenty-Fifth Infantry and talked to Jesup, who confirmed the
news about Scott. Unable to delay any longer because of his wounds, Brown
dispatched his surviving aide, Captain Loring Austin, to find Ripley and order him to collect the wounded and retire, "and, in case the enemy pressed
upon him [to] face about and fight him."[4] Then, "supported on his horse,"
Brown rode slowly back over the field and south down the Portage Road.[5]

Ripley was at this time somewhere on the crest of the hill. After the last

British attack, he maintained his position for thirty minutes until he was certain that the enemy were not going to return. His mind then turned to the captured artillery and he ordered Porter to send a detachment of fifty men from his brigade to get them away. There being no horses or drag-ropes available, the Volunteers pushed the guns down the slope of the hill, although only one brass 6-pdr. was taken to the very bottom. They were ordered to bring down the rest but, in the words of one of their number, "being tired out and half dead for want of water, the most of our faces scorched with powder, we refused to do any more," and were put to work collecting the wounded.[6] Ripley next looked for Hindman, the officer most concerned with the removal of the guns, and only then realized that the American artillery had left the hill.[7]

Hindman had pulled his guns out on Brown's orders. Just after the fighting had ended, he had ridden to the rear to fetch his spare ammunition wagons; and he was directing them forward when he encountered Brown, who ordered him to return to Chippawa. After searching in vain for Ripley, he ordered his three artillery companies to withdraw. As most of the horses had been killed, the gunners had difficulty in getting their pieces away; and in the end they used bricoles (shoulder straps attached to the gun carriages) to move them down the hill onto the Portage Road. Here Harris offered the use of his cavalry horses but was refused as there was no harness to attach the dragoons' mounts to the carriages. One of Towson's 6-pdr. guns, a howitzer with a damaged carriage and two ammunition wagons were left behind because of a lack of horses to move them. Biddle, however, spotted the British brass 6-pdr. rolled to the bottom of the hill by Porter's detachment and decided to keep it as a trophy. As his company had not been involved in the close fighting on the top of the hill, more of his horses had survived and he was able to hook the British piece to one of his own gun carriages and get it back to camp.[8]

When he realized that the artillery had gone, Ripley had not yet received Brown's order to withdraw, and as far as he knew Brown was still in command on the field. Brown's order was delayed in transmission because the bearer, Austin, unable to find Ripley, had given it to his brigade major, Captain Newman S. Clarke, and it took Clarke some time to find his superior in the darkness. After receiving the order, Ripley called the remaining senior officers together for a conference and, while they assembled, he gave orders to collect the wounded, whose groans and pleas could be heard in the night. Those able to walk were helped to wagons which had come up earlier on Brown's order; those unable to move were carried on stretchers improvised from blankets, coats, fence rails and muskets. As the wagons were filled, they were sent back to the camp. Widow Willson, whose tavern had been turned into an emergency dressing station, counted sixty wagon-loads that passed that night on their way to Chippawa. Unfortunately many of the wounded were left on the ground as they were scattered and darkness made it difficult to find them.[9]

In pain from his four wounds, Jesup carefully picked his way through the dead and dying men and horses, broken carriages and wagons that littered the hill to confer with Ripley. Porter also rode up. Ripley informed them that he had a "most positive order" from Brown to withdraw the army and asked their opinions.[10] Jesup, now commanding the remnants of the First Brigade, was inclined to agree; his command, including Leavenworth's fragments, consisted of only two hundred men "exhausted with fatigue and the want of water."[11] Ripley's brigade was in similar case and he doubted if they could "withstand another charge."[12] But Porter was against a withdrawal which he felt would turn victory into defeat. As for Brown's "positive order" to withdraw, Porter later remarked that Ripley "should, without hesitation, have disobeyed ... for he commanded the battle and was answerable for its issue, and ought not to have been dictated to by a wounded man four miles from the scene of action."[13] Always hesitant away from the fighting, Ripley pondered whether "to obey or disobey."[14] If he disobeyed and his army was destroyed by another British attack, "what would have been the consequences to himself personally and the army?"[15] Deciding that his force was too weak to remain on the field, he ordered a withdrawal to Chippawa. Exasperated, Porter "almost wished that fate had swept another General from the combat."[16]

The men of the Left Division were tired and taut from hours of fighting. The withdrawal was made as quietly as possible for fear that the British would be tempted to attack. The infantry formed on the road and the march began, Porter's brigade going first, followed by the remnants of the two regular brigades. The rear guard was formed by Harris's dragoons and a scratch company commanded by Captain Merrill Marston of the Twenty-First that had arrived too late to take part in the fighting and had served as a provost unit during the action. The strength of this column was estimated to be only six to seven hundred men, but as many had earlier left the ranks to help the wounded or to search for water, there were more survivors still on their feet. Shortly after midnight, the march back to Chippawa began.

When all the infantry had passed, Harris wheeled his dragoons and brought up the rear.[17]

But there were still unwounded Americans on the field. After he had got his three companies away, Hindman decided that he wanted one of the British brass 24-pdrs. and ordered First Lieutenant John J. Fontaine and Second Lieutenant John W. Kincaid of the artillery to take a detachment of gunners and bring one of them to the camp. Hindman next directed two wagon drivers to take their vehicles up the hill and assist the two officers and then went looking for horses. When he later came up to check on Fontaine's progress, Hindman discovered the 24-pdr. and the wagons in the possession of the British and discreetly withdrew. On his way back to camp he encountered Towson returning to the field with horses and harness to bring the British guns away and the two artillery officers rode together to Chippawa.[18]

The Left Division's withdrawal was without incident. Leavenworth remembered that "Not a shot was fired from the enemy, and our troops moved in as good order, and with as much regularity *from*, as to the field, and arrived at Chippawa between one and two on the morning of the 26th."[19] As the weary men shuffled across the bridge, they were a far cry from the proud troops who had marched up the Portage Road that afternoon under the "influence of fine martial music."[20] And there were not nearly as many of them. Lieutenant F.A. Sawyer took his company of the Eleventh Infantry into action, fifty strong, but only marched thirteen back. The commander of that regiment at the end of the battle, Lieutenant David Crawford, estimated that his unit had about thirty able-bodied men when it returned to camp. Lieutenant Samuel Brady of the Twenty-Second noted that all that remained of his regiment were himself, Major John Arrosmith and thirty privates. Leavenworth recorded that there were now present less than half of his Ninth Infantry, including men who had remained in camp, still available for service.[21]

Not all those missing from the ranks were casualties or prisoners. First Lieutenant Samuel Tappan of the Twenty-Third Infantry had forty-five in his company when he returned to camp, but of the missing thirty-six men only seventeen were killed or wounded; the remaining nineteen had simply left the ranks for one reason or another during the action. This phenomenon seems to have been widespread throughout the division: when McMullen's company of the Pennsylvania Volunteers paraded in camp before being dismissed, a number of men who had run away during the fighting tried to enter the ranks, but were prevented from doing so by the company commander.[22]

The camp held some surprises for the survivors of the action. In the lines of the Eleventh, Crawford was amazed to find Lieutenant Henry Blake, the senior unwounded officer of the regiment, who had disappeared midway through the action. Blake offered him a meal which he had prepared but Sawyer coldly refused to touch it. McMullen and his comrades were shocked when their company commander, Lieutenant William Patton from Waynesboro, Pennsylvania, berated them for not standing their ground during the battle: "This was too much" for the company, who "believed that we had done all that men could do," and they "broke loose on him with a volley of insulting language."[23] Not at all intimidated, the unfeeling Patton "with a smile told us we were dismissed and might go to the river and get drunk on the water."[24]

After his final attack had failed, Drummond retired to the bottom of the hill about two hundred yards distant from the American line. He remained in this position for some time and then withdrew farther back, putting some distance between his troops and the Americans to prevent surprises. Save for the 89th Foot which was withdrawn north up the Portage Road, the main body of the Right Division moved between a quarter and half-mile up Lundy's Lane, there to spend the night. Like their enemy, the British "remained for some time doubtful whether the contest had yet ended" and the light companies of the 89th and 104th were left in the former British positions as an outpost line.[25] Rumours were rife that the Americans were going to attack and, in the position of the 104th, Lieutenant Colonel William Drummond ordered his men "to draw all the dead horses into a line ... and if attacked to kneel behind them as a breast-work, a capital one it would have proved."[26] When it became known that the Americans had left the area, the British and Canadians began to relax.[27]

Men remembered the night that followed as "chilling cold."[28] Those not on duty slept "on their arms" while those on duty, including Lieutenant John Le Couteur, tried to help the wounded.[29] "Fatigued, weak, cold and wretched" was how the young Jerseyman felt after "36 hours, marching, fasting, and Fighting."[30] "What a dismal night," he later wrote, "there were 300 dead ... and about a hundred of ours – besides several hundred wounded ... groaning and imploring us for water."[31] He found an American officer (probably Captain John Pentland of the Twenty-Second Infantry) shot

Lieutenant John Le Couteur, 104th Regiment of Foot, c. 1812
A 19-year-old light infantry officer, John Le Couteur remembered in later years how his company, part of British reinforcement column, ran in their efforts to get into a battle that they could hear being waged in the dark. As they came close to the firing, Le Couteur said his prayers. (Courtesy, Société Jersiaise, St. Helier, Jersey)

through both legs and got him carried away. Nearby, he saw the corpse of "a magnificent man a Field Officer of the Yankee army," and he found another "old Yankee who I relieved much" who told him "it was a judgement on him for leaving his happy home, wife & Children."

He then came upon twenty-eight-year-old Captain Abraham Hull of the Ninth Infantry lying where he had fallen at the furthermost point of Scott's last, futile charge. Le Couteur gave him some brandy and water and the two young officers talked for a few moments. They discovered that they had much in common besides their youth – both were the sons of generals, Hull's father being the General William Hull who had surrendered Detroit in 1812, while Le Couteur's was the governor of Curaçao. The young American "told me much about himself," remembered Le Couteur, but the British officer could see that Hull was mortally wounded. As Le Couteur had to attend to his duties and as the Indians were starting to "prowl about scalping and plundering," he asked the American to give him his "watch, rings and anything He wished sent to his family." Desperately clinging to life, Hull told Le Couteur to return in the morning "when He would give them to me in charge" and the young Jerseyman left. "A Soldier's life is very horrid sometimes," was his feeling about that night.[32]

Between 4:00 and 5:00 A.M. the sky began to lighten. As the field became revealed, the "scene of the morning was not more pleasant than the night's horrors."[33] Hundreds of men lay sprawled where they had fallen. In places the lines had been so close that Le Couteur noted our "Men's heads and those of the Americans were within a few yards of each other."[34] Another witness remarked that "such ... carnage I never beheld ... as at Lundy's Lane. Red coats, blue & grey were promiscuously intermingled, in many places three deep & around the Hill ... the carcasses of 60 or 70 horses disfigured the ground."[35] For Lieutenant Duncan Clark of the Incorporated Militia, the "sight next morning of mutilated human bodies scattered over the battleground, men and horses nearly cut in two by our rockets together with the groans of the wounded, rendered me more dispirited than even the hottest parts of the engagement."[36] Trampled crops, torn-down fences and buildings "perforated with a thousand bullets" marked the progress of the fighting. True to his promise, Le Couteur looked for Hull only to find him "a beautiful Corpse, stripped stark naked – amongst a host of friends and foes."[37]

Just after sunrise, Drummond formed his troops in three lines north of the hill – the forward one in the open fields, the other two in the woods behind it. There was no sign of the Americans and, to the delight of the British and Canadian soldiers, they discovered all but one of their lost artillery pieces scattered on various parts of the battlefield and two American pieces besides. If British troops had retaken possession of the guns during the previous night, as Hindman believed, they must have abandoned them again. The enemy were nowhere to be seen and Drummond dispatched John Norton with a party of warriors to reconnoitre. Moving south down the Portage Road, Norton found bodies that had fallen from the wagons the night before and picked up a few stragglers, before ascertaining that the Left Division was still in its camp at Chippawa.[38]

Between 7:00 and 8:00 A.M., Drummond moved the division forward to the hill and commenced the job of "cleaning up" the battlefield. The wounded were taken to nearby farmhouses or loaded onto wagons for the long fourteen-mile journey to Fort George. At that place, Surgeon William Dunlop of the 89th Foot was preparing to ride south to join his regiment when he was "told by an officer who had come from the field on the spur" to remain where he was, for "I would have quite enough to do at home without going abroad to look for adventures."[39] Late in the morning, the first wagonloads of wounded began to arrive and by noon the twenty-one-year-old Scotsman found himself in charge of two hundred and twenty British, Canadian and American casualties.[40]

At the same time the grim but necessary task of disposing of the dead began, the warm weather dictating that this be done as soon as possible. British and Canadian corpses were placed in trenches hastily dug in the sandy soil of the hill. Perhaps as a sign of respect for his bravery, perhaps because he was known to at least one British officer, Hull was buried on the hill not far from where he had fallen, but the greater part of the American dead were burned. They were too numerous, remembered Thomas Connolly of the Canadian militia, "and time precious" so "we followed the example of the Romans, made a funeral pile, and set fire to it."[41] Lieutenant Duncan Clark of the Incorporated Militia watched as American corpses "were collected and piled up on the Hill in three heaps of something upwards of 30 lifeless bodies, each with layers of dried oak rails, the torch was applied and the whole reduced to ashes."[42]

As the smoke billowed up from the funeral pyres, the hillside was permeated with the sickly stench of roasting flesh. Working parties carried the wounded to the wagons or dragged corpses to the trenches or pyres. Lampman of the Incorporated Militia was strolling with another officer across the hill when a loaded musket that some fool had thrown on the flames "went off and the bullet struck at [their] feet, showering them with sand."[43] Remarking that "when dead Yankees began to shoot, it was time to retreat," both men quickly withdrew.

There were many such macabre sights on the hill that morning. Sergeant Commins of the 8th and Private Byfield of the 41st watched with horror as an Indian "busy in plundering came to an American that had been severely wounded and not being able to get the man's boots threw him into a fire."[44] A nearby British soldier, "filled with indignation for such barbarity shot the Indian and threw him on the fire to suffer for his unprincipled villainy."[45] In the midst of this "slaughterhouse," as he termed it, Le Couteur and his men enjoyed "a great Camp Kettle of thick chocolate" that "revived us mercifully – though we devoured it among dead bodies in all directions."[46]

All activity suddenly ceased when word came back from the pickets that the Americans were returning. Urged on by their officers and sergeants, the men on the hill dropped shovels, corpses and chocolate, gathered up their arms and equipment and searched for their proper places in the ranks.[47]

The Left Division had spent a restless night. A British attack was a probability and preparations were made to receive it. Douglass positioned his two 18-pdr. guns to cover the bridge over the Chippawa and had "the furniture, equipments, and munitions inspected and arranged, for instant service," while the Twenty-Third Infantry was stationed on the north side of the bridge to guard the approaches to the camp.[48] Anxiety about a possible attack led to most of the British and Canadian officer prisoners, including Riall, being taken across the Niagara to Schlosser for safety. At the same time, their swords, taken from them by their captors, were restored.[49]

When he returned to camp between 1:00 and 2:00 A.M., Ripley was surprised to see that there were, by his calculation, nearly one thousand able-bodied men at Chippawa who had not taken part in the fighting. He wondered why staff officers had not been sent to collect these men and lead them to the field; with such a reinforcement he would not have had to withdraw from his position. Still pondering this question, he reported to Brown, who had had his wounds dressed and was lying on his camp bed. The two officers agreed that the division had gained a victory and that British losses must have been severe. After further discussion, Brown ordered Ripley to re-organize and refresh the division and then, with every available man, to "put himself on the field of battle as day dawned, and there to meet and beat the enemy if he appeared."[50] He "was to be governed by circumstances" but was "at all events to bring off the captured cannon."[51] Ripley made no objection to this order and left for his own tent.[52]

Brown then sent for Hindman. The artillery commander could not be found, but when Towson arrived in his stead, Brown ordered him to prepare the artillery for action. The Marylander harnessed what horses he could find, filled the caissons with ammunition, refreshed his gunners with food and whisky and moved out onto the road to wait for the infantry. By now the "night was fast advanced" and the artillery were no sooner formed then the exhausted men threw themselves on the ground and went to sleep.[53]

The Left Division was not ready to move when daylight arrived. It was "late" when "the drum beat to arms" recalled Second Lieutenant Edward B. Randolph, the divisional inspector-general.[54] Ripley had made few exertions to prepare the division and the available evidence suggests that he issued orders only to his own and not to the other brigades. According to Lieutenant Samuel Tappan of the Twenty-Third, the division was slow forming due to "the death or disability of many of our ablest officers, the extreme fatigue of the troops, and the dispersed and deranged state of the different corps."[55] Angry at what he saw as being yet another example of Ripley's dilatory behaviour, Brown sent a staff officer to the commander of every unit to order "them to be promptly prepared to march."[56] Leavenworth, now commanding the First Brigade, did not receive this order until after 7:00 A.M. and it was nearly two hours later that the three brigades and the artillery, an estimated fifteen to sixteen hundred men, crossed the Chippawa bridge and moved north.[57]

The officers and men who marched out that morning knew the Left Division was in no condition to fight another major engagement. Leavenworth recorded that "every officer with whom I conversed, ... expressed their astonishment" at any attempt to renew the fighting.[58] McMullen, ordered to stay behind to tend the wounded and who "had no wish to go with them as I became satisfied the previous day," watched "with sorrow" as the remnant of his company from Franklin County, Pennsylvania, marched by "with slow and melancholy steps."[59] Ripley was aware of these feelings and his actions that morning demonstrate that he never seriously intended to renew the fighting. As soon as the column had crossed the Chippawa, he ordered Leavenworth to remain with the First Brigade, over a third of his strength, at the old British fieldworks on the north side of the bridge. The other two brigades and the artillery continued as far as the Bridgewater Mills, where Ripley halted and ordered Tappan to take his company of the Twenty-Third and Riddle's company of the Nineteenth "through the woods on our left, advance toward the enemy, and reconnoitre his position, strength and movements."[60]

On learning of the American approach, Drummond had moved part of his force to Willson's and it was this detachment that Tappan saw when he emerged from the woods. He advanced to within musket shot of the British, who "seemed to have no inclination to re-commence the engagement."[61] The New York native reported that the British force outnumbered Ripley by as much as one-third, although this was a considerable exaggeration. In Tappan's opinion it would "have been an act of rashness bordering on insanity, to have attempted an attack."[62] Ripley convened another conference of his senior officers. The majority, including Porter and Towson, were against any attempt to renew the fighting; but when Ripley suggested that perhaps the army should cross over to the United States, Porter, Towson, McRee and Wood were vehemently opposed and it was decided only to withdraw in the direction of Fort Erie. Although they had no military value, Ripley gave orders to burn the Bridgewater Mills and in a few minutes the little community was a mass of flames.[63]

The column slowly marched back to Chippawa while Ripley rode on ahead to report to Brown. He informed him of the decision not to return to Lundy's Lane but apparently not of his intention to move to Fort Erie. Brown was furious and insisted that Ripley take the division back to the battlefield; but when Ripley added that Porter, the other unwounded general officer, also opposed any such movement, Brown capitulated, and with the words "Sir, you will do as you please," dismissed him.[64]

For the next few hours, the Left Division was busy breaking up its camp, destroying the earthworks on the northern bank of the Chippawa and burning the barracks in the village as well as the bridge over the river. They put torches to the buildings of Samuel Street's Pine Grove farm, which the division had used as a landing point for boat traffic to and from Buffalo since 5 July. The wounded officers, including Brown, Scott and Jesup, were placed in boats and rowed upstream to Buffalo. Due to the "feeble and inexperienced" rowers manning it, Scott's boat "narrowly escaped passing over the Falls," but disaster was averted just in time and a "tedious and distressing" voyage up the river commenced.[65] Forty supply wagons were filled with wounded enlisted men, and after the soldiers were allowed to take what they wanted, their loads were dumped into the river. This act gave rise to the later British claim that the American withdrawal was done in fear and haste.[66]

By 3:00 P.M. all was ready and the march for Fort Erie commenced, a march that was "as quiet as if it had passed through friendly territory."[67] McMullen, himself stricken with fever, thought that the suffering of the wounded in the bouncing, jolting, springless wagons was "dreadful and their groans were distressing."[68] Before long, weakened by illness, he had to give up his musket and knapsack and join them in one of these torturing conveyances. The Left Division arrived near Fort Erie at around 11:00 P.M. and made camp as the exhausted men "slept where and how they could."[69]

The British and Canadians remained on the "Blood Stained field" for several hours after the last Americans disappeared from view.[70] They were in no better shape than their opponents – "worn out with fatigue and destitute of ammunition."[71] Le Couteur and others watched with "mortification" the "smoke rising in minute column" from the Bridgewater Mills, but there was nothing that could be done, as they "were not in force sufficient to punish them [the Americans] further."[72] At 3:00 P.M., when he was certain that the enemy had retreated, Drummond sent his light troops and Indians forward to Chippawa and then withdrew the remainder of his exhausted army seven miles north to Queenston.[73]

At this time many of the militia serving with the army were released to return to their homes and farms until they were needed again. Twenty-seven-year-old Rebecca Biggar, sheltering with her young family at the Lundy house, had tended the wounded throughout the battle. Now she took her children back to her own farm before going to the battlefield to search for her husband, William, fighting with the 2nd Lincolns. Unable to find him and distraught that he had been killed or wounded, she returned home with heavy footsteps only to find him there, unharmed, with their children. The battle of Lundy's Lane was over.[74]

Part IV

Aftermath

Cemetery and church at Lundy's Lane, 1860
The cemetery on top of the present-day Drummond Hill was the scene of the heaviest
fighting during the battle. This drawing, done in 1860, shows the cemetery and the post-
battle church which was erected on the site. (From Benson Lossing, *Pictorial Field Book of
the War of 1812*, New York, 1869)

CHAPTER 12

The Cost and the Accounting

*There is hardly on the face of the earth a less enviable situation than that of
an Army Surgeon after a battle – worn out and fatigued in body and mind,
surrounded by suffering, pain and misery, much of which he knows it is not in
his power to heal or even to assuage. While battle lasts these all pass unnoticed,
but they come before the medical man afterwards in all their sorrow and horror,
stripped of all the excitement of the "heady fight."*

SURGEON WILLIAM DUNLOP, 89TH FOOT

For many years after it ended, there was confusion over the name of the action fought on 25 July 1814 along a pretty country lane near the falls of Niagara. British documents termed it the battle of Niagara while, in the United States, it was called either the battle of the Falls, or the Cataract or, sometimes, the battle of Bridgewater after the little hamlet that Ripley burned to the ground on 26 July. In Canada it has always been the battle of Lundy's Lane and it is now universally known by that homely title with its pleasing alliteration.

There was nothing pleasant about the pain and loss that resulted from the fighting. Drummond compiled his casualty return on 26 July and appended it as part of a District General Order dated at the "Falls of Niagara" on 26 July 1814. According to this return, the Right Division lost 84 officers and men killed, 559 wounded, 193 missing and 42 taken prisoner – a total of 878 casualties or approximately one quarter of the British force engaged. A second and later return dated 5 August, which accompanied Prevost's report on the battle to his superiors in London, gives the same totals but provides a breakdown by unit. Not surprisingly, the regular infantry, who had born the brunt of the fighting, paid the highest price – the 1st, 8th and 89th Foot together lost 510 officers and men killed, wounded, prisoners and missing, nearly 60 per cent of the total British casualties. The 89th was particularly hard hit, losing 253 all ranks from 425 and 13 of its 18 officers. Of the Canadian units, the Incorporated Militia suffered most, losing 142 of a total strength of 402 all ranks. In contrast the Glengarry Light Infantry got off lightly with only 56 casualties while the 1st Militia Brigade had only 22 casualties and the 2nd Brigade none.[1]

Drummond's total of 878 British and Canadian casualties has generally been accepted, but there is some evidence that this figure may not be entirely accurate. There exists a separate casualty return for the Canadian militia units, apparently compiled somewhat later than the two British returns, and it provides some interesting information. The British returns of 26 July and 5 August state that the Incorporated Militia suffered a total of 142 casualties, but this later return lists only 97 men lost. The earlier returns report 75 men of the battalion as being missing; the later return lists only 3 officers and 33 men. As the Incorporated Militia broke formation during the action, many of those described as "missing" in the earlier lists either returned to the ranks or were among the killed and wounded. This interpretation is borne out by the figures for those types of losses – the official return states that 1 officer and 6 men of the Incorporated Militia were killed and 8 officers and 36 men wounded; the corresponding figures in the later return are 1 officer and 16 men killed and 8 officers and 36 men wounded.[2] The higher number of dead in the later return no doubt reflects the fact that some of those described as wounded in the earlier returns later died.

If the discrepancies in the figures for the Incorporated Militia are an indication of the accuracy of Drummond's casualty figures, it is probable that more British and Canadians died as a result of the battle than was officially stated but about the same number were wounded.

The official British return records 193 men missing and 42 known to have been taken prisoner, a total of 235. This return, however, was compiled only a few hours after the battle ended and it is possible that many of those listed as prisoners or missing later rejoined the ranks. The American figures for British prisoners taken at the battle list 19 officers and 150 other ranks. If these figures are accurate, than the actual number of British missing was 55, most of whom were actually killed or wounded. Taking all these factors in consideration, Drummond's loss on 25 July 1814 was probably less than was stated in the official return but still in the neighbourhood of 800 men.[3]

The American casualty return was not compiled until five days after the battle. Brown reported a total of 860 casualties: 173 dead, 571 wounded and 117 missing. Many British and Canadian historians have questioned these figures in the belief that Brown tried to cover up his actual losses.[4] There is a striking disparity between the figure of 173 American soldiers killed compared to the 84 British and Canadians killed at Lundy's Lane. This discrepancy can be explained by a number of factors: the British made more effective use of their artillery during the early part of the battle when visibility was greater; the British musket ball, larger and heavier than its American counterpart, inflicted more mortal wounds; and, finally, the later date of the American return meant that many of those listed as killed may have been wounded during the action and later died. Of the 117 men listed as missing in the American return, most were prisoners of war; British records state that 4 officers and 75 American other ranks captured at Lundy's Lane were imprisoned at Quebec in the autumn of 1814. The remainder of the missing were probably the wounded or dead left on the field after Ripley withdrew.[5]

As might be expected, over half the Left Division's casualties were suffered by Scott's First Brigade: 109 killed, 350 wounded and 57 missing, a total of 416 from the brigade's engaged strength of between 1100 and 1200. With 116 casualties, the Twenty-Fifth Infantry got off lightly compared to the three regiments that had born the brunt of the British artillery fire. Ripley's Second Brigade suffered less, losing a total of 228 casualties, nearly half of them (104 men) from Miller's Twenty-First Infantry. The lethality of the British artillery fire can be demonstrated by comparing the casualties of the Twenty-First, not exposed to its full effect, with those of the Twenty-Second which suffered heavily from it. Of Miller's 104 casualties, only 16 men, or 15 per cent, were killed; of the Twenty-Second's 143 casualties, 37 or 26 per cent were killed. Porter's Volunteers suffered the least, taking only 67 casualties, but this was still 22 per cent of the strength that Porter brought on the field. The staff, light dragoons and artillery lost a total of 46 men.[6]

The cold statistics are bad enough – the reality was infinitely worse. Only the most primitive arrangements existed for the removal of the wounded – there were no ambulances; common supply wagons served instead. The wounded American enlisted personnel had to suffer the agonies of a nearly twenty-mile ride in unsprung and uncovered vehicles to Fort Erie, while the British wounded faced a similar tortuous journey to Fort George. Some were fortunate enough to receive quick medical treatment. Lieutenant Henry Ruttan of the Incorporated Militia, hit during the first major British counterattack, "remembered nothing more until after 2 O'Clock next morning, when I found myself lying on my back on the floor of a room ... being examined by a Surgeon who pronounced me 'done for'."[7] Ruttan survived but others were less fortunate – Sergeant Dean Weymouth of the Twenty-First Infantry lay on the field all night and did not reach a hospital until after 6 P.M. on 26 July.[8]

Most of the Left Division's wounded ended up at Williamsville, near Buffalo, where a tented general hospital had been established.[9] The wounded collected by the British were taken to Fort George and placed in the charge of Surgeon William Dunlop of the 89th Foot. When Dunlop inquired where he was to put them, he was "shown a ruinous fabric, built of logs" known as Butler's Barracks and erected as a temporary structure some thirty years before. "Nothing could be worse constructed for a military hospital," remembered Dunlop. The small buildings were so crowded that the wounded "had to be laid on straw on the floor ..." and "their comrades ... put into berths one above another ... where it was impossible to get around to dress their wounds, and their removal gave them excruciating pain."[10] As circumstances permitted, the wounded were sent on to York, where they soon filled the army hospital in the garrison and overflowed into adjacent buildings.

Conditions in these hospitals were appalling. Lacking any form of anaesthesia, medical personnel could do little to lessen the misery and had to

Surgeon William Dunlop, 89th Foot (1792-1848) Nicknamed "Tiger," Surgeon Dunlop found himself in charge of more than 200 badly wounded men after the battle and toiled without rest for three days and nights to alleviate their terrible suffering. Witty, irreverent and fun-loving, Dunlop preferred fighting to doctoring and left one of the most readable memoirs of the War of 1812. (Courtesy, Archives of Ontario, Toronto, S.17142)

leave the wounded in pain until they lapsed into unconsciousness or died. In 1814 military hospitals after a major battle resembled nothing so much as noisy charnel-houses and an American surgeon has left a graphic description of the sights and sounds in such a place where,

> ... nothing but the Groans, of the wounded & agonies of the Dying are to be heard. The Surgeons, wading in blood, cutting of[f] arms, legs & trepanning heads to rescue their fellow creatures from untimely deaths – to hear the poor creatures, crying – Oh, Dear! Oh Dear! Oh My God! my God! Do, Doctor, Doctor! Do cut of[f] my leg! my arm! my head! to relieve me from misery! I cant live! I cant live! – would have rent the heart of Steel & shocked the insensibility of the most harden'd assassin & the cruelest savage.[11]

To alleviate such suffering, medical personnel laboured without cease. The American Surgeon William Horner, responsible for one hundred and seventy-three wounded at Williamsville, operated until his fingers were so sore that he was "constantly liable to let articles fall, from the sudden twinges of agony in touching them."[12] Dunlop "never underwent such fatigue" as he did during the first week after the battle. With over two hundred patients to care for and only a sergeant to assist him, he had not finished his rounds before he had to begin again. He toiled without rest for two days but,

> On the morning of the third day, however, I fell asleep on my feet, with my arm embracing the post of one of the berths. It was ... impossible to awaken me, so a truss of clean straw was laid on the floor, on which I was deposited ... and there I slept soundly for five hours without ever turning.[13]

Most of the wounds were caused by projectiles, either musket balls or artillery rounds. While there is no evidence available on the nature of the wounds treated by British surgeons, there is a descriptive list of the wounds suffered by forty-six American officers which permits some analysis of the effectiveness of period weaponry. Eleven of these men suffered multiple wounds; one, Thomas Jesup, received four, two others suffered three and eight men had two. Of the sixty-one wounds for which some detail is given in this list, only one injury was caused by an edged weapon – a bayonet wound in the thigh suffered by Lieutenant Barony Vasques of the First Infantry. Of the remaining sixty, thirty-seven are described as being caused by "shot," whether musket or artillery is not specified; four are described as caused by canister shot while the remaining nineteen were caused by "contusion" (probably the result of spent shot) or are unspecified. The vast majority of the wounds, seventy-five per cent, were inflicted in the torso and legs.[14]

Surgeon Horner thought that, of the projectile wounds, the most difficult to treat were those caused by the jagged fragments of howitzer and shrapnel shells which created severe damage to the area surrounding their entry point. Canister bullets also caused massive injury, but such was their velocity that they often passed clean through the body. In contrast, the smaller, slower-moving musket balls were deflected if they struck bone, cartilage or muscle and caused great internal damage. But if they did not penetrate major body cavities or break bones, the wounds they caused often healed well. Horner and other American surgeons noted that the British musket ball "tears and shatters more severely" and was more likely to break bones.[15] Many of the British wounded had been hit by buckshot, which was extensively used by the American army, either in a cartridge with twelve pellets or in one that combined three pellets with a ball, the so-called "buck and ball" round. Although these wounds were "annoying and perhaps disabled for a time a greater number of men," they were "less destructive" than those caused by the standard ball.[16]

To treat such wounds, military surgeons possessed only their professional knowledge and a basic surgical kit containing amputating saws, knives, scalpels, forceps, probes, tourniquets and some specialized instruments. Medical care was rudimentary. For abdominal wounds, there was no treatment in 1814 as, without anaesthesia to relax the body, major internal surgery was impossible. Such wounds were stitched and plastered and the recipient left, while the surgeon devoted himself to those whom he had a better chance of saving. Neither were head wounds extensively touched beyond trepanning to remove fluid pressure on the brain. To probe for embedded musket balls or shell fragments, the surgeon used either his fingers or a special forceps with flattened, rounded jaws. If possible, extraction of a ball or fragment was performed with the wounded man standing in the same position as when he was hit – it was thought to make the operation easier. Simple fractures were set with splints, but compound fractures and indeed any complicated wound of the limbs often resulted in an operation at which field surgeons excelled – amputation.[17]

Surgeon's amputation kit, War of 1812 period
Amputation was the quickest and most effective way to convert complicated wounds of the limbs into relatively simple injuries that were easier to treat. Military surgeons of the Napoleonic period were well practised in this operation and, with the help of trained assistants, could have a man's leg off above the knee in about ten minutes. (Courtesy, Parks Canada)

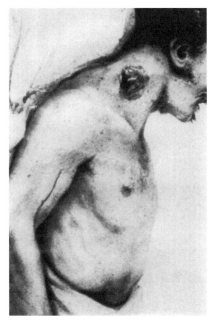

Canister wound
Canister shells were filled with large lead bullets which were sprayed from the muzzles of period artillery when the shell was fired. The result is shown in this 1815 drawing. (Drawing by Surgeon Bell, courtesy Parks Canada)

Wound caused by round shot.
A sketch by Surgeon Bell in 1815 shows a traumatic amputation of this soldier's right arm by round shot. Such a wound, located near the shoulder joint, was extremely difficult to treat with period medical practice and the prognosis for this casualty was not good. (Drawing by Surgeon Bell, courtesy Parks Canada)

Amputation solved the problem of too many wounded and not enough time to properly care for them. It was a fairly simple procedure that converted a troublesome wound into one easily treated. It was also relatively quick – an important consideration in a time before the widespread introduction of anaesthesia. Period medical opinion generally agreed on the primacy of amputation as the best method of treating serious limb wounds although there was beginning to be some dissent. Most military surgeons followed the dictates of Baron Larrey, surgeon general of the French Army, who urged that amputation be performed as soon as possible. If the operation was delayed, he and other medical professionals argued, the wounded man would be further weakened by the primitive transport or would run the risk of contracting diseases in overcrowded hospitals. Others were not so sure. Surgeon General James Tilton of the U.S. army later observed that during the war he performed fewer amputations, either because of the obstinacy of a patient or other reasons, and noted that "limbs might be saved, which the best authorities directed to be cut off."[18]

Horner and Dunlop believed in amputation for a basic reason – it was their most effective treatment and they simply lacked the time for more lengthy or complicated procedures. As Dunlop remarked, "many a poor fellow had to submit to amputation whose limb might have been preserved had there been only time to take reasonable care of it."[19]

Once the operation was decided upon, it was quickly carried out. If there were no undue complications, a good military surgeon with a trained assistant could have a soldier's leg off above the knee in less than ten minutes. Speed was essential because the medical regulations of neither army made any provision for the use of anaesthesia during amputation, although many surgeons tried to provide their patients with at least some alcohol. Surgeon John Hennen, a veteran of the Peninsular campaign, always carried a canteen of wine because he felt that many men died "for want of a timely cordial before, during, and after operations ... [which were] rendered much more favorable in their results, by the administration of a single glass of wine."[20] If alcohol did not have the desired effect, the wounded man was either held or strapped down and given a block of wood, a leather belt or a musket ball to bite while the surgeon performed his business – hence the origin of the expression "to bite the bullet."[21]

This procedure may seem barbaric to the modern reader but it was not regarded so in a time when men expected to experience pain in the course of their lives and they often bore it without complaint. In addition, the soldier's personal code was to endure such pain as stoically as possible. Horner noted that the wounded he treated were "much disposed to repress the expression of pain considering it unmanly" but felt that "this natural mode of easing the circulation of the lungs by groans and expiration was withheld, which can only be done by holding the breath ...... it was highly disadvantageous to the individual."[22] Some men took stoicism to extreme lengths. Horner recorded amputating the leg of a soldier "who was smoking tranquilly during the whole operation, his ease not seeming to be an exaggeration."[23] Although he may have been cool only in retrospect, Private Shadrach Byfield, who had his arm removed in August 1814, was almost nonchalant about the experience:

> ... our doctor informed me that my arm must be taken off, as mortification had taken place. ...... They prepared to bind me, and had men to hold me; but I told them there was no need of that. The operation was tedious and painful, but I was enabled to bear it pretty well. I had it dressed and went to bed. They brought me some mulled wine, and I drank it ..... The stump of my arm soon healed, and three days after I was able to play a game of fives, for a quart of rum.[24]

Unfortunately, for those who survived such operations, worse horrors often lay ahead. The medical profession in 1814 possessed no concept of antisepsis; surgeons did not wash their hands or instruments from one operation to the next. Another problem in the military hospitals at Williamsville, Fort George and York was the hot, humid weather, which brought flies "in myriads" that "lighting on the wounds, deposited their eggs, so that maggots were bred in a few hours, producing dreadful irritation."[25] In contrast to medical experience in Europe, however, there was mercifully little trace of gangrene or tetanus in North America, although the surgeons were not sure why this was so. There are no reliable mortality statistics available for Lundy's Lane but British Surgeon George Guthrie, who served in Spain during this period, recorded that in 1813, forty-eight per cent of the men who underwent amputation later died. The rate for the wounded from Lundy's Lane could only have been marginally lower.[26]

Officers had a much better chance of survival. Of the forty-one officers listed as wounded in the British casualty return, only one, Ensign John McDonnel of the Incorporated Militia, is known to have later died from his wounds. Similarly of the fifty-five American officers listed as wounded, only

Captain Ambrose Spencer, Brown's aide, and Second Lieutenant John Armstrong of the Twenty-Second Infantry are recorded as having died from their wounds. The reason for the officers' better survival rate is simple – they received better treatment. American officers were spared the harrowing wagon journey to Fort Erie, being taken instead by boat, a gentler means of transport, to Buffalo. Here they were nursed in private homes, unlike the wounded soldiers who were placed in tents at Williamsville. Scott convalesced at the home of a friend in Batavia, where he was attended by a single surgeon who, at Scott's insistence and for the "honour of the army," also treated Riall and another captured British officer staying in the same house. His shoulder wound continuing to trouble him, Scott hired a litter and eight bearers and was "taken in triumph" to the home of another friend in Geneva, N.Y., where he remained some time before travelling slowly and in stages to Philadelphia to consult Dr. Philip Physick, one of the most eminent medical professionals in the United States.[27]

Brown recovered at the home of a friend near Buffalo where he was attended by a personal surgeon and nursed by his wife. Two weeks after the battle he was able to walk and he expected to resume command of the division in another two weeks. Drummond had the ball cut out of his neck at Queenston on 27 July and wrote his wife that he suffered more from a head cold he had contracted than from the wound, although he may have downplaying the seriousness of the injury to spare her undue concern. While recuperating, the two generals corresponded on the subject of exchanging their personal aides, Spencer and Loring, who had both been taken prisoner. The proposed trade fell through when Spencer died from his wounds.[28]

What saved many of the wounded, officers and enlisted men alike, was the presence of female relatives and friends who came to the hospitals to nurse them. With his keen eye for clinical detail, Horner noted that, under such care, "recoveries took place which would scarcely have followed in the ordinary hospital practice."[29] The presence of civilians in the hospitals led to scenes of both rejoicing and sorrow. On learning that her husband had been wounded, the young wife of Major Titus G. Simons of the Canadian militia picked up her baby and rode from their home in Flamboro, near Burlington Bay, to care for him. She was fortunate enough to find him on the road and he made a fairly quick recovery, although he lost the use of his right arm.[30] Surgeon Dunlop witnessed a sad scene in his hospital after another wife came to nurse her husband, an American prisoner who "was ly-

ing on a truss of straw, writhing in agony, for his sufferings were most dreadful." As he watched, the woman took the man's head in her lap and sobbed
until,

> ... awakened by a groan from her unfortunate husband, she clasped her
> hands, and looking wildly around, exclaimed, "O that the King and
> President were both here this moment to see the misery their quarrels
> lead to – they surely would never go to war without cause that they
> could give as a reason to God at the last day, for thus destroying the
> creatures that He hath made in his own image."[31]

The man died shortly afterward.

The lot of those captured was much happier, as both nations treated their
prisoners with scrupulous respect. The British and Canadian officer prisoners were taken first to Buffalo and later to Pittsfield, Massachusetts, and its
neighbouring villages, where they spent the next six months as gentlemen
of leisure, riding, reading, drinking, playing cards, writing letters, fishing,
attending social events and holding a few of their own to which they invited the local beauties. Partially recovered from his wound, Riall arrived at
Pittsfield in October and charmed his captors with his courteous manners.
Having given his own sword to Jesup "as a small testament of his regard,"
Riall offered to have the sword of Ritchie, the American artillery captain
killed at the battle, returned to his family.[32] The British general was generous in his praise of the fighting qualities of the American soldier, which by
now he had good reason to respect. Riall was not a prisoner for long; he was
exchanged in November, 1814 and sailed for England. The Americans captured at the battle were, officers and men, confined at Quebec until November when most of them were transferred to Halifax. All prisoners were
released in March 1815 when hostilities ceased.[33]

While recovering from their wounds, the commanders of both armies wrote
their official reports of the battle and both claimed a victory. Drummond
dated his the 27th of July at "Upper Canada near Niagara Falls," revealing a
somewhat tenuous sense of geography as in actual fact he was that day at
Queenston, seven miles to the north.[34] Here he remained for three days.
The reason for his inactivity may have been his state of health – the British
general could not ride because he was confined to his bed by both his wound
and his cold.[35]

The single most important piece of evidence for the British and Canadian side of the battle, Drummond's official report has been accepted almost without question by the historians of those countries. Unfortunately his account of the action is incomplete, confused and in some places a little short of the truth. Beginning with his landing at the river mouth on the morning of 25 July, Drummond provides a concise and accurate account of the movements of the Right Division toward Lundy's Lane. Upon arriving on the field, he states that he "found it almost in the occupation of the Enemy, whose Columns were within 600 yards of the top of the hill, and the surrounding woods filled with his Light Troops." He does not add that the American troops, Scott's brigade, did not advance much further during the first part of the action. After this factual beginning, however, the report degenerates into a catalogue of disconnected events described out of sequence. Drummond does not admit withdrawing from the hill but writes only that in "the Centre, the repeated and determined Attacks of the Enemy were met ... with the most perfect steadiness and intrepid gallantry, and the Enemy was constantly repulsed with very heavy loss." No mention is made of the unsuccessful British counterattacks; according to Drummond, "the Enemy's efforts to carry the Hill were continued until about midnight when ... he gave up the contest and retreated with great precipitation to his Camp." The British commander estimates the American strength as being about five thousand; his own force he states as about twenty-eight hundred "of all description" – actually a fairly accurate number for the regular infantry engaged but excluding the artillery, cavalry, militia and Indians.

When describing events after the battle, Drummond takes some liberty with the facts. He makes no mention of Ripley's advance on 26 July but instead states that the enemy "abandoned his Camp, threw the greatest part of his Baggage, Camp Equipage and Provisions into the rapids, and ... continued his retreat in great disorder, towards Fort Erie." Drummond reports that he detached his "Light Troop[s], Cavalry and Indians ... in pursuit and to harass [the enemy's] retreat, which I doubt not he will continue until he reaches his own Shores." In fact, Drummond's light troops, after advancing on Chippawa on 26 July, moved back with the rest of the Right Division to Queenston on 26 July and did not push south until late in the evening of the next day and only crossed the Chippawa on the morning of the 28th. On 3 August, *nine days after the battle*, they were still out of musket range of Fort Erie.[36]

Unable to disguise the fact that the Americans captured one of his guns,

Drummond resorts to prevarication. "Our Troops having for a moment been pushed back, some of our Guns *for a few minutes* remained in the Enemy's hands" but were "quickly recovered."[37] This is possibly a reference to Glew's temporary recapture of some of the British artillery but Drummond does not report that at the end of the action his guns were in American hands. Nor does he report that they were in those hands for more than three hours and in the possession of neither army for four or five hours after that. Drummond claims the capture of two American pieces, but to account for the loss of his own gun he stoops to a rather cumbersome fiction:

> ... in limbering up our Guns at one period, one of the Enemy's Six Pounders was put, by mistake upon a limber of ours, and one of our six [pounder guns] limbered on one of his, by which means the pieces were exchanged, and thus, though we captured two of his Guns, yet, as he obtained one of ours, we have gained only *one* Gun.[38]

To accept this statement, one would have to believe that, even allowing for darkness, smoke and tension, trained Royal Artillerymen would have confused an American iron 6-pdr. gun with a British brass 6-pdr. gun. The gunners would also have had to overlook other major differences between the artillery equipments of the two nations including different carriages and limbers, different methods of attaching the carriages to their limbers and differences in the sizes of the wheels and the placement of ammunition chests on both carriages and limbers. American and British artillery equipment was so dissimilar that a gunner could differentiate between them at a glance. It was possible, although very difficult, for an American carriage to be attached to a British limber but those attempting such a connection would have been only too aware that the two pieces of equipment were not designed to be connected together.[39]

For his part, Brown did not finish his report until 7 August. During the interval between the action and that date there was considerable scratching of pen on paper by the senior officers of the division. On 29 July Brown's aide, Austin, wrote a brief note to Armstrong informing him that the division had fallen back on Chippawa and the British, unmolested by Chauncey's fleet, were able to concentrate their forces and bring "against us a superior force" which was defeated.[40] The brigade commanders, with the exception of Scott, obeyed an order to report on the performance of their troops during the battle, as did Hindman and Harris for their commands.

Porter also made a separate report to New York Governor Daniel D. Tompkins, stating that the "victory was complete, but, alas, this victory gained by exhibitions of bravery never surpassed in this country, was converted into a defeat by a precipitate retreat"[41] Gardner wrote to Parker informing him that the division had gained a glorious victory "if the glory of an action is commensurate with it being bloody."[42] He felt constrained to complain about Brown, who, although he "has the esteem of us all," did not know how to command an army, otherwise "we should not have wasted our forces by detachment when no advantages could be gained nor have fought by accident when we might have had a planned attack."[43] Gardner excused himself because of sickness, otherwise he would "perhaps have had the other troops in a better situation to support" Scott.[44] Thus, even before their commander had his say, there was considerable jockeying for position among the senior officers of the Left Division.[45]

In contrast with Drummond's effort, Brown's report, dated 7 August 1814 at Buffalo, was a clear, concise and literate document. He began by describing how, on learning that Chauncey's fleet would not be co-operating with him, he withdrew to Chippawa on the 24th to draw supplies from Schlosser, directly across the river, and to disguise his intention of marching on Burlington. He recounts the events leading up to his decision to put Scott in motion but his description of the early part of the battle is vague. He states that Scott's brigade "skilfully and gallantly maintained the conflict" but does not mention that they were decimated. Understandably his narrative becomes more coherent after his arrival on the battlefield. The preparation for the attack on the hill, the attack itself and the repulse of the British counterattacks are described in correct sequence but no report is made of the loss of two pieces of artillery. Brown expresses his "mortification" at the behaviour of Nicholas's First Infantry and notes that the Twenty-Third also faltered during the action. He singles out Scott, Porter, Miller and Jesup for special praise but Ripley is barely mentioned until near the end of the report when Brown states that he ordered him to return to the field at sunrise – an order, adds Brown, that "was not executed." He then adds a damning indictment of the commander of the Second Brigade: "I feel most sensibly how inadequate are my powers in speaking of the troops to do justice either to their merits or to my own sense of them – under able direction, they might have done more or better."[46]

When this report was published in the newspapers, Ripley's friends and family were appalled – his wife threatened to "spit fire in Brown's face and sink him to the bottomless pit with a grin."[47] A trained lawyer, Ripley immediately began to collect affidavits concerning his performance from officers who were present and continued this process for the next eight months. An attempt to enlist Scott's aid was rebuffed but Ripley did complain to Armstrong about the statements in Brown's report. When Armstrong relayed these complaints to Brown, Brown was firm. "If Ripley demands a Court of Enquiry upon his conduct," he told the secretary, "he will be removed [from the service]." He added that he had been "greatly embarrassed" by his subordinate "on more than one occasion" and "He is one of the few men in whom I have been disappointed."[48] Brown then began to draw up charges to be preferred against Ripley.[49]

Ripley was not the only officer dissatisfied with the official report. Nicholas of the First Infantry and Brooke of the Twenty-Third resented Brown's slights on their units. Feeling was so high in the ranks of the First that Captain John Symmes of that regiment was forced to give "a pacifying harangue" to his company.[50] Even Miller, who had been praised, thought that Brown had done "a great injustice" to Ripley "who had acted agreeably to his orders."[51] As for Brown, Miller did not consider him "entitled to the least credit as a General for his conduct in any one action which has been fought here since we have been in Canada for they have been brought on and fought without any arrangements on his part of consequence."

Some of the worst malcontents were in the First Brigade. As Scott never submitted an official report on the conduct of his troops at Lundy's Lane, Brown limited his description of the actions of the First Brigade to what had passed before his own eyes. He gave prominent mention to Scott and Jesup but ignored Leavenworth, Brady and McNeil, who complained. Scott acidly commented that "it requires as much ability to report a successful action, as to fight one" but Brown "has not afforded sufficient evidence to the Army, that he is competent to either task."[52] There was also a considerable degree of bad feeling in the First Brigade against Scott, who some considered should have been cashiered for proving "himself utterly regardless of human life and willing to make any sacrifice for his own personal renown."[53] Nonetheless, the neglected regimental commanders pinned their hopes on Scott submitting a report that would rectify Brown's omissions. They were disappointed and their anger gradually became directed against Winfield Scott himself, who seemed to want "to deprive his companions of their justly acquired fame, and ... take it all to himself."[54]

Despite the confident claims of the two opposing generals, the outcome of the battle was not clear to many of the men who had fought in it. Lieutenant Edward B. Randolph of the Left Division staff thought that, though both armies "claimed the victory ... it was one that neither army could much boast on" though they "deserved the credit of fighting to the death."[55] Drummer Jarvis Hanks agreed, commenting that the action "has often been called a 'drawn game' as it was difficult to decide which [side], inflicted or received the greatest amount of injury."[56] In the opinion of Colonel Hercules Scott of the 103rd Foot, neither army could boast of a "Great Victory" as "it was nearly equal on both sides."[57]

Others were more confident. Lieutenant Daniel Clark of the Incorporated Militia thought the British victory "complete."[58] Captain John Weeks of the Eleventh Infantry, on the other hand, termed the American victory "glorious and complete."[59] Whatever their opinions on the outcome, almost all the participants testified to the ferocity of the fighting and the heavy casualties; the theme that Lundy's Lane was the bloodiest battle ever fought appears constantly in their comments. Lieutenant Henry Blake, who had not played a very notable part in the action, wrote that the fighting was "such a Scene I hope may never again be witnessed by *human* beings – Thank God I have survived it."[60]

Perhaps the best assessment of Lundy's Lane and one that applies equally to the men of both armies, was Brown's statement that "the battle of the 25th, it is believed, will find but few parallels. More desperate fighting has rarely been known. I hope the nation will be satisfied by our conduct – we have endeavoured to do our duty."[61]

CHAPTER 13

The Siege of Fort Erie and
the Close of the Campaign

*If you are pursuing a retreating enemy, let him get a few days march
a-head, to shew him that you have no doubt of being able to overtake him,
when you set about it: and who knows but this proceeding may encourage
him to stop? After he has retired to a place of security, you may then go
in quest of him with your whole army.*
"Advice to General Officers, Commanding in Chief" in
[Francis Grose], *Advice to the Officers of the British Army,* 1783

Duing the four days that followed the battle, Drummond remained at
Queenston and did not pursue the Americans. His lack of energy may have
been due to his health as he was suffering both from his wound and a bad
head cold that confined him to his bed. The wound appears to have been
more serious than Drummond acknowledged and he was to complain of its
effects for the remainder of the campaign. The British general also had
other worries – "Jonathan Chauncey" had finally emerged from his lair and
Yeo disappeared from Lake Ontario. American warships were now off the
mouth of the Niagara, interdicting his waterborne line of communications
and increasing his supply difficulties. Concerned about the safety of the three
forts, he reinforced their garrisons and then turned to his main objective: "the
defeat and expulsion of the Enemy's force which has taken post at Fort Erie."[1]

But he did not push very hard toward this objective. The Right Division
remained out of contact with the Americans for more than a week after the
battle. Norton and his Indian scouts, for example, did not leave Queenston
until 27 July and advanced only as far as Bridgewater where they camped
overnight before crossing the Chippawa the following morning. As Ripley
had burned the bridge, Norton floated his warriors across on rafts while an

accompanying detachment of the 19th Light Dragoons swam their horses over.[2]

Moving cautiously down the Portage Road on 28 July, Norton encountered two American officers under a flag of truce with letters from Brown to Drummond. He detained them until the dragoons, who were making a reconnaissance of Fort Erie, had returned from this mission. His task accomplished, Norton withdrew north a few miles and there remained until he was joined by Drummond and the remainder of the division which left Queenston on 30 July. By 2 August, they had reached Palmer's House, six miles north of Fort Erie.[3]

Drummond's desultory pursuit granted the Left Division seven days of much-needed grace. It was in poor case, mustering only 2125 men fit for duty on 31 July and the recent fighting had created a desperate shortage of officers. Miller, now commanding the Second Brigade, was the only unwounded colonel left and there was only one lieutenant-colonel on duty. Convinced that the division could no longer undertake heavy fighting, Ripley wanted to withdraw to the United States but the other senior officers were firmly opposed to such a move. An anxious Ripley visited Brown at Buffalo on 27 July and asked permission to cross over from Canada. Losing his temper, Brown treated Ripley "with justifiable indignation and scorn" and ordered him to stay put at Fort Erie. At Ripley's request, he put this order in writing and followed it with another telling Ripley that he must not contemplate surrender, and if the enemy attacked, "I expect you to ruin him."[4] Ripley returned to the west bank of the river and on 28 July the Left Division began to entrench at Fort Erie.[5]

Although he was incapable of active command, Brown spent much of his convalescence trying to get reinforcements. He sent all the troops he could find across to Fort Erie, retaining only Major Lodowick Morgan's battalion of the First Rifle Regiment, which had just arrived from Sackets Harbor, to protect the batteries at Black Rock that dominated the approaches to Fort Erie. The most promising source of troops was the New York militia and, informing Governor Tompkins that he was "resolved not to order my army out of Canada under existing circumstances without further instruction from the War Department," he appealed to the governor to call out militia to reinforce him.[6] When Tompkins agreed to this request, Brown worked with politicians and officials in an effort to raise men.[7]

He also found time to answer the acrimonious statements of Chauncey, who, stung by the taunts contained in Brown's dispatches, some of which had been published in the papers, had complained directly to Armstrong. The commodore insisted he had "never been under any pledge to meet General Brown" but had "told him distinctly that I should not visit the head of the lake unless the enemy's fleet did," which was no less than the truth.[8] Writing to Brown, Chauncey accused him of courting the public "in case of disaster to your army" and reminded the general that, although he might think the fleet "somewhat of a convenience" to transport supplies, it really had a "higher destiny ... to seek and to fight the enemy's fleet."[9] In reply, Brown acknowledged that Chauncey's complaints would be justified if the fleet was the commodore's private property but as "it was the property of the nation" and "as the Government led me to believe" that Chauncey would "co-operate with my division ... by the first week of July," Brown deemed it "but proper to let the nation know that the support I had the right to expect was not afforded."[10]

While it is true that Chauncey had never promised to appear at a certain date and that, once on the lake, his main object had to be the defeat of the British fleet, it is also true that Chauncey, prostrate by illness, refused to let a subordinate take the squadron out after it was ready to sail. Although Brown and, to a lesser extent, Armstrong, had to bear the responsibility for invading Canada before the fleet could render support, Chauncey's behaviour in the matter was not beyond reproach. His procrastination had prevented Brown from exploiting his victory at Chippawa and had left him unsupported on the Canadian side of the river for nearly three weeks. Brown's aggressiveness, Chauncey's caution and the lack of clear communication between the two was a combination fatal to American aspirations in 1814.[11]

Armstrong himself was undecided about the Left Division's future. He was worried about the arrival of strong British reinforcements from Europe and contemplated shifting operational emphasis east to take advantage of Chauncey's newly-acquired superiority on Lake Ontario. He was receptive, therefore, when Major General George Izard, commanding the American Right Division at Plattsburgh, expressed his "unease" about the situation in the Niagara and suggested that, should "any accident occur in that quarter, ought I not move to the St. Lawrence, and threaten the rear of Kingston?"[12] On 2 August Armstrong directed Izard to head for Sackets Harbor and co-operate with Chauncey in an attack on the secretary's favourite objective, Kingston. If such an attack was not possible, he informed Brown, then Izard was to sail for Burlington Bay, where he "will effect a junction with your division when the whole force [both divisions] will be employed in beating Drummond & reducing Forts George & Niagara."[13] Brown agreed that this plan offered "the best chance of assailing the enemy with success."[14]

All this, of course, was unknown to Drummond. What he did know was that he lacked the resources in men, materiel and supplies for a prolonged siege of Fort Erie. He therefore decided to make a move against the American supply depots at Black Rock and Buffalo. If the Americans lost their supplies, he reasoned, their position at Fort Erie would be untenable and they would either have to withdraw to the United States, surrender, or come out and fight a pitched battle.

Drummond ordered Lieutenant Colonel John Tucker of the 41st Foot to carry out this raid with a force of five hundred and eighty men. Tucker's primary objective was Buffalo and Drummond cautioned him to move during the night so as to be in position to attack that place at dawn. On 2 August at 11:00 P.M., Tucker embarked his men, who were "in expectation of making lots of prize money, *plunder*, etc.," in boats and crossed the river without incident.[15] Tucker, whose army nickname was "Brigadier Shindy," was not a well-respected officer and there is reason to question his competence. After landing, he did nothing for four hours then, without advance or flank guards, moved south towards Black Rock.[16]

At about 4:30 A.M. on 3 August, Tucker's leading element, composed of his own 41st Foot, was approaching the bridge over the Conjocta Creek. They suddenly came under heavy and accurate rifle fire from Morgan's battalion, which forewarned by Tucker's dilatory advance, had entrenched itself on the south side of the stream. Suffering casualties, the 41st broke and fled to the rear. The remainder of Tucker's troops remained steady and after the 41st had been reformed, he advanced toward the creek in a long skirmish line but, in Le Couteur's words, the riflemen "shot every Fool that came near the Bridge."[17] Although the creek was fordable a mile upstream, Tucker contented himself with exchanging shots for about two and a half hours before withdrawing and recrossing to Canada. His ineptitude had cost forty-four casualties, including Private Shadrach Byfield of the 41st Foot, who had survived Lundy's Lane only to lose an arm in this sordid little action.[18]

Drummond was furious. His hopes of levering the enemy out of Canada cheaply were dashed and, as the Americans would be on the alert, any future attempt to cross the river would have to be made in strength. When

Tucker complained about his own troops, who "had displayed an unpardonable degree of unsteadiness, without possessing one solitary excuse to justify their want of discipline," Drummond overreacted.[19] Enraged by the "failure of an expedition, the success of which, by destroying the enemy's means of subsistence," would have forced the Americans to withdraw from Fort Erie, he issued a general order severely censuring the men who had fought at Conjocta. Attributing the defeat "solely" to the "misbehavior of the troops employed," he directed his officers "to punish with death on the spot" any man who, in future, wavered in the face of the enemy."[20] Drummond forbade "crouching, ducking or laying down when advancing under fire," against riflemen or not. The miscreant 41st Foot were sent back to the forts and replaced by the thousand-strong De Watteville's regiment, a foreign unit in British service, just arrived from Kingston.[21]

Drummond now had to contemplate seriously an attack on Fort Erie. On 3 August his light troops drove in the American pickets to permit him to make a closer examination of the defences. He did not like what he saw. The Americans had put the respite he had given them to good use. Working day and night, they had strengthened and defended the original small stone fort with a series of earthworks that connected it with Lake Erie and extended some eight hundred yards south to Snake Hill, a sand mound that had been levelled and re-shaped into a strong battery. Most of the perimeter was protected by a ditch and an abatis, a man-made obstacle formed of tangled trees with sharpened branches and weighed down by logs. The entire position was surrounded by an open area, cleared of vegetation, out to a distance of between three and four hundred yards. Approximately eighteen pieces of artillery were positioned to cover the defences and, in addition, the northern approaches were exposed to fire from the American batteries at Black Rock and three USN schooners anchored in the lake.[22] In the words of one British officer, Fort Erie was an "Ugly customer."[23]

Drummond had no illusions about the difficulty of assaulting such a position: it would be an operation of "great hazard" given "the strength of the enemy's position and the number of men and guns by which it is defended."[24] He decided to wait, as after the debacle at Conjocta he had become somewhat apprehensive about the "Stamina and firmness" of his troops and wanted to "soften" up the American position with artillery fire.[25] To do this, he needed engineer officers skilled in siegecraft but this type of warfare was not one of the British army's strong suits in 1814. Unlike other European powers, Britain had conducted few large sieges during the previous half century and had accumulated limited experience in this type of operation. This lack of specialized expertise was compounded by a shortage of Royal Engineer officers – there were only nineteen serving in North America in August 1814 and they were apparently not the cream of the crop. As Surgeon Dunlop remarked, any engineer whom the Duke of Wellington "deemed unfit for the Peninsula was considered as quite good enough for the Canadian market."[26] Drummond quickly became dissatisfied with his senior engineer and dismissed him, making do with two very junior officers, Lieutenants George Phillpotts and Joseph Portlock. To assist them, he assigned any officers who possessed some technical knowledge to the task, including Le Couteur, who found himself "working in his shirt like the men" to build fieldworks.[27]

Ordered to construct a battery to breach the walls, Philpotts chose a site near the lake north of the American position. He was hampered by a lack of entrenching tools – there were only enough for one hundred and twenty men to work at any given time – and by long-range fire from the batteries across the river at Black Rock and the American warships.[28]

On the night of 12 August, the annoying fire from the three American schooners was stopped. Captain Alexander Dobbs, RN, having moved six boats by wagon to the shore of the lake south of the American position, led a force of sailors and marines that attacked and captured two of these vessels. That same night, Philpotts completed the siege battery and began cutting down the trees in front of it to prepare for the bombardment. The battery was armed with three 24-pdr. guns, a 24-pdr. carronade[29] and an 8-inch iron mortar, which opened fire at daylight on 13 August.[30]

Once begun, the British bombardment continued throughout the 13th but it was obvious that it was not doing much damage. The reason was simple: Philpotts had located it about eleven hundred yards from the American position, extreme range for a breaching battery, not normally placed more than seven hundred yards from its target. At this range, roundshot had little effect on earthworks and stone buildings – to Le Couteur, "our fire, instead of affecting a breach seemed to me, and others, to ram the earth harder."[31] Another witness remembered that not "one shot in ten reached the rampart at all, and the fortunate exceptions that struck the stone building at which they were aimed, rebounded from its sides as innocuous as tennis balls."[32] Of the five pieces in the battery, a 24-pdr. iron gun and the 8-inch mortar were the most effective but the latter split its wooden bed "almost as often as it was fired."[33] In contrast, the

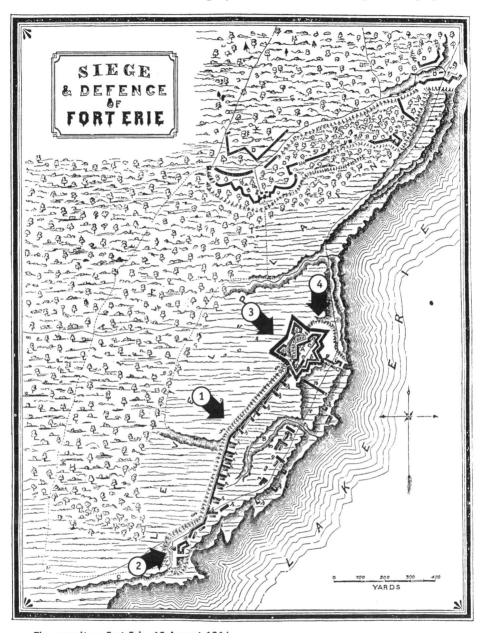

The assault on Fort Erie, 15 August 1814

1. Indian deception attack force
2. Snake Hill assault force (De Watteville's Regiment, 8th Foot and attachments) commanded by Lt. Col. Viktor Fisher, De Watteville's Regiment
3. Fort Erie assault force (104th Foot, light infantry attachments, Royal Marines and Royal Navy sailors) commanded by Lt. Col. William Drummond, 104th Foot
4. Northern assault force (103rd Foot) commanded by Col. Hercules Scott, 103rd Foot

American guns "managed to pitch shot and shell ... in a way that was anything but pleasant."[34]

The British guns ceased firing at dusk on 13 August, resumed again at dawn and continued throughout 14 August. During this time eight Americans were killed and forty-four wounded. Late in the afternoon of the 14th, a mortar shell exploded a small magazine inside the fort and Brigadier General Edmund P. Gaines, who had assumed command at Armstrong's request, "persuaded that this explosion would lead the enemy to assault," prepared to receive them.[35]

Gaines had read the British intentions correctly. Drummond, believing "that a sufficient impression had been produced" on the American position, decided to attack that night.[36] Philpotts disagreed with his superior's assessment of the bombardment, recording in his journal on 14 August that the effect of the battery's fire "was very trifling" and "no injury of any consequence appears to have been done."[37] But Drummond was determined to assault and, as darkness fell on 14 August, the troops selected for the attack moved into their start positions under a torrential downpour of rain.

The plan for the assault was a complicated business involving four separate forces. A few minutes before 2:00 A.M., a party of Indians would mount a demonstration at a point midway between Snake Hill and the stone fort to distract the garrison. Then the right, or southern, column under Lieutenant Colonel Victor Fischer with about fifteen hundred men drawn mostly from De Watteville's regiment and the 8th Foot would attack Snake Hill at precisely 2:00 A.M. To achieve surprise, Drummond suggested that Fischer order his men to remove the flints from their muskets so that no accidental discharges would give them away. This would force Fischer's column "to use the Bayonet with the effect which that valuable weapon has been ever found to possess in the hands of British soldiers."[38]

After Fischer had taken Snake Hill and entered the American perimeter, two more columns would move in from the north. The centre under Lieutenant Colonel William Drummond of the 104th, with about three hundred sailors, marines and light infantry, would attack the stone fort itself, while the left column under Colonel Hercules Scott of the 103rd, with about seven hundred men drawn mostly from his own regiment, would attack the entrenchments that ran from the stone fort to the lake. If all three attacks succeeded, the two anchors of the American position would be in British hands and the reserve, under Tucker, would move in to mop up. Drummond assured his assault commanders that the defenders did not exceed fifteen hundred "much dispirited" men and recommended they make "a free use of the bayonet."[39] As they assembled in the rain, the men in the assault force were "in high spirits and certain of conquest" although both William Drummond and Hercules Scott had premonitions of disaster.[40]

The attack went wrong from the outset. The Indian force ordered to make the demonstration failed to come up on time and Fischer's column was thirty minutes late getting up to Snake Hill. Here it encountered an alert American picket commander outside the abatis who opened fire to alert the garrison and then fell back by stages under fire from his own gunners. Following close on his heels, the lead British elements got to the battery, threw their scaling ladders against the wall and clambered up only to find the ladders were too short. Unable to come to grips with the enemy, unable to fire because they had no flints, but unwilling to withdraw, Fischer's men milled around in confusion until the Americans, realizing their plight, got up on the ramparts and shot them down "like so many sheep."[41] The British panicked and fled back into the darkness.[42]

The northern columns fared no better. Alerted, the Americans were ready when Hercules Scott and William Drummond's men emerged out of the dark at about 3:00 A.M. and Scott was mortally wounded by the defenders' withering fire. Some of his men surged west along the ditch in front of the American earthworks to encounter Drummond's men, who had been bloodily repulsed in several attempts to scale the curtain wall of the stone fort.

William Drummond decided to make another try. Throwing their ladders against the northeast bastion of the stone fort, his men, crazed by the fighting at the curtain wall, climbed over the wall screaming "no quarter!" With cutlasses, pikes and bayonets, they cut down the American gunners in the bastion and gained a lodging in the fort. But it did little good as the only way out of the bastion was a narrow passageway overlooked by the upper storey of a stone building in which the defenders "cut loopholes in the Floor, and everyone that entered them were killed, or wounded."[43] For the next half hour, British attempts to get further into the fort and American attempts to get into the bastion were equally futile. During one of these rushes, William Drummond's luck ran out and he was shot dead.[44]

The attackers' situation was growing desperate; dawn was approaching and daylight would expose them to a cross fire from the American artillery. Lieutenant George Charlton, RA, who had accompanied the assault force, swung one of the captured guns in the bastion around and fired two rounds at the American positions. It was probably sparks from the muzzle blast of this weapon that fell through cracks in the wooden floor of the bastion and ignited the ammunition stored below. Witnesses remembered that "every sound was hushed by the sense of an unnatural tremor beneath our feet, like the first heave of an earthquake" and then, before startled eyes, "the centre of the bastion burst up, with a terrific explosion and a jet of flame, mingled with fragments of timber, earth, stone and bodies" rose a hundred feet in the air "and fell, in a shower of ruins."[45] Sixty-four years later, one American could still clearly see in his mind's eye the sight of men flying through the air, "their cartridge boxes filled with fixed ammunition ignited and spangled out in every direction."[46]

The few survivors of the explosion found themselves lying dazed in the ditch in front of the fort. By now it was daybreak, and as they attempted to regain the safety of their own lines, the defenders opened a furious fire on them. Surgeon Dunlop remembered scouring "along the road at the top of my speed, with a running accompaniment of grape, canister and musketry whistling about my ears, and tearing the ground at my feet."[47] Norton, who had come up with his party too late to take part in the attack, witnessed the retreat of his comrades and became "enraged at their misfortune."[48] One of the few lucky ones to reach the safety of the British lines was John Le Couteur who, reacting to the horror he had just been through, threw down his sword and sobbed, "This is a disgraceful day for Old England!"[49]

The night assault on Fort Erie, 15 August 1814, was, for the British and Canadians, the most "unfortunate business that happened [to] us during the war."[50] The casualties were appalling – from an assault force of about 2500 men, Drummond reported 57 dead, 309 wounded and 539 missing, a total of 905 men. Most of the missing were victims of the explosion and most were dead; Gaines reported that the bodies of 222 British and Canadians were found the next morning. The losses surpassed those suffered at Lundy's Lane, and only at New Orleans on 8 January 1815 did the British army lose more men in a single engagement during the war. Of the units involved, the 103rd had suffered the worst, having 424 casualties including 14 of their 18 officers. The two flank companies of the 104th lost 54 out of 77 and, when their roll was called the evening after the attack, the survivors, to a man, burst into tears.[51]

In his official report to Prevost, Drummond attributed the failure of the attack to the explosion. In a private letter, however, confessing that he had a "most painful and distressing duty to perform," Drummond placed the blame squarely on De Watteville's regiment complaining that, "by the failure of this Foreign Corps has the opportunity been totally lost for the present of striking such a blow at the Enemy's force in this neighbourhood."[52] Worried that the defeat at Conjocta Creek and the disastrous assault of 15 August reflected badly on him as commanding general, he confessed to Prevost that the "agony of mind I suffer, from the present disgraceful, and unfortunate conduct of the Troops, committed to my superintendence, wounds me to the Soul!"[53] No mention was made of the scaling ladders that were too short, no mention was made of the removal of the flints and no mention was made of the fact that the assault force was unsupported for the half hour or so they were in possession of the northeast bastion.

Gaines was ecstatic about his "handsome victory" which cost him only sixty-two casualties, as well he might be.[54] The morning after the attack, the demolished bastion presented a frightful spectacle. Drummer Hanks "counted 196 bodies lying in the ditch and about the fort, most of them dead; some dying."[55] Many of the corpses were horribly mutilated; the young teenager was transfixed by the sight of "legs, arms and heads lying, in confusion, separated, by the concussions, from the trunks to which they had long been attached."[56] When the British artillery did not resume firing for a number of days, Gaines put the time to good use repairing and strengthening his defences. A week after the assault, he confidently reported that "our position is growing stronger every day."[57]

Although Drummond decided to remain before Fort Erie, he was beset by problems. Chauncey's intermittent blockade of the river mouth worsened his supply situation, he was running low on artillery ammunition and there were no tents to shelter his men from the almost constant rainfall. On 27 August his chief commissary officer informed him that only two and a half weeks of provisions were left and in desperation Drummond appealed to Yeo to get out on Lake Ontario and secure the army's supply line as "nothing but the assistance of the whole of H[is].M[ajesty's]. squadron ... can enable it to continue it operations against the enemy, or even retain its present position on this frontier."[58] The strain was beginning to tell on the British commander, still suffering from the wound he had received at Lundy's Lane, and his senior staff officer, Lieutenant Colonel John Harvey, worried that his superior's responsibilities were "evidently hurting his constitution & health."[59]

The siege continued. Philpotts, ordered to construct a second battery, chose a site in the woods about four hundred and fifty yards to the southwest of the first battery but still about eight hundred yards from the fort. This battery, armed with four pieces of artillery, opened fire on 29 August but its fire proved ineffective because Philpotts had neglected to properly examine the levels in front of the battery and it was discovered "that a rise of ground ... prevented us from seeing the fort."[60] Wishing to preserve ammunition, Drummond ordered his gunners to restrict their fire.[61]

Philpotts then sited a third battery a further five hundred yards southeast of the second and only four hundred yards from the fort. At this distance, Drummond hoped to be able "to open the rear face [of Fort Erie] and complete the destruction of the stone building" which had proved so formidable during the ill-fated assault of 15 August.[62] The new position was completed on 4 September and Drummond intended to open fire on the morning of 6 September and attack at dawn the following day, but before the woods in front were cut away, he changed his mind and postponed the assault.[63]

To Prevost he explained that he was waiting for infantry reinforcements and more artillery ammunition. But the delay probably had more to do with Drummond's state of mind than with any deficiencies of men and materiel. By now he had amassed two hundred rounds per gun and his division had recently been joined by twelve hundred veterans of the 6th and 82nd Foot, first-class regiments just arrived in North America after service with Wellington in Spain. In addition, Chauncey had retired into Sackets Harbor and Yeo now ruled Lake Ontario, easing his logistical difficulties.[64]

The plain truth seems to have been that Drummond was reluctant to risk another assault without receiving a definite order, or at least clear approval, from Prevost. Complaining he was ignorant of the commander in chief's "views and plans with regard to the general operations of the campaign," especially concerning a second attack, he queried Prevost whether it might be more "politic" to simply blockade the fort in preference to mounting an assault which, even if successful, would entail "a severe loss."[65] He assured his superior that he would certainly take advantage "of any favorable opportunity of attacking the enemy" but if such an opportunity did not occur, Drummond felt "it incumbent on me to prepare Your Excellency for the possibility of my being compelled by sickness or suffering of the troops ... to withdraw them from their present position to one which may afford them the means of cover."

While Drummond kept his options open, the rain continued to fall and the "Trenches filled with Water, & the chilling blasts of Autumn began to be felt."[66] The mutual exchange of artillery fire went on and there was almost daily skirmishing "that served no purpose to the parties except to harass one another."[67] A sharp action occurred on the afternoon of 4 September when a detachment from Porter's brigade sallied out to attack the second battery. They were repulsed but the fighting lasted for nearly six hours until a "tremendous rain and thunder storm broke over the combattants about 5 and tended to cool both parties."[68] The Americans came close enough to kill one of Philpotts's assistants but lost their leader, Joseph Willcocks, who was shot in the chest. There was much rejoicing in the British camp that evening when news was learned of the "death of that arch-rebel."[69]

The weather continued bad. From 11 September, it rained almost daily. Having observed numbers of boats gathered on the American shore and learning from deserters that a strong force of New York militia had crossed over to Fort Erie, Drummond feared that the Americans would either mount a major sortie from the fort or attempt to cross the Niagara and land in his rear. The third battery had still not opened fire and on 15 September Drummond restricted his gunners to one round per gun per hour as no "direct fire from the small numbers of guns which I have could produce any material effect on such mounds of earth."[70] By now he had totally lost heart and recited a litany of complaints to Prevost: weather, supply shortages, the health of his troops and his apprehension of an American attack. He would have to meet such an attack "under every possible disadvantage" but hoped it would take place as "it will bring us into contact with the enemy at a far cheaper rate than if we were to be the assailants, and may at the same time ... bring to a happy crisis a campaign which has been marked by a series of unlucky circumstances."[71]

His senior officers were of similar mind. Harvey thought an assault would entail "great loss & some *risque* of a failure."[72] Drummond's new second-in-command, Major General Louis De Watteville, a thirty-eight-year-old Swiss with two decades of active service in Europe, did not even seriously contemplate another attempt. Arriving at the beginning of September, De Watteville went to Drummond on the 16th of that month and bluntly told him that the Right Division should abandon the siege and withdraw. This seems to have tipped the scale and that same day Drummond ordered Philpotts to start removing the guns from the batteries. The engineer was engaged in this task on the rainy afternoon of the following day when the Americans boiled out of the fort and attacked.[73]

This attack was made by the orders of Brown, who had resumed command of the Left Division on 2 September after Gaines had been wounded. He at first set up his headquarters in Buffalo, leaving Ripley in command at Fort Erie, but crossed over to Canada at the request of the senior officers of the division who felt it "could not be trusted" with that officer. At Fort Erie Brown found about twenty-two hundred men of all ranks fit for duty and growing very "impatient." He expressed his annoyance with the government in Washington, which he felt was ignoring his division which, "struggling with the Enemies of their Country and devoting themselves for its Honor and its safety," had been "left by that Country to struggle alone within sight & within hearing."[74]

But Washington's gaze was focused elsewhere in the late summer of 1814. By the time he had received Armstrong's order to march to the west, Izard had realized that a massive British troop build-up was under way at Montreal and warned the secretary that Plattsburgh was in danger. Nonetheless, Izard marched on 29 August with four thousand men for Sackets Harbor and almost immediately Prevost moved south from Montreal with ten thousand veterans of Wellington's peninsula army. Brushing aside American resistance, the British arrived before Plattsburgh on 6 September. Prevost, convinced that he needed naval superiority before assaulting, harried his naval commander into a premature attack on the American Lake Champlain squadron. The result was a resounding defeat and the loss of most of the British vessels. Feeling he could not sustain himself this deep inside American territory without naval support, Prevost ordered the finest army Britain ever sent to North America to retrace its steps to Canada.[75]

Izard's warning had gone unheeded in Washington because the American capital itself was in danger. Vice Admiral Alexander Cochrane, commander of the Royal Navy's America and West Indies station, was not obliged to respond to a request made by Prevost in June to "inflict that measure of retaliation" on America that would prevent a recurrence of incidents such as the destruction of Dover. But it had met with a measure of sympathy from the senior British naval officers and on 18 July 1814 Cochrane issued an "Order for Retaliation" to his subordinates "to destroy and lay waste such towns and cities upon the coast as you may find assailable" and "to spare merely the lives of the unarmed inhabitants of the United States."[76]

On 19 August a small but veteran British force under the command of Major General Robert Ross landed at the mouth of the Patuxent. Five days later, at Bladensburg, Maryland, Ross encountered a scratch American force composed mainly of militia with a leavening of regulars and put them to flight after a three-hour action. That evening Ross occupied Washington and ordered the destruction of the White House, the Capitol and other government and military buildings. On 25 August Ross marched out of the American capital and five days later he safely re-embarked on Cochrane's fleet.

This fiasco led to Armstrong's replacement on 4 September by James Monroe, the secretary of state. American morale was bolstered by the successful defence of Baltimore by its citizens which resulted in a British rebuff at the battle of North Point on 12 September but the nation was verging on collapse. After two years of war, the treasury was empty and there were no funds to pay the regular army, which dwindled as recruiting dropped off. Monroe's talk of conscription raised the ire of the New England states, whose support for the war had never been strong and, led by Massachusetts, they began to discuss secession from the federal government. The British government was quick to take advantage of the American disarray and British representatives to the peace negotiations, which had finally got under way in August at Ghent in Holland, went on the offensive. They demanded territorial concessions from the United States and the establishment of an Indian barrier state in the northwest as the price of peace. By September 1814 America's cup was becoming increasingly bitter.

All this was not clear to Brown on the Niagara. He was concerned that Fort Erie would fall before he received reinforcements and urged Izard to come to his aid as the future of the Left Division was "very doubtful unless speedy relief is afforded."[77] But Izard moved slowly, reaching Sackets Harbor only on 17 September. Here he embarked his division on Chauncey's squadron but was delayed by contrary winds. Worried about the third British battery whose fire would be able to enfilade his entire position, Brown decided to sortie in an effort to save a division "neglected by a country for which it had devoted itself."[78] On 9 and 10 September he was gratified to receive a reinforcement of fifteen hundred New York militia that crossed over from Buffalo and camped south of the Snake Hill battery.[79]

In the evening of 16 September Brown informed Porter and Miller of his intentions. Porter, with a force consisting of Volunteers, regular infantry and riflemen, would move from Snake Hill through the woods on a trail to be cut the night before and take the British in the flank. As soon as he had commenced his assault, Miller, with a force of regulars, would attack directly west from the centre of the American position. The object of the sortie was "to storm the batteries, destroy the cannon, and roughly handle the [British] brigade on duty" before Drummond could bring up reinforcements.[80]

Preparations went smoothly. Rain and mist covered the working party that cleared a trail from Snake Hill to a point south of the extreme right of the British right and they remained undetected. As the troops moved into their forming up positions on the morning of 17 September, Brown, feeling guilty because he had not taken Ripley into his confidence, told that officer what was about to take place. Ripley's reaction was predictable – he thought the sortie "hopeless" and was "well satisfied to escape from the disgrace that in his judgement would fall upon all engaged in it." After this statement, Brown was "gratified to find that his second in command claimed no situation in the attack, as such claim at the moment would have been most embarrassing." But when Ripley later changed his mind and asked for command of the reserve. Brown granted this request.[81]

At midday on 17 September Porter advanced cautiously along the trail. The drizzling rain increased to a downpour that masked their movement and put the British sentries off guard. By 2:30 P.M. Porter had outflanked the British entrenchments and gave the signal for the attack. Appearing out of the mist and woods, Porter's men were soon inside the third battery and the defenders either fled or surrendered. When he heard the noise of the attack, Brown ordered Miller forward from his position in a ravine in front of the American camp. Moving quickly, Miller's men joined Porter's column in an attack on the second battery and it too fell into American hands. In both batteries, working parties spiked the guns, knocked off their trunnions and blew up the ready-use powder magazines.[82]

Up to this point the operation had gone well but the British and Canadians recovered from their surprise and counterattacked. Two companies of the 82nd Foot under twenty-six-year-old Captain Robert Patteson moved on the second battery and poured a concentrated fire into the mass of attackers who were crowded so close together that they found it difficult to use their weapons. Seeing an American officer, Patteson demanded that he surrender and some of the attackers started to ground their muskets when Patteson was shot dead. Enraged at what they took to be a dishonourable act, his men moved in with the bayonet and slaughtered many Americans. Fighting then became general and, due to the thick woods, the rain and the confusion of the fighting, Porter and Miller began to lose control of their commands, which had become intermingled.[83]

Sensing something was amiss, Brown sent Ripley and the reserve forward but Ripley lost his way in the tangled thickets and was seriously wounded. As more British counterattacked, Miller and Porter, unable to make any headway against the first battery, began to take heavy casualties. Having gained most of his objectives, Brown ordered them to fall back and they did so in a running fight with the Glengarries and British-allied Indians who were in hot pursuit.

As Drummond had already decided to lift the siege, the sortie was a needless operation although Brown could not know that. He was pleased with the results as he had disabled most of the British heavy ordnance and in his own mind saved the Left Division from certain disaster. But the success was costly: Brown admitted the loss of 79 dead, 216 wounded and 216 missing, a total of 511. Drummond's losses were 115 killed, 183 wounded and 316 missing, for a total of 516. Over half the British casualties were from the 8th Foot and De Watteville's regiment, the units on duty when the attack began. Ironically the sortie cost the lives of some of the prominent survivors of Lundy's Lane including Lieutenant Colonel John Gordon of the 1st Foot, the sixth battalion commander of the Right Division to be killed or wounded since 3 July 1814. On the American side, that invaluable officer Eleazar D. Wood was killed while Porter and Ripley were wounded.[84]

The British buried the dead of both sides and then resumed the task of getting the heavy guns out of the batteries. Delayed by rain, this work was not completed until the evening of 21 September when the Right Division withdrew from its lines and retired north by stages. Three days later the bulk of the division was behind the Chippawa with strong pickets posted between the river and Fort Erie. Drummond reported to Prevost that "now unencumbered with heavy guns" his division was "again moveable and ready, and most anxious" to show that it was "only behind works or in thick woods" that his opponents "gain any advantage over British troops."[85] These words ignored the fact that the initiative was back squarely in American hands.[86]

Brown waited for Izard before pursuing but it was not until 21 September that Izard sailed from Sackets Harbor and, instead of heading for Burlington Bay as had been Armstrong's intention, he landed on the south shore of Lake Ontario at the mouth of the Genesee river. He then marched to Batavia where he met with Brown a week later. Brown wanted him to lay siege to Fort Niagara while he operated on the Canadian side of the river, but Izard was reluctant to do so because he had no heavy artillery. He therefore resumed his westward march and by 10 October had reached Black Rock, where his troops began to cross the Niagara River. As he was senior to Brown, the Left Division came under his orders and, "at the head of the most efficient army the United States have possessed during this war," Izard moved north to the Chippawa, halting at the site of Brown's old camp south of Street's Creek.[87]

For three days Izard demonstrated before the British positions on the north bank of the Chippawa hoping to lure Drummond out of his entrenchments. But the British commander refused to rise to the bait and, unwilling to attack the strong enemy position, Izard withdrew to the south on 17 October.

The following day he dispatched Brigadier General Daniel Bissell with about a thousand regulars to Cook's Mills, on Lyon's Creek, to seize supplies believed to be stored at that place. Learning of this movement, Drummond dispatched a force of seven hundred light infantry under Lieutenant Colonel Christopher Myers, including Le Couteur, who remembered marching "knee deep in mud in a pitch dark night ... an exquisite enjoyment for those who have never tried it."[88] Early in the morning of 19 October Myers neared the mills and drove in Bissell's pickets but Bissell quickly formed and the two sides manoeuvred for some time trying to gain an advantage. Realizing he was outnumbered, Myers withdrew in good order and Bissell did the same.[89]

Izard confessed to Secretary of War Monroe that he was "greatly embarrassed" as "much must be expected from me, and yet I can discern no object which can be achieved at this point worthy of the risk which attend its attempt."[90] Further operations were pointless without the support of Chauncey but that officer had, with his usual prudence, withdrawn into Sackets Harbor after Yeo had emerged on the lake with his new warship, the 104-gun *St. Lawrence*. Wanting to procure good winter quarters for his troops, Izard decided to cross back to the United States and, seeing no advantage in holding Fort Erie other than as a "trophy," had it prepared for demolition.[91]

He ordered Brown to march to Sackets Harbor and on 24 October the Left Division returned to the United States. It had won great renown but the price had been high. Miller wrote to his wife that, since the division had crossed into Canada on 3 July, "every major, save one, every lieutenant-colonel, every colonel that was here when I came and has remained here, has been killed or wounded, and I am now the only general officer out of seven that has escaped."[92]

Drummond made no attempt to interfere with Izard's movements. This lack of aggression on the part of the British puzzled Izard, who attributed it to an exaggerated opinion of the strength of his army as he could not "otherwise account for their cautious conduct in keeping behind their intrenchments."[93] But Drummond had no intention of attacking. Writing to Prevost, he regretted that it was not within his power to inflict "an additional momento" on the Americans but "it would be imprudent, without good information, to attempt it and ... sufficient had been done by this gallant division during this campaign ... to deter the enemy from ever again attempting the invasion of this frontier."[94] Worn out, he complained of his "indifferent state of health" which did not permit "the exertion I felt necessary to make in the important discharge of my duty."[95] Requesting permission to give up the command in Upper Canada and return to Britain, he boarded Yeo's squadron on 30 October and sailed for York leaving the Right Division in the charge of Major General Richard Stovin.[96]

It was not the same division that had fought throughout the summer. The units that had been at Lundy's Lane, reduced by sickness and casualties, had gradually been withdrawn and replaced by fresh troops from Europe. One of the last of the veteran regiments to leave was the 89th Foot and, as he trudged up the river road to Fort George, Surgeon William Dunlop remembered how, over four hundred strong, they had gone into action at Lundy's Lane three months before. "Now we retired," wrote Dunlop, "about sixty rank and file, commanded by a Captain, two of the senior Lieutenants carrying the colours and myself marching in the rear – *voila*, His Majesty's 89th Regiment of Foot!"[97]

On 5 November 1814, Izard evacuated his troops from Canada and blew up the entrenchments at Fort Erie. After one hundred and twenty-five days, four major battles, two minor actions and countless skirmishes, the Niagara campaign of 1814, the most hard-fought military operation of the War of 1812, came to an end. In the apt words of the American Surgeon William Horner, "there was never a campaign in which the belligerents came to a better understanding of what they might expect in battle at each other's hands; and where the leaders, though under the excitement of a state of war, left off with more military respect for one another."[98]

CHAPTER 14

The End of the War
and the Fates of Men

*The War of 1812 is one of those episodes in history that make
everybody happy, because everybody interprets it in his own way.
The Americans think of it primarily as a naval war in which the
pride of the Mistress of the Seas was humbled by what an
imprudent Englishman had called "a few fir-built frigates
manned by a handful of bastards and outlaws." Canadians think
of it equally pridefully as war of defence in which their brave
fathers ... saved the country from conquest. And the English are
the happiest of all because they don't even know it existed.*
C.P. STACEY, "THE WAR OF 1812 IN CANADIAN HISTORY"

Almost from the time the echoes of the last shots died away in the
darkness around the hill, the battle of Lundy's Lane has been the subject of
controversy. This is not surprising for it was an unplanned encounter, a
meeting engagement in which two armies made contact, fought desperately
and fed continual reinforcements into that fight. Because it continued into
the night, a most unusual event in 1814, and because both forces withdrew
after the fighting ceased, the events of the action and its outcome were
bound to become controversial. It is tempting to leave the matter unsettled
but clearly a decision must be made as to which army won the battle and
what was the result?

Major General Jacob Brown has good claim to having won a tactical victory at Lundy's Lane. His division took the hill, the key to the British position, and Drummond's artillery – and held them against repeated counterattacks. Brown's decision to withdraw from the ground his men had fought
so hard for and the confusion of that withdrawal resulted in the proof of his
triumph, the captured British artillery, being left behind.

The American withdrawal allowed Lieutenant General Gordon Drummond to also claim a tactical victory but this assertion has less validity. Drummond did not succeed in either recapturing the hill or his artillery, only repossessing them after Brown left the field. It is Drummond's repossession, not recapture, of his artillery that has been the source of much of the debate about who won the battle.[1]

Matters are less certain when the battle is judged in terms of the effect it had on the outcome of the campaign of 1814. If, as Brown stated, he intended to move on Burlington Bay after he had withdrawn from Queenston on 24 July to re-supply at Chippawa, Lundy's Lane doomed that intention. On the other hand, if his intention was to lure his opponents into an open battle, then Lundy's Lane, a tactical American victory, can only be regarded as a defeat for Brown as, far from continuing to threaten the British field force, Burlington Bay or the forts at the river's mouth, he ended up at Fort Erie, his initial crossing point.

In one sense, Lundy's Lane can be considered a British victory. Although the invaders were not expelled from Canada, they advanced no further and their withdrawal to Fort Erie placed the military initiative squarely in Drummond's hands. What advantage Drummond gained on 25 July 1814, however, he threw away by not actively pursuing and harrying his enemy. Instead he chose to withdraw in the opposite direction to Queenston, giving the Left Division time to consolidate its position at Fort Erie. When his bid to pry the Americans out of their entrenchments came to grief at Conjocta Creek and his attempt at a *coup de main* failed during the assault of 15 August, Drummond was doomed to a frustrating and ineffectual blockade of an American bridgehead while at the end of a tenuous and lengthy supply line. Thus, for neither army, can Lundy's Lane be considered a decisive military action.

Neither did the battle, nor indeed the entire campaign, have any real impact on the outcome of war. This is not surprising as the campaign itself was not based on any clear strategic aim. It had begun almost as an afterthought, a suggestion by Secretary of War Armstrong to Brown that he keep his army occupied until Chauncey had naval superiority on Lake Ontario by crossing the Niagara, advancing to the Chippawa and being "governed by circumstances either in stopping there or going further."[2] Under the mistaken impression that Chauncey would meet him at a certain date, Brown decided to go further – with little to show for it. His tactical successes took place in a vacuum because the campaign in which they occurred lacked clear strategical and operational foundations. As a result, Brown accomplished little except to establish that, properly trained and led, American soldiers were capable of beating a skilled and professional opponent in open battle.

Certainly the Niagara campaign had little influence on the course of the peace negotiations at Ghent which had continued throughout the summer of 1814. For the United States, these talks were critical – two years of war had left her bankrupt, her merchant marine captured or blockaded and parts of her territory under enemy occupation. The young republic was fortunate that Britain, weary from nearly two decades of continuous struggle against France, had entered negotiations with the intention of signing a treaty that would restore the *status quo ante bellum*. The momentary advantage granted by the British victories at Bladensburg and Washington in August 1814 encouraged her delegates to take a harder stance and demand extreme concessions but these demands dissolved in the face of Prevost's fiasco at Plattsburgh in September. Thereafter, the British position softened, real progress was made and, on Christmas Eve, 1814, the two nations signed the Treaty of Ghent which brought hostilities to a close. Fighting continued in Louisiana until news of the cessation of hostilities reached North America, but by March 1815, the war was over.[3]

Thus ended the "incredible War of 1812," as one of its chroniclers has termed it.[4] For Britain, it had been an unwanted conflict and would be remembered, when it was remembered, as a sideshow of the greater fight she had waged against revolutionary and imperial France. For the United States, the success of her negotiators at the bargaining table and the late victory at New Orleans allowed Madison's government to claim victory in this "Second War of Independence" – but it had been a very near run thing. The republic had plunged into war woefully unprepared and only the efforts of her sailors and soldiers had averted disaster. The excellent record of the U.S Navy in a series of single-ship engagements was matched by the performance of the United States Army in the Niagara campaign of 1814, and although that campaign had little real effect on the outcome of the war, it did win that army the respect of its opponents. As one senior British officer remarked, it was "but justice" to the American soldier,

> ... to observe that he seems to have wonderfully improved in the last year of the war. The American troops at Street's Creek [Chippawa], Lundy's Lane, and at the sortie at Fort Erie, appear to have shown all the discipline as well as spirit of enterprize, that could be wished for.[5]

In Brown's words, the operations of the Left Division in the Niagara campaign of 1814 had restored the "tarnished military character" of the United States.[6] Brown and his men would have thought that enough.

While historians fought over who had won the battle, the survivors of the action got on with their lives. Most of the British veterans of the Niagara campaign were long-service professionals who continued in the military after the war. As a group, they did not receive the recognition accorded their counterparts who had fought in Europe and took a somewhat perverse pride in being "forgotten soldiers." Their attitude was sardonically summed up by one of their number, Surgeon William Dunlop, who quipped about the Duke of Wellington, "thank God he managed to do without us at Waterloo."[7]

Of these "forgotten soldiers," their commander in chief, Lieutenant General Sir George Prevost, perhaps fared worst. He was recalled to Britain in April 1815 and retired to his estate in Hampshire. When the members of the court martial of the naval commander at Plattsburgh in September 1814 blamed Prevost for bringing on the naval action too soon, he requested an army court martial to clear his name. Exactly one month before it was scheduled to convene in early 1816, he died suddenly at the age of forty-eight. For decades after the war, Prevost was a subject of scorn in Canada and it has only been in recent times that historians have re-evaluated the man and his actions.[8]

In contrast, Lieutenant General Gordon Drummond was showered with honours. He was knighted in January 1815 and the following April succeeded Prevost as commander-in-chief of the Canadas. He served in this position for a year and then asked to be relieved for reasons of ill health. Through seniority, he achieved promotion to full general in 1825 and at the time of his death was the senior general of the British army. Drummond was awarded a large grant of land by the Legislative Assembly of Upper Canada which he bestowed, along with his wartime prize money, on the widows and orphans of the men who had fallen. One of his two sons joined the Royal Navy, the other the army, and both died on active service. In his later life Drummond resided mainly in his town house in London and he died in 1854 in his eighty-second year.[9]

Major General Phineas Riall never again held an important military command although through seniority he gained promotion to lieutenant general in 1835 and general in 1841. From 1816 to 1823 Riall was governor of Grenada but this was his only diplomatic post. He was married in 1819, knighted in 1831 and died without issue in 1850 at the age of seventy-five.[10]

John Harvey, Drummond's adjutant-general, continued in the army reaching the rank of major-general and commanding the Irish Constabulary by 1828. He then returned to Canada and held a series of lieutenant-governorships: Prince Edward Island from 1831 to 1837, New Brunswick from 1837 to 1841 and Newfoundland from 1841 to 1846. While lieutenant governor of New Brunswick, he negotiated with his old adversary, Winfield Scott, the successful settlement of a border dispute with the United States. Harvey died in 1852 in his seventy-fourth year.[11]

Lieutenant Colonel Thomas Pearson, the commander of the light brigade at the battle, returned to England after the war but saw no more active service. He suffered much from his wounds, a thigh bone shattered in the Peninsula in 1811 and a rifle ball in the head at Fort Erie in 1814. He was knighted in 1835 and through seniority had reached the rank of lieutenant general when he died at Bath in 1847.[12]

Lieutenant Colonel Joseph Morrison, who commanded the 89th Foot at Lundy's Lane, returned to Britain but, unable to carry out his duties because of the wound he received at the battle, was placed on half pay in 1816. He returned to active service in 1821 as commanding officer of the 44th Foot and participated with his regiment in the Burma campaign of 1824-1825. At the age of forty-two, he died of malaria on board the ship returning him to England.[13]

Lieutenant Colonel Francis Battersby, the commanding officer of the Glengarry Light Infantry during the battle, remained with that unit until they were disbanded in 1816. He then went on to command the 64th Foot but ill health forced him to go on half pay in 1826. In 1845 Battersby died at the age of seventy on his estate near Drogheda, Ireland, and was survived by a wife and son.[14]

Lieutenant Colonel William ("Billy") Robinson of the 8th Foot, the irrepressible Irishman who commanded the Incorporated Militia Battalion, never fully recovered from the severe wound he received at Lundy's Lane. He tried to continue in service but was forced to sell his commission in 1824 and shortly afterward became paralysed in his lower limbs. Robinson died at the age of forty-eight in 1827, his last years being marred by "painful imbecility."[15]

Major Thomas Evans, who commanded the 8th Foot at Chippawa and Lundy's Lane, had a long and distinguished career in the army and retired from active service in 1838 with the rank of major general. Married to a

Canadian woman from Montreal, he settled in that city in 1848 and remained there the rest of his life, dying in 1863 at the ripe old age of eighty-six. During his long military life, Evans participated in forty-two general actions and minor affairs.[16]

The two senior Royal Artillery officers at Lundy's Lane, Captains James Maclachlan and James Mackonochie, did not long survive the war. Mackonochie died at Plymouth in September 1815, shortly after his return from Canada, while Maclachlan suffered the "rupture of a blood vessel" at Tunbridge Wells in 1827 and "expired simultaneously."[17]

Captain Joseph Barry Glew, the light company commander of the 41st Foot who recaptured some of the British guns for a brief period during the battle, was commanding the Incorporated Militia Battalion by the end of the war. Little is known about his postwar career but he never received the knighthood one officer thought he should have been awarded for his deeds during the battle. Glew went on half pay and died in 1838 in his fifty-fifth year.[18]

Of the three British soldiers who had black marks on their records when they fought at Lundy's Lane – Captain William Brereton of the 1st Foot, Captain James Basden of the 89th and Volunteer Winslow of the 104th – later life brought some vindication. Brereton was tried by court martial for cowardice and insubordination on charges stemming from his behaviour at the Battle of Chippawa; he was acquitted of the first charge and reprimanded for the second. He left the 1st Foot and served briefly with the 2nd West India Regiment before going on half pay and dying unmarried in 1837. Basden, the light company commander of the 89th Foot, went on to a very successful military career, serving thirty-seven years with that regiment, the last five, from 1838 to 1843, as its commanding officer. He saw active service again in Canada during the rebellion of 1837-1838 and, during discussions over border incidents with American authorities, came face to face again with his old enemy, Hugh Brady. Twice married, Basden died in his seventy-first year in his villa in Hampshire in 1856. John Winslow was the former lieutenant of the 41st Foot who had been forced to resign his commission after an altercation in the officer's mess and who fought in the action as a gentleman volunteer in the ranks of the 104th. On the basis of his war record and following the intercession of Prevost and other senior officers, Winslow was restored to a half-pay lieutenancy in 1819. In 1832 he became sheriff of Woodstock County, New Brunswick, a post he held until 1856. Winslow died in 1859 at the age of sixty-six.[19]

One veteran of the battle settled within musket shot of the ground over which it was fought. This was Captain Richard Leonard, the commander of the grenadier company of the 104th Foot, who became sheriff of the Niagara district. He suffered severely from a wound received during the assault on Fort Erie which left him in constant pain. As a result, his temper was liable to be, as one acquaintance said, a bit "peppery," especially when American tourists accosted him on his daily rides along Lundy's Lane to ask directions to the place "where we whipt the British."[20] Leonard died at the age of fifty-six in 1833, leaving a widow and several children.[21]

Surgeon William Dunlop remained in military service until 1817 and then supported himself as a newspaper editor, a contributor to *Blackwood's Magazine* and lecturer. He returned to Canada in 1826 as "Warden of the Woods and Forests," basically agent, for the Canada Land Company, a private firm which had purchased some two and a half million acres in the western part of Upper Canada. He was later elected to the provincial legislative assembly and ended up as the superintendent of the Lachine Canal. Dunlop, a fun-loving and sophisticated man who loved to play the rustic, was known for his wit, including his famous three reasons why a man should not attend church – first, he would "be sure to find his wife there, secondly, he could not bear any meeting where one man engrossed the whole of the conversation and thirdly, that he never liked singing without drinking." Dunlop was the author of several books, including a memoir of his wartime experiences, notable for their self-deprecating humour. He died unmarried in 1848 in his fifty-sixth year.[22]

Lieutenant John Le Couteur left the army in 1817 and returned to his native Jersey to marry his cousin. He lived a long and productive Victorian life devoted to public and private good works and there was scarcely a single aspect of his native island that he did not leave improved. Among other things, Le Couteur established the breeding points of the Jersey cow, an accomplishment for which he is primarily remembered on his home island. Le Couteur spent much of his leisure hours writing a lengthy and detailed memoir of his experiences during the War of 1812 which he based on the daily diary he kept throughout the conflict. In 1875, surrounded by children and grandchildren, he died at Belle Vue, his Jersey estate, at the green old age of eighty-two.[23]

Private Shadrach Byfield, who lost an arm at Conjocta Creek, was unable to work at his trade as a weaver until one night he had a vision in a dream of a device that would permit him to practise his craft. Using this artificial aid, supplemented by a pension of nine pence a day, Byfield was able to eke out a living sufficient to support his wife and children. He added to this income by selling copies of his wartime memoir which he dictated in the 1840s. The old soldier became religious in his later years and died in 1874 at the age of eighty-four.[24]

Almost all the Canadians who fought at Lundy's Lane returned to civilian pursuits when peace returned. Their postwar lives were characterized by involvement in public life and strong loyalty to the Crown. Many served in the militia and took an active part in suppressing the abortive rebellion of 1837-1838 in Upper Canada.

Major James Kerby, who assumed command of the Incorporated Militia after Robinson was wounded, settled near Fort Erie. He held several public positions, serving as postmaster, magistrate and town warden and was also a member of the Legislative Council of Upper Canada. For many years he was the collector of customs at Fort Erie and his zealous pursuit of the most minor transgressors made him the subject of numerous complaints. Kerby reached the rank of colonel in the militia and commanded the local regiment. He died in 1854 and is buried in the churchyard of St. Paul's Church, Fort Erie.[25]

Hamilton Merritt, the young Canadian cavalry officer captured at Lundy's Lane, was released from captivity in March 1815. Following his return to Canada, he married an American woman, Catharine Prendergast, and they had four sons and two daughters. Merritt settled on the Twelve-Mile Creek and became a merchant, sawmill owner, distiller and potash producer. The need for water to run his mills caused him to build a feeder canal and this early project gave him the idea of connecting Lakes Ontario and Erie by means of a canal that would bypass the obstacle of the falls of Niagara. Construction commenced on this waterway in 1824 and, after considerable difficulties, the first boat passed through to Lake Erie in 1834. Merritt went on to promote other transportation projects: railways, a canal on the St. Lawrence; and a suspension bridge over the Niagara gorge. He took a leading part in public life, was elected several times to the Legislative Assembly and was instrumental in raising funds for the erection of Brock's memorial on Queenston Heights and promoting pensions for the veterans of the war. Merritt maintained a life-long interest in history and was a founder of the Historical Society of Upper Canada. He died in 1862.[26]

Titus Geer Simons of the 2nd York Militia returned to his residence at

Flamboro where he owned extensive property and mills, and served as sheriff of the district and colonel of the local militia regiment. He died at the age of sixty-four in 1829, "the officers of the Militia attending in uniform; his favourite hunter being led behind the hearse by his groom, both of which spent their remaining years on the old homestead."[27] He was survived by his wife and three daughters.[28]

Lieutenant Henry Ruttan of the Incorporated Militia Battalion recovered from the wound he received at Lundy's Lane but saw no further action during the war. He married in 1816 and had five children. Ruttan returned to Northumberland County, where he led a very active public life, serving as a member and later Speaker of the Legislative Assembly, sheriff and senior provincial militia officer. In 1871 he died in his seventy-eighth year and was buried in St. Peter's church yard, Cobourg.[29]

His fellow Incorporated Militia officer, Lieutenant Duncan Clark, was employed by the Northwest Fur Company until 1825 and then operated as a merchant in Matilda near Prescott, Upper Canada. Clark was also prominent in the militia, rising to the rank of colonel, and saw active service again during the rebellion of 1837. He never married and died in 1862 at the age of seventy-seven.[30]

Lieutenant John Kilborn of the same regiment set up as a merchant at Unionville near Brockville, Upper Canada. He was employed by the Crown to assist new settlers coming to open up the Rideau Lakes area and also held the positions of postmaster, justice of the peace and, later, judge. Kilborn married in 1816 and had nine children, four of whom survived him. He was active in the militia, rising to the rank of colonel and was called out during the rebellion. He was still alive in 1878, at the age of eighty-four, and was at that time the last surviving officer of the Incorporated Militia.[31]

That natural leader, John Norton, was promoted major and given a pension of £200 per annum for his outstanding wartime services. In 1815 he travelled to Britain with his wife and son and, during his stay, wrote a lengthy memoir of his experiences and of the history and customs of the native peoples of North America. Intended for publication, this manuscript ended up in the library of the Duke of Northumberland, where it was discovered in the 1960s. Returning to Canada, Norton settled on a large tract of land overlooking the Grand River and occupied himself farming and translating the Gospels into Mohawk. In 1823 he fought a duel with another man who was rumoured to have been making undue advances to Norton's wife. His opponent was mortally wounded and, although he was cleared by the courts, Norton left Canada and travelled to the west to live with the Cherokee nation. He never returned to Canada and is believed to have died in the late 1820s.[32]

As a group, most of the officers of the Left Division who remained in military service after the war had long and distinguished careers. They played a significant role in increasing the professionalism of the U.S. army during the nineteenth century. The statistics speak for themselves. During the forty-six years between 1815 and 1861, veterans of the Left Division served in the position of general-in-chief of the army for twenty-eight years, as adjutant-general for twenty-seven years, paymaster for forty-two and quartermaster for forty-two years. The Left Division left its stamp and, thanks to the efforts of its officers, the United States would never again go to war in such a wretched state of preparation as it had in 1812.[33]

Along with the other general officers who had fought in the Niagara campaign, the divisional commander, Major General Jacob Brown, received the official "thanks" of the nation and a special gold medal. He remained in the peacetime service and commanded the Northern Division until 1821 when he was appointed general-in-chief. As long as his health was good, Brown was a competent, practical and effective senior officer of the army.

It was unfortunate that Brown, having won a number of actual victories during the 1814 campaign, lost a postwar paper battle with Ripley. By the close of the campaign, Brown had drawn up formal court martial charges against his subordinate but was talked out of preferring them by senior members of the cabinet who were anxious to smooth over any difficulties with Ripley, one of the few New Englanders to play a prominent part in the war. Hearing of these charges, Ripley demanded and received a court of inquiry into his conduct during the campaign but it had hardly begun to hear evidence in February 1815 when it was discharged by the president. At the behest of the cabinet, Brown signed a confidential letter in May 1815 addressed to acting Secretary of War Alexander J. Dallas. Stating that his official report of the battle dated 7 August 1814 had created doubts about Ripley, Brown explained that he had not intended to implicate his "courage, his talents, or his zeal" and that Ripley could not be criticized for his actions on 26 July because Brown had already turned over command of the Left Division to him.[34]

This letter was shown to Ripley and the two officers made their peace. Brown was later angered when Ripley's friends published the text of it in a pamphlet entitled *Facts Relative to the Campaign on the Niagara Frontier in 1814* which came out a few months later. This pamphlet included all of the testimony at the court of inquiry favourable to Ripley as well as other testimonials from former officers of the division and created a great deal of sympathy for Ripley who appeared in the public eye to be a brave but unjustly maligned officer. By this very adroit manoeuvre, Ripley not only defused the case against him but made it appear that Brown was in the wrong to criticize him. There was nothing Brown could do except clench his teeth.

Brown's later years were marred by financial and physical problems. He suffered a stroke that partially incapacitated him and some of his business ventures went sour, leaving him in debt. These troubles probably hastened his end, which came in 1828 in his fifty-third year. He is buried in the Congressional Cemetery in Washington and his grave is marked with a marble column engraved with the words "In War his services are attested by the fields of Chippewa, Niagara, Erie; in Peace by the improved organization and discipline of the army."[35] It is a fitting epitaph.

Brown's adjutant-general, Colonel Charles K. Gardner, also fell afoul of Ripley. While in Boston in 1816, Gardner made some intemperate remarks about Ripley, who was the local commander, and was charged with insubordination among other things. A court martial was held in the autumn of 1816 and Gardner was found not guilty but, as happened with Brown, the proceedings, including all the most damaging testimony against Gardner (but not the verdict) soon appeared in the form of a pamphlet. Disgusted, Gardner resigned his commission and turned to literary pursuits, publishing military treatises and becoming the editor of the *New York Patriot*. In 1829 he re-entered government service and held a number of positions in the post office until his death in 1869 at the age of eighty-two. Among his other services, Gardner deserves mention for first suggesting the use of letter designations for the companies of U.S. infantry regiments.[36]

Major Roger Jones, the assistant adjutant general of the division, received a brevet promotion to lieutenant-colonel. In 1825 he was appointed adjutant general of the army and held this post until 1852 when he died in his sixty-third year.[37]

William McRee, the divisional engineer, was given a brevet promotion to colonel and sent on a European inspection tour following the war. He then worked on the design of coastal fortifications before resigning from the army in 1819 to become surveyor general of the United States. McRee died, unmarried, in 1833 in St. Louis at the age of forty-six.[38]

The divisional artillery commander, Jacob Hindman, ended the war as a brevet colonel. Of the sixteen officers in his battalion when it crossed the Niagara on 3 July, Hindman and Towson were the only ones not killed, wounded or taken prisoner before the campaign ended. Hindman remained in the artillery and died in 1827 at the young age of thirty-eight.[39]

Captain Nathan Towson ended the war as a brevet lieutenant colonel. In 1819 he became paymaster general and remained in this position for thirty-four years during which time he disbursed seventy-nine million dollars without incident. Ironically, as a brigadier general, one of Towson's last official duties in 1848 was to preside over a court of inquiry called against his former commander, Winfield Scott, on charges that Scott had misappropriated public funds to bribe Mexican generals. The matter was eventually dropped but, for his discretion, Towson received a brevet promotion to major general. Nathan Towson died at Washington in 1854 in his seventieth year.[40]

His fellow artilleryman, Captain Thomas Biddle, received a brevet promotion to major for his services at the siege of Fort Erie. Biddle stayed in the army and in 1819 was sent to St. Louis where he served as a paymaster. He married shortly afterward and lived happily until 1831 when he got into a violent argument over politics with Missouri congressman Spencer Pettis. A duel resulted, and because of his poor vision Biddle requested that the opposing parties stand only five feet apart, and both men were mortally wounded in the ensuing exchange of shots. Biddle was forty-one when he died.[41]

David Bates Douglass, the young engineer officer who so admired the captured British guns on the hill, received a brevet promotion to captain and was appointed to the faculty of the military academy at West Point. Ultimately, Douglass held the chairs of Mathematics and Engineering but outside work as a consulting engineer led him to resign from the army in 1831 and join the staff of New York University as professor of civil engineering. In 1840 Douglass began delivering a series of lectures on his wartime experiences which proved very popular and were later published. In 1849, at the age of sixty, he died suddenly from a stroke.[42]

Winfield Scott, who began the war as a captain, ended it as a brevet major general. He took some time to recover from the wound he received at Lundy's Lane, but by December 1814 he was well enough to preside over a board created to choose a new tactical system for the infantry. After he was fully recovered, he embarked on a tour of Europe and returned full of admiration for European, especially French, military practices. For the next three decades Scott translated each current French infantry manual for adoption by the army, as well as other technical material. Scott served in the Seminole War but, like many others, did not come away with his reputation enhanced. In 1846 he was sent to command the army in Mexico, where he planned and mounted a daring campaign that brought the surrender of the enemy capital and a quick peace. It also provided a graduate course in the school of war for a new generation of officers with names like Lee, Grant, Jackson, Johnston, Sherman, McClellan and Beauregard who would rise to later prominence.

But Scott had his dark side. A thoroughgoing professional of the best kind, his arrogance and unyielding obstinacy brought him into conflict with almost every senior officer in the army at some point in his career. For over three decades he carried on a feud with Gaines so acrimonious that, when Brown died in 1828, the government bypassed both men for the post of general-in-chief and instead appointed a more junior officer, Alexander Macomb. Scott also clashed with Jesup and in Mexico he clashed with two of his divisional commanders, Worth and Pillow, in a puerile display of temper that was unworthy of his position.[43]

Scott never filed a report on the actions of his brigade at Lundy's Lane and this neglect came back to haunt him in 1852 when he was an unsuccessful candidate for the presidency of the United States. His supporters used a recently published and adulatory biography of Scott by John Mansfield as campaign literature.[44] In response, Scott's opponents published a carefully crafted pamphlet that rebutted many of Mansfield's exaggerated statements. This pamphlet made much of the missing report and the fact that, of the four regimental commanders in the First Brigade, McNeil, Leavenworth, Brady and Jesup, only Jesup had been mentioned in Brown's report because he happened to come under Brown's notice. Jesup was the only former regimental commander still alive in 1852 and the pamphlet included letters from Jesup to McNeil and to the Pension Committee on McNeil's behalf concerning his role in the battle. They emphasized the fact that Scott never gave his regimental commanders the credit they deserved. The pamphlet was highly critical of Scott's generalship at Lundy's Lane:

[Towson's company] stood and were shot down, and fired to animate the infantry to stand and be shot down. And this continued to be the case until Gen. Brown came and saw that the battery must be taken, or the whole army sacrificed. Scott sees that *now*, although he did not see it when he might have preserved his gallant brigade by rushing on the battery, with the bayonet in the beginning, instead of standing 200 or 300 yards off, plying it ineffectually with musketry, and equally ineffectually with artillery.[45]

Scott survived this tempest as he had so many others and in the end simply outlived his critics. He was still on the active service list as commanding general of the army when the Civil War began and, although a native Virginian, his loyalty never wavered for a moment. It was now that he rendered perhaps his greatest service when he devised the "Anaconda" plan to crush the rebellion by isolating it using a blockade along the coasts and a powerful amphibious thrust up the Mississippi. If the south was cut off from foreign aid and not invaded, Scott reasoned, the rebellion would wither from lack of supplies and sheer boredom. It was a good plan but the politicians wanted immediate action and other younger and more ambitious generals were willing to give it to them. In the end, Scott realized that it was time to go and on a rainy night in November 1861, after fifty-three years in the army, he boarded a train at Washington station and went into retirement. Five years later, in his eightieth year, the old warrior died at West Point.[46]

His aide, Captain William Worth, recovered from the wound he received at Lundy's Lane and gained steady promotion in the postwar army. He fought in the Seminole War of the 1830s and by the time of the war with Mexico he was a brigadier general leading a division under his old commander. Sadly, relations between the two men became strained and they ended up preferring charges against each other, charges that were later dropped. In 1849, at the age of fifty-five, Worth died from cholera at San Antonio.[47]

Henry Leavenworth, the commander of the Ninth Infantry, ended the war as a brevet colonel and remained in the army although he resigned for a brief period to sit in the New York State Legislature before returning to the service in 1818. For the next sixteen years Leavenworth served on the western frontier, becoming commandant of the southwestern department before dying in 1834 at the age of fifty-one after a short illness. Fort Leavenworth, Kansas, is named after him.[48]

Major John McNeil of the Eleventh Infantry, who fought bravely at Chippawa but was badly wounded in the opening moments of the battle of Lundy's Lane, never fully recovered the use of his right leg. He had reached the rank of brigadier general by 1830 when he resigned to become collector of the port of Boston. McNeil was proud of his wound and took it for granted that everyone knew how it had occurred. He did not suffer fools gladly and when a small, rather voluble stranger asked the six foot, two inch, McNeil one day why he limped, he received the reply: "I fell through a barn floor, you devilish fool! Did you never read the history of your country?"[49] The tall, former general died in 1850 at the age of sixty-six.[50]

Hugh Brady of the Twenty-Second Infantry was so badly wounded at Lundy's Lane that he was not fit for service until the war ended. He remained in the army and held a series of commands on the northern border and western frontier. In 1837 Brady helped to maintain peace along the border during the rebellions in Upper Canada and found himself involved in a near incident with Lieutenant Colonel James Basden of the British army whom he had previously opposed at Lundy's Lane. Brady set a record, thirty years, for time in grade as a colonel, and was still on the rolls in 1851 as an eighty-three-year-old brevet major general when he died from injuries received in an accident.[51]

Thomas S. Jesup of the Twenty-Fifth Infantry, wounded four times during the action, was semi-convalescent for only a few weeks and returned to partial duty by September 1814. He never recovered the use of his right hand and learned to write with his left. At the end of the war, Jesup was a brevet colonel and in 1818 he was promoted brigadier general and appointed quartermaster general. He served in this appointment for forty-two years and was an efficient and effective administrator. Jesup held field commands during the Creek and Seminole Wars but his postwar career was clouded by an altercation with Winfield Scott. At the age of seventy-two, after fifty-two years of service, Jesup was still quartermaster-general when he died from a stroke at his home in Washington in 1860.[52]

Brigadier General Eleazar Wheelock Ripley, badly wounded in the sortie from Fort Erie, was slow to recover. He received a brevet promotion to major general and command of the Boston area although his reputation had suffered because of his record during the 1814 campaign. But Ripley's political instincts were sound and he was able not only to outmanoeuvre Brown and his adherents but also to gain much sympathy. To keep him away from Brown, Ripley was sent to Louisiana and was still there in 1820 when he resigned from the army. He returned to his original profession of law and was twice elected from Louisiana to the House of Representatives. Ripley died in 1839 in his fifty-seventh year.[53]

Lieutenant Colonel Robert C. Nicholas of the First Infantry who had the courage to disobey an impossible order, was court-martialled but acquitted. He resigned from the army in 1819 and two years later became Indian Agent to the Chickasaw. Nicholas died in 1836.[54]

Colonel James Miller, the modest but enterprising commander of the Twenty-First Infantry, whose unit captured Drummond's artillery at the battle, was one of the few senior officers of the Left Division to survive the campaign unscathed. He received a gold medal from Congress, a brevet promotion to major general and was lionized throughout the United States. Miller remained in the army until 1819 when he resigned to become governor of the Arkansas Territory, holding that office until 1824 when he was appointed Collector of the Port of Salem. He retained that appointment until 1849 when he was paralyzed by a stroke. Miller died at the age of seventy-five in 1851.[55]

Major George Brooke, who commanded the Twenty-Third Infantry during the latter part of the battle, ended the war as a brevet colonel. He remained in the army after the war, was promoted brigadier general in 1824 and major general in 1848. In 1824 he established Fort Brooke in Florida, the site of the future city of Tampa. Brooke's last command was Texas and he died at San Antonio in 1851 at the age of sixty-six.[56]

Brigadier General Peter B. Porter returned to politics after the war. He was re-elected to Congress in 1815, ran unsuccessfully for governor of New York in 1818 and served on the United States-Canada boundary commission before spending a year as secretary of war in the cabinet of John Quincy Adams. Porter retired from political life in the 1830s and passed his remaining years on the extensive property he owned along the Niagara River. He died in his seventy-first year in 1844 and was universally mourned.[57]

There were also those members of the division with less illustrious records. Lieutenant Henry Blake of the Eleventh Infantry, who disappeared in the midst of the battle, was tried by court martial and resigned from the army in 1816. Captain Joseph Treat of the Twenty-First, who was dismissed from the army after Brown witnessed him leaving a wounded man behind on the morning of the Battle of Chippawa, persisted for months in trying to obtain a court martial to vindicate his name. He was finally successful in April 1815 and, after hearing evidence, the court honourably acquitted him of the charge of "Cowardice before the enemy."[58]

And finally there was young Drummer Jarvis Hanks. In March 1815 news of the peace reached Jarvis at Sackets Harbor, where he had spent the winter in garrison with the Eleventh Infantry. "All the soldiers rejoiced," he remembered, "but none so heartily" as those, including Hanks, who had only enlisted for the duration of the war. An extra ration of whisky was distributed "to make merry" and young Jarvis, contrary to his custom, "drank mine, so that I might feel good." The following May the fifteen year-old was honourably discharged and returned home to his family in Pawlet.[59]

Intrigued with army life, Jarvis wanted to go to West Point, but his father being against the idea, he relinquished all hope of a military career and instead attended the Pawlet Academy and learned to play the violin in his spare time. In 1817 he became restless and left for Ohio where he eked out a living as a painter and chair-maker. For the next six years, he led a somewhat gypsy existence, moving between Ohio and Philadelphia, working as a painter and studying art and medicine, before ending up in Charles Town, Virginia, as a music teacher. Here he fell in love with a local girl, Charlotte Garber, and they married in 1823 much against the wishes of her family, who were concerned about Jarvis's financial prospects.

Determined to make a living as an artist, Jarvis moved to New York City and for a time prospered as a sign and portrait painter. But the lure of the west was too much and in 1835 he moved to Ohio and settled near Cleveland. Unfortunately for Jarvis, the practical midwesterners saw little use for such luxuries as portraits and he had to struggle to support his wife and family, which eventually numbered eight children. Charlotte's father, however, was generous in his assistance and, though there was never much to spare in the Hanks household, it did not want. It would be nice to record that the former drummer boy's later years were easier but in middle age he became afflicted by a brain tumour that robbed him first of his sight and then his life. Jarvis Hanks died at Cleveland in 1858 in his fifty-seventh year.

Where Right and Glory Lead!

*Horace Tower was killed in the sanguinary battle of Bridgewater
and was buried in "the corn field," as the soldiers were accustomed
to denominate the grounds where the slain were interred.*
JOSIAH GOODHUE, *History of the Town of Shoreham*, 1861

In the years immediately following the war, as modern tourism was born
in the Niagara area, the battlefields of the summer of 1814 became popular
attractions for the thousands who flocked to see the falls. Guides, often veterans of the engagements, took the curious around the scenes of the fighting and one American visitor remembered with excitement that "every attack and retreat was detailed to us" while we stood "on the very spot of
action."[1] By 1838 a standard sightseeing guide for the area solemnly assured
its readers that "the battles at Fort Erie, Chippewa, and Lundy's Lane, were
among the most bloody and hard-fought, that are recorded in history."[2]

Being close to the falls, Lundy's Lane was the most visited site but also
the first to be encroached upon by development. In 1831 the straggling little hamlet at the junction of the Portage Road and the lane became incorporated as the village of Drummondville and five years later the old meeting house on the hill was replaced by a more elaborate Presbyterian church.

A decade later, Charles Anderson, a former lieutenant in the Canadian
Provincial Artillery Drivers who had been present on 25 July, conducted
tours of the battlefield. Dressed in a red jacket and a broad-brimmed white
hat, the affable Anderson was a fixture on the hillside. He was also a man
who liked his dram, and in 1844 when two visitors from Montreal went
with him to view the battlefield one Sunday morning, they found that
Anderson had spent some time fortifying himself in a local hotel. Taking up
position on the steps of the Presbyterian church on top of the hill, he
launched into a fiery description of the events of the fighting which he

Lundy's Lane
Lundy's Lane looking westward from Portage Road as it appeared in 1915. This pleasant, tree-shrouded street has long since disappeared under concrete. (Courtesy, *Niagara Falls Review*)

punctuated with frequent loud exclamations of "Hurrah, boys!" as in "Hurrah, boys! There comes the 89th redcoats, at a mad charge, with a wild, ringing British cheer!" To his listeners' embarrassment, the congregation rapidly emptied out of the church, the worshippers "being anxious to learn what was going on outside."[3]

It was Anderson who conceived the idea of building an observation tower on top of the hill (possibly because he was no longer allowed to use the church as a viewing point). He constructed a primitive structure about

Observation towers erected along Lundy's Lane in the 1860s
For decades after the war, the battlefield at Lundy's Lane was a major tourist attraction and the operators of these observation towers enjoyed a brisk business. (From James Morden, *Historical Monuments and Observatories of Lundy's Lane and Queenston Heights*, Niagara Falls, Lundy's Lane Historical Society, 1929.. Courtesy of the Lundy's Lane Historical Society)

forty feet high on the north side of the lane but it collapsed soon afterward. In 1846 a local resident, Donald McKenzie, erected a more substantial tower, eighty feet in height, west of the church. McKenzie charged twenty-five cents admission and made additional profit by exposing his customers to a choice assortment of souvenirs including native beadwork, barkwork, bows and arrows, and muskets balls picked up from the hillside. This edifice burned in 1851 but, soon after, two more were built on the north side of the lane. The owners employed veterans as guides and these wily gentlemen first ascertained a visitor's nationality before describing the battle which, depending on that nationality, would see the "stars and stripes wave in triumph" or "the Cross of St. George float in glory."[4]

In 1867 the American historian Benson Lossing visited the site of the battle, and after he "climbed wearily to the top," he was "richly rewarded for the toil by a magnificent panoramic view of the surrounding country."[5] Lossing and his companions were less pleased with the elderly guide they encountered at the top of the tower who,

... began his well-learned task of repeating the record of historical events there. We only wanted to know the exact locality of certain incidents of the battle, and, after four times preventing him from going farther in his tedious details than the words "In the year one thousand eight hundred and fourteen," we obtained what we wished, and descended.

The Civil War sounded the death knell for the tower operators as American tourists now had more recent, and closer, battlefields to visit. Although the falls continued to grow in popularity as a tourist attraction, the military aspect of a visit began to lose its appeal and by 1870 one of the towers had been dismantled and the other had fallen into disuse. In 1893 prominent local citizens erected a steel structure with an elevator and it lasted for nearly thirty years although it was operated only intermittently. By this time the city of Niagara Falls had swallowed Drummondville and the lanes and trails of 1814 had become paved streets framed by business blocks or residential housing.[6]

The graveyard on the hill and a vacant lot that adjoins it to the south were now the only part of the former battlefield that remained relatively untouched. The Drummond Hill cemetery, as it came to be called, functioned as the major local burial ground and was gradually increased over the nineteenth century from its original half-acre to four acres in size. But it contained no memorial to commemorate those who had fallen in the battle and, in 1887 the Lundy's Lane Historical Society launched an appeal to "British Canadians" for funds for the construction of a monument.[7]

This appeal fell on fertile ground for the memory of the War of 1812 was still very much alive in Canada and the response was steady enough for the historical society to commence construction in 1895. The finished monument was a forty-foot-high granite shaft mounted on a twenty-foot square base with six steps. Its inscription, composed during the full flower of imperial glory, read: "In Honour of the Victory Gained by the British Canadian Forces on this Field on the 25th Day of July, 1814 And in Grateful Remembrance OF THE BRAVE MEN WHO DIED ON THAT DAY FIGHTING FOR THE UNITY OF THE EMPIRE." On 25 July 1895, a crowd of two thousand gathered in the cemetery to listen to officials and dignitaries dedicate the monument.[8]

With some foresight, the society had incorporated a vault into the foundations of the monument. It was needed as from time to time human remains from the battle had come to light. Early tourists had actually un-

Grim mementoes of the battle
William Dalton, sexton of the Drummond Hill cemetery from 1877 to 1898, poses with some of the mementoes of the battle he uncovered on the battlefield. The two human skulls have since been properly interred. (Courtesy, Lundy's Lane Historical Society)

earthed bones from the shallow graves "and carried them away as reliques" and, in the late nineteenth century, expansion of the city of Niagara Falls led to the discovery of some gruesome reminders of the battle.[9] On 3 September 1891, workmen digging a sand pit on the north side of the hill uncovered eleven skeletons identified from their buttons as being men of the 89th and 103rd Foot. Uniform fragments also indicated that one of the eleven was an officer of the 89th Foot, either Captain Robert Spunner or Lieutenant John Latham. Word spread quickly and a crowd of souvenir hunters soon gathered. The caretaker of the local museum tried to prevent the curious from stealing the remains although he was unable to save the bits of uniform, boot heels, belt plates, cap badges and buttons which were spirited away. Later this same caretaker learned of "a medical student who had a bag of bones (89th) in his bedroom."[10] An ingenious man, "he employed a half-witted fellow to place a ladder to the window and steal the bag," thus adding the missing members of the 89th to those he had already preserved.[11]

Headstone of Captain Abraham Hull, U.S. Army
The only American soldier killed in the battle to have a marked grave, Abraham Hull was a captain in the Ninth Infantry who was mortally wounded towards the close of the action. He was the son of General William Hull, who surrendered Detroit in 1812, and the nephew of Captain Isaac Hull, captain of the famous USS *Constitution*. Behind his stone are the graves of nine American servicemen whose remains were accidentally uncovered in 1901 and reburied with full military honours. (Author's photo)

These remains were re-interred in the cemetery with appropriate ceremony in October 1891. Subsequent discoveries were made in April 1893 of the skeletons of seven men of the 1st Foot at the corner of Lundy's Lane and the Portage Road and in October 1899 of an officer, possibly Ensign John Campbell of the Incorporated Militia. All were ultimately placed in the vault of the newly constructed memorial along with the remains of the eleven soldiers who had been disinterred in 1891.[12]

In 1900 a unique ceremony took place when the recently discovered remains of nine soldiers of the Ninth United States Infantry were laid to rest beside the grave of Abraham Hull, which had been marked early in the century with a stone erected by his family and comrades. On this occasion, Company K of the Fourteenth U.S. Infantry, stationed at Fort Niagara, were given permission to enter Canada with their weapons and fired three volleys over the grave while a band played "Nearer, My God to Thee."[13]

The high point of Canadian fervour over the War of 1812 was the centenary of the battle. The Lundy's Lane Historical Society began a year in advance to prepare for the event and by the great day, Saturday, 25 July 1914, all was ready. Volunteers had decorated the junction of the lane and the Portage Road and the Lane north to Drummond Hill Cemetery with red, white and blue bunting and banners inscribed "Drummond" and "Brown." The cemetery and memorial were bedecked with more bunting, flags and small pennants bearing the names of every officer who had played a prominent part in the action. The invited official guests and notables assembled in the late morning and, following an extended lunch at a good hotel, rode by carriage to the hill, where a crowd estimated at ten thousand was waiting. In the van of the procession marched detachments from the regular Canadian army and various militia regiments.[14]

The ceremonies got under way at 3:00 P.M. sharp. Dignitary after dignitary rose to deliver (if the official programme is to be believed) long-winded speech after speech on the bravery shown by Canadians at the battle. The speech making was broken by patriotic interludes. School children sang "O Canada" and "The Maple Leaf Forever" and at one point twelve white-clad maidens, six from Canada and six from the United States, laid wreaths on the various tombs in the cemetery. Sonnets and poems by local authors were then declaimed including one by Duncan Scott with such wretched lines as "But, O the joy of that battle – it was worth the whole of life. You felt immortal in action with the rapture of the strife."[15] The afternoon passed in a general mood of self-satisfaction and the only sour note was sounded by Chief Josiah Hill of the Grand River Nations, one of twelve chiefs invited to the ceremony, who asked all present "to use their influence with those in power" to rectify the grievances of his people who were "brothers who had shared in the defence of Canada."[16]

Such was the feeling in 1914 Canada. The coming years, however, would provide that nation with new and unwelcome national experiences to commemorate. Twenty-seven days before the centenary ceremonies, a young Serb had assassinated an Austrian archduke and lit the fuse that was to ignite the first of the great conflicts that would mark the next four decades. For Canadians there would be other hills and other confused and bloody night battles to remember with sorrow and pride, and gradually, the aura around Lundy's Lane diminished.

Today there is little physical evidence of the battle in the modern city of Niagara Falls. The shaded country lane of 1814 is now a busy four-lane artery crowded with motels, fast food outlets and souvenir emporiums. The Lundy farmhouse still exists but is almost hidden from view by a large gift shop. You can sleep in air-conditioned comfort in a motel near the same spot where the four-times wounded Jesup formed the Twenty-Fifth into a single rank to repel Drummond's last desperate attack. The area where Miller's Twenty-First Infantry formed for their attack on the British artillery is partly school yard and partly residential backyard. The only thing unchanged is the distant, constant roar of the falls – if you can hear it over the roar of the traffic.

Memories of that bloody battle are kindled, however, when the visitor enters Drummond Hill Cemetery. For this ground is the last resting place of many who participated in the events of that far-off summer of 1814. It contains the family plots of some of the local people over whose land the battles of 1814 were fought: Samuel Street, Philip Bender, Christopher Buchner, William Lundy and many of his family, Haggai Skinner and many of his, and, finally, William and Rebecca Biggar and their children.

Centennial celebration, 1914
The centennial of the battle, held on 25 July 1914, saw an impressive gathering of distinguished speakers, military units and large crowds at the Drummond Hill cemetery. At one point during the ceremonies, twelve white-clad maidens, six from the U.S. and six from Canada, adorned the graves of the dead from the battle. Here they pose with their chaperons. (From *Centennial Celebration of the Battle of Lundy's Lane,* Niagara Falls, 1919. Courtesy of the Lundy's Lane Historical Society)

Canadian soldiers return to the battlefield, 1914
Regulars from the Royal Canadian Regiment march up Lundy's Lane during the centennial celebrations of 25 July 1914. Within months, many of these men would be in action on the Western Front. (From *Centennial Celebration of the Battle of Lundy's Lane*, Niagara Falls, 1919. Courtesy of the Lundy's Lane Historical Society)

Here too, lying "in the corn field" under tombstones marred by time, vandals and pollution, are the soldiers. Captain Richard ("Old Dick") Leonard of the 104th Foot rests alongside his family. Close by is Captain S.B. Torrens of the 1st Foot killed at the disastrous night assault on Fort Erie of 15 August, and Lieutenant Colonel John Gordon of the same regiment, wounded at Chippawa, present at Lundy's Lane and killed at the sortie from Fort Erie. Not far away is the grave of Captain Robert Patteson of the 6th Foot, killed leading the British counterattack on 17 September 1814. Scattered throughout the older section of the cemetery are various "trenches" – the common graves of some of the British dead from the battle. Separated by the monument, and somewhat apart from the rest, are the Americans. In front of the burial plot of the men of the Ninth Infantry is the grave of Captain Abraham Hull, whom Le Couteur of the 104th tried to succour in the last hours of his young life during the "chilling cold" night after the battle.

Whether soldiers or civilians, whether friends or enemies – they all now lie together in the place where right and glory lead.

Where Right and Glory Lead.
Memorial erected by the Lundy's Lane Historical Society in 1895. In a vault beneath the obelisk are interred the remains of British soldiers killed during the action which were un-covered in the late 19th century. (Courtesy, National Archives of Canada, C-9896)

Order of Battle and Strength, Left Division, United States Army, 25 July 1814

Commanding Officer	Major General Jacob Brown

Divisional Staff

Aides to Gen. Brown:	Capt. Loring Austin
	Capt. Ambrose Spencer
Adjutant General:	Col. Charles K. Gardner
Assistant Adjutant General:	Maj. Roger Jones
Chief Engineer:	Lt. Col. William McRee
Assistant Engineer:	Maj. Eleazar D. Wood
Quartermaster:	Capt. John Camp
Acting Inspector General:	Second Lt. Edward B. Randolph

First Brigade (est. 1080 men)

Commanding Officer:	Brigadier General Winfield Scott
Aide to Scott:	First Lt. William Jenkins Worth
Brigade Major:	Lieutenant J.D. Smith
Ninth Infantry (200)	Maj. Henry Leavenworth
Eleventh Infantry (200)	Maj. John McNeil
Twenty-Second Infantry (300)	Col. Hugh Brady
Twenty-Fifth Infantry (380)	Maj. Thomas S. Jesup

Second Brigade (est. 882 men)

Commanding Officer:	Brigadier General Eleazar W. Ripley
Aide:	First Lt. William MacDonald
Brigade Major:	First Lt. Newman S. Clarke
First Infantry (150)	Lt. Col. Robert C. Nicholas
Twenty-First Infantry (432)	Lt. Col. James Miller
Twenty-Third Infantry (300)	Maj. Daniel McFarland

Note: The First Infantry only arrived with the division on the day of the battle and was later placed in the Second Brigade. Single companies of the Seventeenth Infantry under Capt. John Chunn and the Nineteenth Infantry under Lt. David Riddle were attached to the Twenty-First Infantry on 25 July 1814.

Third Brigade (546)

Commanding Officer:	Brig. Gen. Peter B. Porter, New York Militia
Aide:	Maj. Jacob Dox, New York Militia
Brigade Major:	Maj. John Stanton, New York Militia
Regiment of Detached New York Militia (250):	Lt. Col. Hugh W. Dobbin
5th Pennsylvania Regiment (Fenton's Pennsylvanians) (246):	Maj. James Wood, Pennsylvania Militia
Canadian Volunteers (50)	Lt. Col. Joseph Willcocks, U.S. Volunteers

Note: Half of New York regiment was at Lewiston on 25 July 1814 under the regimental commander, Colonel Philetus Swift, N.Y. Militia. Colonel James Fenton, commander of the Pennsylvania regiment, was on leave on 25 July 1814.

Artillery (est. 200 gunners in action)

Major Jacob Hindman's Battalion, Corps of Artillery
    Captain Thomas Biddle's Company (probably three 12-pdr. guns)
    Captain John Ritchie's Company (two 6-pdr. guns, one 5½-inch howitzer)
    Captain Nathan Towson's Company (two 6-pdr. guns, one 5½-inch howitzer)
    Captain Alexander Williams's Company (probably three 18-pdr. guns)
    Lieutenant David B Douglass's Company of Sappers, Bombardiers and Miners
        (two 18-pdr. guns)
    Artillery Reserve (unknown numbers and calibres)

Notes: Only Biddle, Ritchie and Towson's companies came into action on 25 July 1814. Towson accompanied Scott's First Brigade. See below for a discussion of the number and types of weapons in the three companies that came into action.

Cavalry (70)

Captain Samuel D. Harris's Company (Troop), U.S. Light Dragoons
Captain Claudius V. Boughton's Company, New York Volunteer Dragoons

Note: Harris commanded both mounted units at the battle.

Recapitulation of Number of U.S. Troops Present at Lundy's Lane

1st Brigade	1080
2nd Brigade	882
3rd Brigade	546
Artillery	est. 200 and nine guns
Cavalry	70
Total	2778 men and nine guns

Note: The last full muster of the Left Division was made on 23 July 1814, two days before the battle. On that day, the division possessed 5009 officers and men, of which

4232 were fit for duty. Of this latter total, Brown estimated that he had about 2800 men available for action on 25 July 1814 after deducting the garrisons of Buffalo, Fort Erie, Schlosser and Lewiston as well as those units left in camp during the battle (two companies of Volunteers, one company of artillery, the company of sappers, bombardiers and miners and the companies on picket). This figure was used as a check against the totals worked out above which are extracted from the reports, correspondence, memoirs and court martial testimony of brigade, regimental and company commanders.

The numbers and calibres of the artillery in Hindman's battalion constitute a problem. A not entirely reliable source states that each of the four companies had three pieces of ordnance. If so, this would be in accordance with current U.S. regulations in which field artillery was to be organized in divisions (batteries) or half-divisions (half batteries). Each division was to consist of four guns of the same calibre and two howitzers, or six guns of not more than two different calibres. Each half-division was to consist of two guns of the same calibre and one howitzer, or three guns of the same calibre.

What is known is that Towson commanded two 6-pdr. guns and one 5½-inch howitzer at Chippawa on 25 July and it is presumed that he had the same number and types on 25 July 1814. On 15 July, Ritchie's company provided the artillery support for Porter's reconnaissance of Fort George and the British ascertained that he had one 6-pdr. gun and one 5½-inch howitzer; it is presumed that he had the same calibres ten days later. Williams's company is known to have been equipped with 18-pdr. guns as was Douglass's company, but neither participated in the action of 25 July. This leaves Biddle's company, and an officer of that company is known to have brought an 12-pdr. gun into action at Chippawa.

Taking all this into consideration, it seems likely that Towson and Ritchie's companies constituted half-divisions, each equipped with two 6-pdr. guns and one howitzer, while Biddle's company constituted another half division and was probably equipped with three 12-pdr. guns. It is therefore probable that the American artillery brought nine guns into action at Lundy's Lane.

Sources

Overall Divisional Strength
Strength of the American Army Commanded by Major General Jacob Brown on the 23d of July 1814, Brown Papers, Library of Congress; Guards and Pickets on Duty Roster, 25 July 1814, RG 98, E50, Brigade Orders Issued, vol. 452, 351, National Archives; Strength of the American Army July 25th 1814, *Facts Relative to the Campaign on the Niagara in 1814* (Boston: Patriot Office, 1815).

First Brigade Units
Thomas S. Jesup, Memoir of the Campaign Upon the Niagara, Jesup Papers, Library of Congress; Letter of Leavenworth, 15 Jan. 1815, *Facts*, 19; Certificate of Foster, *Facts*, 42; Strength of Scott's Brigade, 31 July 1814, Henry Adams, *History of the United States during the Administration of James Madison* (New York: A.C. Boni, 1930, 4 vols.), IV, Book 8, 68.

Second Brigade Units
Miller to wife, 28 July 1814, War of 1812 Papers, Clements Library, University of Michigan; Ripley to Brown, 29 July 1814, War of 1812 Mss., Lilly Library, Indiana University; Evidence of McDonald, *Facts*, 42; Court Martial of Lt. Col. R.C. Nicholas, RG 153, K-1, 115, 169, National Archives; Adams, *History*, IV, Book 8, 69.

Third Brigade Units
Porter to Brown, 28 July 1814, War of 1812 Papers, Lilly Library, Indiana University; Hugh Dobbin, Memoir, Geneva Historical Society; Muster Rolls, RG 94, Entry 55, National Archives; Morning Reports, Peter B. Papers, Buffalo & Erie County Historical Society; Volunteer Organizations and State Militia, War of 1812, RG 94, Box 207, Fenton, National Archives.

Artillery and Cavalry Units
Sketch of the Life of General Nathan Towson (Baltimore: N. Hickman, 1842), 14; Harris to Brown, 29 July 1814, War of 1812 Mss., Lilly Library, Indiana University; David B. Douglass, "An Original Narrative of the Niagara Campaign of 1814," ed., John F, Horton, *Niagara Frontier* 46 (1964), 13; Report of Capt. Samuel D. Harris, 2 Aug. 1814, War of 1812 Papers, Lilly Library, Indiana University; Strength of Hindman's battalion, 30 June 1814, Adams, *History*, IV, Book 8, 69.

Numbers and Types of Artillery
"Biographical Sketch of Maj. Thomas Biddle. Late of the United States' Army," *Illinois Monthly Magazine* 1 (1831), 549; Regulations of the Ordnance Department, 1 May 1813, *The Army Register of the United States* (Boston: Chester Stebbins, 1814), 73-74; Hindman to Adjutant General, n.d., Ernest A. Cruikshank, ed., *Documentary History of the Campaigns upon the Niagara Frontier in 1812-1814* (Welland, Canada: Tribune Press, 1896-1907, 9 vols.), I, 44; General Order, 9 July 1814, Left Division Order Book, Mss. 11225, New York State Library, Albany; Porter to Brown, *Doc. Hist.*, I, 16 July 1814; Tucker to Riall, 15 July 1814, *Doc. Hist.* I, 66; marginal notations on: Strength of the American Army commanded Major General Jacob Brown on the 23d of July 1814, Brown Papers, Library of Congress.

Order of Battle and Strength, Right Division, British Army in Canada, 25 July 1814

Commander, Upper Canada	Lt. Gen. Gordon Drummond
Commanding Officer, Right Division	Maj. Gen. Phineas Riall

Staff

Aides to Lt. Gen. Drummond:	Capt. William Jervois
	Capt. Robert Loring
Aide to Maj. Gen. Riall:	Capt. J.H. Holland
Deputy Adjutant General:	Lt. Col. John Harvey
Assistant Adjutant General:	Maj. John Glegg
Deputy Assistant Adjutant General:	Lt. Henry Moorsom
Assistant Quartermaster General:	Maj. John Maule
Deputy Assistant Quartermaster General:	Lt. John LeBreton

PEARSON'S FORCE (est. 1157 men)

2nd or Light Brigade (est. 857)	**Lt. Col. Thomas Pearson**
19th Light Dragoons (squadron, 95)	Maj. Robert Lisle
Provincial Light Dragoons (30)	Capt. W.H. Merritt, Militia
Glengarry Light Infantry (376)	Lt. Col. Francis Battersby
Incorporated Militia Battalion of Upper Canada (336)	Lt. Col. William Robinson
Royal Artillery (est. 20)	
Two brass 6-pdr. guns	
One brass 5½-inch howitzer	

1st Militia Brigade (est. 300)	**Lt. Col. Love Parry**
1st Lincoln Regiment, detachment	–
2nd Lincoln Regiment, detachment	Maj. David Secord, Militia
4th Lincoln Regiment, detachment	–

| 5th Lincoln Regiment, detachment | Lt. Col. Andrew Bradt, Militia |
| 2nd York Regiment, detachment | Maj. Titus G. Simons, Militia |

Force of Mohawk Warriors (est. 50) Capt. John Norton, (Snipe)

MORRISON'S FORCE FROM THE FORTS AT THE RIVER MOUTH (est. 761 men)

1st Foot (3 companies, 171)	Capt. William Brereton
8th Foot (1 company, est. 65)	Capt. Francis Campbell
41st Foot (light company, est. 60)	Capt. Joseph B. Glew
89th Foot (8 companies, 425)	Lt. Col. Joseph W. Morrison & Major Miller Clifford
Artillery (est. 40)	Capt. James Machlachlane, RA

Two 24-pdr. brass guns under Lt. Richard Tomkyns, RA
Congreve rocket section, under Sergt. Austin, RMA
Force of Mohawk and Western Warriors (numbers unknown, possibly 400–500)

COLONEL HERCULES SCOTT'S FORCE (est. 1720 men)

1st Brigade (est. 1070 men)	**Col. Hercules Scott**
8th Regiment of Foot (5 companies, 275 men)	Maj. Thomas Evans
103rd Regiment of Foot (7 companies, 635 men)	Maj. William Smelt
104th Foot (2 companies, 120 men)	Capt. Richard Leonard
Royal Artillery (est. 40) Three 6-pdr. brass guns	Capt. James Mackonochie, RA

Reserve, (est. 400 men), Lt. Col. John Gordon

| 1st Foot (7 companies, 400 men) | Lt. Col. John Gordon |

2nd Militia Brigade (est. 250 men), Lt. Col. Christopher Hamilton
1st Norfolk Regiment, detachment
2nd Norfolk Regiment, detachment
1st Essex Regiment, detachment
1st Middlesex Regiment, detachment
Caldwell (Western) Rangers, detachment

Recapitulation

	British Regulars	Canadian Regulars	Militia	Totals
Pearson's Force:	115	742	300	1157
Morrison's Force:	761	–	–	761
Hercules's Scott's Force:	1350	120	250	1720
Totals:	2226	852	550	3638

Note: Because they were long-service units recruited for the duration of the war, Merritt's Provincial Light Dragoons and the Incorporated Militia have been counted as

"Canadian Regulars" along with the Glengarry Light Infantry Fencibles and 104th Foot, British units recruited in Canada.

Drummond's large force of Indian warriors did not see much action in the battle and have not been included in the totals above.

Ascertaining the correct number and calibres of the British artillery at Lundy's Lane is a problem. According to the order which re-organized the division on 16 July, two 6-pdr. guns were assigned to Pearson's Brigade and three 6-pdr. guns and one 5½-inch howitzer to Hercules Scott's brigade. If Pearson had two guns and Drummond added two there should have been four guns on the hill in the early stages of the battle. However, in a "Sketch of the action fought on the night of 25 July near the falls of Niagara" by Capt. G.A. Eliot who was present, five guns are shown on the hill in the early part of the action.

It is likely that Pearson brought along a 5½-inch howitzer as well as two 6-pdr. guns. There are numerous American accounts of shells being fired during the early part of the battle and one American witness clearly stated that there was a howitzer firing from the hill. Ensign John Kilborn, a member of Pearson's brigade, recalled that two or three pieces of artillery with the brigade. The balance of the evidence seems to suggest that there were five pieces of artillery on the hill in the first stages of the battle and that one of them was a howitzer. With the addition of Hercules Scott's three 6-pdr. guns that would make a total of eight British artillery pieces in the action. This is the number that Lieutenant David Douglass of the American army, who was able to inspect the captured ordnance several times, states was on the hill.

Sources

Sources on Organization and Strength of the Right Division
Return and Distribution of Ordnance, Carriages, etc., 1 April 1814, WO 44, vol. 250, 530, Public Record Office, London; Weekly Distribution of Right Division, 8 July 1814, Ernest A. Cruikshank, *Documentary History of the Campaigns upon the Niagara in 1812-1814* (Welland, Canada: Tribune Press, 1896-1908, 9 vols.), I, 50; Drummond to Prevost, 10 July 1814, *Doc. Hist.*, I, 35; Riall to Drummond, 15 July 1814, *Doc. Hist.*, I, 65; General Order, 16 July 1814, MG 19, A34, vol. 3, Right Division Order Book, Clark Papers, National Archives of Canada; Riall to Drummond, 17 July 1814, *Doc. Hist.*, I, 69; Riall to Drummond, 22 July 14, *Doc. Hist.* I, 65; Harvey to Riall, 23 July 1814, *Doc. Hist.*, I, 82; Arrangements for collecting a force at Burlington, RG 8 I, vol. 684, 91, National Archives of Canada; District General Order, 1 Aug. 1814, RG 8 I, vol. 231, 128, National Archives of Canada; Duncan Clark, The Battle Lundy's Lane, MG 19, A34, National Archives of Canada; Shadrach Byfield "Recollections", in John Gellner, ed., *Recollections of the War of 1812: Three Eyewitness Accounts* (Toronto: Baxter Publishing, 1964), 38; John Norton, *The Journal of John Norton 1816*, eds., J.J. Talman & C.F. Klinck (Toronto: Champlain Society, 1970), 355-356; Richard Cannon, compiler, *Historical Records of the First or Royal Regiment of Foot* (London: Furnivall & Parker, 1847), 199; and *Historical Records of The Eighth, or, The King's Regiment of Foot* (London: Furnivall & Parker, 1844), 97-98; William James, *A Full and Correct Account of the Military Occurrences of the Late War Between Great Britain and the United States* (London: Black, 1818, 2 vols.), II, 141-142; Ernest A. Cruikshank: "Record of the Serv-

ices of Canadian Regiments in the War of 1812 – II. The Glengarry Light Infantry," *Selected Papers of the Canadian Military Institute* 6 (1894-1895), 17; "V. The Incorporated Militia, " *Selected Papers of the Canadian Military Institute* 9 (1897-1899), 70-80; "XI. The Militia of Norfolk, Oxford, and Middlesex," *Canadian Military Institute Selected Papers* 15 (1907), 66-67.

Sources on Numbers and Calibres of British Artillery at Lundy's Lane
Right Division Order, 16 July 1814, MG 19, A34, vol. 3, Right Division Order Book, National Archives of Canada; Drummond to Prevost, 27 July 1814, RG 8 I, vol. 684, 235, National Archives of Canada; NMC H2/407-1814, Sketch of the Action, 25 July 1814, National Archives of Canada; Letter on the battle of Niagara, *NWR*, Supplement to Vol. VIII, 174; John Kilborn, "Biographical Sketch," in Thaddeus Leavitt, *History of Leeds and Grenville* (Belleville: 1879, reprinted Mika Press, 1972), 70; David B. Douglass, "An Original Narrative of the Niagara Campaign of 1814," John F. Horton, ed., *Niagara Frontier* 46 (1964), 19.

The Problem of the Guns

The most vexing aspect of any detailed study of Lundy's Lane is deciding which army was in possession of the British artillery at the end of the battle. Most British and Canadian historians either accept Drummond's statement that "some of our guns remained for a few minutes" in American hands but were "quickly recovered," or, while admitting that the Left Division held those guns for a longer period, conclude that they were recaptured before the fighting ended.[1] Those authors who state that the guns were retaken usually base their argument on two pieces of primary evidence – the account of Private Shadrach Byfield of the 41st Foot and a statement made by Major Jacob Hindman in 1815 – or on a secondary source: Robert Gourlay's *Statistical Account of Upper Canada*, published in 1822.

Gourlay, who visited the battlefield in the immediate postwar period, stated that the "British line made three vigorous but unsuccessful efforts to regain their artillery."[2] He then continued:

> Captain Glew of the 41st, with two companies, having fallen in with and dispersed the American rear guard, and taken possession of the artillery, the British line remained near the battle ground through the night.[3]

Of greater value, however, is the statement made by Jacob Hindman, the Left Division's artillery commander, while testifying at Ripley's court of inquiry. Hindman described his efforts to remove all the artillery after the fighting had ended and then went on:

> Immediately after this, I turned my attention to getting off the enemy's brass 24 pounder, and for this purpose detached Lieut. Fontaine, of the artillery, with orders to take it from the field, and afterwards ordered Lieut. Kincaid, of the artillery, to assist him. I then rode to the bottom of the hill, and after great difficulty, procured some horses, and at the same time ordered several waggons to the top of the hill, to bring off the wounded. On my return to the gun, some of the waggons having previously reached the hill, I discovered the gun and waggons in possession of the enemy; some of the men and horses were captured. I left the field at the same time. When I reached the troops on their return to camp, Lieut. Fontaine informed me, that I had left him but a few minutes, before the enemy charged his little party at the gun, and made them all prisoners. He escaped by dashing through their ranks on horseback, it being dark.[4]

Although Hindman makes it clear that the artillery was in American hands when the fighting ended, many British and Canadian authors have been extremely reluctant to accept any evidence, primary or secondary, that this was so.[5] In his pamphlet on the battle, first published in the 1890s and unfortunately still being treated as a reliable source by some modern historians, Ernest Cruikshank wrote that:

> Almost all American writers, following the cue furnished by General Brown in his official letter, convey the impression that their forces retired voluntarily, and were not expelled from the position they had won, and none of them admit the loss of any artillery. The statements on these points, however, are fully substantiated by affidavits published in General Ripley's pamphlet already referred to, as well as by several letters from officers and men in the American army, which appeared in different contemporary newspapers.[6]

Combining Gourlay and Hindman, Cruikshank concluded that the battle ended as follows:

> Finally, when it was about midnight, the thinned and wearied ranks were again closed and urged up the hillside. Headed by the light company of the 41st, led by Captain Glew, they pressed steadily up the slope, and at length stood triumphantly upon the summit. Their opponents were surprised in the act of retiring, and their rearguard was easily overthrown and dispersed. The two 24-pounders they had lost were recovered, but the 6-pounder had already been removed. ......
> The officer commanding the party at the guns put spurs to his horse and escaped, but most of his men were taken prisoner beside them.[7]

When he wrote this passage, Cruikshank appears to have been unaware of the memoir of Private Shadrach Byfield, first published in 1840.[8] Byfield, a soldier in Glew's light company of the 41st Foot, recorded how he and his comrades captured some artillery during the battle:

> We then moved on for the field of action. We had a guide with us and when we came near the field, our captain was called upon, by name, in a loud voice, to form on the left of the speaker. It being night, we could not discover what regiment it was. The guide positively asserted that it was one of the enemy. Our bugle then sounded for the company to drop. A volley was then fired upon us, which killed two corporals, and wounded a sergeant, and several of the men. The company then arose, fired, and charged. The enemy quitted their position; we followed and took three field pieces.[9]

Note that, according to Byfield, his company first received and then returned fire although neither Hindman nor Le Couteur of the 104th, who were both in the vicinity of the hill after the Left Division had withdrawn, mentions hearing any musketry after the battle ended.

Thus, according to Cruikshank and those who follow him, the "Canadian" historiographic tradition, if it can be called that, of the end of the battle of Lundy's Lane, appears to be based on two assumptions. First, that the Left Division did not voluntarily give up possession of the guns but lost them as the result of a final British bayonet charge. Second, that this charge was led by Glew's light company of the 41st Foot which dispersed the American rear guard and recaptured most of the guns.

Based on the evidence quoted above, the "Canadian" school would appear to have good proof for these assumptions. However, neither Cruikshank nor any of the many historians who have blindly followed his work, seem to have consulted the original manuscript of Thomas S. Jesup's "Memoir of the Campaign on the Niagara," now in the Jesup Papers at the Library of Congress. Cruikshank certainly knew of the existence of this document, which was partially published by the American historian Ingersoll in his 1849 *Historical Sketches of the Second War Between the United States and Great Britain*, because Cruikshank included portions of it in Volume II of his *Documentary History*.[10] Unfortunately he was either unaware of or chose to omit, a crucial paragraph which described the immediate aftermath of the action:

> All that now remained of the 1st Brigade did not exceed two hundred & twenty men. Major Jesup's position in the rear of General Rial's [sic] line, early in the action, had enabled him to observe his as well as Genl. Drummond's force. He believed each to be equal, and he knew the whole to be greatly superior to our whole force. Our loss in officers had been unusually great, and being more than five hours continuously engaged, both officers and soldiers were completely exhausted. They were suffering with thirst and there was no water nearer than the Chippewa – the necessity of falling back to camp was apparent to everyone. Major Leavenworth was sent to endeavour to find General Ripley – he returned with a message from the Genl. desiring the presence of Major Jesup – the Major, though suffering severely from his wounds joined him immediately, and found him surrounded by officers apparently in consultation. He informed Major Jesup that General Brown had ordered him to conduct the troops to camp, and the wounded being first removed, we marched slowly and in good order, to our camp behind the Chippewa.[11]

This statement by one of the senior surviving American officers of the action makes it clear that, when the fighting ended, the Left Division was in possession of both the hill and the British guns and withdrew of its own accord.

As for Cruikshank's claim that American expulsion from the hill is "fully substantiated by affidavits published in General Ripley's pamphlet," this same source (the proceedings of Ripley's court of inquiry) actually contains considerable evidence to the contrary. For example, Captain William McDonald, Ripley's aide, testified that, after the fighting had ceased, the Left Division remained on the hill "for three fourths, or one half an hour," during which time men from Porter's brigade were detailed to remove the captured British guns and collect the wounded, before the division "retired unmolested."[12] The veracity of McDonald's testimony was attested by Captain Newman Clarke, brigade major of the Second Brigade, Lieutenant John Livingston, adjutant of the Twenty-Third Infantry and Lieutenant John Holding, adjutant of the Twenty-

First.[13] Leavenworth of the Ninth, after confirming many of the statements made by Jesup in his "Memoir," stated that not "a shot was fired from the enemy, and our troops moved in as good order, and with as much regularity *from*, as to the field."[14] Miller of the Twenty-First testified that the division remained "near an hour" after the fighting had ceased before a withdrawal was effected "in perfect order."[15] Finally. Marston of the same regiment, who commanded the American rearguard, stated that the troops "passed in good order" and made no mention of British presence or pressure.[16] It is clear from this evidence that the Left Division was not expelled from the hill but left in its own good time.

If this is true, then how are we to account for the second assumption of the "Canadian" tradition of the ending of the battle – that all or part of the British artillery was recaptured at bayonet point by a charge led by Glew's company of the 41st? It is certain that Glew's men did take some artillery during the battle; Byfield, a member of Glew's company, states so while Gourlay, who may have heard it from participants in the battle, recounted this event as early as 1822.

Newly uncovered evidence suggests that Glew's feat probably took place in the middle of the engagement, not at its end. Lieutenant John Le Couteur of the 104th Foot, who was part of Hercules Scott's column, kept a diary throughout the war and, from it, compiled a memoir of his wartime service. According to Le Couteur, as Scott's column,

> ... marched up, to my utter astonishment, I saw the Captain of Artillery passing me. "What, in the name of fortune, brings you from your guns?" "Two of them were taken at the Bayonet's point and my Gunners are despatched. They made me a Prisoner, shoved me in that church above there, but as I saw a window at the other end and on one watching, I jumped out and here I am." Captain Glew of the 41st Light Company who was on the left under the crest of the hill, saw all this. When Jonathan thought he had the Guns safe, and like a raw fool had bayonetted the horses as well as what men he could catch, and fancied the centre of the battle won – bold Capt. Glew charged them with his gallant light bobs and retook our Guns and one from the enemy. He ought to have been made a Knight Bannaret or a Major on the spot.[17]

The artillery captain in question was James Mackonochie, who had accompanied Scott's force to the battle. Le Couteur then goes on to describe other incidents in the battle and the implication is clear that Glew's attack took place in the middle of the action. Le Couteur confirms this in a letter written on 27 July 1814 in which he states that, midway in the fighting,

> ... Three pieces of artillery which we had just brought up were charged and carried by the enemy. They had driven on to the enemy without knowing, where they were taken.[18]

This new evidence demonstrates that Glew's achievement did not take occur at the end of the action and that the guns he recaptured were the pieces that arrived with Hercules Scott's column *midway* through the action. The event described by Byfield and Gourlay took place but Gourlay and Cruikshank, and every other author who has followed them, has the timing wrong. The guns taken by Glew, however, were retaken by the Left Division, as we have the American Lieutenant David B. Douglass's evidence that *toward the close of the action* he rode in perfect safety among the captured British artillery, which, he says, were "eight in number – brass guns, of the most beautiful model, of different calibres, from six to twenty-four pounders."[19] This is an accurate description of the number and type of the British guns by an officer familiar with field artillery.

But what of Hindman's statement that one of the brass 24-pdr. guns was in British hands following the withdrawal of the American main force. Hindman implies that Lieutenant John Fontaine escaped while Lieutenant John Kincaid and some of the working party were captured. This is not borne out by the records – in the official casualty return, Kincaid is not noted as being either a prisoner nor missing while only one American artilleryman is reported as missing at Lundy's Lane.[20] If they did fall into British hands, the men of Fontaine and Kincaid's party seem to have later escaped. Nonetheless it appears that some British troops were on the hill after the Left Division had withdrawn and that they retook one piece of artillery, a brass 24-pdr. gun. Who were these troops?

Evidence concerning Drummond's movements and dispositions after the fighting ended is fragmentary. It is certain that Le Couteur's company of the 104th was on picket the night after the battle but Le Couteur does not mention seeing either the British guns or unwounded Americans.[21]

John Norton remembered that at the end of the battle "We now perceived that the Enemy had retired, leaving the field covered with the Dead & Dying – they also left our Guns, with some that had belonged to themselves."[22] This would seem to indicate that Norton at least was aware of the location of the British guns immediately after the fighting had ended.

But we also have some contradictory evidence. Private John Costello of the grenadier company of the 104th Foot testified at Ripley's court of inquiry that, after "the action closed the British army lay during the remainder of the night in Lundy's Lane, about a quarter of a mile from the heights" and did not advance before "sun-rise on the morning of the 26th."[23] Sergeant Weymouth of the Twenty-First Infantry, who lay wounded on the hill all night, testified at the same inquiry that the British army did not reoccupy the hill until 9 A.M. the following morning at which time they removed all the artillery.[24] Surgeon Bull of the U.S. Army stated that he "rode to the battle ground about daylight without witnessing the presence of a single British officer or soldier."[25]

There is more. In December 1815 Captain William Worth, Scott's aide, reported to Brown the substance of a conversation Worth had with a Major Powell of the "militia of Upper Canada" (probably Surgeon Grant Powell of the Incorporated Militia) who "expressed his astonishment, at the Conduct of the Com[mandin]g Officer of our force in abandoning the Captured Cannon" at Lundy's Lane[26] Worth made a point of asking the Canadian "if the proximity of the British Army did not render the removal of it impracticable?" Powell replied that the Right Division "was ordered to retreat up the Lundy's road with the exception of the 89th Regt." which left one company,

... in the Vicinity of the Battle ground in order to obtain information at dawn of day of our [the American] movements – when to his great surprize [sic] [the commander of this company] discovered that the Battle ground and captured artillery, were abandoned by the American forces – he immediately repossessed the heights at the same time dispatched express to Lt. Genl. Drummond.[27]

Taking all the above into consideration, it would seem that the bulk of the Right Division did not re-occupy the hill during the night that followed the action. At most, the light company of the 104th Foot (Le Couteur's company) and a company of the 89th Foot remained in the immediate vicinity during the early morning of 26 July 1814. When daylight came, the British and Canadians discovered to their great delight that the captured weapons had been left on the battlefield and repossessed them.[28]

In sum, the balance of evidence indicates that the Left Division voluntarily gave up both the hill and the captured artillery with the exception of one 6-pdr. gun and one 24-pdr. gun. The latter weapon was retaken by the British, not from the rearguard of the Left Division but from a small working party sent by Hindman to collect it after all American combat troops had left the field. This is the sequence of events that has been recounted in Chapter 11 above.

The Accuracy of the American Casualty Figures

There has been a tendency on the part of some British and Canadian historians to disparage the accuracy of the total American casualty figure of 860 (173 dead, 571 wounded and 117 missing). They take their cue from William James, an early commentator writing in 1818, who stated that the British counted 210 American dead on the field after the action and later discovered a number of fresh graves on the site of the Left Division's camp at Chippawa "in which the bodies had been so slightly covered, that the arms and legs were, in many instances, exposed to view."[1] The Canadian historian Ernest A. Cruikshank is, as usual, foremost among the doubters and quotes letters by American officers published in the press immediately after the battle as evidence that Brown's losses were greater than publicly stated. Written before the official return was compiled, these letters understandably exaggerate the losses suffered in a confusing night action. Cruikshank also infers that, since officers from the Second Rifle Regiment and the Seventeenth and Nineteenth Infantry are named as being among the wounded in Brown's return, those units fought in the battle but that Brown did not include their unit casualties in his return.

Cruikshank was unaware that a single company each from the Seventeenth and Nineteenth Infantry was attached to the Twenty-First Infantry and the casualties suffered by these two "orphan" companies were included in the general figure for the Twenty-First. He was also unaware that it was American practice to detach officers from their regiments to serve with other units – thus Lieutenant David Riddle of the Fifteenth Infantry commanded the company of the Nineteenth attached to the Twenty-First Infantry and thus Ensign William Camp of the Second Rifle Regiment also served with the Twenty-First during the action. This tendency of historians unfamiliar with American military practice to question Brown's statement of his losses shows no signs of diminishing.[2]

The fact is that Brown's return was probably as accurate as it could be, given the vagaries of period record keeping and the circumstances under which it was compiled. By 30 July 1814 many of the men who had absented themselves from the battle for one reason or another had returned to the ranks, showing the first estimates of losses to be exaggerated. As one member of the division wrote on 1 August 1814, "our loss ... was not so great as first apprehended" because of the "battle being fought at night, many of our men scattered and secreted themselves in the woods, and have not until within a day or two all been collected."[3] More evidence of the accuracy of the American figures is found in a statement made by Colonel Charles K. Gardner, adjutant-general of the Left Division and the officer responsible for the accounting of casualties, to Daniel Parker, chief clerk of the War Department in Washington and *de facto* adjutant-general of the U.S. army. Writing "in confidence," Gardner informed Parker on 29 July that "our loss is upwards of 800."[4] If Brown was trying to hide his actual losses, he would have needed the co-operation of Gardner but that officer gives no indication of such an action on Brown's part.

Additional evidence is provided by documents not intended for the public. Thus, an undated return of the casualties of the First Brigade gives a total of 502 as opposed to the 516 in the official return. Separate casualty returns for the Twenty-Second Infantry dated 1 August and the Twenty-Fifth Infantry dated 27 July 1814 give total casualties of 144 and 116 men respectively, compared to the official figures of 143 and 116 respectively. Porter and Harris, commanding the volunteers and the cavalry respectively, included casualty figures in letters they wrote shortly after the battle that correspond almost exactly to the official figures. Porter also proudly stated that his brigade "in proportion to the numbers engaged ... lost more than any other corps, and I believe, small as we were, we actually lost more officers killed then either of the other brigades."[5] These are not the words of an officer trying to hide his losses.[6]

Endnotes

RCMI   Royal Canadian Military Institute
RDOB   Right Division Order Book. This is MG 19, A39, vol. 3, Duncan Clark Papers, NAC.
RG   Record Group
RLB   Letter Book of Maj. Gen. Phineas Riall, Buffalo and Erie County Historical
        Society
SJ   Société Jersiaise
USMA   Library, United States Military Academy, West Point
USMHI   United States Military History Institute
WHS   Wisconsin Historical Society
WO   War Office
WRHS   Western Reserve Historical Society

Prologue
1. Wilkinson to Armstrong, 16 Nov. 1813, ASPMA, I, 475.
2. The Thirteenth Infantry were known as the "Snorters" because one of their previous commanders, Colonel Robert Chrystie, had insisted that all officers and enlisted men wear moustaches.
3. Mordecai Myers, *Reminiscences. 1780-1814* (Washington: Crane, 1900), 41-42.
4. Letter of Lt. Col. John Harvey, 12 Nov. 1813, quoted in Matilda Edgar, *Ten Years of Upper Canada in Peace and War* (Toronto: William Briggs, 1890), 252.
5. George C. Salisbury, *The Battle of Chrysler's Farm* (Ottawa: Library of Parliament, n.d. [c. 1955]), 7. See also Reynold M. Kirby, "Reynold M. Kirby and His Race to Join the Regiment: A Connecticut Officer in the War of 1812," John C. Fredriksen, ed., *Connecticut History* 32 (November, 1991), 70-72.
6. Letter of Lt. Col. John Harvey, 12 Nov. 1813, Edgar, *Ten Years*, 252.
7. Salisbury, *Chrysler's Farm*, 7.
8. Narrative of Lt. John Sewell, 49th Foot, 11 Nov. 1860, quoted in Ronald Way, "The Day of Crysler's Farm," *Canadian Geographic Journal* 62 (1961), 208.
9. *Ibid.*
10. Letter from an officer, 13 Nov. 1813, *Quebec Mercury*, 23 Nov. 1813.

Chapter 1 – "A Mere Matter of Marching": The Coming of War
1. Jarvis Hanks, Biography, 6-7, 14-15, BECHS. A newly annotated version of Hanks's memoir is now available in: Donald E. Graves, ed., *Soldiers of 1814: American Enlisted Men's Memoirs of the Niagara Campaign* (Youngstown: Old Fort Niagara Press, 1995).
    On American military drums, see H.C. McBarron and John Elting, "Musicians, 1st U.S. Infantry, Winter Uniform, 1812-1813," *Military Historian* 2 (1950), 24-25.
2. James F. Zimmerman, *Impressment of American Seamen* (New York: Columbia University, 1925), 266-267.
3. Madison to Congress, 5 Nov. 1811, quoted in Donald Hickey, *The War of 1812. A Forgotten Conflict* (Chicago: University of Illinois, 1989), 32.
4. My discussion of the reasons for war follows John Stagg, *Mr Madison's War: Politics, Diplomacy, and Warfare in the Early American Republic* (Princeton: Princeton University, 1983), 3-47; and Jeffrey Kimball, "Strategy on the Northern Frontier", PhD. Dissertation, University of Louisiana at Baton Rouge, 1969, chapter III. Another American historian takes a different view, see Hickey, *War of 1812*, 26-47. Canadian historians have traditionally put more emphasis on the conquest of Canada as a reason for war, see George Stanley, *The War of 1812: Land Operations* (Ottawa: National Museums, 1983), 29-42; and J.M. Hitsman, *The Incredible War of 1812* (Toronto: University of Toronto, 1965), 21-22.
5. Jefferson to Duane, 4 Aug. 1812, Jefferson Papers, reel 46, LC.
6. Summary of American military problems from Kimball, "Strategy", 81-97; and Stagg, *Madison's War*, 227-244.
7. Kimball, "Strategy", 81-97.
8. Return of the number of troops in Service on the Peace Establishment and Additional Mili-

tary Force of 1808, 6 June 1812; Eustis to Anderson, 8 June 1812, both *ASPMA*, I, 320; Stagg, *Madison's War*, 175.

9. Duane to Jefferson, 26 Sep. 1812, "Letters of William Duane," Frederick Worthington, ed., *Proceedings of the Massachusetts Historical Society* 20 (1906), 362.

10. Clark to Eustis, 4 June 1813, RG 107, Micro 222, reel 5, NA.

11. Age of generals extracted from biographical information contained in James Wilson & John Fiske, eds., *Appleton's Cyclopedia of American Biography* (New York: Appleton, 1888, 7 vols); Roger Spiller and Joseph Dawson, eds., *Dictionary of American Military Biography* (Westport: Greenwood, 1984, 3 vols); *Dictionary of American Biography* (New York: Scribner, 1958-1964, 22 vols); Francis B. Heitman, *Historical Register and Dictionary of the United States Army* (Washington: Government Printing Office, 1902, 2 vols), vol. I; ; *National Cyclopedia of American Biography* (Clifton, NJ: J.T. White, 1891, 63 vols); and Rossiter Johnson, ed., *The Twentieth Century Biographical Dictionary of Notable Americans* (Boston: Biographical Society, 1904, 10 vols). Also, Armstrong to Eustis, 2 Jan. 1812, John Armstrong, *Notices of the War of 1812* (New York: Wiley, 1840, 2 vols), I, 234; Irvine to Armstrong, 17 Mar. 1812, RG 107, Micro 221, reel 46, NA; Stagg, *Madison's War*, 165-168.

12. On Prevost, see *DCB*, V, 693-698. Strength for the British army extracted from: General Monthly Returns of ... the several Corps serving in Canada, 25 June 1812, WO 17, vol. 1516, and General Monthly return of the several corps serving in Nova Scotia and its dependencies, 25 June, 1812, WO 17, vol 2359, both PRO. This figure includes only enlisted men fit for duty; it excludes officers, and troops serving in Newfoundland and Bermuda. On the state of Canada's military defences, see Hitsman, *Incredible War*, 25, 38-41; and Stanley, *War of 1812*, 49-82.

13. Prevost to Drummond, 30 Apr. 1814, quoted in Hitsman, *Incredible War*, 184.

14. MacEwan to Wife, 31 Mar. 1814, William MacEwan, *Excerpts from Lieut. and Adjutant William MacEwan To His Wife, 1813-1814* (n.p, n.d.), 12.

15. Harvey to McClure, 14 Dec. 1813, RG 8 I, vol. 681, 261, NAC.

16. *Proceedings and Reports of the Loyal and Patriotic Society of Upper Canada* (York, Upper Canada: The Society, 1815), 391.

17. In March 1994, nearly 120 years after it was captured at Fort Niagara, the large American "Stars and Stripes" which flew over the fort that fateful night was returned to that place through the generosity of the descendant of Lady Strange, the descendant of Lieutenant General Sir Gordon Drummond, whose family kept it safe in the ancestral home at Megginch Castle in Scotland.

18. Drummond to Prevost, 2 Jan. 1814, RG 8 I, vol. 682, 1, NAC.

19. Kimball, "Strategy", 106-115; Stagg, *Madison's War*, 98; Armstrong to Wilkinson, 24 Jan. 1814, and Armstrong to Wilkinson, 30 Jan. 1814, both RG 107, Micro 6, Reel 7, NA.

20. Although the Left Division was actually a geographic area, the term came, through usage, to mean the force Brown commanded in the field.

21. John Morris, "General Jacob Brown", Unpublished paper read before the 50th Anniversary Conference, Siena College, NY, 1987.

22. Brown to Tompkins, 27 July, 1811, Franklin Hough, *A History of Jefferson County* (Albany: Little, 1854), 423.

23. Armstrong to Brown, 28 Feb. 1814, Armstrong, *Notices*, II, Appendix II, 213.

24. Kimball, "Strategy", 118-123; Charles W. Elliott, *Winfield Scott: The Soldier and the Man* (New York: MacMillan, 1937), 190.

25. Armstrong to Brown, 20 Mar. 1814, RG 107, Micro 6, reel 7, NA.

26. Kimball, "Strategy", 127-129.

27. Brown to Armstrong, 8 Apr. 1814, RG 107, Micro 221, reel 51, NA.

28. Alexander McMullen, "The Narrative of Alexander McMullen, a Private Soldier in Colonel Fenton's Regiment of Pennsylvania Volunteers", *Doc. Hist.*, II, 372. An annotated version of McMullen's memoir is available in Donald E. Graves, ed., *Soldiers of 1814: American Enlisted Men's Memoirs of the Niagara Campaign* (Youngstown: Old Fort Niagara Press, 1995).

29. Hanks, Biography, 15, BECHS.

30. Kimball, "Strategy", 132-134.
31. Brown to Armstrong, 8 Apr. 1814, RG 107, Micro 221, reel 51, NA. Also, Brown to Armstrong, 20 Apr. 1814, Brown Papers, LC; Gaines to Brown, 14 Apr. 1814, RG 107, Micro 221, reel 61, NA.
32. Kimball, "Strategy", 182-191.
33. In Cabinet, 7 June 1814, *Letters and Other Writings of James Madison* (New York: R. Worthington, 1884, 4 vols.) III, 403-404, quoted in Kimball, "Strategy", 184-185.
34. Armstrong to Brown, 10 Jun. 1814, Parker Papers, PHS.
35. Brown to Chauncey, 21 June 1814, *CBD*, 38.
36. Chauncey to Brown, 25 June 1814, *CBD*, 40.
37. Chauncey to Brown, 25 June 1814 [second letter], *CBD*, 41. Also, Brown to Armstrong, 22 June 1814, *CBD*, 39; Armstrong to Brown, 19 July 1814, *CBD*, 47.
38. Brown to Williams, 2 July 1814, Brown Papers, CL.
39. Thomas S. Jesup, Memoir of the Campaign on the Niagara in 1814, 2, LC.
40. *Ibid.*; Brown to Armstrong, 22 June 1814, *CBD*, 39; Brown to Armstrong, 26 June 1814, RG 107, Micro 221, Reel 59, NA.

Chapter 2 – Major General Jacob Brown's Left Division, United States Army

1. Benjamin F. Perry, *Reminiscences of Public Men* (Greenville, SC: 1889), 121, quoted in John C. Fredriksen, *Officers of the War of 1812 with Portraits and Anecdotes* (Lewiston, NY: Edgar Mellen, 1989), 50.
2. Winfield Scott, *Memoirs of General Scott, written by himself* (New York: Sheldon, 1864, 2 vols), I, 51.
3. 3. Hindman to Uncle, 19 Feb. 1815, War of 1812 Mss., LL. On Scott's prewar life and career, see John M. Hallahan, "No Doubt Blamable: The Transformations of Captain Winfield Scott," *Virginia Cavalcade*, 40 (1991), 160-171.
4. General Order, 7 Apr. 1814, LDOB, NYSL.
5. Brown to Armstrong, 17 Apr. 1814, RG 107, Micro 222, reel 10, NA.
6. Brigade Order, 7 Apr. 1814, LDOB, NYSL.
7. Scott to Winder, 6 May 1814, Elliott Collection, NYPL. Also, Donald E. Graves, "I have a handsome little army: A Re-examination of Winfield Scott's Camp at Buffalo in 1814," in R.A Bowler, ed., *War Along the Niagara: Essays on the War of 1812 and its Legacy* (Youngstown: Old Fort Niagara Association, 1991), 43-52; "Biography of Colonel Jacob Hindman," *Portico*, 3 (1816), 38-52; "Biographical Memoirs of General Ripley," *Portfolio*, 14 (1815), 108-136. There is a myth current to this day that the bulk of the regular troops present at Scott's camp were raw recruits, see, for instance, Russel F. Weigley, *History of the United States Army* (New York: MacMillan, 1967), 129; and Charles F. Heller, "Those are Regulars, by God!," *Army* 37 (1987), 52-54. For a contrasting view, see Graves, "Handsome little army", 44-46.
8. Scott, *Memoirs*, I, 351.
9. Graves, "Handsome little army", 46; John S. Hare, "Military Punishments in the War of 1812," *Journal of the American Military Institute* IV, No. 4 (Winter 1940), 225-239.
10. Cromwell Pearce, "'A Poor But Honest Sodjer': Colonel Cromwell Pearce, the 16th U.S. Infantry and the War of 1812," John C. Fredriksen, ed., *Pennsylvania History* 52 (July, 1985), 134-135. Age of U.S. generals extracted from sources listed in Chapter I, note 11.
11. Weigley, *History of the U.S. Army*, 113-114; John R. Jacobs, *The Beginnings of the United States Army, 1783-1812* (Princeton: Princeton University, 1947), 343-352; John Douglas, *Medical Topography of Upper Canada* (London, 1819, reprinted Science Publications, 1985), 44, 65, 72; James Mann, *Medical Sketches of the Campaigns of 1812, 1813, and 1814* (Dedham, Mass: H. Mann, 1816), 66-67; Elliott, *Scott*, 146.
12. General Order, 23 June 1814, LDOB, NYSL.
13. General Order, 13 June 1814, LDOB, NYSL.
14. Report of Surgeon Lovell in Mann, *Medical Sketches*, 160.
15. Brown to Armstrong, 17 Apr. 1814, RG 107, Micro 221, reel 59, NA; Elliott, *Scott*, 146-147; Statement of Surgeon Lovell in Mann, *Medical Sketches*, 160; Morning Report of the Division,

23 June, 1814, Louis Babcock, *The War of 1812 on the Niagara Frontier* (Buffalo: Buffalo Historical Society, 1927), 149.

16. Scott to Armstrong, 27 Apr. 1814, RG 107, Micro 221, reel 57, NA.

17. Scott to Armstrong, 7 May 1814 and 17 May 1814, both RG 107, Micro 221, reel 57, NA; General Orders, 19 May 1814;, 24 May 1814; Brigade Order, 23 June 1814, all LDOB, NYSL; René Chartrand, *Uniforms and Equipment of the United States Forces in the War of 1812* (Youngstown, NY: Old Fort Niagara Association, 1992), 42-50.

18. *Buffalo Gazette*, 3 May 1814, quoted in William Ketchum, *An Authentic and Comprehensive History of Buffalo* (Buffalo: Rockewell, Baker S. Hill, 1864, 2 vols.), II, 418.

19. Scott to Brown, 4 May 1814, Brown Papers, CL.

20. General Order, 31 May 1814, LDOB, NYSL.

21. General Order, 3 June 1814, LDOB, NYSL.

22. *Ibid.*

23. *Ibid.* Also, Sarah Lemmon, *Frustrated Patriots: North Carolina and the War of 1812* (Chapel Hill: University of North Carolina, 1977), 55; Hare, "Military Punishments", 238.

24. Hanks, Biography, 16-17, BECHS.

25. "Winfield Scott", *Harper's Magazine*, 462.

26. General Order, 4 June 1814, LDOB, NYSL; Morning Report, 23 June 1814, Babcock, *War on the Niagara*, 149.

27. Chartrand, *Arms and Equipment*, 86-90; James Hicks, *Notes on U.S. Ordnance* (Mt. Vernon, 1940;, reprinted, Green Farms, Conn: Modern Books & Crafts, 1971, 2 vols.), I, 19; Howard Blackmore, *British Military Firearms, 1650-1850* (London: Herbert Jenkins, 1961), 277.

28. Loading and firing movements extracted from Alexander Smyth, *Rules Regulations for the Field Exercise, Manoeuvres and Conduct of the Infantry of the United States* (Philadelphia: T. & G. Palmer, 1812). Also, Peter Hofschromb, "Flintlocks in Battle," *Military Illustrated* No. 1 (June/ July 1986), 30-31; B.P. Hughes, *Open Fire. Artillery Tactics from Marlborough to Wellington* (Strettington: Antony Bird, 1983), 8; William Duane, *American Military Library* (Philadelphia: author, 1809, 2 vols), I, 175.

29. "Artillero Viejo", "How to Fight Brother Jonathan," *Museum of Foreign Literature, Science and Art*, 42 (May-August 1841), 211; Hofschromb, "Flintlocks", 32-35; Matti Lauerma, *L'Artillerie campagne française pendant les guerres de la Révolution* (Helsinki: Sumolaisen Tiedakatemian Tormituksia, 1956), 31; George Bell, *Soldier's Glory* (London: Bell & Sons, 1956), 32.

30. B.P. Hughes, *Firepower: Weapons Effectiveness on the Battlefield, 1630-1850* (London: Arms & Armour, 1974), 26, 127-133; Lauerma, *L'artillerie de campagne*, 32; Philip Haythornewaite, *Weapons and Equipment of the Napoleonic Wars* (Poole: Blandford, 1979), 20; Brent Nosworthy, *Battle Tactics of Napoleon and His Enemies* (London: Constable, 1995), 204-205.

31. Horse Guards, *General Regulations and Orders for the Army* (London: T. Egerton, 1811), 71; Myers, *Reminiscences*, 16; General Orders, 20 June, 22 June, 23 June 1814; Brigade Orders, 24 June 1814, all LDOB, NYSL.

32. Hughes, *Firepower*, 133; Hofschromb, "Flintlocks", 35; William Greener, *The Gun; or, A Treatise on the Various Descriptions of Small Fire-Arms* (London: Longman, Rees, Orme, Brown, Green, 1835), 222.

33. British battalion organization and formation from: War Office, *Rules and Regulations for the Formation, Field-Exercise, and Movements of His Majesty's Forces* (London: T. Egerton, 1808), 63-78. American organization and formation from Smyth, *Regulations*, 1-6; and Component Parts of Regiments, Corps, Troops and Companies, *The Army Register of the United States. Corrected Up to the First Day of June, 1814* (Boston: Chester Stebbins, 1814), 59.

34. War Office, *Rules and Regulations*, 66-69.

35. Smyth, *Regulations*, 1-3.

36. *Ibid.*, 29. See Irenée Amelot De Lacroix, *Rules and Regulations for the Field Exercises and Manoeuvres of the French Infantry* (Boston: T.B. Wait, 1810, 3 vols), I, 173-174, for the functions of sub-units in battle. This manual was used by Scott at Buffalo, see Donald E. Graves, "From Steuben to Scott: The Adoption of French Infantry Tactics by the U.S. Army, 1807-1816," *Acta*, XIIIth International Colloquy on Military History, Helsinki, 1988.

37. Jean Colin, *L'Infanterie au XVIIIe siècle: La Tactique*, (Paris: Berger-Levrault, 1907), xvii-cii; John Lynn, *Bayonets of the Republic: Motivation and Tactics in the Army of Revolutionary France, 1791-1794* (Chicago: University of Chicago, 1984), 253; Scott to Parker, 14 Feb. 1814, Parker Papers, PHS. During the War of 1812, American manuals were based on French originals, see Graves, "Steuben to Scott"; "Handsome little army"; and "'Dry Books of Tactics': U.S. Infantry Manuals of the War of 1812 and After," *Military Historian* 38, (1986), 50-61.

38. Quotation from Paddy Griffith, *Forward into Battle: Fighting Techniques from Waterloo to Vietnam* (Strettington: Antony Bird, 1981), 28-29.

39. *Ibid.*, 25-31; Hew Strachan, *From Waterloo to Balaclava: Tactics, Technology and the British Army, 1815-1834* (Cambridge: University Press, 1985), 26-29.

40. David B. Douglass, "An Original Narrative of the Niagara Campaign of 1814," John F. Horton, ed., *Niagara Frontier*, 46 (1964), 19.

41. George J. Guthrie, *Commentaries on the Surgery of War* (London: Burgess & Hill, 1855), 15-16.

42. On the reluctance to use the bayonet, see John Keegan, *The Face of Battle* (New York: Viking, 1976), 165-167; Gunther Rothenberg, *The Art of Warfare in the Age of Napoleon* (Bloomington: University of Indiana, 1978), 69-70; and Griffiths, *Forward*, 38-41.

43. Material on artillery from Donald Graves, "Field Artillery of the War of 1812: Equipment, Organization, Tactics and Effectiveness," *Arms Collecting*, 30, No. 2 (May 1992), 39-48.

44. Scott to Walbach, 21 Apr. 1814, RG 98, vol. 555, 56, NA.

45. General Order, 22 Apr. 1814, LDOB, NYSL. Also, Graves, "Dry Books of Tactics"; "Handsome little army" and "Steuben to Scott".

46. Murdock to Gardner, 26 May 1814, Gardner Papers, NYSL; General Orders, 22 Apr., 23 Apr., 7 May, 19 May, 15 June 1814, all LDOB, NYSL; Scott to Brown, 30 Apr. 1814, Brown Papers, CL.

47. Scott, *Memoirs*, I, 121.

48. Hanks, Biography, 15-16, BECHS. On training at Flint Hill, see also: General Orders, 21 June, 23 June 1814, LDOB, NYSL; Scott to Brown, 30 Apr. 1814, Brown Papers, CL; "The Pennsylvania Volunteers in the War of 1812: An Anonymous Journal of Service for the Year 1814," John C. Fredriksen, ed., *Western Pennsylvania Historical Magazine* 70, No. 2 (1987), 150; Jesup, Memoir, 1-2, LC; Joseph Henderson, Narrative, LL; Graves, "Handsome little army".

49. Brown to Scott, 20 Apr. 1814, *CBD*, 8.

50. Sinclair to Jones, 27 May 1814, *CBD*, 23.

51. Scott to Armstrong, 19 May 1814, RG 107 Micro 221, reel 52, NA; Sinclair to Jones, 27 May 1814, *CBD*, 23; Snyder to Fenton, 8 Mar. 1814, *Doc. Hist.*, IX, 215; Sinclair to Jones, 13 May 1814, quoted in Ernest A. Cruikshank, "The County of Norfolk in War of 1812," *Proceedings, Ontario Historical Society* 20 (1923), 29; Scott to Armstrong, 7 May 1814, RG 107, Micro 221, reel 57, 7, NA; Campbell to Harrison, 7 Apr. 1814, quoted in Ross P. Wright, *The Burning of Port Dover* (Erie, PA: author, 1948), 13; Sinclair to Cocke, 6 May 1814, Sinclair Papers, ALUV.

52. Campbell to Armstrong, 18 May 1814, RG 107, Micro 221, reel 51, NA.

53. Amelia Harris (nee Ryerse), "Memoir", in James J. Talman, ed., *Loyalist Narratives from Upper Canada* (Toronto: Champlain Society, 1946), 148.

54. McMullen, "Narrative", 371.

55. Campbell to Riall, 16 June 1814, RLB, BECHS.

56. Armstrong to Brown, 2 June 1814, RG 107, Micro 6, reel 7, NA; General Order, 30 June 1814, LDOB, NYSL.

57. McDonald to Morris, 6 Sept. 1814, Ross County Historical Society, Ohio, quoted in Fredriksen, *Officers*, 77.

58. Brown to Armstrong, 8 May 1814, *CBD*, 13. Also, General Order, 19 May 1814, LDOB, NYSL; "Memoirs of Ripley", 120-121. Brown's first choice to command the Second Brigade was Brigadier General Joseph Swift, an engineer officer, see Brown to Armstrong, 17 Apr. 1814, RG 107, Micro 222, reel 10, NA.

59. Tompkins to Armstrong, 2 Jan., 9 Jan. 1814, Hugh Hastings, ed., *Public Papers of Daniel D. Tompkins, Governor of New York, 1807-1817* (New York: Wynkoop, Hallenbeck, Crawford,

1898-1902), III, 411; Armstrong to Scott, 12 Jan. 1814, RG 107, Micro 6, reel 7, NA; Porter to Armstrong, 27 Mar. 1814, *Doc. Hist.*, II, 382; General Order, 13 Mar. 1814, *Doc. Hist.*, IX, 231.

60. Benson J. Lossing, *Pictorial Field Book of the War of 1812* (New York: Harpers, 1869), 426; Porter, *DAB*, VIII, 99-100.

61. Porter to Armstrong, 27 Mar. 1814, *Doc. Hist.*, II, 382.

62. *Ibid.*

63. Granger to Porter, 28 May 1814, Porter Papers, BECHS.

64. Brown to Armstrong, 3 June 1814, *CBD*, 26.

65. Porter to Tompkins, 3 May 1814, *Doc. Hist.*, II, 390; Porter to Brown, 17 May 1814, *Doc. Hist.*, II, 398; Scott to Porter, 29 May 1814, *Doc. Hist.*, II, 400; Brown to Armstrong, 28 June 1814, *CBD*, 41; Porter to Tompkins, 3 July 1814, *Doc. Hist.*, I, 26.

66. Porter to Tompkins, 3 July 1814, *Doc. Hist.*, I, 116.

67. Porter to Tompkins, March 1814, *Doc. Hist.*, II, 380.

68. Scott to Brown, 23 May 1814, Brown Papers, CL.

69. *Ibid.* Also, Elliott, *Scott*, 152-154.

70. McMullen, "Narrative", 371.

71. "Pennsylvania Volunteers", 150.

72. William Horner, "Surgical Sketches: A Military Hospital at Buffalo, New York, in the Year 1814," *Medical Examiner and Record of Medical Service*, 16 (Dec. 1852), 761.

73. John Witherow, "A Soldier's Diary for 1814," *Pennsylvania History*, 12 (1945), 299.

74. "Pennsylvania Volunteers", 149.

75. Scott to Winder, 6 May 1814, Elliott Collection, NYPL.

76. Ages and physical descriptions from Prisoner of War Registers, Quebec, 1813-1815, RG 8 I, vols. 694A & 695B, NAC. Ethnic origins and occupations from John Stagg, "Enlisted Men in the United States Army, 1812-1815: A Preliminary Survey," *William and Mary Quarterly*, 3rd Series, 43 (1986), 616-645; recruiting origins from *Army Register, 1814*, xi.

77. General Orders, 22 Apr., 23 Apr., 17 June, 21 June 1814, Brigade Orders 15 June, 17 June 1814, all LDOB, NYSL; McMullen, "Narrative", 372; Smyth, *Regulations*, 173-175; "Garrison Orders, Burlington, Vermont, July 13 – August 4, 1813," *Moorsfield Antiquarian* 1, No. 2 (1937), 79-103.

78. Pay of soldiers from *Army Register 1814*. On U.S. army supply and rations, see Joseph Whitehorne, "The Battle of Fort Erie. Reconstruction of a War of 1812 Battle," *Prologue* 22 (1990), 451-466.

79. Brigade Order, 23 June 1814, LDOB, NYSL.

80. On uniforms and equipment of the Left Division, see Chartrand, *Uniforms*, 42-50, 90-91, 103-106.

81. Alexander Williams to Jonathan Williams, 8 June 1814, Williams Papers, LL.

82. For sources on the organization and strength of the units of the Left Division, see Appendix A.

83. General Orders, 19 May, 16 June, 29 June, 30 June 1814, LDOB, NYSL; Samuel D. Harris, "Service of Captain Samuel D. Harris. A Sketch of his Military Career in the Second Regiment of Light Dragoons during the War of 1812," *Publications of the Buffalo Historical Society* 24 (1920), 333; "Pennsylvania Volunteers", 150; Witherow, "Diary", 199.

84. Component parts of regiments, *Army Register, 1814*, 58-59; Monthly Returns of the First and Second Brigades, 30 June 1814, Henry Adams, *History of the United States during the Administration of James Madison* (New York: A.C. Boni, 1930, 4 vols), IV, Book 8, 35-36.

85. For sources on the organization and strength of the units of the Left Division, see Appendix A.

86. Lossing, *Field Book*, 804-808; Fredriksen, *Officers*, 33-38; George W. Cullum, *Campaigns of the War of 1812-15 … with Brief Biographies of the American Engineers* (New York: James Miller, 1879), 102-103, 203-204; Heitman, *Register*, I, 682, 1054. McRee's name is often spelled McRae or McRea but he signed himself as McRee.

87. Jesup, Memoir, 2, LC.

88. "Pennsylvania Volunteers", 149.

89. Horner, "Military Hospital", 761.

90. General Order, 2 July 1814, LDOB, NYSL.

91. Jesup, "Memoir", 2, LC. Also, Charles Walker, "Engineers in the War of 1812,", 13, Type-script, Historical Division, Engineer School, Fort Belvoir, VA; Jacob Brown, Memoranda of Occurrences and some important Facts pertaining to the Campaign on the Niagara, 2-3, Gardner Papers, NYSL; Samuel White, *History of the American Troops during the late war under Colonels Fenton and Campbell* (Baltimore: author, 1829), 12.

Chapter 3 – The Defenders of Upper Canada

1. Earl of Stanhope, *Notes of Conversations with the Duke of Wellington* (London: G. Murray, 1888), 182. Also, Drummond, DCB, VIII, 236-239; Marchioness of Tullibardine, *A Military History of Perthshire, 1660-1902* (Perthshire: R. & J. Hay, 1908, 2 vols), I, 487-488.

2. Strachan to Gore, 1 Jan. 1814, John L. Henderson, *John Strachan, 1778-1867* (Toronto: University of Toronto, 1969), 50.

3. Drummond to Prevost, 21 Jan. 1814, vol. 632, 32; Prevost to Drummond, 10 Apr. 1814, vol. 1222, 89, both RG 8 I, NAC; Riall to Drummond, 6 May, 28 June 1814, RLB, BECHS.

4. Drummond to Prevost, 19 Jan. 1814, vol. 682, 27; Drummond to Prevost, 21 Jan. 1814, vol. 682, 32; Prevost to Drummond, 29 Jan. 1814, vol. 1222, 32; Drummond to Prevost, 3 Feb. 1814, vol. 682, 90; Prevost to Drummond, 17 Feb. 1814, vol. 1221, 48; Drummond to Prevost, 5 Mar. 1814, vol. 682, 163, all RG 8 I, NAC; Christopher Hagerman, Diary, 19 Feb. 1814, TPL.

5. Address of President Gordon Drummond, 15 Feb. 1814, *Seventh Report of the Bureau of Archives for Ontario, 1910* (Toronto: King's Printer, 1911), 435. On Willcocks, see Donald E.Graves, "Joseph Willcocks and his Canadian Volunteers: An Account of Political Disaffection in Upper Canada during the War of 1812," Unpublished M.A. Thesis, Carleton University, Ottawa, 1982.

6. Foster to Robinson, 19 Jan. 1814, RG 7, G 16 C, vol. 6, NAC; Robinson to Foster, 21 Jan. 1814, RG 5, A1, vol. 16, NAC; Address of Drummond, 15 Feb. 1814, *Seventh Ontario Archives Report*, 435, 455-456; Notice to President's Office, 24 Mar. 1814, Doc. Hist., IX, 251; W.R. Riddell, "The Ancaster 'Bloody Assize' of 1814," *Papers and Records of the Ontario Historical Society*, 20 (1923), 108-125; "Eight Men were Sentenced to be 'Hanged-Drawn-Quartered'", *Cuesta*, (Spring 1981), 31-32.

7. Drummond to Bathurst, 5 Apr. 1814, Doc. Hist., IX, 279; Proclamation, 11 Jan. 1814, Doc. Hist., IX, 107; District General Order, 25 Mar. 1814, RDOB, NAC; Proclamation, 26 Apr. 1814, Doc. Hist., IX, 308; Riall to Drummond, 13 Apr. 1814, RLB, BECHS; John Norton, *The Journal of Major John Norton*, C.F. Klinck & J.J. Talman, eds., (Toronto: The Champlain Society, 1970), 347; Drummond to Prevost, 2 Apr. 1814, vol. 732, 90; Prevost to Drummond, 19 Mar. 1814, vol. 682, 163; Drummond to Prevost, 5 Mar. 1814, vol, 682, 163; Drummond to Prevost, 3 Feb. 1814, vol. 682, 104, all RG 8 I, NAC; Proclamation, 12 Apr. 1814, Doc. Hist., IX, 292.

8. Platt to Merritt, 21 Feb. 1814, Doc. Hist., IX, 195.

9. Yeo to Prevost, RG 8 I, vol. 683, 19, NAC.

10. Drummond to Prevost, 2 Apr. 1814, RG 8 I, vol. 683, 1, NAC; John Le Couteur, Journal, 10 Apr. 1814, SJ; Hagerman, Diary, 4 May 1814, TPL; Drummond to Prevost, 25 Apr. 1814, Doc. Hist., I, 11.

11. Prevost to Drummond, 30 Apr. 1814, RG 8 I, vol. 1222, 112, NAC.

12. Drummond to Prevost, 4 June 1814, RG 8 I, vol. 683, 234, NAC; Hagerman, Diary, 4 May, 6 June 1814, TPL.

13. Drummond to Yeo, 6 June 1814, RG 8 I, vol. 683, 242.

14. Drummond to Prevost, 25 Apr. 1814, Doc. Hist., I, 11.

15. Prevost to Drummond, 28 June 1814, RG 8 I, vol. 1222, 146.

16. Notation on Drummond to Prevost, 21 June 1814, RG 8 I, vol. 683, 295.

17. Riall, DCB, VII, 744-746; Robert. J. Jones, *A History of the 15th (East Yorkshire) Regiment (The Duke of York's Own), 1685 to 1914* (Beverly, 1958)

18. York to Prevost, 10 Aug. 1813, RG 8 I, vol. 682, 382, NAC.

19. William H. Merritt, *Journal of Events Principally on the Detroit and Michigan Frontiers during the War of 1812* (St. Catharines: Historical Society of British North America, 1863), 79. Also, Riall, DCB, VII, 744-746.

20. Riall to Drummond, 10 Mar. 1814, RG 8 I, vol. 682, 258, NAC.

21. Harvey to Riall, 23 Mar. 1814, RG 8 I, vol. 682, 269, NAC.

22. Isaac Weld, *Travels through the States of North America and the Province of Upper Canada during the Years 1795, 1796, and 1797* (London: Stockdale, 1799), 326. Also, John Maude, *Visit to the Falls of Niagara in 1800* (London: Longman, Rees, Orme, Brown and Green, 1826), 142; John Howison, *Sketches of Upper Canada, Domestic, Local, and Characteristic* (Edinburgh: Oliver & Boyd, 1825), 83; George Heriot, *Travels through the Canadas* (London, 1807), 69.

23. Riall to Drummond, 10 Mar. 1814, vol. 682, 258; Riall to Drummond, 15 Mar. 1814, vol. 388, 44, both RG 8 I, NAC; Riall to Young, 27 Apr. 1814, RLB, BECHS.

24. Riall to Drummond, 5 Mar. 1814, RG 8 I, vol. 682, 258, NAC; Riall to Talbot, 31 Mar. 1814, RLB, BECHS.

25. Young to Riall, 14 Mar. 1814, RG 8 I, vol. 833, 112, NAC.

26. Riall to Drummond, 15 Mar. 1814, vol. 388, 44; Drummond to Prevost, 15 Mar. 1814, vol. 682, 202; Drummond to Prevost, 22 Mar. 1814, vol. 833, 119; Drummond to Prevost, 28 June 1814, vol. 1222, 71, all RG 8 I, NAC.

27. Riall to Drummond, 6 May, 5 June, 15 June 1814, all RLB, BECHS.

28. Riall to Drummond, 15 June 1814, RLB, BECHS.

29. Riall to Drummond, 28 June 1814, RLB, BECHS. Also, Riall to Drummond, 15 June 1814, RLB, BECHS.

30. Drummond to Prevost, 2 July 1814, RG 8 I, vol. 684, 12, NAC.

31. Weekly Distribution Return of the Right Division, 22 June 1814, *Doc. Hist.*, I, 28; Weekly Distribution of the Right Division, 8 July 1814, *Doc. Hist.*, I, 51.

32. For brief summaries of the services of British units in Canada during the War of 1812, see Charles A. Stewart, *The Services of British Regiments in North America* (Ottawa: Department of National Defence Library, 1962). On the poor conduct of the 103rd Foot, see General Order, 19 Mar. 1814, RG 8 I, vol. 1171, 216, NAC; Prevost to Bathurst, 10 Mar. 1814, CO 42, vol. 156, 133, NAC.

33. Size, age and service of British regulars of the Right Division extracted from the following inspection returns: 2nd Battalion, 8th Foot, 1 June 1815; 41st Foot, May 1815; 2nd Battalion, 89th Foot, 16 May 1815; 103rd Foot, 24 May 1815; 104th Foot, 18 May 1815, all WO 27, volume 133, PRO. Inspection returns for 1815 were used as there appear to be no surviving returns from 1814.

34. Unknown recruiting sergeant quoted in H. De Watteville, *The British Soldier. His Daily Life from Tudor to Modern Times* (London: J.M. Dent, 1954), 97.

35. William Wheeler, *The Letters of Private Wheeler, 1809-1828*, ed. B.H. Liddell Hart, (London: Michael Joseph, 1954), 19.

36. Le Couteur, Journal, 5 Jan. 1813, SJ. A published edition of this memoir is available in Donald E. Graves, editor, *Merry Hearts Make Light Days: The War of 1812 Memoir of Lieutenant John Le Couteur, 104th Foot* (Ottawa: Carleton University Press, 1993). Also Inspection Return of the 2nd Battalion, 8th Foot, 1 June 1815, WO 27, vol. 133, PRO; Tullibardine, *Military History*, I, 489-490.

37. William B. Lighton, *Narrative of the Life and Sufferings of a Young British Captive* (Concord, NH: author, 1836), 90.

38. Soldier's pay from Charles James, *The Regimental Companion; Containing the Pay, Allowances and Relative Duties of Every Officer in the British Service* (London: T. Egerton, 1811, 2 vols.), I, 272-273. Desertion figures for Right Division extracted from General Monthly Returns of the Several Corps serving in Canada, January to June 1814, vols. 1516-1518, all WO 17, PRO.

39. R.M. Grazebrook, "The Wearing of Equipment, 1801," *Journal of the Society of Army Historical Research* 24 (1946), 38.

40. William Dunlop, *Tiger Dunlop's Upper Canada* (Toronto: McClelland & Stewart, 1967), 19. On the reforms of the British army, see Richard Glover's magisteral *Peninsular Preparation: The Reform of the British Army, 1795-1809* (Cambridge: University Press, 1963).

41. Ages from WO 27 Inspection Returns from the PRO cited in note 32; Michael Glover, *Wellington as Military Commander* (London: Sphere, 1973), 24-28; Inspection Return of the 2nd

Battalion, 89th Foot, 16 May 1815, WO 27, vol. 133, PRO; Career of Col. Hercules Scott, MG 24, F15, NAC; Morrison, *DCB*, VI, 520-524; W.J. Patterson, "A Forgotten Hero in a Forgotten War," *Journal of the Society for Army Historical Research* 68 (1990) 7-21; Evans, *DCB*, IX, 245-246; George Hay, "Recollections of the War of 1812 by George Hay, Eighth Marquis of Tweeddale," ed. Lewis Einstein, *American Historical Review* 32 (1926), 69-78; George Hay, *DNB*, XXV, 263-265.

42. Prevost to Bathurst, 26 May 1812, CO 42, vol. 146, 205, NAC.

43. Dunlop, *Tiger Dunlop*, 45. On the history of the Glengarry Light Infantry and the Incorporated Militia, see Ernest Cruikshank, "Record of the Services of Canadian Regiments in the War of 1812 - II. The Glengarry Light Infantry," *Selected Papers of the Canadian Military Institute* 6 (1894-1895), 9-23; and; and "V. The Incorporated Militia," *Selected Papers of the Canadian Military Institute* 9 (1897-1899), 70-80. On the uniforms of the Glengarries, see René Chartrand and Jack Summers, *Military Uniforms in Canada, 1665-1970* (Ottawa: National Museums, 1981), 71-74.

44. Weekly Distribution Return of the Right Division, 22 June 1814, *Doc. Hist.*, I, 28; Weekly Distribution Return of the Right Division, 8 July 1814, *Doc. Hist.*, I, 51; M.E.S. Laws, *Battery Records of the Royal Artillery. 1716-1859* (Woolwich: Royal Artillery Institution, 1952), 158-161; W.H. Askwith, *List of Officers of the Royal Regiment of Artillery From the Year 1716 to the Year 1899* (London: Royal Artillery Institution, 1900), 27, 34; Dunlop, *Tiger Dunlop*, 40-41; Return of the Dismounted Brass Guns and Iron Ordnance, Quebec, 30 April 1807, WO 44, vol. 250, 14, PRO. On numbers and types of weapons and organization of the British artillery, see Appendix B.

45. Paul Couture, "The Non-Regular Military Forces on the Niagara Frontier: 1812-1814," (Cornwall: Parks Canada, 1985), 141-144.

46. R. David Edwards, *The Shawnee Prophet* (Lincoln: University of Nebraska, 1983), 143-146; List of Warriors who have gone to Fort George by their Tribes, 22 June 1814, RG 10, vol. 28, 17032, NAC; Statement of Five Nations Inhabiting the Grand River, 16 June 1814, RG 10, vol. 3, 1447, NAC; Norton, *DCB*, VI, 550-553. On Norton's parentage, see John Lang, Diary, 22 July 1813, PLDU.

47. The name derived from a British corruption of the Ojibway salutation, "Sha'kan, Niiji" – "Hello Friend" or "Hello Comrade". For use of this term by the British, see Le Couteur, Journal, 5 June-6 Oct. 1813, SJ.

48. James Commins, "The War on the Canadian Frontier, 1812-1814. Letters written by Sergt. James Comins [sic], 8th Foot," Norman Lord, ed., *Journal of the Society for Army Historical Research* 18, no. 72 (Winter 1939), 199-211.

49. Le Couteur to Bouton, 24 Oct. 1813, Le Couteur, Journal, SJ.

50. On the relationship between the British military and the Indians, see Colin Calloway, *Crown and Calumet: British-Indian Relations, 1783-1815* (Norman: University of Oklahoma, 1987). On Drummond, see Donald E. Graves, "William Drummond and the Battle of Fort Erie," *Canadian Military History* 1 (1992), 1-18.

51. Norton, *Journal*, 348.

Chapter 4 – Opening Moves and Battle at Chippawa

1. Scott, *Memoirs*, I, 123.

2. *Ibid.*; Porter to Stone, 26 May 1840, *Doc. Hist.*, II, 358; Brown, Memoranda, 2-4, Gardner Papers, NYSL.

3. *Ibid.*; Jesup, Memoir, 3-4, LC.

4. Merritt, *Journal*, 77.

5. Porter to Stone, 26 May 18140, *Doc. Hist.*, II, 358. Buck was court martialled for his actions and, although found not guilty, his conduct was considered "reprehensible" as he had sent out a flag of truce before being summoned to do so. See York to Drummond, 25 Sept. 1815, RG 8 I, vol. 167, 148, NAC.

6. Return of the British prisoners of war surrendered at Fort Erie, 3 July 1814, *Doc. Hist.*, I, 42; David Owen, *Fort Erie (1764-1823). An Historical Guide* (Fort Erie: Niagara Parks Commission, 1986), 49; Instructions to the officer commanding at Fort Erie, May 1814, RLB, BECHS; Brown

to Armstrong, 7 July 1814, *Doc. Hist.*, I, 38; Jesup, Memoir, 3-4, LC; John Livingston, *Sketches of Eminent Americans* (New York: Craighead, 1854), 399; Benjamin Ropes, "Benjamin Ropes' Autobiography," Mary Cates, ed., *Essex Institute Historical Collections* 91 (April 1955), 116.

7. "Pennsylvania Volunteers", 151; Harris, "Service", 333-334; Scott, *Memoirs*, I, 124.

8. Norton, *Journal*, 348; Riall to Drummond, 6 July 1814, RG 8 I, vol. 684, 51, NAC; Lang, Diary, 29 June 1814, PLDU.

9. Brown to Armstrong, 7 July 1814, *Doc. Hist.*, I, 38.

10. Scott, *Memoirs*, I, 124; "Pennsylvania Volunteers", 151.

11. *Ibid.*, 124; Obituary of Pearson, *United Service Journal* 2 (1847), 479; David Thompson, *History of the Late War Between Great Britain and the United States of America* (Niagara, Canada: T. Sewell, 1832), 223.

12. Riall to Drummond, 6 July 1814, RG 8 I, vol. 684, 51, NAC; Norton, *Journal*, 349; Merritt, *Journal*, 55; Scott, *Memoirs*, I, 24; Jesup, Memoir, 4-5, LC.

13. John Livingston, *Sketches*, 400.

14. Jesup, Memoir, 4, LC; Scott to Brown, 15 July 1814, *Doc. Hist.*, I, 44.

15. Porter to Stone, 26 May 1840, *Doc. Hist.*, II, 360; John Melish, *Military and Topographical Atlas of the United States* (Philadelphia: G. Palmer, 1813), 14; Norton, *Journal*, 349; Extract of Captain Martin's report on the defences in Upper Canada, 3 July 1814, RG 8 I, vol. 388, 139, NAC; Memoir of the Defence of Canada by Captain Frederick Gaugreben, MG 24 F23, NAC.

16. Scott, *Memoirs*, I, 125-128.

17. George Howard, Letter Book, 109, CHS.

18. Ropes, "Autobiography", 117. Also, Ridout to Ridout, 10 July 1814, Edgar, *Ten Years*, 288.

19. Babcock, *War on the Niagara*, 153; Scott, *Memoirs*, I, 127; Porter to Stone, 26 May 1840, *Doc. Hist.*, II, 260; Norton, *Journal*, 351; Hanks, Biography, 18, BECHS; Jesup, Memoir, 5, LC; "Biographical Sketch of Major Thomas Biddle," *Illinois Monthly Magazine* 1 (Sept. 1831), 553.

20. Merritt, *Journal*, 56.

21. Norton, *Journal*, 349. Also, Merritt, *Journal*, 56; Drummond to Prevost, 11 July 1814, RG 8 I, vol. 684, 72, NAC.

22. Norton, *Journal*, 349: Henderson, Narrative, LL.

23. Henderson, Narrative, LL.

24. Norton, *Journal*, 349; Joseph Treat, *The Vindication of Joseph Treat, late of the Twenty First Regiment* (Philadelphia: author, 1815), 15-16, 33; "Sketch of Biddle," 553; General Order, 5 July 1814, LDOB, NYSL; Brown, Memoranda, 5, Gardner Papers, NYSL; Ropes, "Autobiography", 117-118.

25. Drummond to Prevost, 11 July 1814, RG 8 I, vol. 684, 72, NAC; Norton, *Journal*, 349-350; Merritt, *Journal*, 56; Thompson, *History*, 223-224.

26. Brown to Armstrong, 7 July 1814, *Doc. Hist.*, I, 38; Porter to Stone, 26 May 1840, *Doc. Hist.*, II, 362; Porter to Brown, n.d., *Doc. Hist.*, I, 149.

27. White, *History of American Troops*, 14; McMullen, "Narrative", 373.

28. Brown to Armstrong, 7 July 1814, *Doc. Hist.*, I, 38; Porter to Stone, 26 May 1840, *Doc. Hist.*, II, 363; Porter to Brown, n.d., *Doc. Hist.*, I, 149; White, *History of American Troops*, 14-15; McMullen, "Narrative", 373.

29. Porter to Stone, 26 May 1840, *Doc. Hist.*, II, 363-364; Porter to Brown, n.d. *Doc. Hist.*, I, 149; White, *History of American Troops*, 15.

30. Porter to Stone, 26 May 1840, *Doc. Hist.*, 364.

31. *Ibid.*; Porter to Brown, n.d., *Doc. Hist.*, I, 149; White, *History of American Troops*, 15-16.

32. Merritt, *Journal*, 56; Norton, *Journal*, 349; Thompson, *History*, 225; Lang, Diary, 29 June 1814, PLDU.

33. Captured letter printed in the *Federal Gazette and Baltimore Daily Advertiser*, 2 Aug. 1814.

34. Merritt, *Journal*, 56; Dickson to Coffin, 7 Mar. 1820, RG 9, I B 1, vol. 8, NAC; Letter from a captain in Fenton's Regiment, 7 July 1814, *Columbian Centinel*, 13 Aug. 1814.

35. Riall to Drummond, 6 July 1814, RG 8 I, vol. 684, 51, NAC; Hay, "Recollections", 73; Norton, *Journal*, 349; Mackonochie to Maclachlan, 11 July 1814, WO 55, vol. 1223, 311, PRO; Lang, Diary, 29 June 1814, PLDU; White, *History of American Troops*, 14.

36. Gardner to Brown, 10 Mar. 1825, Gardner Papers, NYSL.
37. *Ibid.*; Scott, *Memoirs*, I, 128; Brown to Armstrong, 7 July 1814, *Doc. Hist.*, I, 38.
38. Scott, *Memoirs*, I, 128.
39. *Ibid.*; Brown to Armstrong, 7 July 1814, *Doc. Hist.*, I, 38.
40. Hay, "Recollections", 73-74; Mackonochie to Maclachlan, 11 July 1814, WO 55, vol. 1223, 311, PRO; White, *History of American Troops*, 14-15; Douglass, "Narrative", 9; Jesup, Memoir, 6, LC; Joseph Baker, Memory Book, 5 July 1814, NAC; Thompson, *History*, 226.
41. Henderson, Narrative, LL.
42. Hanks, Biography, 18, BECHS. Also, Henderson, Narrative, LL; Scott to Adjutant General (Gardner), 15 July 1814, *Doc. Hist*, I, 44; Hanks, Biography, 19, BECHS; Scott, *Memoirs*, I, 130; Jesup, Memoir, 6-7, LC.
43. Jesup, Memoir, 6-7, LC. Also, Scott to Adjutant General, 15 July 1814, *Doc. Hist.*, I, 44; Hanks, Biography, 18-19, BECHS; Scott, *Memoirs*, I, 129-130.
44. Mackonochie to Glasgow, 19 Aug. 1814, WO 55, vol. 1224, 332, PRO.
45. Scott to Adjutant General, 15 July 1814, *Doc. Hist.* I, 44.
46. Mackonochie to Glasgow, 19 Aug. 1814, WO 55, vol. 1224, 332, PRO; Livingston, *Sketches*, 400; Drummond to Prevost, 10 July 1814, RG 8 I, vol. 684, 59, NAC; Ropes, "Autobiography", 117.
47. Scott, *Memoirs*, I, 128. The author has never been able to find a primary source for this famous exclamation.
48. Riall to Drummond, 6 July 1814, RG 8 I, vol. 684, 51, NAC; Hay, "Recollections", 73-74; Lang, Diary, 29 June 1814, PLDU. Strength of British units extracted from Drummond to Prevost, 10 July 1814, RG 8 I, vol. 684, 59, NAC. The two battalions numbered approximately 950 rank and file (figure excludes officers, sergeants and drummers) less the approximately fifty men in each of the two light infantry companies detached on the right under Pearson.
49. Scott, *Memoirs*, I, 130. Also, Hindman to Adjutant General, n.d., *Doc. Hist.*, I, 44.
50. Hay, "Recollections", 73.
51. *Ibid.*; Henderson, Narrative, LL; Hanks, Biography, 18-19, BECHS.
52. William L. Stone, *The Life and Times of Red Jacket* (New York: Wiley, Putnam, 1841), 264; Henderson, Narrative, LL; Hanks, Biography, 19, BECHS.
53. George Howard, Letter Book, 110-111, CHS. Also, Jesup to Brown, 12 July 1814, draft of letter in Gardner Papers, NYSL; Jesup, Memoir, 7-9, LC.
54. *Ibid.*
55. "Memoirs of Ripley", 121; Brown to Armstrong, 7 July 1814, *Doc. Hist.*, I, 38; Hindman to Adjutant General, n.d., *Doc. Hist.*, I, 44; James Wilkinson, *Memoirs of My Own Times* (Philadelphia: Abraham Small, 1816, 3 vols.), I, 650-651; Porter to Stone, 26 May 1840, *Doc. Hist.*, II, 364-365; Lossing, *Field Book*, 807n.
56. Gardner to Brown, 10 Mar. 1825, Gardner Papers, NYSL; Porter to Stone, 26 May 1840, *Doc. Hist.*, 365; Brown to Armstrong, 7 July 1814, *Doc. Hist.*, I, 38; "Biographical Sketch of Hindman", 44.
57. Hay, "Recollections", 73-74; Ridout to Ridout, 10 July 1814, Edgar, *Ten Years*, 288.
58. Letter of Lt. John Stevenson, 100th Foot, 5 July 1814, Niagara Historical Society Papers, AO.
59. Scott to Adjutant General, 15 July 1814, *Doc. Hist.*, I, 44. Also, Ridout to Ridout, 10 July 1814, Edgar, *Ten Years*, 288.
60. Scott, *Memoirs*, I, 131.
61. Hay, "Recollections", 73-74; Merritt, *Journal*, 56; Riall to Drummond, 6 July 1814, RG 8 I, vol. 684, 51, NAC; Norton, *Journal*, 350-351; Ropes, "Autobiography", 118.
62. Baker, Memory Book, 5 July 1814, NAC.
63. McMullen, "Narrative", 373.
64. Porter to Stone, 26 May 1840, *Doc. Hist.*, II, 365; "Sketch of Hindman" 44; Brown to Armstrong, 7 July 1814, *Doc. Hist.*, I, 38.
65. Report of the killed and wounded of the Left Division ... in the action of the 5th July, 1814, *Doc. Hist.* I, 43; Return of the Killed, Wounded and Missing of the Right Division ... 5th July 1814, appended to Riall to Drummond, 6 July 1814, RG 8 I, vol. 684, 51, NAC; Ridout to Ridout, 10 July 1814, Edgar, *Ten Years*, 288.

The American casualty figures provided in the text are the official figures. Recent research has revealed that the actual figures were much lower, see Donald E. Graves, *Red Coats and Grey Jackets: The Battle of Chippawa, 1814* (Toronto: Dundurn, 1994), Appendices D and E.

66. Brown to Armstrong, 7 July 1814, *Doc. Hist.*, I, 38; Report of the Killed and Wounded of the Left Division, Chippawa, 9 July 1814, *Doc. Hist.*, I, 43; Return of Killed, Wounded and missing of Capt. George Howards Company 25 U.S. Infy., 5 July 1814, Howard, Letter Book, CHS.
67. Ropes, "Autobiography", 119.
68. Porter to Stone, 26 May 1840, *Doc. Hist.*, II, 367. Also, Henderson, Narrative, LL; "Pennsylvania Volunteers", 299.
69. Norton, *Journal*, 351.
70. Merritt, *Journal*, 57.
71. White, *History of American Troops*, 25.
72. Merritt, *Journal*, 56.
73. Riall to Drummond, 6 July 1814, RG 8 I, vol. 684, 51, NAC.
74. Drummond to Prevost, 10 July 1814, RG 8 I, vol. 684, 59, NAC.
75. Prevost to Drummond, 12 July 1814, RG 8 I, vol. 1222, 162, NAC.
76. Prevost to Glasgow, 26 Aug. 1814, WO 55, vol. 1222, 338, PRO.
77. Brown to Armstrong, 10 July 1814, RG 107, Micro 221, reel 59, NA.
78. Henderson, Narrative, LL.
79. Douglass, "Narrative", 9.
80. *Ibid.*

Chapter 5 – March and Countermarch
1. Riall to Drummond, 8 July 1814, RG 8 I, vol. 684, 54, NAC.
2. *Ibid.*; Merritt, *Journal*, 57; Norton, *Journal*, 352.
3. Brown, Memoranda, 10, Gardner Papers, NYSL; Ropes, "Autobiography", 119.
4. *Ibid.*, 10-11; Hugh Dobbin, Memoir, 8 July 1814, GHS; "Biographical Sketch of Biddle", 554-555.
5. White, *History of American Troops*, 25.
6. Riall to Drummond, 8 July 1814, RG 8 I, vol. 684, 54, NAC; Merritt, *Journal*, 57; Brown to Armstrong, 11 July 1814, Cruikshank, *CBD*, 48; Ropes, "Autobiography", 119.
7. White, *History of American Troops*, 26.
8. John Kilborn, "Biographical Sketch", in Thaddeus Leavitt, *History of Leeds and Grenville* (1879, reprinted Mika, Belleville, 1972), 69.
9. *Ibid.*; Riall to Drummond, 8 July 1814, RG 8 I, vol. 684, 54, NAC; Merritt, *Journal*, 57.
10. Brown, Memoranda, 11-12, Gardner Papers, NYSL; Harris, "Service", 336; General Order, 9 July 1814, LDOB, NYSL; Dobbin, Memoir, 8-10 July 1814, GHS; McMullen, "Narrative", 374; Baker, Memory Book, 8-10 July 1814, NAC.
11. Brown to Armstrong, 23 July 1814, Brown Papers, MHS.
12. Brown to Nathan Williams, 10 July 1814, Nathan Williams Paper, OHS.
13. Brigade Orders, 11 July 1814, 16 July 1814, LDOB, NYSL; Hanks, Biography, 19-20, BECHS; Jesup, Memoir, 7-8, LC.
14. Brigade Order, 13 July 1814, LDOB, NYSL; George McFeely, "Chronicle", 281-282; Gardner to Brooke, 13 July 1814, Gardner Papers, NYSL; Douglass, "Narrative", 4-5.
15. Douglass, "Narrative", 5.
16. Jesup to Trimble, 23 July 1814, Trimble Papers, OHS.
17. Scott to Brown, 10 July 1814, Brown Papers, CL.
18. General Order, 6 July 1814, LDOB, NYSL; Jesup to Trimble, 23 July 1814, Trimble Papers, OHS; Scott to Brown, 10 July 1814, Brown Papers, CL; Brown to Scott, 10 July 1814, Brown Papers, CL; Scott to Brown, 10 July 1814 [second letter], Brown Papers, CL.
19. Merritt, *Journal*, 58; General Order, 2 July 1814; General Order, 12 July 1814, both LDOB, NYSL; Porter to Stone, 26 May 1840, *Doc. Hist.*, II, 367; Letter of McFarland quoted in William James, *A Full and Correct Account of the Military Occurrences of the Late War between Great Britain and the United States* (London: Black, 1818, 2 vols.), II, 134. This often quoted letter was almost certainly found on McFarland's body the morning after the battle of Lundy's Lane.

20. Brown to Williams, 16 July, 1814, Nathan Williams Papers, OnHS.

21. Brown, Memoranda, 13-15, Gardner Papers, NYSL; Dobbin, Memoir, 21 July 1814, GHS; Witherow, "Diary", 16 July 1814.

22. Brown to Chauncey, 13 July 1814, *Doc. Hist.*, I, 64.

23. Brown, Memoranda, 15, Gardner Papers, NYSL; Unknown [Gaines?] to Armstrong, 20 July 1814, *Doc. Hist.*, I, 77; Lossing, *Field Book*, 815.

24. Riall to Drummond, 12 July 1814, vol. 684, 124; Evans to Riall, vol. 684, 127; Riall to Drummond, 15 July 1814, vol. 684, 131, all RG 8 I, NAC.

25. Arrangements for Collecting a Force at Burlington, vol. 684, 88; Drummond to Prevost, 13 July 1814, vol. 684, 90; Drummond to Prevost, 15 July 1814, vol. 684, 101, all RG 8 I, NAC; Drummond to Prevost, 16 July 1814, *Doc Hist.*, I, 60.

26. Right Division Order, 16 July 1814, RDOB, NAC.

27. Riall to Drummond, 19 July 1814, RG 8 I, vol. 684, 179, NAC.

28. Right Division Order, 16 July 1814, RDOB, NAC.

29. Norton, *Journal*, 354-355; Riall to Drummond, 17 July 1814, RG 8 I, vol. 684, 134, NAC.

30. Merritt, *Journal*, 58. Also, Return of the Killed, Wounded and Missing of the Militia in Skirmishing with the Enemy between the 15th and 24th July 1814, RG 9, I B 1, vol. 2; vol. 3, NAC; Return of the Militia Wounded in Reconnoitering the position of the Enemy on the 22nd July 1814, RG 9 I, B1, vol. 3, NAC; Right Division Militia Order, 18 July 1814, RG 9 I B 1, vol. 8, NAC.

31. Riall to Drummond, 17 July 1814, *Doc. Hist.*, I, 71.

32. Porter to Brown, 16 July 1814, *Doc. Hist.*, I, 68.

33. Letter of McFarland, James, *Full and Correct Account*, II, 134; Merritt, *Journal*, 58-59; Riall to Drummond, 17 July 1814, RG 8 I, vol. 684, 134, NAC; Morning Order, 13 July 1814, LDOB, NYSL; Porter to Brown, 16 July 1814, *Doc. Hist.*, I, 68; Porter to Orne, 13 July 1814, *Doc. Hist.*, II, 414.

34. Extract of Memorial of David Secord to the Assembly of Upper Canada, *Doc. Hist.*, I, 72.

35. Letter of McFarland, James, *Full and Correct Account*, II, 134.

36. General Order, 19 July 1814, LDOB, NYSL.

37. Jesup, Memoir, 7, LC.

38. Lossing, *Field Book*, 814-815; Wilkinson, *Memoirs*, I, 669, 671; "Memoirs of Ripley", 123; Porter to Brown, 16 July 1814, *Doc. Hist.*, I, 68.

39. Jesup, Memoir, 7-8, LC; Brown to Gaines, 23 July 1814, Brown Papers, MHS; Porter to Stone, 26 May 1840 *Doc. Hist.*, II, 367-368; Parrish to Porter, 27 July, 1814, *Doc. Hist.*, II, 419.

40. Howard, Letter Book, 23 July 1814, CHS.

41. Hanks, Biography, 20-21, BECHS.

42. Merritt, *Journal*, 60.

43. Howard, Letter Book, 23 July 1814, CHS.

44. *Ibid.* Also, General Order, 23 July 1814, LDOB, NYSL; Merritt, *Journal*, 59-60.

45. Riall to Drummond, 20 July 1814, RG 8 I, vol. 684, 182, NAC.

46. Riall to Drummond, 22 July 1814, *Doc. Hist.*, I, 79.

47. Andrew Warffe, Diary, 22-23 July 1814, BHL; Riall to Drummond, 21 July 1814, vol. 684, 182; Riall to Drummond, 20 July 1814, vol. 684, 182, both RG 8 I, NAC.

48. Riall to Drummond, 21 July 1814, *Doc. Hist.*, I, 80; Information of American deserters to Fort George, *Doc. Hist.*, I, 80; Riall to Drummond, 22 July 1814, RG 8 I, vol. 684, 184, NAC; Gardner to Brooke, 13 July 1814, Gardner Papers, NYSL.

    The salt battery was erected on the American side of the Niagara in the autumn of 1812. Its name came derived from the fact that it was originally partly constructed from kegs of salt.

49. Harvey to Tucker, 23 July 1814, vol. 684, 167; Harvey to Riall, 23 July 1814, vol. 684, 169.

50. Harvey to Riall, 23 July 1814, RG 8 I, vol. 684, 169, NAC.

51. Brown to Armstrong, 25 July 1814, Brown Papers, LC.

52. Brown to Gaines, 23 July 1814, Brown Papers, MHS.

53. Brown, Memoranda, 14-16, Gardner Papers, NYSL. Also, Brown to Armstrong, 25 July 1814, Brown Papers, LC; Brown to Armstrong, 7 Aug. 1814, Parker Papers, PHS; Brown to Gaines,

23 July 1814, Brown Papers, MHS; Gaines to Armstrong, 20 July 1814, RG 107, Micro 221, reel 61, NA; Allen to Thompson, 24 Oct. 1816, BECHS.

54. Douglass, "Narrative", 13.

Chapter 6 – Advance to Contact, 24–25 July 1814

1. Norton, *Journal*, 355.
2. Kilborn, "Biographical Sketch", 70; Right Division Orders, 21 July 1814, Right Division Orders, 22 July 1814, both RDOB, NAC; Clark, Lundy's Lane, NAC; Warffe, Diary, 24 July 1814, BHL.
3. For sources on the composition and strength of Pearson's brigade, see Appendix B.
4. Warffe, Diary, 25 July 1814, BHL; Merritt, *Journal*, 61; Norton, *Journal*, 356.
5. Norton, *Journal*, 356; Merritt, *Journal*, 61.
   An American officer who served with the Left Division in 1814 has left an excellent description of "pickets", which he defines as: "small detachments of Infantry or Cavalry ... thrown out, at various points, beyond the line of camp sentinels. These pickets are often again divided into small parties, which are thrown still further forward, and which may again be subdivided into individual guards. In this method, the whole range of country, for one, two, or three miles, in every direction, may be completely under the surveillance of a military encampment." See Douglass, "Narrative", 11n.
6. A vedette is an outpost of mounted troops.
7. Merritt, *Journal*, 61; Mary Agnes Fitzgibbon, *A Veteran of 1812 ... The Life of James Fitzgibbon* (Toronto: William Briggs, 1894), 122; Norton, *Journal*, 356; Kilborn, Biographical Sketch, 70; "Recollections of Lundy's Lane," *Army and Navy Chronicle* 3 (1836), No. 14; [James Richardson], *The Letters of Veritas* (Montreal, A. Gray, 1815), 127; Drummond to Lady Drummond, 27 July 1814, letter in possession of Lady Strange, U.K.
8. Drummond to Prevost, 27 July 1814, RG 8 I, vol. 684, 235, NAC.
9. Byfield, "Recollections", 37; James, *Full and Correct Account*, II, 142; Withrow, "Diary", 25 July 1814; [Richardson], *Veritas*, 150.
10. James, *Full and Correct Account*, II, 142; [Richardson], *Veritas*, 150.
11. Drummond to Lady Drummond, 27 July 1814, letter in possession of Lady Strange, U.K.
12. James, *Full and Correct Account*, II, 142; Drummond to Prevost, 27 July 1814, RG 8 I, vol. 684, 235, NAC; Richard Cannon, compilor, *Historical Records of the First or Royal Regiment of Foot* (London: Furnivall & Parker, 1847), 199; *Historical Records of the Eighth, or, The King's Regiment of Foot* (London: Furnivall & Parker, 1844), 97; Byfield, "Recollections", 36. For sources on the composition and strength of Morrison's force, see Appendix B.
13. Le Couteur, Journal, 24-25 July 1814, SJ; James, *Full and Correct Account*, II, 144. For sources for the composition and strength of Hercules Scott's force, see Appendix B.
14. Norton, *Journal*, 356.
15. Douglass, "Narrative", 13.
16. Evidence of Captain William McDonald, *Facts*, 10; Letter of Leavenworth, 15 Jan. 1815, *Facts*, 18; Letter of Odell, *Facts*, 33.
17. Letter of Odell, *Facts*, 33; Letter of Leavenworth, 15 Jan. 1815, *Facts*, 19; John L. Thomson, *Historical Sketches of the Late War* (Philadelphia: T. Donilever, 1817), 286.
18. Brown, Memoranda, 15-16, Gardner Papers, NYSL.
19. Brown to Armstrong, 7 Aug. 1814, Parker Papers, PHS.
20. Gardner to Parker, 31 July 1814, Gardner Papers, NYSL; Dobbin, Memoir, 19 July 1814, GHS; Randolph, Autobiography, MDAH.
21. Dobbin, Memoir, 25 July 1814, GHS.
22. *Ibid.*; Ropes, "Autobiography", 121.
23. Brigade Orders, 16 July 1814, LDOB, NYSL.
24. Brigade Orders, 11 July 1814, LDOB, NYSL.
25. Charles J. Ingersoll, *Historical Sketches of the Second War between the United States of American and Great Britain.* (Philadelphia: Lee, Blanchard, 1849, 2 vols.), II, 95; Brigade Orders, 11 July and 14 July 1814, LDOB, NYSL; Scott, *Memoirs*, I, 137.
26. Douglass, "Narrative", 13; General Order, 10 July 1814, LDOB, NYSL.

27. Scott, *Memoirs*, I, 137; Letter of Leavenworth, 15 Jan. 1815, *Facts*, 19; Letter of Odell, *Facts*, 33; Jesup, Memoir, 8, LC; Brown to Armstrong, 7 Aug. 1814, Parker Papers, PHS.

28. Brown, Memoranda, 15, Gardner Papers, NYSL.

29. Scott, I, *Memoirs*, 137; Brown to Armstrong, 7 Aug. 1814, Parker Papers, PHS.

30. Thomson, *Historical Sketches*, 286.

31. Letter of Leavenworth, 15 Jan. 1815, *Facts*, 19; Brady to Vincent, 28 July 1814, John B. Linn, *Annals of Buffalo Valley, Pennsylvania, 1755-1855* (Harrisburg: Lane & Haupt, 1877) 419. For sources on the strength of the American units, see Appendix A.

32. Scott, *Memoirs*, I, 137.

33. Douglass, "Narrative", 13.

34. Hanks, Biography, 21, BECHS. Also Brady to Vincent, 28 July 1814, Linn, *Annals*, 419; Douglas, "Narrative", 13; Letter of Odell, *Facts*, 34; Statement of McDonald, *Facts*, 10, Scott, *Memoirs*, I, 137.

35. Letter from an officer of the 11th Regiment, 2 August 1814, *Doc. Hist.*, I, 110-111; Jesup, Memoir, 8, LC; Letter of Leavenworth, 15 Jan. 1815, *Facts*, 19.

36. Douglass, "Narrative", 13.

37. Report of Capt. Harris, 2 Aug. 1814, War of 1812 Mss, LL; Douglass, "Narrative", 13.

38. Map in Weld, *Travels*.

39. Le Couteur, Journal, Le Couteur to Bouton, 24 Oct. 1813, SJ. A naiad is a water nymph. Also, Livingston, *Sketches*, 403; Myers, *Reminiscences*, 35; Hall, Livre de voyage, 27 Aug. 1816. MG 24, F 17, NAC.
    Either Mrs. Willson's American birth, her protestations of neutrality, or the nature of the entertainment available in her tavern, annoyed the authorities. On the cover of her claim for losses suffered during the war, some anonymous official scribbled the comment: "Reputed Character Destroyed and Infamous". See Claim of Debora Willson, RG 19, E5(a), vol. 3749, file 3, claim 794, NAC.

40. Myers, *Reminiscences*, 35; Douglass, "Narrative", 13-14.

41. Scott, *Memoirs*, I, 139.

42. *An Interesting Account of the Campaign of 1814* (n.p. n.d.), 5; Richard Bonnycastle, *Canada, As It Was, Is, and May Be* (London: Colburn, 1852, 2 vols.), I, 52; Report of Capt. Harris, 2 Aug. 1814, War of 1812 Mss, LL; Wilkinson, *Memoirs*, I, 685.

43. Hanks, Biography, 22, BECHS.

44. Jesup, undated draft report, Gardner Papers, NYSL.

45. Brown to Armstrong, 7 Aug. 1814, Parker Papers, PHS; Jesup, Memoir, 9, LC; Letter of Leavenworth, 15 Jan. 1815, *Facts*, 20; Wilkinson, *Memoirs*, I, 685; Blake Court Martial, RG 153, K-4, 48, NA.

46. On U.S. Regimental colours, see Chartrand, *Uniforms and Equipment*, 111-115; Hanks, Biography, 22-23, BECHS.

47. Scott, *Memoirs*, I, 137.

48. "Recollections of Lundy's Lane"; Scott, *Memoirs*, I, 137. American troops played "Yankee Doodle" when they attacked at Fort George in May 1813, see Norton, *Journal*, 325.

49. Kilborn, "Biographical Sketch", 70.

50. Clark, Lundy's Lane, NAC; Merritt, *Journal*, 61; Kilborn, "Biographical Sketch", 70; Drummond to Prevost, 27 July 1814, RG 8 I, vol. 684, 235, NAC.

51. Norton, *Journal*, 356.

52. Drummond to Prevost, 27 July 1814, RG 8 I, vol. 684, 235, NAC; Drummond to lady Drummond, 27 July 1814, letter in possession of Lady Strange, U.K.

53. Howison, *Sketches*, 83; Bonnycastle, *Canada*, I, 52; Clark, Lundy's Lane, NAC; Pentland to Wilkinson, 14 Oct. 1816, War of 1812 Miscellaneous Papers, PHS.

54. Weld, *Travels*, 311. Also, Green, "Township No. 2", 273; Norton, *Journal*, 357; Ernest A Cruikshank, *The Battle of Lundy's Lane* (Welland, 1893), 31; Statement of Miller, 31 July 1814, War of 1812 Mss., LL; McMullen, "Narrative", 375; Howison, *Sketches*, 83; MacEwen to wife, 31 July 1814, MacEwan, *Excerpts*, 14.

55. Green, "Township No. 2", 286; Mabel Warner, "Memorials at Lundy's Lane," *Ontario History*

51 (59), 47; Petition of Stephen Peer, 18 July 1797, RG 1, L3, vol. 399, NAC; Petition of Lydia (Skinner) Peer, 1 March 1811, RG 1, L3, vol. 402a, NAC.

56. Lieutenant John Le Couteur of the 104th Foot, who fought at the battle, made a detailed inspection of the site a few months later. It was his opinion that "it was a very good position" and "if the church had been occupied and loop holed, the position would have been empragnable, and of easy defence." See Le Couteur, Journal, 15 Oct. 1814, SJ.

57. Warffe, Diary, 25 July 1814, BHL. Also, Drummond to Lady Drummond, 27 July 1814, letter in possession of Lady Strange, U.K.; Clark, Lundy's Lane, NAC.

58. "Artillero Viejo", "How to Fight Brother Jonathan", 211.

59. Green, "Canadians at Lundy's Lane"; Norton, *Journal*, 357.

60. War Office, *Rules and Regulations*, 33.

61. District General Order, 1 Aug. 1814, RG 8 I, vol. 231, 128, NAC. Although promulgated after the battle, this order had been issued on a previous occasion and predated the action.

62. Byfield, "Recollections", 38.

63. Maude, *Visit*, 131, states that the horseflies were bad in the area of the falls in August, but worse in July.

64. Norton, *Journal*, 357.

65. Couture, "Non-Regular Military Forces", 143; Return of the Militia Men who were Killed and Wounded in the Sortie which took place on the 5th Instant, RG 9, IB4, vol. 1, 98-99; *Proceedings and Report of the Loyal and Patriotic Society*, 292, 380.

66. Green, "Township No. 2", 287; Muster Roll and Pay List of Capt. John Birch's Company, 2nd Lincolns, 26 June to 27 July 1814, RG 9, I B 7, vol. 22; Biggar, *Tale of Early Days on Lundy's Lane* (n.p., n.d.), no pagination.

67. Merritt, *Journal*, 61.

68. Clarke, Lundy's Lane, NAC; Drummond to Prevost, 27 July 1814, RG 8 I, vol. 684, 235, NAC; Letter of Leavenworth, 15 Jan. 1815, *Facts*, 20. Hugh Brady, in his "The Battle of Lundy's Lane," *Historical Magazine* 10 (1866), 272, states unequivocally that Towson's artillery was the first target of the British gunners.

Chapter 7 – The First Brigade Stands and Dies

1. Scott, *Memoirs*, I, 140.

2. *Ibid.*

3. Letter from an officer to his friend in Alexandria, 28 July 1814, *Doc. Hist.*, I, 108.

4. Letter of Leavenworth, 15 Jan. 1815, *Facts*, 20.

5. Janet Carnochan, "Early Churches in the Niagara Peninsula, Stamford and Chippawa, with Marriage Records of Thomas Cummings and Extracts from the Cummings Papers," *Papers and Records of the Ontario Historical Society* 8 (1907), 223.

6. Letter of Leavenworth, 15 Jan. 1815, *Facts*, 20.

7. Hanks, Biography, 22, BECHS.

8. Blake Court Martial, RG 153, K-4, 48, NA, emphasis in the original. Also Blake, Court Martial, 44, 48, 73, NA; Report of the Killed, Wounded & Missing of the Left Division, 25 July 1814, Parker Papers, PHS.

9. Jesup to Phelps, 2 Jan. 1840, *Memoir of General Scott contemporaneous with events* (Washington: C. Alexander, 1852), 8.

10. Blake, Court Martial, RG 153, K-4, 44, NA; Letter of Leavenworth, 15 Jan. 1815, *Facts*, 20-21; Jesup to Phelps, 2 Jan. 1840, *Memoir of Scott*, 8.

11. Livingston, *Sketches*, 381-422; *Sketch of the Life of General Nathan Towson* (Baltimore: Hickman, 1842), 13; Heitman, *Register*, I, 968.

12. Letter of Leavenworth, 15 Jan. 1815, *Facts*, 20-21.

13. *Ibid.*, 21; *Sketch of Towson*, 13; Charles J. Peterson, *The Military Heroes of the War of 1812* (Philadelphia: James Smith, 1858), 172; Livingston, *Sketches*, 403; Louis de Tousard, *American Artillerist's Companion, or Elements of Artillery* (Philadelphia: C. & A. Conrad, 2 vols.), II, 238-241.

14. Hughes, *Firepower*, 38, 159; Ralph W. Adye, *The Bombardier and Pocket Gunner* (London: T. Egerton, 1813), 17; Askwith, *List*, 27.

15. Glasgow to Prevost, 27 Dec. 1814, RG 8 I, vol. 745, 122, NAC.

16. Riall to Drummond, 6 July 1814, vol. 684, 51; Mackonochie to Glasgow, 19 Aug. 1814, vol. 745, 123E, both RG 8 I, NAC.

17. Hughes, *Firepower*, 166; [Amos Stoddard] *Exercise for Garrison and Field Ordnance* (Philadelphia: A. Finlay, 1812), 59-60; Duane, *Military Library*, II, 292; Otto von Pivka, *Armies of the Napoleonic Period* (Newton Abbot: David & Charles, 1979), 50. Maclachlan would have hoarded his shrapnel as, according to a Return and Distribution of Ordnance, Carriages, and Ammunition, 1 April 1814, WO 44, vol. 250, 276, PRO, there was only 84 rounds of 6-pdr. shrapnel, 10 rounds of 5 1/2 in. howitzer shrapnel and no rounds of 24-pdr. shrapnel in the Niagara peninsula.

18. Albert Ellis, "Fifty-four Years Recollections of Men and Events in Wisconsin," *Wisconsin Historical Collections* 7 (1876), 260, quoted in Fredriksen, *Officers*, 65.

19. Brady to Vincent, 28 July 1814, Linn, *Annals*, 419. Also, Smyth, *Regulations*, 1-3; Blake, Court Martial, RG 153, K-4, 50, NAC; Horner, "Military Hospital", 3; Letter of Leavenworth, 15 Jan. 1815, *Facts*, 20; Return of the Killed and Wounded and missing of the 22nd Regiment, 25th July 1814, BECHS; Heitman, *Register*, I, 239.

20. Henry Parker, "Henry Leavenworth, Pioneer General," *Military Review* 59 (1970), 58-59.

21. Scott to Adjutant General [Gardner], 15 July 1814, *Doc. Hist.*, I, 46.

22. Parker, "Leavenworth", 59.

23. Hanks, Biography, 24, BECHS. Also, letter of Leavenworth, 15 Jan. 1815, *Facts*, 21; Smyth, *Regulations*, 1-3.

24. Report of Capt. Samuel Harris, 2 Aug. 1814, War of 1812 Mss, LL.

25. Hanks, Biography, 23-24, BECHS; Jesup to Phelps, 2 Jan. 1814, *Memoir of Scott*, 11.

26. Brady to Vincent, 28 July 1814, Linn, *Annals*, 419. Also, Report of the Killed, Wounded and Missing of the Left Division, 25 July 1814, Parker Papers, PHS; Blake, Courtmartial, RG 153, K-4, 31, NA; Letter of Leavenworth, 15 Jan. 1815, *Facts*, 20-21.

27. Smyth, *Regulations*, 1-3, 19; Norton, *Journal*, 357.

28. Blake, Court Martial, RG 153, K-4, 18, 31, NA; William Congreve, *Details of Rocket System* (London: J. Whiting, 1814, reprinted Museum Restoration Service, 1970), 21.

29. Abraham Paul, RA, Manuscript Note Book, 100, RCMI.

30. Cavalie Mercer, *Journal of the Waterloo Campaign* (London: Peter Davies, 1927), 153.

31. David Yarrow, "A Journal of the Walcheren Expedition," *Mariner's Mirror* 61 (1975), 188.

32. Mercer, *Journal*, 153.

33. [Stoddard], *Exercises*, 31.

34. Tousard, *Artillerist's Companion*, I, 320.

35. Report of Capt. Samuel Harris, 2 Aug. 1814, 1812 Mss., LL.

36. *Ibid.* Also, Adye, *Bombardier*, 20; *Sketch of Towson*, 14; Report of Major Hindman, 29 July 1814, War of 1812 Mss., LL; Letter of Leavenworth, 15 Jan. 1815, *Facts*, 20-21.

37. Norton, *Journal*, 357. Also, Brown, Memoranda, 17, Gardner Papers, NYSL.

38. Letter of Leavenworth, 15 Jan. 1815, *Facts*, 21.

39. *Ibid.* Leavenworth thought that the cancellation of the order to advance may have been due to the poor condition of the Eleventh and Twenty-Second Infantry. The movement of the brigade forward and their final position is clearly shown in Wilkinson, *Diagrams and Plans*, Battle of Bridgewater, No. 13, View 2nd.

40. *Ibid.*; Question for Lieutenant George Chisholm, n.d., RG 9, I B 1, 10, NAC.

41. Question for Major Titus G. Simons, n.d., RG 9, I B 1, 10, NAC.

42. Questions for Major Titus G. Simons and Lieutenant George Chisholm, n.d., RG 9, I B 1, 10, NAC.

43. H.H. Robertson, "Some Historical and Biographical Notes on the Militia within the Limits now Constituting the County of Wentworth ...," *Transactions of the Wentworth Historical Society* 4 (1905), 20; H.H. Robertson, "Major Titus Geer Simons at Lundy's Lane," *Transactions of the Wentworth Historical Society* 2 (1899), 52; Foster to Robinson, 10 July 1814, RG 9, I B 1, vol. 4, file, Incorporated Militia, NAC.

44. Torrens to Prevost, 17 June 1815, RG 8 I, vol. 167, 79, NAC. In his official report on the bat-

tle, Drummond displays a maddening imprecision about British dispositions and movements during the battle. Where other evidence is lacking, I have relied on two period British maps: Sketch of an Action fought on the Night of the Twenty-fifth of July, near the Falls of Niagara ... contained in Prevost to Bathurst, 5 Aug. 1814, CO 42, vol. 157, 116, NAC; Sketch of the action fought on the night of 25 July 1814 near the Falls of Niagara, NMC H2/407/1814, NAC. This later map is by Captain G.A. Elliott who was present at the battle. The two maps are similar but the legends which contain information on the troops and their movements differ, the map sent with Prevost's dispatch being more informative.

45. Letter of Leavenworth, 15 Jan. 1815, *Facts*, 21.

46. Norton, *Journal*, 357.

47. *Ibid*; Robertson, "Simons at Lundy's Lane", 52; Medical Certificate of Major Simons, 3 July 1814, RG 9, I B 4, vol. 1, 14, NAC; Leavenworth, letter of 15 Jan. 1815, *Facts*, 21.

48. Brigade Order, 6 July 1814, LDOB, NYSL; letter of Leavenworth, 15 Jan. 1815, *Facts*, 21.

49. Blake, Court Martial, RG 153, K-4, 18-28, 31-44, 48, 73, 104, NA.

50. *Ibid.*, 22, 31, 42, 104; Douglass, "Narrative", 14; Gardner, *Proceedings of a Court Martial Held at Fort Independence ... for the Trial of Major Charles K. Gardner* (Boston: n.p., 1816), 46; W.F. Scarborough, "William Worth – Soldier," *Americana (American Historical Magazine)* 23 (1929), 561-562; Leavenworth letter of 15 Jan. 1815, *Facts*, 21.

51. Letter of Leavenworth, 15 Jan. 1815, *Facts*, 21.

52. Wilkinson, *Memoirs*, I, 695n; *Facts*, Appendix.

53. Letter of Leavenworth, 15 Jan. 1815, *Facts*, 21.

54. Drummond to Prevost, 27 July 1814, RG 8 I, vol. 684, 235, NAC.

55. Jesup to Phelps, 2 Jan. 1815, *Memoir of Scott*, 10-11.

56. Hughes, *Firepower*, 166, calculates that the standard rate of fire for artillery during the Napoleonic period was one round per minute for light pieces and one round every two minutes for heavy pieces. These calculations are partially confirmed by Towson's ammunition expenditure at Chippawa where the American gunner fired 120 rounds from his two light 6-pdr. guns during an action that lasted one hour, see Extract of a letter, 7 July 1814, *Doc. Hist.*, I, 49.

　　The casualty figures in the text exclude the Twenty-Fifth Infantry but include men who were unharmed but may have left the ranks. These figures are derived from the number of men, the Ninth, Eleventh and Twenty-Second are estimated to have taken into action, less the 240 men known to have still been in the ranks after the British artillery ceased firing. See Blake, Court Martial, RG 153, K-4, 31, NA; Wilkinson, *Memoirs*, I, 689, 701.

　　Hughes, *Firepower*, 167, calculates that a well-placed artillery piece usually caused between one and two casualties for every round fired or between 60 and 120 casualties for every hour it was in action. Thus, Maclachlan's gunners who, in one hour, had fired about 180 rounds from their guns and possibly another 30 rounds from the howitzer, a total of 210, had inflicted about 500 casualties of all types, a little above average for artillery of this period.

57. Appendix, *Facts*. This unsigned appendix, which discusses some of the high level decisions made during the battle, was almost certainly the work of Ripley.

58. Statement of McDonald, *Facts*, 13; Drummond to Lady Drummond, 27 July 1814, letter in the possession of Lady Strange, U.K.

59. Jesup, undated draft report, Gardner Papers, NYSL; Heitman, *Register*, I, 573, 870; Chester L. Kieffer, *Maligned General. The Biography of Thomas Sidney Jesup* (San Rafael: Presidio Press, 1979), 2-6, 27.

60. Jesup, undated draft report, Gardner papers, NYSL. The northernmost extension of this road is clearly marked in James Wilkinson, *Diagrams and Plans, illustrative of the Principal Battles and Military Affairs Treated of in Memoirs of My Own Times* (Philadelphia: Abraham Small, 1816), Plates 12, 13, 14, 15, Views of the Battle of Bridgewater. A more accurate depiction is in NMC 3790, HB-440-Drummondville 1838, Sketch of Drummondville, 22 Aug. 1838, NAC, which shows it joining the present Ferry Street, Niagara Falls about six hundred yards east of the junction of Lundy's Lane and Portage road.

61. Jesup, undated draft report, Gardner Papers, NYSL.

62. *Ibid.*; Number of companies from Report of the Killed, Wounded & Missing of the 25th Inf in the Action ... on the 25th of July, 1814, BECHS.

63. Clark, Lundy's Lane, NAC.

64. Warffe, Diary, 25 July 1814, BHL.

65. Sketch of an Action, CO 42, vol. 157, 116 and Sketch of the Action, NMC H2/407, both NAC; Ruttan, "Memoir", 302; Clark, Lundy's Lane, NAC; Warffe, Diary, 25 July 1814, BHL; Kilborn, "Biographical Sketch", 70.

66. Clark, Lundy's Lane, NAC; Ruttan, "Memoir", 307; Warffe, Diary, 25 July 1814, BHL; District General Order, 26 July 1814, Names of Officers Killed, Wounded and Missing, RDOB, NAC; Kilborn, "Biographical Sketch", 70; Proceedings of Medical Board on Lieutenant McDougall, 7 Mar. 1816, RG 9, IB4, vol. 1, 24-25, NAC.

67. Dunlop, *Tiger Dunlop*, 46. Also, 45; Ruttan, "Memoir", 307; Clark, Lundy's Lane, NAC; Kilborn, "Biographical Sketch", 70; Ernest A. Cruikshank, "A Memoir of Colonel The Honourable James Kerby. His Life in Letters," *Welland County Historical Society, Papers and Records* 4 (1931), 32. The light company of the 8th Foot which was to the east of the Portage road almost certainly participated in this action.

68. Marcus Cunliffe, *The Royal Irish Fusiliers, 1793-1850* (London: Oxford University Press, 1950), 150; Drummond to Prevost, 27 July 1814, RG 8 I, vol. 684, 235, NAC; Sketch of an Action, CO 42, vol. 157, 116, NAC; Sketch of the Action, NMC H2/407, NAC; John Biddulph, *The Nineteenth and their Times* (London: John Murray, 1899), 202; Merritt, *Journal*, 62.

69. Jesup, Memoir, 10-11, LC; Jesup, undated draft Report, Gardner Papers, NYSL; Biddulph, *Nineteenth and their Times*, 202; Merritt, *Journal*, 62; Livingston, *Sketches*, 401.

    William Fitch Arnold, the son of Benedict Arnold and Peggy Shippen, entered the British army in 1811 and by 1814 was serving as a lieutenant in Lisle's squadron of the 19th Light Dragoons. See WO 17, vol. 257 and 272, WO 25, vol. 749, 164 and his obituary in the *Gentleman's Magazine*, 1847, 216.

70. Livingston, *Sketches*, 401.

71. *NWR*, 27 Aug. 1814.

72. *Ibid.*; Jesup, Memoir, 11, LC; Kilborn, "Biographical Sketch", 70; Jesup, undated draft report, Gardner Papers, NYSL. On being told Ketchum's name, Riall is said to have remarked: "Captain Ketchum! Ketchum! Well, you have caught us sure enough!" See Douglass, "Narrative", 21.

73. Holland to William Riall of Clonmel, 31 July 1814, letter in possession of Mr. Nicholas Riall of Alton, Hampshire; Kilborn, "Biographical Sketch", 71; James Morden, *Historical Monuments and Observatories of Lundy's Lane and Queenston Heights* (Niagara Falls: Lundy's Lane Historical Society, 1929), 46; Jesup, Memoir, 11, LC; Jesup, undated draft Report, Gardner Papers, NYSL; Livingston, *Sketches*, 401.

74. Livingston, *Sketches*, 401.

75. *Ibid.*

76. *Ibid.*

77. Jesup, undated draft Report, Gardner Papers, NYSL; Morden, *Historical Monuments*, 46; Gardner to mother, 16 Aug. 1814, Gardner Papers, NYSL.

78. Jesup, undated draft Report, Gardner Papers, NYSL. Jesup does not state who gave him this information.

Chapter 8 – "I'll try, sir!": Brown Renews the Battle

1. Douglass, "Narrative", 14.

2. Statement of Lt. Shaw, *Doc. Hist.*, II, 357; Smyth, *Regulations*, 175, 206; Dobbin, Memoir, 25 July 1814, GHS; Testimony of McDonald, *Facts*, 10; Testimony of Odell, *Facts*, 33; Douglass, "Narrative", 14.

    According to Smyth, *Regulations*, 206: "The retreat will always be beat fifteen minutes before sun-setting".

3. Douglass, "Narrative", 14.

4. Brown, Memoranda, 18-19, Gardner Papers, NYSL. Also, Douglass, "Narrative", 14; Testi-

mony of McDonald, *Facts*, 14; Brown to Armstrong, 7 Aug. 1814, Parker Papers, PHS; *Proceedings of a Court Martial Held at Fort Independence ... for the Trial of Major Charles K. Gardner by Major General Ripley* (Boston: n.p., 1816), 62.

5. Dobbin, Memoir, 25 July 1814, GHS; Brown, Memoranda, 18, Gardner Papers, NYSL; Wilkinson, *Memoirs*, I, 699-700, 704n; Testimony of McDonald, *Facts*, 10; Testimony of Odell, *Facts*, 33; Thomson, *Historical Sketches*, 286.

6. Nicholas Court Martial, RG 153, Box 17, K-4, 107, 282, NA. For sources on the composition and strength of the First Infantry, Second and Third Brigades, see Appendix A.

7. Howard, Letter Book, 17, Howard Papers, CHS.

8. Recollections of William Hodge Jr., Edward B. Hein, "The Niagara Frontier and the War of 1812," Unpub. PhD. dissertation, University of Ottawa, 323.

9. Brown, Memoranda, 18, Gardner Papers, NYSL.

10. *Ibid.*

11. Le Couteur, Journal, 25 July 1814, SJ.

12. Cruikshank, *Lundy's Lane*, 35; [Richardson], *Veritas*, 151.

13. Le Couteur, Journal, 25 July 1814, SJ.

14. *Ibid.*

15. Sketch of an Action, CO 42, vol. 157, 116, and Sketch of the Action, NMC H2/407, both NAC.

16. Brown, Memoranda, 18, Gardner Papers, NYSL.

17. *Ibid.*

18. Brown to Armstrong, 7 Aug. 1814, Parker Papers, PHS.

19. *Ibid.*; Brown, Memoranda, 19, Gardner Papers, NYSL; Douglass, "Narrative", 15.

20. Brown, Memoranda, 19, Cullum, *Campaigns*, 102-104; Gardner to Parker, 31 July 1814, Gardner Papers, NYSL; Douglass, "Narrative", 16.

21. Goodell to his father, 3 Aug. 1814, NYHS; Wilkinson, *Memoirs* , I, 699; Testimony of McDonald, *Facts*, 11, 16.

22. Testimony of McDonald, *Facts*, 11.

23. Unsigned letter to Fosdick, 28 July 1814, Gardner Papers, NYSL.

24. Brown, Memoranda, 19-20, Gardner Papers, NYSL.

25. Testimony of McDonald, *Facts*, 11; Wilson, *Military Heroes*, I, 259; Brown, Memoranda, 19, Gardner Papers, NYSL; Wilkinson, *Memoirs*, I, 701; Letter of Leavenworth, 15 Jan. 1815, *Facts*, 22.

26. Letter in *The Yankee*, 2 Sept. 1814.

27. Baker, Memory Book, 25 July 1814, NAC.

28. Ruttan, "Memoir", 308.

29. Clark, Lundy's Lane, NAC; Green, "Canadians at Lundy's Lane"; Norton, *Journal*, 357.

30. [Richardson], *Veritas*, 151.

31. John DeCew, "Reminiscences of the Late Capt. John DeCew," *Annual Transactions of the United Empire Loyalists Association* 4 (1901), 98.

32. For information on the organization and strength of Hercules Scott's force, see Appendix B.

33. Testimony of McDonald, *Facts*, 11.

34. Facts relative to dispositions made, for carrying the Enemy's Park of Artillery, 25 July 1814, by Lt. Newman S. Clark, 31 July 1814, War of 1812 Mss., LL.

35. Ripley to Brown, 29 July 1814, War of 1812 Mss., LL.

36. Brown, Memoranda, 19, Gardner Papers, NYSL.

37. *Ibid.*; Brown, to Armstrong, 7 Aug. 1814, Parker Papers, PHS.

38. Brown, Memoranda, 19, Gardner Papers, NYSL.

39. Ripley to Brown, 29 July 1814, War of 1812 Mss, LL. Also, Brown, Memoranda, 19, Gardner Papers, NYSL; Brown to Armstrong, 7 Aug. 1814, Parker Papers, PHS.

40. Testimony of McDonald, *Facts*, 12; Statement of facts by Miller, 31 July 1814, War of 1812 Mss., LL.

41. Douglass, "Narrative", 16.

42. Holden, "Miller", 282-285; Heitman, *Register*, I, 710.

43. Miller to wife, 28 July 1814, War of 1812 Papers, CL.

44. Douglass, "Narrative", 16. Douglass was present when this exchange took place. Miller's reply is today the motto of the Fifth Infantry Regiment, U.S. Army, the modern descendant of the Twenty-First Infantry of 1814.

45. Trimble to Symmes, 8 Apr. 1815, Draper Mss., WHS. Also, Nicholas Court Martial, RG 153, K-1, 115, 169, NA.

46. Brown, Memoranda, 19, Gardner Papers, NYSL..

47. Symmes to Trimble, 8 Apr. 1815, Draper Mss., WHS. Also, Nicholas Court Martial, RG 153, K-1, 108, 111, 113, 174, NA.

48. Letter of Leavenworth, 15 Jan. 1815, *Facts*, 22.

49. Nicholas Court Martial, RG 153, K-1, 108, 111, 113, 174, NA; Ruttan, "Memoir", 308.

50. Nicholas Court Martial, RG 153, K-1, 109, NA.

51. *Ibid.* Also, *Ibid.*, 112-113; Symmes to Trimble, 8 Apr. 1815, Draper Mss., WHS; Bissell to Shepherd, 20 July 1866, Kingsbury Collection, MissHS.

52. Ripley to Brown, 29 July 1814, War of 1812 Papers, LL.

53. Soldier's letter from the battle of Bridgewater, *NWR*, VIII, 174. Also, Wilson, *Military Heroes*, II, 256.

54. John G. Jacobs, *The Life and Times of Patrick Gass* (Wellsburg, Va.: Jacobs, Smith, 1859), 171-172.

55. *Ibid.*

56. Miller to wife, 28 July 1814, War of 1812 Papers, CL.

57. *Ibid.*

58. Norton, *Journal*, 357.

59. *Ibid.*, 357. The British guns must have ceased firing as Miller does not mention seeing their muzzle flashes when he reached the fence. Both Norton and Le Couteur state that Mackonochie's guns were still limbered when they were captured which would indicate that he was not yet in position when Miller attacked.

   Norton could distinguish American troops by their shako plates which were rectangular in shape with straight edges. British troops wore brass plates with a curved shape and scalloped edges. See Chartrand, *Uniforms and Equipment*, 147.

60. Miller to wife, 28 July 1814, War of 1812 Papers, CL.

61. Jacobs, *Gass*, 172. Also Miller to wife, 28 July 1814, War of 1812 Papers, CL; Douglass, "Narrative", 16; Ripley to Brown, 29 July 1814, War of 1812 Mss., LL. British artillery casualties from Return of the Killed, Wounded, Missing and Taken Prisoners of the Right Division, 25 July 1814, CO 42, vol. 158-1, 132a. This is the total for the RA, Royal Marine Artillery and Royal Artillery Drivers during the action. As the British gunners were nearly out of musketry range during the first part of the battle and were unable to perform their duties after their weapons were captured, I have assumed that almost all of their casualties were incurred during Miller's attack.

62. Norton, *Journal*, 357.

63. Miller to wife, 28 July 1814, War of 1812 Papers, CL.

64. *Ibid.* Also, Jacobs, *Gass*, 172.

65. Miller to wife, 28 July 1814, War of 1812 Papers, CL.

66. Soldier's letter from the battle of Bridgewater, *NWR*, VIII, 174.

67. Miller to wife, 28 July 1814, War of 1812 Papers, CL; Drummond to Prevost, 27 July 1814, RG 8 I, vol. 684, 235, NAC; Le Couteur to Robison, 27 July 1814, War of 1812 Papers, CL; Drummond to Lady Drummond, 27 July 1814, letter in possession of Lady Strange, U.K.

68. *Ibid.* (all sources).

69. Le Couteur, Journal, 25 July 1814, SJ.

70. Graves, "William Drummond"; Letter of William Drummond, undated, *Edinburgh Annual Register*, 1814, 354. Also, Miller to wife, 28 July 1814, War of 1812 Papers, CL.

71. Byfield, "Recollections", 38; Drummond to wife, 27 July 1814, letter in possession of Lady Strange, U.K.; Le Couteur, Journal, 25 July 1814, SJ; Le Couteur to Robison, 27 July 1814, War of 1812 Papers, CL; Norton, *Journal*, 357; Miller to wife, 28 July 1814, War of 1812 Papers, CL.

72. Jacobs, *Gass*, 172.

73. Miller to wife, 28 July 1814, War of 1812 Papers, CL.

74. Miller to Brown, 26 Nov. 1818, Brown Papers, LC.

75. *Ibid.* Also, Le Couteur, Journal, 25 July 1814, SJ.

76. Daniel McFarland, "The Papers of Daniel McFarland. A Hawk of 1812," John N. Crombie, ed., *Western Pennsylvania Historical Magazine* 51 (1968), 105.

77. Ripley to Brown, 29 July 1814, War of 1812 MSS, LL. On the movements and detachments of the Twenty-Third Infantry, see McFeely, "Chronicle of Valor", 282-283; General Order, 14 July 1814, LDOB.

78. Testimony of McDonald, *Facts*, 12.

79. Amasiah Ford, Memorandum, USAMHI. This memoir is now available in new and annotated version. See Donald E. Graves, *Soldiers of 1814. American Enlisted Men's Memoirs of the Niagara Campaign* (Youngstown, NY: Old Fort Niagara Press, 1995).

80. Ripley to Brown, 29 July 1814, War of 1812 Mss., LL; Testimony of McDonald, *Facts*, 12-13.

81. Ford, Memorandum, USAMHI.

82. Ripley to Brown, 29 July 1814, War of 1812 Mss., LL; Testimony of McDonald, *Facts*, 12-13.

83. Goodell to father, 3 Aug. 1814, NYHS.

Chapter 9 – Both Armies Make Ready

1. Douglass, "Narrative", 17; Ruttan, "Memoir", 308; "Recollections of Lundy's Lane".

2. Symmes to Trimble, 8 Apr. 1815, Draper Mss., WHS; Nicholas Court Martial, RG 153, K-1, 178, 181, NA; Statement of McDonald, *Facts*, 13; Miller to Brown, 26 Nov. 1815, Brown Papers, LC.

3. "Biographical Sketch of Hindman", 46; "Sketch of Biddle", 555; Randolph, Autobiography, MDAH; Wilkinson, *Diagrams and Plans*, 14, Battle of Bridgewater, View 3rd; Statement of McDonald, *Facts*, 13.

4. Brown, Memoranda, 20, Gardner Papers, NYSL.

5. Jesup, Memoir, 11, LC.

6. Miller to wife, 28 July 1814, War of 1812 Mss., LL.

7. Douglas, "Narrative", 24. None of the American accounts mention seeing Congreve rocket equipment on top of the hill although there is considerable evidence as to its being there.

8. Towson to Brown, 12 Nov. 1815, Brown Papers, MHS.

9. Statement of McDonald, *Facts*, 13; Miller to wife, 28 July 1814, War of 1812 Mss., LL; Towson to Brown, 12 Nov. 1815, Brown Papers, MHS; Le Couteur, Journal, 25 July 1814, SJ.

10. Brown, Memoranda, 21, Gardner Papers, NYSL; Appendix, *Facts*.

11. Brown, Memoranda, 21, Gardner Papers, NYSL.

12. *Ibid.* The occurrence of this exchange was confirmed by Lt. Henry Ruttan of the Incorporated Militia who heard it from the other side, see Ruttan, "Memoir", 308.

13. *Court Martial of Gardner*, evidence of Brown, 62.

14. McMullen, "Narrative", 374-375. Also, Porter to Tompkins, 29 July 1814, *Doc. Hist.*, I, 103; Porter to Brown, 28 July 1814, *Doc. Hist.*, II, 417; Wilkinson, *Maps and Diagrams*, No. 14, Battle of Bridgewater, View 3rd; Dobbin, Battle of Lundy's Lane, Dobbin Papers, GHS.

15. Dobbin, Lundy's Lane, GHS.

16. Clark, Battle of Lundy's Lane, NAC.

17. Dobbin, Lundy's Lane, GHS; McMullen, "Narrative", 375; Clark, Lundy's Lane, NAC.

18. On Hercules Scott's movements, see James, *Full and Correct Account*, II, 145.

19. Sketch of an Action, 25 July 1814, CO 42, vol. 157, 116, NAC; Sketch of the Action, 25 July 1814, NMC H2/407, NAC; Drummond to Prevost, 27 July 1814, RG 8 I, vol. 684, 235, NAC; Norton, *Journal*, 355; Le Couteur, Journal, 25 July 1814, SJ; Perry to Ripley, 9 June 1815, *Facts*, 36; Letter of William Drummond, *Edinburgh Annual Register*, 1814, 354.

20. Sketch of an Action, 25 July 1814, CO 42, vol. 157, 116, NAC; Sketch of the Action, 25 July 1814, NMC H2/407, NAC; Drummond to Prevost, 27 July 1814, RG 8 I, vol. 684, 235. For information on the organization and strength of the Right Division, see Appendix B.

21. Symmes to Trimble, 8 April, 1815, Draper Collection, WHS.

22. Letter from William Drummond, *Edinburgh Annual Register*, 1814, 354.

23. Douglas, "Narrative", 21.
24. Report of Capt. Harris, 2 Aug. 1814, War of 1812 Mss, LL; "Sketch of Biddle", 556.
25. Le Couteur to Robison, 27 July 1814, War of 1812 Papers, CL. Also, Lang, Diary, 29 June 1814, PLDU.
26. Norton, *Journal*, 357.
27. Green, "Canadians at Lundy's Lane"; Biggar, *Tale of Early Days*, no pagination; "Reminiscences of Mr. Daniel Field," *Reminiscences of Niagara*, Niagara Historical Society No. 11 (Niagara-on-the Lake: n.d.).
28. Bradt to Adjutant General, 23 Aug. 1814, RG 9, B 1, vol. 3, NAC. Also, Green, "Canadians at Lundy's Lane"; L. Homfray Irving, *Officers of the British Forces in Canada during the War of 1812-1815* (Welland: Canadian Military Institute, 1908), 88.
29. Basden to Prevost, 2 Aug. 1813, RG 8 I, vol. 1004, 49.
30. Drummond to Prevost, 5 Mar. 1814, RG 8 I, vol. 682, 164, NAC.
31. Sheaffe to [illegible], 20 Oct. 1812, RG 8 I, vol. 911, 86, NAC; Memorial of John Winslow to the Duke of York, 19 Dec. 1816, RG 8 I, vol. 1026, 71, NAC.
32. Commands from War Office, *Rules and Regulations*, 221-223; Le Couteur, Journal, 25 July 1814, SJ; Letter from an officer in the army, 29 July 1814, *American Watchman*, 20 Aug. 1814; Letter from an officer in Ripley's brigade, *Chillicothe Supporter*, 13 Aug. 1814.

Chapter 10 – A Conflict Obstinate Beyond Description

1. War Office, *Rules and Regulations*, 220-221.
2. General Order, Right Division, 1 Aug. 1814, RG 8 I, vol. 231, 128.
3. *Ibid.*
4. On protecting the line with light infantry, see War Office, *Rules and Regulations*, 276-281. By this time, Drummond had under command the light infantry companies of the 1st, 8th, 41st, 89th, 103rd and 104th Regiments of Foot, as well as the Glengarry Light Infantry.
5. General Order, Right Division, 1 Aug. 1814, RG 8 I, vol. 231, 128.
6. For a description of Drummond's dispositions at this time, see Chapter 9 above.
7. Testimony of McDonald, *Facts*, 14.
8. Elihu Shepherd, *The Autobiography of Elihu Shepherd* (St. Louis: George Knapp, 1869), 68-69; "Biographical Sketch of Hindman", 46.
9. Scott, *Memoirs*, I, 143.
10. Testimony of McDonald, *Facts*, 14.
11. *Ibid.*, 14. Also, Brown, Memoranda, 22, Gardner Papers, NYSL; Clark, Lundy's Lane, NAC.
    The best evidence for the entire latter part of the battle is American in origin. Beyond Drummond's official dispatch, itself a confused jumble of individual incidents reported out of sequence, the available British and Canadian accounts consist of participants' recollections of varying quality and reliability. These observations were restricted by the limitations of their personal vision, the press of other duties, the tension of combat, darkness, and the ever-present clouds of powder smoke. The significantly more numerous accounts by American participants suffer from similar restrictions but there is, however, a considerable body of excellent evidence contained in the transcripts of the courts martial and court of inquiry that arose out of the Niagara campaign. Factual, undramatic, detailed and reliable, this documentation forms the basis for much of the following account of the close of the battle.
12. Randolph, Autobiography, MDAH.
13. Livingston, *Sketches*, 406; "Biographical Sketch of Hindman", 46.
14. Ruttan, "Memoir", 308.
15. John Lampman, "Memoirs of Captain John Lampman (1790) and his wife Mary Secord (1797)," R.I. Warner, ed., *Welland County Historical Society Papers and Records* 3 (1927), 131-132.
16. Clark, Lundy's Lane, NAC.
17. Ruttan, "Memoir", 308.
18. *Ibid.*; Testimony of McDonald, *Facts*, 14; McMullen, "Narrative", 368; Norton, *Journal*, 358; Thompson, *History*, 233-234; Medical Certificate of Lt. Henry Ruttan, 12 Feb. 1816, RG 9,

IB1, vol. 1, NAC; Proceedings of a Medical Board on Capt. Thomas Fraser, 1 Mar. 1816, RG 9, IB4, vol. 1, NAC.

19. McMullen, "Narrative", 375.

20. Letter in *American Watchman*, 20 Aug. 1814.

21. Lt. Henry Blake to his father, 9 Aug. 1814, quoted in John W. Blake to Mrs. Cabot, 22 Aug. 1814, MHS.

22. Le Couteur to Robison, 27 July 1814, War of 1812 Papers, CL.

23. Commins, "Letters", 209.

24. Letter of an officer of the Eleventh Regiment, 2 Aug. 1814, *Doc. Hist.*, I, 110.

25. Testimony of McDonald, *Facts*, 14.

26. Ropes, "Autobiography", 120.

27. Letter in the *American Watchman*, 20 Aug. 1814.

28. Evidence of McDonald, *Facts*, 14. Also, "Memoirs of Ripley".

29. Donald McLeod, *A Brief Review of the Settlement of Upper Canada by the U.E. Loyalists and Scotch Highlanders* (Cleveland: author, 1841), 65

30. Clark, Lundy's Lane, NAC.

31. Le Couteur, Journal, 25 July 1814, SJ.

32. Jesup, Memoir, 12, LC; McMullen, "Narrative", 375; Testimony of McDonald, *Facts*, 14.

33. McMullen, "Narrative", 375.

34. Douglass, "Narrative", 19. Also, Testimony of McDonald, *Facts*, 14-15.

35. Jesup, "Memoir", 12, LC; McMullen, "Narrative", 375; *Court Martial of Gardner*, 55, 61, 62; Harris to Gardner, 2 Aug. 1814, War of 1812 Mss., LL; Le Couteur, Journal, 25 July 1814, SJ; James Browne, *England's Artillerymen. An Historical Narrative of the Services of the Royal Artillery* (London: Hall, Smart & Allen, 1865), 187.

36. Ford, Memorandum, USAMHI.

37. Brown to Armstrong, 7 Aug. 1814, Parker Papers, PHS.

38. Brown, Memoranda, 22, Gardner Papers, NYSL.

39. Brown to Armstrong, 7 Aug. 1814, Parker Papers, PHS.

40. Letter of Leavenworth, 15 Jan. 1815, *Facts*, 22. Also, Appendix, *Facts*.

41. Letter of Leavenworth, 15 Jan. 1815, *Facts*, 22; Blake Court Martial, RG 153, K-4, 20, 27, 31-32, 59, NA; Weeks to Romayne, 25 Sept. 1814, Weeks Papers, DCL. In the Left Division, the average strength of a platoon, or half-company, was between 25-30 men. This gave Scott's new formation a strength of between 200 and 240 men.

42. Wilkinson, *Memoirs*, I, 703. Also, Blake Court Martial, RG 153, K-4, 104; Pentland to Wilkinson, 14 Oct. 1814, Misc. Collection, War of 1812, PSH.

43. Letter of Leavenworth, 15 Jan. 1815, *Facts*, 22.

44. Brown, Memoranda, 22, Gardner Papers, NYSL.

45. Testimony of McDonald, *Facts*, 14.

46. *Ibid.* Also, Brown, Memoranda, 22, Gardner Papers, NYSL; Scott, *Memoirs*, I, 143; Letter of Leavenworth, 15 Jan. 1815, *Facts*, 22.

47. Hindman to Gardner, 29 July 1814, War of 1812 Mss., LL. Also, Letter of E.L. Allen, 26 July 1814, *Doc. Hist.*, I, 106; Testimony of McDonald, *Facts*, 16; Testimony of Hindman, *Facts*, 44; Towson to Brown, 12 Nov. 1815, Brown Papers, MHS.

   My calculation for the amount of ammunition available to Hindman is extracted from: Regulations for the Ordnance Department, *Army Register, 1814*, 73-74; [Stoddard], *Exercises*, 35; Jean-Jacques Basilien de Gassendi, *Aide-Memoire a l'usage des Officiers d'Artillerie de France* (Paris: Magimel, 1801, 2 vols.) I, 215-217. The two latter sources list the amount of ammunition that could be carried on the types of carriages used by Hindman's gunners.

48. Testimony of McDonald, *Facts*, 14.

49. McMullen, "Narrative", 375.

50. *Ibid.*

51. Symmes to Trimble, 8 Apr. 1815, Draper Mss, WHS; Ripley to Brown, 29 July 1814, War of 1812 MSS.

52. Testimony of McDonald, *Facts*, 14.

53. Kieffer, *Maligned General*, 37; Jesup, Memoir, 12-13, Gardner Papers, NYSL.
54. Scott, *Memoirs*, I, 143.
55. Letter of Leavenworth, 15 Jan. 1815, *Facts*, 23.
56. *Ibid.*
57. *Ibid.*
58. Scott, *Memoirs*, I, 143.
59. Pentland to Wilkinson, 14 Oct. 1816, Misc. Papers, War of 1812, PHS.
60. *Ibid.*
61. *Ibid.*; Letter of Leavenworth, 15 Jan. 1815, *Facts*, 23, 25; Wilkinson, *Memoirs*, I, 709.
62. Testimony of McDonald, *Facts*, 14.
63. *Ibid.*
64. Le Couteur to Robison, 27 July 1814, War of 1812 Papers, CL.
65. Testimony of McDonald, *Facts*, 14.
66. Randolph, Autobiography, MDAH.
67. Goodell to his father, 3 Aug. 1814, NYHS.
68. Letter from an officer in Ripley's brigade, *Chillicothe Supporter*, 13 Aug. 1814.
69. Letter from an officer in the Eleventh Regiment, 2 Aug. 1814, *Doc. Hist.*, I, 106.
70. Appendix, *Facts*; Ripley to Brown, 29 July 1814, War of 1812 Mss., LL; Jesup, 13, Memoir, 13, LC.
71. McMullen, "Narrative", 375-376.
72. Wilkinson, *Memoirs*, I, 703.
73. Pentland to Wilkinson, 14 Oct. 1816, Misc. War of 1812 Papers, PSH.
74. Brown to Armstrong, 7 Aug. 1814, Parker Papers, PHS. Also, Letter of Leavenworth, 15 Jan. 1815, *Facts*, 23.
75. Letter of Leavenworth, 15 Jan. 1815, *Facts*, 23.
76. Le Couteur, Journal, 25 July 1814, SJ.
77. Pentland to Wilkinson, 14 Oct. 1816, Misc. Papers, War of 1812, PSH.
78. Leavenworth to Brown, 21 Sept. 1814, Gardner Papers, NYSL. Also, Perry to Ripley, 9 June 1815, *Facts*, 37.
    It may have been at this time that an incident occurred which Drummond later recounted to Prevost. "In the night action of the 25th", Drummond wrote, "their boasted 1st Brigade laid down their arms & called that they had surrendered – this being believed by us to be a ruse de Guerre, & the Enemy compelled to save themselves by flight." See Drummond to Prevost, 8 Aug. 1814, RG 8 I, vol. 685, 47.
79. Jesup, Memoir, 13, LC; Hanks, Biography, 24, BECHS; Heitman, *Register*, I, 956.
80. John Brown to brother, 4 Aug. 1814, Brown Papers, MHS.
81. Horner, "Military Hospital", 24; Wilkinson, *Memoirs*, I, 712; Brown, Memoranda, 23, Gardner Papers, NYSL; Austin to Armstrong, 29 July 1814, *Doc. Hist.*, I, 96; Shepherd, *Autobiography*, 68.
82. Brown, Memoranda, 23, Gardner Papers, NYSL.
83. *Ibid.*
84. Brown to Armstrong, 7 Aug. 1814, Parker Papers, PHS; Report of the Killed, Wounded and Missing of the Left Division, 25th July 1814, Parker Papers, PHS; Testimony of McDonald, *Facts*, 15; McMullen, "Narrative", 376-377; Dobbin, Battle of Lundy's Lane, GHS; Porter to Brown, 29 July 1814, War of 1812 Mss., LL.
85. Dobbin, Lundy's Lane, GHS; Brown to Armstrong, 7 Aug. 1814, Parker Papers, PHS; Symmes to Trimble, 8 Apr. 1815, Draper Mss., WHS.
86. Jesup, Memoir, 14, LC.
87. *Ibid.*; Scott, *Memoirs*, I, 143.
88. Jesup, "Memoir, 12-13, LC; Scott, *Memoirs*, I, 143.
89. Appendix, *Facts*.
90. Dunlop, *Tiger Dunlop*, 19. Also, Towson to Brown, 12 Nov. 1815, Brown Collection, MHS.
91. Abstract of the Services of Major Miller Clifford, 14 Dec. 1814, RG 8 I, vol. 1004, 79, NAC; Thomas, *Glory of America*, 328; "Sketch of Hindman", 146.

92. Letter from an officer in the Eleventh Regiment, 2 Aug. 1814, *Doc. Hist.*, I, 110.
    Porter and Miller to Brown, 29 July 1814, in Douglass "Narrative", 18n.

Chapter 11 – Disengagement, 26 July 1814

1. Brown, Memoranda, 24, Gardner Papers, NYSL; "Recollections of Lundy's Lane".
2. Letter of Leavenworth, 15 Jan. 1815, *Facts*, 21.
3. *Ibid.*
4. Clarke to Ripley, 15 Mar. 1815, *Facts*, 30.
5. Brown, Memoranda, 24-25, Gardner Papers, NYSL.
6. McMullen, "Narrative", 376.
7. Statement of McDonald, *Facts*, 15; Ripley to Brown, 29 July 1814, War of 1812 Mss., LL.
8. Statement of Hindman, *Facts*, 43; Letter from an officer to his friend in Alexandria, 28 July 1814, *Doc. Hist.* I, 108; Statement of Harris, *Facts*, 44; Randolph, Autobiography, MDAH; Wilkinson, *Memoirs*, II, 723; "Biographical Sketch of Biddle", 556; Letter from unknown author to Fosdick, 28 July 1814, Gardner Papers, NYSL.
    The brass 6-pdr. gun which Biddle took off the field is now on display at Fort McNair in Washington, D.C.
9. Letter of Leavenworth, 15 Jan. 1815, *Facts*, 22; Brown, Memoranda, 24-25, Gardner Papers, NYSL; Le Couteur to Robison, 27 July 1814, War of 1812 Papers, CL; Evidence of MacDonald, *Facts*, 16.
10. Jesup, Memoir, 14-15, LC.
11. Letter of Leavenworth, 15 Jan. 1815, *Facts*, 25.
12. Appendix, *Facts*.
13. Porter to Tompkins, 29 July 1814, *Doc. Hist.*, I, 101.
14. Appendix, *Facts*.
15. *Ibid.*
16. Porter to Tompkins, 29 July 1814, *Doc. Hist.*, I, 101.
17. Dobbin, Lundy's Lane, GHS; McMullen, "Narrative", 376; Letter of Marston, 15 Mar. 1815, *Facts*, 32; Evidence of McDonald, *Facts*, 32; Brown, Memoranda, 25, Gardner Papers, NYSL.
18. Statement of Hindman, *Facts*, 43; Towson to Brown, 12 Nov. 1815, Brown Papers, MHS.
19. Letter of Leavenworth, 15 Jan. 1815, *Facts*, 25. Emphasis in the original.
20. Hanks, Biography, 21, BECHS.
21. Letter of an officer of the Eleventh Infantry, 2 Aug. 1814, *Doc. Hist.*, I, 110; Blake Court Martial, RG 153, Box 17, K-4, 45 NAC; Brady to Vincent, 28 July 1814, Linn, *Annals*, 419; Letter of Leavenworth, 15 Jan. 1815, *Facts*, 25.
22. Tappan to Ripley, 20 Mar. 1815, *Facts*, 34; McMullen, "Narrative", 376.
23. McMullen, "Narrative", 377.
24. *Ibid.* Also, Blake Court Martial, RG 153, K-4, 45-46, NA.
25. Norton, *Journal*, 355.
26. Le Couteur, Journal, 25 July 1814, SJ.
27. Appendix, *Facts*; Statement of Costello, 21 Mar. 1815, *Facts*, 37; Statement of Weymouth, *Facts*, 38; Worth to Brown, 25 Dec. 1815, Brown Papers, MHS; Le Couteur, Journal, 25 July 1814, SJ; Robert Gourlay, *Statistical Account of Upper Canada Compiled with a View to a Grand System of Immigration* (London: Simpkin & Marshall, 2 vols., 1822) , I, 74. See also Appendix D.
28. Norton, *Journal*, 358.
29. W.A. McCollom, "McCollom Memories," *Ontario Historical Society, Papers and Records* 6 (1909), 90.
30. Le Couteur to Robison, 27 July 1814, War of 1812 Papers, CL.
31. Le Couteur, Journal, 25 July 1814, SJ.
32. Le Couteur to Robison, 27 July 1814, War of 1812 Papers, CL. Also, Journal, 25 July 1814, SJ.
33. Le Couteur, Journal, 25 July 1815, SJ.
34. *Ibid.*
35. Bull to Williams, 31 July 1814, Nathan Williams Papers, OCHS.
36. Clark, Lundy's Lane, NAC.

37. Le Couteur, Journal, 25 July 1814, SJ. Another British officer stated that Hull's body was not stripped but, as this officer was writing to the man's family, he may have been trying to exercise some tact, see unknown officer to Hickman, 7 Oct. 1814, BECHS.

38. Statement of Costello, 21 Mar. 1815, Facts, 38; Statement of Weymouth, 7 Aug. 1815, Facts, 7 Aug. 1815; Le Couteur to Robison, 27 July 1814, War of 1812 Papers, CL; Lang, Diary, 29 July 1814, PLDU; Hercules Scott to his sister Helen, 30 July 1814, MG 24, F15, NAC; Worth to Brown, 25 Dec. 1815, Brown Papers, MHS; Norton, Journal, 358.

39. Dunlop, Tiger Dunlop, 33-34.

40. Ruttan, "Memoir", 309.

41. Account of Thomas Conolly, War of 1812 Collecton, WRHC.

42. Clark, Lundy's Lane, NAC. Also, "A Canadian Battlefield" in Daily Globe, Clark Papers, AO; Lampman "Memoirs", 132; Unknown British officer to Hickman, 7 Oct. 1814, BECHS; Commins, "Letters", 18; Byfield, "Recollections", 38.

43. Lampman, "Memoirs", 132.

44. Commins, "Letters", 200. Byfield of the 41st also witnessed this incident, see Byfield, "Recollections", 38.

45. Commins, "Letters", 200.

46. Le Couteur, Journal, 25 July 1814, SJ.

47. Norton, Journal, 358; Statement of Weymouth, 7 Aug. 1815, Facts, 38.

48. Douglass, "Narrative", 21.

49. Tappan to Ripley, 20 Mar. 1815, Facts, 34; Merritt, Journal, 63; Jesup to Ketchum, 12 April 1853, USAMHI, Coco Collection.

50. Brown to Armstrong, 7 Aug. 1814, Parker Papers, HSP.

51. Brown, Memoranda, 25-25, Gardner Papers, NYSL.

52. Appendix, Facts; McDonald to Ripley, 20 Mar. 1815, Facts, 29.

53. Towson to Brown, 12 Nov. 1815, Brown Papers, MHS. Also, Livingston, Sketches, 407.

54. Randolph, Autobiography, MDAH.

55. Tappan to Ripley, 20 Mar. 1815, Facts, 34.

56. Brown, Memoranda, 26, Gardner Papers, NYSL.

57. Thomas, Glory of America, 329; Tappan to Ripley, 20 Mar. 1815, Facts, 34; Letter of Leavenworth, 15 Jan. 1815, Facts, 26-27.

58. Letter of Leavenworth, 15 Jan. 1815, Facts, 26.

59. McMullen, "Narrative", 377.

60. Tappan to Ripley, 20 Mar. 1815, Facts, 34.

61. Ford, Memorandum, USMHI.

62. Tappan to Ripley, 20 Mar. 1815, Facts, 34.

63. Statement of Weymouth, 7 Aug. 1815, Facts, 38; Livingston, Sketches, 407; Brown, Memoranda, 26-27, Gardner Papers, NYSL; Towson to Brown, 12 Nov. 1815, Brown Papers, MHS; Douglass, "Narrative", 21; Jesup, Memoir, 13, LC. On the Bridgewater Mills, see Ray C. Bond, Peninsula Village. The Story of Chippawa (n.p., n.d. [c. 1964]), 24.

64. Brown, Memoranda, 26, Gardner Papers, NYSL. Also, Douglass, "Narrative", 21.

65. Scott, Memoirs, I, 146.

66. Dobbin, Diary, 26 July 1814, Dobbin Papers, GHS; Buffalo Gazette, 2 Aug. 1814; Ropes, "Autobiography", 121-122; Scott, Memoirs, I, 146; McMullen, "Narrative", 377-378. Also notes attached to Brown to Ripley, 27 July 1814, Gardner Papers, NYSL. These notes describe Brown's movements and actions, 26-27 July 1814, and appear to have originally been part of Brown's Memoranda.

67. Douglass, "Narrative", 21.

68. McMullen, "Narrative", 377.

69. Ibid. Also, Douglass, "Narrative", 21-22.

70. Norton, Journal, 359.

71. Ibid.

72. Le Couteur, Journal, 26 July 1814, SJ.

73. Ibid.; Norton, Journal, 359; Statement of Weymouth, 7 Aug. 1815, Facts, 38.

74. District General Order, 26 July 1814, RDOB, NAC; Biggar, *Tale of Early Days*, no pagination.

Chapter 12 – The Cost and the Accounting

1. District General Order, Falls of Niagara, 26 July 1814, RDOB, NAC; Return of the Killed, Wounded, Missing and taken Prisoners of the Right Division ... near the Falls of Niagara, 25 July 1814, dated 5 Aug. 1814, CO 42, vol. 158-1, 132a, NAC; Rolph to McDonnell, 31 Aug. 1814, RG 8 I, vol. 688D, 79, NAC. On British strengths, see Appendix B. Calculations for British casualties omit Drummond's Indian force which was apparently not heavily engaged.

2. Return of the Killed, Wounded, Missing and taken Prisoners of the Right Division ... near the Falls of Niagara, 25 July 1814, dated 5 Aug. 814, CO 42, vol. 158-1, 132a, NAC; Incorporated Militia, Monthly Return, 25 July 1814, RG 9, I B 7, vol. 3, NAC.

3. Returned of Killed, Wounded and Missing of Militia in action with the Enemy at Lundys lane on the ... 25th July 1814, RG 9, I B 7, vol. 3, NAC. This return is not dated.

4. The accuracy of the American casualty figures is discussed in Appendix D below.

5. Report of the killed, wounded and missing of the Left Division ... in the action of the ... 25th July 1814, dated 30 July 1814), Parker Papers, HSP; Entry Book, Prisoners of War, Quebec, RG 8 I, vol. 694B, NAC, entries for August, September and October, 1814.

6. Report of the killed, wounded and Missing of the Left Division ... in the action of the ... 25th July 1814, dated 30 July 1814, Parker Papers, PHS.

7. Ruttan, "Memoir", 309.

8. Statement of Weymouth, *Facts*, 38-39.

9. Horner, "Military Hospital", 768.

10. Dunlop, *Tiger Dunlop*, 33.

11. Surgeon William Beaumont, "General Notebook", 27 Apr. 1813, in Genevieve Miller, ed., *William Beaumont's Formative Years. Two Early Notebooks 1811-1821* (New York: Henry Schuman, 1946), 46.

12. Horner, "Military Hospital", 1, 767.

13. Dunlop, *Tiger Dunlop*, 35-36.

14. Report of the Killed, wounded and missing of the Left Division ... in the action of the ... 25th July 1814, dated 30 July 1814, Parker Papers, PHS.

15. Horner, "Military Hospital", 3, 1.

16. Samuel Holmes, A Pedestrian Tour to the Falls of Niagara in Upper Canada, MG 40, R110, 139, NAC. Also, Horner, "Military Hospital", 3, 1; 2, 2.

17. Great Britain, Horse Guards, *Instructions to Regimental Surgeons for Regulating the Concerns of the Sick and the Hospitals* (London: Horse Guards, 1808), 37; Richard Blanco, *Wellington's Surgeon General: Sir James McGrigor* (Durham, NC: University of North Carolina, 1974), 18; Charles G. Roland, "War Amputations in Upper Canada," *Archivaria*, 10 (1980), 75.

18. Blanco, *Surgeon-General*, 19; Baron Larrey, *Memoires de chirugie militaire* (Paris, 1808), quoted in James Phalen, "Landmarks in Surgery. Surgeon James Mann, U.S. Army; Observations on Battlefield Amputations," *Surgery* 66 (1938), 1072; Douglas, *Medical Topography*, 32; Mann, *Medical Sketches*, 212; James Tilton, *Economical Observations on Military Hospitals; and the Prevention and Cure of Diseases Incident in an Army* (Washington, 1813), quoted in Roland "Amputations", 77; Dunlop, *Tiger Dunlop*, 34; Horner, "Military Hospital", 2, 7.

19. Dunlop, *Tiger Dunlop*, 34.

20. John Hennen, *Principles of Military Surgery* (London: Constable, 1820), 77.

21. Procedure for amputation from George Guthrie, *A Treatise on Gun-Shot Wounds* (London: Burgess & Hill, 1827), 400-403; Blanco, *Surgeon-General*, 18.

22. Horner, "Military Hospital", 2, 7.

23. *Ibid.*

24. Byfield, "Recollections", 40-41.

25. Dunlop, *Tiger Dunlop*, 35.

26. *Ibid.,*; Roland, "Amputation", 75-76; Douglas, *Medical Topography*, 30-31, 103-104; Horner, "Military Hospital", 2, 4.

27. Names of Officers, Killed, Wounded and Missing, attached to District General Order, 26 July

1814, RDOB, NAC; Irving, *Service*, 38; Report of the killed, wounded and missing of the Left Division ... in the action of the ... 25th July 1814, dated 30 July 1814, Parker Papers, PHS; Heitman, *Register*, I, 170, 910; Scott, *Memoirs*, I, 146, 148-151; Scott to Brown, 1 Aug. 1814, quoted in Elliott, *Scott*, 179.

28. John Brown to brother, 4 Aug. 1814, Brown papers, MHS; Gardner to his mother, 16 Aug. 1814, Gardner papers, NYSL; Drummond to Lady Drummond, 27 July 1814, letter in possession of Lady Strange; Lossing, *Field Book*, 825n.

29. Horner, "Military Hospital", 753-754.

30. Robertson, "Simons at Lundy's Lane", 52-53.

31. Dunlop, *Tiger Dunlop*, 35.

32. Jesup to Ketchum, 12 April 1853, USAMHI, Coco Collection.

33. Merritt, *Journal*, 64-82; Warffe, *Diary*, 26 July - 7 Apr. 1815; Entry Book, Prisoners of War, Quebec, entries for August and September, 1814, RG 8 I, vol. 694B, NAC.

34. Drummond to Prevost, 27 July 1814, RG 8 I, vol. 684, 235, NAC.

35. Drummond to Lady Drummond, 27 July 1814, letter in the possession of Lady Strange, U.K. This letter was written and dated at Queenston on the same day that Drummond wrote his official report.

36. All quotations in this and preceding paragraph are from Drummond to Prevost, 27 July 1814, RG 8 I, vol. 684, 235, NAC. On the movements of the Right Division after the battle, see Norton, *Journal*, 359-360; Le Couteur, *Journal*, 26, 27 July 1814, SJ; Byfield, "Recollections", 38-39; Drummond to Prevost, 31 July 1814, vol. 684, 249; District General Order, 1 Aug. 1814, vol. 231, 128; Drummond to Prevost, 31 July 1814, vol. 684, 249; Drummond to Prevost, 4 Aug. 1814, vol. 685, 38, all RG 8 I, NAC.

37. Drummond to Prevost, 27 July 1814, RG 8 I, vol. 684, 235, NAC. The emphasis is mine.

38. *Ibid.*

39. American artillery carriages were modelled on the French Gribeauval pattern and constructed of two brackets or heavy wooden planks placed on end and connected by shorter wooden pieces or transoms. When assembled, the carriage resembled an oblong square, one end of which was mounted on a wooden axle tree with two wheels. The ready-use ammunition was carried in a chest suspended between the brackets and removed when the gun went into action.

    During the early part of the war, the Royal Artillery used a similar type of carriage but by 1814 had largely switched to an improved type known as the "block trail" which utilized a single, solid piece of wood for its trail. On both types of British carriages, the ready-use ammunition was carried in chests placed on either side of the gun, resting on the axle tree.

    There were other differences. American carriages were attached to their limbers by means of an iron ring fixed on the end of the trail that slid down over a pintle mounted on the top of the limber. British carriages used a similar method of attachment but the pintle was mounted on the lower rear of the limber, *not* the top. British gun and limber wheels were the same size but American gun wheels were larger than American limber wheels.

    On the artillery of the two nations in 1814, see Henri Othon De Scheel, *Treatise on Artillery* (Philadelphia: War Department, 1800, reprinted, Museum Restoration Service, 1984), 16-25; Donald E. Graves, "Field Artillery of the War of 1812"; and "A Note on British Field Artillery Equipments of the War of 1812," *Arms Collecting* 20 (1982), 127-1290; David McConnell, *British Smooth-Bore Artillery: A Technological Study* (Ottawa: Environment Canada, 1988), 163-234; and "Early Systems of Artillery," *U.S. Ordnance Notes* 25 (May 1874), 137-167.

40. Austin to Armstrong, 29 July 1814, *Doc. Hist.*, I, 96.

41. Porter to Tompkins, 29 July 1814, *Doc. Hist.*, I, 55

42. Gardner to Parker, 29 July 1814, Gardner Papers, NYSL.

43. *Ibid.*

44. *Ibid.*

45. Brown to Williams, 1 Aug. 1814, Williams Papers, OnHS; Hindman to Gardner, 29 July 1814; Report of Capt. Harris, 2 Aug. 1814; Porter to Brown, 29 July 1814; Ripley to Brown, 29 July 1814, all War of 1812 Mss., LL.

46. Brown to Armstrong, 7 Aug. 1814, Parker Papers, PHS.

47. Miller to wife, 13 Sep. 1814, USMA.
48. Brown to Armstrong, 25 Aug. 1814, Brown Papers, LC.
49. For examples of the evidence gathered by Ripley, see: *Facts Relative to the Campaign Upon the Niagara* (Boston: Patriot Office, 1815); Statement of Captain William McDonald on the events of the battle, 31 July 1814; Statement of Captain Newman S. Clarke, 31 July 1814; Statement of Facts by Lieutenant Colonel James Miller, 31 July 1814, all War of 1812 Mss., LL. Ripley's attempts to gather evidence to support his case were not always successful, see: Scott to Brown, 21 Aug. 1814, Brown Papers, CL; Miller to Brown, 29 July 1814, War of 1812 Mss., LL. Rough drafts of the charges that Brown intended to prefer against Ripley are in the Gardner Papers, NYSL.
50. Symmes to Trimble, 8 Apr. 1815, Draper Mss., WHS.
51. Miller to wife, 13 Sep. 1814, USMA.
52. Scott to Brady, 5 Sep. 1814, Elliott Collection, NYPL.
53. Eber Howe, "Recollections of a Pioneer Printer," *Buffalo Historical Society Publications* 9 (1906), 396.
54. See Jesup to McNeil, 2 Jan. 1840, and Jesup to Phelps, 13 Jan. 1845, in *Memoir of Scott*; Gardner to Leavenworth, 15 Aug. 1814, Gardner Papers, NYSL.
55. Randolph, Autobiography, MDAH.
56. Hanks, Biography, 23, BECHS.
57. Hercules Scott to James Scott, 12 Aug. 1814, MG 24 F15, NAC.
58. Clark, Lundy's Lane, NAC.
59. Weeks to Pearson, 1 Aug. 1814, Weeks Papers, DCL.
60. Blake to his father, 9 Aug 14, quoted in John W. Blake to Mrs. Henry Cabot, 22 Aug. 1814, Cabot Papers, MHS.
61. Brown to Tompkins, 1 Aug. 1814, *Doc. Hist.*, I, 103.

Chapter 13 – The Siege of Fort Erie and the Close of the Campaign
1. Drummond to Prevost, 31 July 1814, RG 8 I, vol. 684, 249, NAC. Other information from Drummond to wife, 27 July 1814, letter in the possession of Lady Strange, U.K.; Harvey to Baynes, 6 Aug. 1814, Harvey Papers, AO; Drummond to Prevost, 19 Sep. 1814, RG 8 I, vol. 685, 216, NAC.
2. Norton, *Journal*, 359.
3. *Ibid.*, 359-360; Drummond to Prevost, 18 Oct. 1814, RG 8 I, vol. 686, 34 NAC; Le Couteur, Journal, 26 July - 2 Aug. 1814, SJ.
4. Brown to Ripley, 27 July 1814, Gardner Papers, NYSL.
5. 5. Left Division strength, 31 July 1814, from returns in Adams, *History of the United States*, IV, Book 8, 68-69; Brown, "Memoranda", *CBD*, 87-88; Dobbin, Diary, 28 July 1814, GHS; Miller to wife, 28 July 1814, War of 1812 Mss., CL.
6. Brown to Tompkins, 1 Aug. 1814, *Doc. Hist.*, I, 103.
7. *NWR*, VI, 415, quoted in *Doc. Hist.* I, 110; Brown, "Memoranda", *CBD*, 88.
8. Chauncey to Armstrong, 10 Aug. 1814, *Doc. Hist.*, I, 128.
9. Chauncey to Brown, 10 Aug. 1814, *Doc. Hist.*, I, 129.
10. Brown to Chauncey, 4 Sep. 1814, *Doc. Hist.*, II, 444.
11. Kimball, "Strategy", 243-244. For a defence of Chauncey's actions in the summer of 1814, see William S. Dudley, "Commodore Isaac Chauncey and U.S. Joint Operations on Lake Ontario, 1813-14," in William B. Cogar, ed., *New Interpretations in Naval History* (Annapolis: U.S. Naval Institute Press, 1990), 139-155.
12. Izard to Armstrong, 19 July 1814, George Izard, *Official Correspondence with the Department of War* (Philadelphia: Thomas Dobson, 1816), 46.
13. Armstrong to Brown, 16 Aug. 1814, *CBD*, 63.
14. Brown to Armstrong, 15 Aug. 1814, *CBD*, 69
15. Le Couteur, Journal, 2 Aug. 1814, SJ.
16. *Ibid.* A "shindy" was period slang for a dance. Tucker's nickname implies that he was excitable and flighty.

17. *Ibid.*, 3 July 1814, SJ.

18. Morgan to Brown, 5 Aug. 1814, *Doc. Hist.*, I, 121; Tucker to Conran, 4 Aug. 1814, RG 8 I, vol. 685, 34, NAC; Le Couteur, Journal, 3 Aug. 1814, SJ; Byfield, "Recollections", 41.

19. Tucker to Conran, 4 Aug. 1814, RG 8 I, vol. 685, 34, NAC.

20. District General Order, Fort Erie, 5 Aug. 1814, Harvey Papers, AO. The Canadian historian, C.P. Stacey, noting that this order was not to be found in the National Archives of Canada, concluded that it was missing because it "was an improper order, and it was probably withdrawn and suppressed", see C.P. Stacey, "Upper Canada at War, 1814: Captain Armstrong Reports," *Ontario History* 48 (1956), 39-40. Stacey was wrong. The order was issued and a copy will be found in the Harvey Papers, AO. Another copy, which fell into American hands, was published in the *Buffalo Gazette* and is reproduced in *Doc. Hist.*, II, 427.

21. Drummond to Prevost, 4 Aug. 1814, vol. 685, 38; Drummond to Prevost, 8 Aug. 1814, vol. 685, 47, both RG 8 I, NAC; Monthly Returns, North America, July 1814, WO 17, General Returns, PRO.

22. Drummond to Prevost, 4 Aug. 1814, RG 8 I, vol. 685, 38, NAC; Dobbin Diary, 28 July to 13 Aug. 1814, GHS. Details of American position at Fort Erie from: Court Martial of Brig. Gen. E.P. Gaines, Court Martial, RG 153, K-2, NA; Lossing, *Field Book*, 839.

23. Le Couteur, Journal, 14 Aug. 1814, SJ.

24. Drummond to Prevost, 8 Aug. 1814, RG 8 I, vol. 685, 47, NAC.

25. This statement did not appear in Drummond's official correspondence but was contained in a letter "entre nous" from Harvey to Baynes, 6 Aug. 1814, Harvey Papers, Ao.

26. Dunlop, *Tiger Dunlop*, 40.

27. Le Couteur, Journal, 8 Aug. 1814, SJ. Also, Monthly Return, Aug. 1814, WO 17, vol. 1518, PRO; Drummond to Prevost, 8 Aug. 1814, vol. 685, 47; and 12 Aug. 1814, vol. 685, 76, both RG 8 I, NAC. On the British army's weakness in siegecraft, see Glover, *Peninsular Preparation*, 96.

28. Position, description and construction of British batteries from: NMC: H3/440, 0003003, Plan of the Country round Fort Erie shewing Entrenchments thrown up by the enemy in August, 1814. Position on the 8th August, 1814; and H2/440, 0022340, Plan of the Attack made Upon Fort Erie by the Right Division of the British Army ... in August and Sept. 1814, both NAC; Lt. George Phillpotts, RE, Journal of the Attack made upon Fort Erie by the Right Division ... in the Months of August & September 1814, WO 55, vol. 860, 135-144, PRO; Le Couteur, Journal, 6-14 Aug. 1814, SJ; Dunlop, *Tiger Dunlop*, 40-42; Drummond to Prevost, 12 Aug. 1814, RG 8 I, vol. 685, 76.

29. A carronade was a type of ordnance cast with a large bore and a short barrel to fire large calibre projectiles at short ranges. It was usually used at sea.

30. Dobbs to Yeo, 13 Aug. 1814, *Doc. Hist.*, I, 135; Phillpotts, Journal, 11 Aug. 1814, PRO.

31. Le Couteur, Journal, 14 Aug. 1814, SJ.

32. Dunlop, *Tiger Dunlop*, 41.

33. *Ibid.*, 41.

34. *Ibid.*, 40-41. Information on siege batteries from Tousard, *Artillerist's Companion*, I, 4; Glover, *Peninsular Preparation*, 96.

35. Gaines to Armstrong, 23 Aug. 1814, *Doc. Hist.*, I, 152. Also, Report of the Killed and Wounded During the Bombardment and Cannonading, 15 Aug. 1814, *Doc. Hist.*, I, 150.

36. Drummond to Prevost, 15 Aug. 1814, RG 8 I, vol. 685, 47, NAC.

37. Phillpotts, Journal, 14 Aug. 1814, PRO.

38. Instructions to Lieut. Col. Fischer, 14 Aug. 1814, RG 8 I, vol. 685, 90, NAC.

39. Arrangements for the attack on Fort Erie, 14 Aug. 1814, RG 8 I, vol. 686, 83, NAC.

40. Le Couteur, Journal, 14 Aug. 1814, SJ. On Hercules Scott and William Drummond's premonitions of disaster see: Young to Scott, 20 Dec. 1814, MG 24, F15, NAC; and Dunlop, *Tiger Dunlop*, 52. Also, Arrangement for the attack on Fort Erie, 14 Aug. 1814, vol. 686, 83; Instructions to Lieut. Colonel Fischer, 14 Aug. 1814, vol. 686, 90, both RG 8 I, NAC; Returns for North America, 25 July 1814, WO 17, vol. 1518, PRO.

41. Le Couteur, Journal, 14 Aug. 1814, SJ.

42. *Ibid.*; Johnathan Kearsley, "The Memoirs of Johnathan Kearsley: A Michigan Hero from the

War of 1812," John C. Fredriksen, ed., *Indiana Military History Journal* 10 (1985), 12-13; Belknap to Brown, 9 Jan. 1821, RG 94, Adjutant General, Letters Received, 14939, NA.

43. John Le Couteur to his mother, 6 September 1814, Le Couteur-Sumner Papers, Box 1, No. 1, Societe Jersiaise, St. Helier, Jersey.

44. Donald E. Graves, "William Drummond and and the Battle of Fort Erie," *Canadian Military History* 1 (1992), 1-18.

45. Douglass, "Narrative", 29-30.

46. "War of 1812-15. Reminiscences of a Veteran Survivor", *Geneva Gazette*, 29 Nov. 1878. Also, Gaines Court Martial, RG 153, Box 17, K-2, 63-64, 196

47. Dunlop, *Tiger Dunlop*, 53.

48. Norton, *Journal*, 363.

49. Le Couteur, Journal, 14 Aug. 1814, SJ.

50. Merritt, *Journal*, 69.

51. Le Couteur, Journal, 15 Aug. 1814, SJ. On British casualties, see: Return of the Killed, Wounded and Missing of the Right Division in the Assault of Fort Erie, 15th of August, 1814, CO 42, vol. 128-1, 182a; MacMahon to Jarvis, 22 Aug. 1814, *Doc. Hist.*, I, 166; Robin Reilly, *The British at the Gates: The New Orleans Campaign in the War of 1812* (New York: G.P. Putnam, 1974), 297; Le Couteur, Journal, 15 Aug. 1814, SJ.

52. Drummond to Prevost, 16 Aug. 1814, private letter, RG 8 I, vol. 685, 101, NAC. Drummond's official report to Prevost, 15 Aug. 1814, is contained in RG 8 I, vol. 685, 94.

53. Drummond to Prevost, 16 Aug. 1814, RG 8 I, vol. 685, 101, NAC.

54. Gaines to Armstrong, 26 Aug. 1814, *Doc. Hist.*, I, 159; Killed, Wounded and Missing of the Left Division ... in the Action of the 15th, *Doc. Hist.*, I, 150.

55. Hanks, Biography, 27-28, BECHS.

56. *Ibid.*

57. Gaines to Armstrong, 26 Aug. 1814, *Doc. Hist.*, I, 159.

58. Drummond to Yeo, 18 Aug. 1814, *Doc. Hist.*, I, 182.

59. Harvey to Baynes, 6 Aug. 1814, Harvey Papers, AO. On Drummond's problems see Drummond to Prevost, 21 Aug. 1814, vol. 685, 123; Drummond to Prevost, 24 Aug. 1814, vol. 685, 134, both RG 8 I, NAC; Robinson to Prevost, 27 Aug. 1814, *Doc. Hist.*, I, 180.

60. Dunlop, *Tiger Dunlop*, 42.

61. Position of second battery from NMC H3/440, Plan of the country around Fort Erie, NAC. Also, Phillpotts, Journal, 26 Aug. to 1 Sept. 1814, PRO; Drummond to Prevost, 21 Aug. 1814, vol. 685, 123, NAC; Drummond to Prevost, 30 Aug. 1814, vol. 685, 158, both RG 8 I, NAC.

62. Drummond to Prevost, 2 Sep. 1814, RG 8 I, vol. 685, 164, NAC.

63. Site of third battery from NMC H3/440, Plan of the Country around Fort Erie, NAC.

64. Drummond to Prevost, 8 Sept. 1814, RG 8 I, vol. 685, 179, NAC.

65. *Ibid.*

66. Norton, *Journal*, 365.

67. Dunlop, *Tiger Dunlop*, 46-47.

68. Le Couteur, Journal, 4 Sept. 1814, SJ.

69. Harvey to Strachan, 8 Sept. 1814, Strachan Papers, AO. Also, General Order, 6 Sept. 1814, *Doc. Hist.*, I, 194; Matteson to Ripley, 5 Sept. 1814, *Doc. Hist.*, II, 445; Le Couteur, Journal, 4 Sept. 1814, SJ; Phillpotts, Journal, 4 Sept. 1814, PRO.

70. Drummond to Prevost, 11 Sept. 1814, RG 8 I, vol. 685, 192, NAC.

71. Drummond to Prevost, 14 Sept. 1814, RG 8 I, vol. 685, 197, NAC.

72. Harvey to Baynes, 5 Sept. 1814, Harvey Papers, AO.

73. Drummond to Prevost, 11 Sept. 1814, vol. 685, 192; Drummond to Prevost, 14 Sept. 1814, vol. 685, 197, both RG 8 I, NAC; Phillpotts, Journal, 16 Sept. 1814, PRO; De Watteville, Journal, 16-17 Sept. 1814, MG 24, F96 De Watteville Papers, NAC; Confidential Memorandum signed by Harvey, 16 Sept. 1814, MG 24, F 96, De Watteville Papers, NAC.

74. Brown to Armstrong, 19 Aug. 1814, CBD, 67. Also, Brown, "Memoranda", CBD, 89-91; Brown to Monroe, 29 Sept. 1814, *Doc. Hist.*, II, 211; Return of the Left Division, 31 Aug. 1814, *Doc. Hist.*, II, 442.

75. On the Plattsburgh campaign, see Alan Everest, *The War of 1812 in the Champlain Valley* (Syracuse: Syracuse University Press, 1981), 155-192.

76. Order by Cochrane, 18 July 1814, RG 8 I, vol. 684, 204, NAC.

77. Brown to Izard, 10 Sept. 1814, Izard, *Correspondence*, 86.

78. Brown, "Memoranda", *CBD*, 90.

79. Douglass, "Narrative", 34; Jesup, Memoir, 16, LC.

80. Brown to Monroe, 29 Sept. 1814, *Doc. Hist.*, II, 211. Also, Brown, "Memoranda", *CBD*, 90.

81. Brown, "Memoranda", *CBD*, 91.

82. Philpotts, Journal, 17 Sept. 1814, PRO; De Watteville to Drummond, 19 Sept. 1814, CO 42, vol. 128-2, 271, NAC; Brown to Tompkins, 20 Sept. 1814, *Doc. Hist.*, I, 207; Porter to Brown, 23 Sept. 1814, *Doc. Hist.*, I, 208; Brown to Monroe, 29 Sept. 1814, *Doc. Hist.*, I, 211; Dunlop, *Tiger Dunlop*, 47.

83. For the sortie of 17 Sept. 1814 see: Dunlop, *Tiger Dunlop*, 47; Brown to Monroe, 29 Sept. 1814, *Doc. Hist.*, I, 211; Drummond to Prevost, 19 Sept. 1814, RG 8 I, vol. 685, 216, NAC.

84. Report of the Killed, Wounded and Missing of the Left Division in the sortie of 17 Sept., *Doc. Hist.*, I, 214; DeWatteville to Drummond, 19 Sept. 1814, enclosing return of British casualties suffered 17 Sept., CO 42, vol. 128-2, 271, NAC.

85. Drummond to Prevost, 19 Sept. 1814, RG 8 I, vol. 685, 216, NAC.

86. Norton, *Journal*, 365; Phillpotts, Journal, 18 Sept. 1814, PRO; DeWatteville, Journal, 21 Sept. 1814, NAC; Drummond to Prevost, 19 Sept. 1814, vol. 685, 216; Drummond to Prevost, 24 Sept. 1814, vol. 685, 266, both RG 8 I, NAC.

87. Izard to Monroe, 16 Oct. 1814, *Doc. Hist.*, II, 254. Also, Izard to Monroe, 28 Sept. 1814, Izard, *Correspondence*, 92.

88. Le Couteur, Journal, 19 Oct. 1814, SJ.

89. Drummond to Prevost, 18 Oct. 1814, vol. 686, 34; Harvey to Myers, 19 Oct. 1814, vol. 686, 70, both RG 8 I, NAC; Izard to Monroe, 16 Oct. 1814, *Doc. Hist.*, II, 254; Harvey to Myers, 18 Oct. 1814, *Doc. Hist.*, II, 258; Bissell to Izard, 22 Oct. 1814, *Doc. Hist.*, II, 270; Le Couteur, Journal, 20 Oct. 1814, SJ.

90. Izard to Monroe, 16 Oct. 1814, *Doc. Hist.*, II, 254.

91. Izard to Monroe, 2 Nov. 1814, Izard, *Correspondence*, 110.

92. Miller to wife, 19 Sept. 1814, *Doc. Hist.*, II, 223.

93. Izard to Monroe, 2 Nov. 1814, Izard, *Correspondence*, 110.

94. Drummond to Prevost, 23 Oct. 1814, RG 8 I, vol. 686, 85, NAC.

95. *Ibid.*

96. District General Order, Niagara Frontier, 30 Oct. 1814, *Doc. Hist.*, II, 281.

97. Dunlop, *Tiger Dunlop*, 54.

98. Horner, "Military Hospital", 762.

Chapter 14 – The End of the War and the Fates of Men

1. For a discussion of the question of which army was in possession of the British artillery at the end of the battle, see Appendix C.

2. Armstrong to Brown, 10 June 1814, Parker Papers, PHS.

3. On the negotiations that ended the war, see John Stagg, "The Politics of Ending the War of 1812," in R.A. Bowler, ed., *War Along the Niagara. Essays on the War of 1812 and Its Legacy* (Youngstown, NY: Old Fort Niagara Association, 1991), 93-104; and Stanley, *War of 1812*, 381-395.

4. J.M. Hitsman, *The Incredible War of 1812* (Toronto: University of Toronto, 1965).

5. James Carmichael-Smyth, *Precis of the Wars in Canada* (London: Tinsley Brothers, 1862), 193.

6. Jesup, Memoir, 2, LC.

7. Dunlop, *Tiger Dunlop*, 62.

8. Prevost, *DCB*, V, 693-698. For a re-evaluation of Prevost, see J.M. Hitsman, "Sir George Prevost's Conduct of the Canadian War of 1812," *Canadian Historical Association Report*, 1962, 34-43.

9. Drummond, *DCB*, VIII, 236-239; Tullibardine, *Military History*, I, 492.

10. Riall, *DCB*, VII, 744-746.
11. Harvey, *Canadian Encyclopedia*, II, 797.
12. *The Royal Military Calendar, or Army Service and Commission Book* (London: T. Egerton, 1820, 5 vols.) IV, 339-341; Obituary, *United Service Journal*, II, July, 1847, 479.
13. Morrison, *DCB*, VI, 520-521; Patterson, "Forgotten Hero", 19-21.
14. Obituary, *Gentleman's Magazine*, 1845, part 1, 454.
15. Dunlop, *Tiger Dunlop*, 46; Obituary, *Gentleman's Magazine*, 1818, part 2, 573.
16. Evans, *DCB*, IX, 245-246.
17. Askwith, *List*, 27, 31.
18. Obituary, *United Service Journal*, February, 1839, 288; Le Couteur, Journal, 25 July 1814. SJ.
19. On Brereton, see Obituary, *United Service Journal*, Dec. 1837, 574; Letter to Half Pay Officers, WO 27, vol. 751, 156, PRO. On Basden, see Statements of the Services of Officers on Full Pay, WO 25, vol. 802, 223-234, PRO; *Gentleman's Magazine*, 1856, Part II, 124; Bates, "Reminiscences of the Brady Guards", 541. On Winslow, see Sheaffe to Winslow, 8 Mar. 1816, RG 8 I, vol. 1026, 74; *Army List, 1819*, 211; W.O. Raymond, ed., *Winslow Papers A.D. 1776-1826* (St. John: New Brunswick Historical Society, 1901), 10.
20. Bonnycastle, *Canada*, I, 88;
21. Ernest Green, *Some Graves in Lundy's Lane* (Ottawa: Niagara Historical Society, 1911), 42.
22. Dunlop, *DCB*, VIII, 236-239.
23. For a detailed study of Le Couteur's life, see Joan Stevens, *Victorian Voices: An Introduction to the Papers of Sir John Le Couteur* (St. Helier: Société Jersiaise, 1969). Le Couteur's lengthy wartime journal has been edited by the author and published as *Merry Hearts Make Light Days: The War of 1812 Journal of Lieutenant John Le Couteur, 104th Regiment of Foot* (Ottawa: Carleton University Press, 1993).
24. Byfield, "Recollections", 44-45.
25. Kerby, *DCB*, VIII, 465-466; David McIntosh, *The Collectors. A History of Canadian Customs and Excise* (Ottawa: National Revenue, 1985), 301-321; E.A. Cruikshank, "Memoir of Kerby", 29.
26. Merritt, *DCB*. IX, 544-548.
27. John R. Simons, "The Fortunes of a United Empire Loyalist Family," *Ontario Historical Society Papers and Records* 23 (1929), 480.
28. *Ibid.*, 480-481.
29. Ruttan, "Memoir", 296-297, 310-311.
30. Life of Duncan Clark, Clark Papers, vol. 2, 1-2, AO.
31. Kilborn, "Biographical Sketch", 71-72.
32. Norton, *DCB*, VI, 550-553.
33. Statistics of postwar careers of Left Division veterans extracted from Heitman, *Register*, I, 37-45.
34. Brown to Dallas, May 1815, *Facts*, 46. A draft of the charges against Ripley are in the Gardner Papers, NYSL.
35. Lossing, *Field Book*, 608n.
36. *Court Martial of Gardner*; Lossing, *Field Book*, 804n.
37. Lossing, *Field Book*, 812; Heitman, *Register*, I, 38.
38. Lossing, *Field Book*, 803n.
39. "Biographical Sketch of Hindman", 52; Fredriksen, *Officers*, 117-118.
40. Lossing, *Field Book*, 809n; Heitman, *Register*, I, 42; Fredriksen, *Officers*, 126.
41. "Biographical Sketch of Biddle", 559-561; Fredriksen, *Officers*, 121-122.
42. Douglass, "Narrative", 1-3; Fredriksen, *Officers*, 109-110.
43. Kieffer, *Maligned General*, 132-141; K. Jack Bauer, *The Mexican War. 1846-1848* (New York: MacMillan, 1974), 371-374.
44. Edward D. Mansfield, *The Life and Services of General Winfield Scott* (New York: A.S. Barnes, 1846).
45. *Memoir of Scott*, 13, emphasis in the original. Also, 6-14.
46. Fredriksen, *Officers* , 49-52.

47. Lossing, *Field Book*, 812n; Scarborough, "Worth", 290-297; Fredriksen, *Officers*, 57-58.

48. Lossing, *Field Book*, 816-817n; Parker, "Leavenworth", 64-68; Fredriksen, *Officers*, 61-62.

49. Fredriksen, *Officers*, 66.

50. Lossing, *Field Book*, 821n; Fredriksen, *Officers*, 65-66.

51. Lossing, *Field Book*, 822n; Fredriksen, *Officers*, 69-70; Bates, "Brady Guards", 541.

52. Kieffer, *Maligned General*; Fredriksen, *Officers*, 73-74.

53. Fredriksen, *Officers*, 77-78.

54. Lossing, *Field Book*, 820n.

55. Holden, "Miller", 294-297.

56. Fredriksen, *Officers*, 93-94.

57. Lossing, *Field Book*, 838n; Fredriksen, *Officers*, 97-98.

58. Treat, *Vindication*, 56-57; Heitman, *Register*, I, 223, 969.

59. This and all other information on Hanks's postwar life from Hanks, Biography, BECHS.

Epilogue – Where Right and Glory Lead

1. William Dalton, *Travels in the United States and Part of Upper Canada* (Appleby, UK: author, 1821), 184-185.

2. Horatio Parsons, *The Book of Niagara Falls* (Buffalo: Steele & Peck, 1838), 75.

3. Morden, *Historical Monuments*, 11, 13: Irving, *Officers*, 60.

4. George W. Holley, 1865, quoted in Morden, *Historical Monuments*, 20.

5. Lossing *Field Book*, 828.

6. *Ibid.*, 24, 31

7. Mabel Kampfoly-St. Angelo and Velma Slagget-Rivard, *Historic Drummond Hill Cemetery Transcriptions* (St. David's: Niagara Research, 1985), ix-xi; Green, *Some Graves in Lundy's Lane*, 3-4; Warner, "Memorials", 43-44; Lossing, *Field Book*, 827-828; Morden, *Historical Monuments*, 31, 34.

8. Morden, *Historical Monuments*, 33-36.

9. Richard Barrett, *Richard Barrett's Journal: New York and Canada, 1816*, Thomas Brott and Philip Kelley, eds., (Winfield, Kansas: Wedgestone Press, 1983), 48.

10. Day to Reeves, 9 Aug. 1897, in Cunliffe, *Irish Fusiliers*, 484-485.

11. The plundering of the battle sites continues to this day. On a recent visit in August 1994 to the vacant lot adjoining the cemetery, the author and two others watched as a souvenir hunter equipped with a metal detector patiently worked the ground of the public school to the south of the cemetery. The author is also in receipt of a letter from another metal detector ghoul enclosing a photograph showing various objects this man had unearthed from the battlefield at Chippawa.

12. Morden, 54-61; *Military Re-Interment of Eleven Soldiers (of the 89th and 103rd Regiments) killed in Battle at Lundy's Lane, July 25th, 1814* (Niagara Falls: Lundy's Lane Historical Society, 1891); *Address by Canon Houston, 25th July, 1893* (Niagara Falls: Lundy's Lane Historical Society, 1893); *A Brief Account of a Third Military Re-Interment at Lundy's Lane, Oct. 13th, 1899, with Notes, etc.* (Niagara Falls: Lundy's Lane Historical Society, 1899).

13. Morden, *Historical Monuments*, 60-61.

14. *The Centenary Celebration of the Battle of Lundy's Lane: July Twenty-Fifth, Nineteen Hundred and Fourteen* (Niagara Falls: Lundy's Lane Historical Society, 1919), 21-33.

15. *Ibid.*, 51-55.

16. *Ibid.*, 68.

Appendix C – The Problem of the Guns

1. For historians who follow Drummond's version, see [Richardson], *Veritas*, 127; James, *Full and Correct Account*, II, 44-45; and Thompson, *History*, 233-234. For those who feel that the guns were recaptured before the fighting ended, see Robert Gourlay, *Statistical Account*, I, 74-75; Gilbert Auchinleck, *A History of the War between Great Britain and the United States in the years 1812-1814* (Toronto: Maclear, 1855), 326; Cruikshank, *Lundy's Lane*, 40-41; Charles P. Lucas, *The Canadian War of 1812* (Oxford: University Press, 1906), 180-181; James Hannay, *History*

of the War of 1812 between Great Britain and the United States of America (St. John: J.A. Bowles, 1901), 310; Hitsman, *Incredible War*, 198-199; and Cresswell, "Near Run Thing", 53. Stanley, *War of 1812*, 323-324, criticizes the accuracy of Drummond's dispatch but feels that the guns were recovered before the Left Division had totally withdrawn from the field.

2. Gourlay, *Statistical Account*, I, 74.

3. *Ibid.*, I, 74-75.

4. Statement of Hindman, *Facts*, 42-43.

5. See particularly Auchinleck, *History of the War*, 326 when the author states that "It has been our good fortune to converse with several of the officers who distinguished themselves in the battle ... and by all we have been assured that, so far from the American troops leaving the hill leisurely, and voluntarily abandoning the guns, ... the real state of the case was, that the Americans did abandon both the top of the hill and the guns, but that it was a vigorous bayonet charge that compelled them, and that the guns were recaptured about one hundred yards from the position originally occupied."

6. Cruikshank, *Lundy's Lane*, 40.

7. *Ibid.*

8. [Shadrach Byfield], A Narrative of a Light Company Soldier's Services in the 41st Regiment of Foot during the late American War ... from 1812 to 1814 (Bradford, UK: John Bubb, 1840). This memoir was reprinted in John Gelner, ed., *Recollections of the War of 1812: Three Eyewitness Accounts* (Toronto: Baxter Publishing, 1964), 1-45.

9. Byfield, "Recollections", 38.

10. Ingersoll, *Historical Sketches*, II, 1849; Cruikshank, *Doc. Hist.*, II, 473-482.

11. Jesup, Memoir, 11-12, LC.

12. Evidence of McDonald, *Facts*, 15-16.

13. Certificate of Clark, Livingston and Holding, *Facts*, 17.

14. Letter of Leavenworth, 15 Jan. 1815, *Facts*, 25. Emphasis is in the original.

15. Extract of a letter from James Miller, 4 Sep. 1814, *Facts*, 30.

16. Marston to Ripley, 15 Mar. 1815, *Facts*, 32.

17. Le Couteur, Journal, 25 July 1814, SJ.

18. Le Couteur to Robison, 27 July 1814, War of 1812 Papers, CL.

19. Douglass, "Narrative", 19.

20. Report of the Killed, Wounded and Missing, 30 July 1814, Parker Papers, PHS.

21. Le Couteur, Journal, 25 July 1814, SJ; British officer to Hickman, 7 Oct. 1814, BECHS.

22. Norton, *Journal*, 358.

23. Statement of Costello, *Facts*, 37. Costello deserted from the 104th Foot on 2 Sep. 1814, see W. Austin Squires, *The 104th Regiment of Foot* (Fredericton: Brunswick Press, 1962), 203.

24. Statement of Weymouth, *Facts*, 38.

25. Statement of Bull, enclosed in Brown to Tompkins, 1 Aug. 1814, *Doc. Hist.*, I, 103.

26. Worth to Brown, 25 Dec. 1815, Brown Papers, MHS.

27. *Ibid.*

28. Hercules Scott to James Scott, 12 Aug. 1814, MG 24, F 15, NAC; Lang, Diary, 29 June 1814, PLDU. Although Lang was not present at the battle, he must have had occasion to discuss the action with those officers of his regiment, the 19th Light Dragoons, who were present. Lang states that "our guns were found on different parts of the field" the following day.

It is interesting that the only prominent British or Canadian historian who feels that the captured artillery was not retaken but discovered the next day is Sir John Fortescue, the author most experienced in musket period warfare. See Fortescue, *History of the British Army*, Vol. X (London: Macmillan, 1920), 115.

Appendix D – The Accuracy of the American Casualty Figures

1. James, *Full and Correct Account*, II, 149.

2. Cruikshank, *Lundy's Lane*, 42. For a recent Canadian historian who has followed Cruikshank's lead, see Cresswell, "Near Run Thing", 53.

3. Letter from Fort Erie, 1 Aug. 1814, *Doc. Hist.*, I, 109.

4. Gardner to Parker, 28 July 1814, Gardner Papers, NYSL. In the summer of 1814, Daniel Parker was serving as adjutant and inspector general of the army as no military officer held that position. In November of that year he was commissioned a brigadier-general and appointed on a permanent basis. On Parker, see Edward Skeen, *John Armstrong Jr., 1758-1843: A Biography* (Syracuse: University of Syracuse, 1981), 171-172; and Heitman, *Register*, I, 38-39, 769.

5. Porter to Tompkins, 29 July 1814, *Doc. Hist.*, I, 101.

6. Report of the Killed, Wounded & Missing of the 1st Brigade in the Action of the 25th July, undated, BECHS; Report of the killed, wounded and missing of the Left Division ... in the action of the ... 25th July 1814, dated 30 July 1814, Parker Papers, PHS; Report of the Kild [sic] wonded [sic] and Missing of the 22nd Regt ... in the late action on the 25th July 1814; Report of Captain Samuel Harris, 2 Aug. 1814, War of 1812 Mss., LL; Porter to Tompkins, 29 July 1814, *Doc. Hist.*, I, 101. Harris states he suffered 3 casualties and Porter states 65 as against the official figures of 3 and 67 respectively.

Bibliography

PRIMARY SOURCES – ARCHIVAL

Alderman Library, University of Virginia, Charlotteville, Virginia
    Arthur Sinclair Papers
Archives of Ontario, Toronto
    Niagara Historical Society Papers
    MU 572, Daniel Clark Papers
    MU 2057, John Harvey Papers
    Strachan Papers
Buffalo and Erie County Historical Society, Buffalo, New York
    Biography of Drummer Jarvis Hanks, Eleventh Infantry
    Peter B. Porter Papers
    Manuscripts Collection, War of 1812, Letterbook of Maj. Gen. Phineas Riall
Burton Historical Library, Detroit, Michigan
    Diary of Ensign Andrew Warffe, Incorporated Militia
Connecticut Historical Society, Hartford, Connecticut
    Letter book of Capt. George Howard, Twenty-Fifth Infantry
Dartmouth College Library, Hanover, New Hampshire
    John W. Weeks Papers
Geneva Historical Society, Geneva, New York
    Papers of Lt. Col. Hugh Dobbin, New York Volunteers
        Account of battle of Lundy's Lane
        Diary, June-August 1814
        Memoir of the Campaign on the Niagara
Library of Congress, Washington, D.C.
    Jacob Brown Papers
    Thomas Jefferson Papers
    Thomas S. Jesup Papers, Twenty-Fifth Infantry
        Memoir of the Campaign on the Niagara
Lilly Library, Indiana University, Bloomington, Indiana
    War of 1812 Manuscripts
    Narrative of Capt. Joseph Henderson, Twenty-Second Infantry
    Williams Papers
Lord Coutanche Library, Societé Jersiaise, St. Helier, Jersey
    Journal of Sir John Le Couteur
Massachusetts Historical Society, Boston, Massachusetts
    Jacob Brown Papers
    Cabot Papers
Metropolitan Toronto Reference Library, Toronto
    Diary of Christopher Hagerman, Provincial ADC to Drummond

Mississippi Department of Archives & History, Jackson, Mississippi
  Autobiography of Lt. Edward B. Randolph, Left Division staff
Missouri Historical Society, St, Louis, Missouri
  Correspondence of Capt. Lewis Bissell, First Infantry, in the Kingsbury Collection
National Archives of Canada, Ottawa
  Manuscript Group 11 (Colonial Office 42), Original Correspondence, Canada
  Manuscript Group 19
    A39, Duncan Clark Papers
      Account of the Battle of Lundy's Lane
      Order Book, Right Division, July 1814
  Manuscript Group 24
    F15, Correspondence of Col Hercules Scott, 103rd Foot
    F17, Livre de voyage, Francis Hall, 1816
    F23, Nicolls Papers, vol. 1, Memoir by Gaugreben, 1815
    F96 De Watteville Papers
      Diary, August-October 1814
    G17, Memory Book of Joseph Baker, Canadian Volunteers
    L8, Viger Papers, Ma Saberdache Bleu, vol. 4
  Manuscript Group 40
    R110, Holmes, Pedestrian Tour to the Falls of Niagara
  Record Group 1, Records of the Executive Council, Upper Canada
  Record Group 5, Records of the Civil Secretary's Office, Upper Canada, 1791-1867
  Record Group 7, Governor-General's Office, 1774-1966
  Record Group 8 I, British Military and Naval Records, 1757- 1903
  Record Group 9, Pre-Confederation Militia Records
  Record Group 10, Records of the Indian Department
  Record Group 19, E5, War of 1812 Loss Board Claims
National Archives of the United States, Washington, D.C.
  Record Group 94, Records of the Adjutant General
  Record Group 98, Records of United States Army Commands
  Record Group 107, Correspondence of the Secretary of War
    Micro 6, Letters Sent
    Micro 221, Letters Received, Registered Series
    Micro 222, Letters Received, Unregistered Series
  Record Group 153, Records of the Judge Advocate General
    K-1, Court Martial of Lt. Col. R.C. Nicholas, 1816
    K-2, Court Martial of Brig. Gen. E.P. Gaines, 1816
    K-4, Court Martial of Capt. Henry Blake, 1815
New York Historical Society, New York
  Correspondence of Capt. Richard Goodell, Twenty-Third Infantry
New York Public Library, New York,
  Charles W. Elliott Collection
New York State Library, Albany, New York
  Mss. 11225, Left Division Order Book, April-July 1814
  Papers of Col. Charles K. Gardner, Left Division staff
    Memoranda of Occurrences and Some Important Facts Attending the Campaign on the
      Niagara
Ohio Historical Society, Columbus, Ohio
  W.A. Trimble Papers
Oneida County Historical Society, Utica, New York
  Nathan Williams Papers
Pennsylvania Historical Society, Philadelphia, Pennsylvania
  Daniel Parker Papers
  War of 1812 Papers

Perkins Library, Duke University, Durham, North Carolina
    Diary of Lt. John Lang, 19th Light Dragoons
Public Record Office, Kew, Surrey, United Kingdom
    War Office 17, Monthly Returns
    War Office 25, Registers, Various
    War Office 27, Inspection Returns
    War Office 44, Ordnance Office, In-Letters
    War Office 55, Ordnance Office, Miscellanea
        Journal of Lt. Phillpotts, RE, Aug.-Sept. 1814
Royal Canadian Military Institute, Toronto, Canada
    Manuscript Notebook of Abraham Paul, RA
United States Army Military History Institute, Carlisle, Pennsylvania
    Memorandum of Amasiah Ford, Twenty-Third Infantry
    Jesup to Ketchum, 12 April 1853, Coco Collection
United States Military Academy Library, West Point, New York
    James Miller correspondence
Western Reserve Historical Society, Cleveland, Ohio
    Memoir of John Conolly, Canadian Militia
William L. Clements Library, University of Michigan, Ann Arbor, Michigan
    Jacob Brown Papers
    War of 1812 Papers
Wisconsin Historical Society, Madison, Wisconsin
    Correspondence of Capt. John Symmes, First Infantry, in the Draper Manuscripts

UNPUBLISHED, MAPS, PLANS AND SKETCHES

National Archives of Canada, Ottawa
    MG 11, CO 42, vol. 157, 116, Sketch of an Action fought on the Night of the 25th of July 1814
    National Map Collection
        NMC HB-440-Drummondville, Sketch of Drummondville, 22 Aug. 1838.
        NMC H2/407, Sketch of the action fought on the night of 25th July, in Plan of Part of the
            Niagara Frontier, 1814
        NMC H2/440, Plan of the Attack made Upon Fort Erie by the Right Division of the Brit-
            ish Army ... in August and Sept. 1814.
        NMC H3/440, Plan of the Country around Fort Erie shewing Entrenchments thrown up
            by the enemy in August, 1814.
        NMC 0021729, Survey of the River Niagara, 1817, corrected to 1836
National Archives of the United States, Washington, D.C.
    National Map Collection
        Drawing 154, Sheet 42-24, Plan of Battle of Chippewa, by "Engineer of General Brown"

PRIMARY SOURCES – PUBLISHED

Newspapers & Periodicals
American Watchman, Wilmington, Delaware
Buffalo Gazette
Chillicothe Supporter
Columbian Centinel, Boston
Edinburgh Annual Register
Federal Gazette and Baltimore Daily Advertizer, Baltimore
Geneva Gazette
Gentleman's Magazine
Niles Weekly Register
Quebec Mercury, Quebec City
The Yankee, Boston
United Service Journal

Published Documents

Cruikshank, Ernest A. ed., *Documentary History of the Campaigns upon the Niagara Frontier in 1812-1814* [titles vary slightly]. Welland: Tribune Press, 1896-1908. 9 vols.

——. *Documents Relating to the Invasion of the Niagara Peninsula by the United States Army, commanded by General Jacob Brown in July and August, 1814.* Niagara-on-the-Lake: Niagara Historical Society, 1920.

Facts Relative to the Campaign on the Niagara in 1814. Boston: Patriot office, 1815.

"Garrison Orders, Burlington, Vermont, July 13 - August 4, 1813," *Moorsfield Antiquarian* 1 (1937), 79-103.

Izard, George. *Official Correspondence with the Department of War.* Philadelphia: Thomas Dobson, 1816.

Loyal and Patriotic Society of Upper Canada. *Proceedings and Reports of the Loyal and Patriotic Society of Upper Canada.* York: the Society, 1815.

Ontario, Province of. *Seventh Report of the Bureau of Archives for Ontario, 1910.* Toronto: King's Printer, 1910.

Proceedings of a Court Martial Held at Fort Independence ... for the Trial of Major Charles K. Gardner ... by Major General Ripley. Boston: n.p., 1816.

Tompkins, Daniel D. *Public Papers of Daniel D. Tompkins, Governor of New York.* Albany: State of New York, 1898-1902. 3 vols.

United States, Congress. *American State Papers: Class V, Military Affairs.* Vol. I. Washington: Gales & Seaton, 1832.

PUBLISHED MEMOIRS, DIARIES, JOURNALS, CORRESPONDENCE

American

An Interesting Account of the Campaign of 1814: By a Musician in the Army. N.p., n.d.

Armstrong, John. *Notices of the War of 1812.* New York: Wiley, 1840. 2 vols.

Barrett, Richard. *Richard Barrett's Journal: New York and Canada, 1816,* ed. Thomas Brott and Philip Kelley. Winfield, Kansas: Wedgestone Press, 1983.

Beaumont, William. *William Beaumont's Formative Years: Two Early Notebooks 1811-1821.* New York: Henry Schuman, 1946.

Dalton, William. *Travels in the United States and Part of Upper Canada.* Appleby, U.K.: author, 1821.

Douglass, David B [U.S. Engineers]. "An Original Narrative of the Niagara Campaign of 1814,", ed. John F. Horton, *Niagara Frontier,* 46 (1964), 1-36.

Duane, William, "Letters of William Duane," ed. Frederick Worthington, *Proceedings of the Massachusetts Historical Society,* 20 (1906), 257-394, ed. Frederick Worthington.

Gass, Patrick [First Infantry]. John G. Jacobs, *The Life and Times of Patrick Gass.* Wellsburg, Va.: Jacobs, Smith, 1859.

Harris, Samuel D. [Light Dragoons]. "Service of Capt. Samuel D. Harris; A Sketch of His Military Career as a Captain in the Second Regiment of Light Dragoons during the War of 1812," *Publications of the Buffalo Historical Society* 24 (1920), 327-342.

Horner, William [Surgeon], "Surgical Sketches: A Military Hospital at Buffalo, New York, in the Year 1814," *Medical Examiner and Record of Medical Service,* 16 (Dec. 1852), 753-774, 17 (Jan. 1853), 1-25.

Howe, Eber. "Recollections of A Pioneer Printer," *Buffalo Historical Society Publications* 9 (1906), 377-406.

Kearsley, Johnathan. "The Memoirs of Johnathan Kearsley: A Michigan Hero of the War of 1812," ed. John C. Fredriksen, *Indiana Military History Journal* 10 (1985), 4-16.

Kirby, Reynald M. "Reynald M. Kirby and His Race to Join the Regiment: A Connecticut Officer in the War of 1812, *Connecticut History* 32 (November 1991), 51-82.

Mann, James [Surgeon]. *Medical Sketches of the Campaigns of 1812, 1813, and 1814.* Dedham, Mass.: H. Mann, 1816.

McFarland, Daniel [Twenty-Third Infantry]. "The Papers of Daniel McFarland. A Hawk of 1812," ed. John N. Crombie, *Western Pennsylvania Historical Magazine* 51 (1968), No. 2, 101-125.

McFeely, George [Twenty-Second Infantry]. "Chronicle of Valour: The Journal of a Pennsylvania Officer in the War of 1812," ed. John C. Fredriksen, *Western Pennsylvania Historical Magazine*, 67 (1984), 243-284.

McMullen, Alexander [Pennsylvania Volunteers]. "The Narrative of Alexander McMullen, a Private Soldier in Colonel Fenton's Regiment of Pennsylvania Volunteers," in E.A. Cruikshank, ed., *Documentary History of the Campaign on the Niagara in 1814*, Vol. II, 368,-379 (see main entry).

Myers, Mordecai [Thirteenth Infantry]. *Reminiscences. 1790 to 1814. Including Incidents in the War of 1812-1814*. Washington: Crane, 1900.

Pearce, Cromwell [Sixteenth Infantry]. "'A Poor But Honest Sodger': Colonel Cromwell Pearce, the 16th U.S. Infantry and the War of 1812," ed. John C. Fredriksen, *Pennsylvania History*, 52 (1985), 131-161.

"The Pennsylvania Volunteers in the War of 1812. An Anonymous Journal of Service for the Year 1814," ed. John C. Fredriksen, ed., *Western Pennsylvania Historical Magazine*, 70 (1987), 123-157.

Ropes, Benjamin [Twenty-First Infantry]. "Benjamin Ropes' Autobiography," *Essex Institute Historical Collections*, 91 (1955), 105-127.

Scott, Winfield. *Memoirs of General Scott, Written by Himself*. New York: Sheldon, 1864. 2 vols.

Shepherd, Elihu. *The Autobiography of Elihu Shepherd*. St. Louis: George Knapp, 1869

Treat, Joseph [Twenty-First Infantry]. *The Vindication of Joseph Treat, late of the Twenty First Regiment*. Philadelphia: author, 1815.

White, Samuel [Pennsylvania Volunteers]. *A History of the American Troops during the Late War under Colonel Fenton*. Baltimore: author, 1829.

Wilkinson, James. *Memoirs of My Own Times*. Philadelphia: Abraham Small, 1816. 3 vols.

Witherow, John [Pennsylvania Volunteers], "A Soldier's Diary for 1814," ed. Joseph Walker, *Pennsylvania History*, 12 (1945), 292-303.

British and Canadian

Bell, George. *Rough Notes of an Old Soldier During Fifty Years Service*. London: Day & Sons, 1867. 2 vols.

Byfield, Shadrach [41st Foot]. "Recollections" in John Gelner, ed., *Recollections of the War of 1812: Three Eyewitness Accounts*. Toronto: Baxter, 1964.

Commins, James [8th Foot]. "The War of 1812 on the Canadian Frontier, 1812-1814. Letters written by Sergt. James Comins, 8th Foot," ed. Norman C. Lord, *Journal of the Society for Army Historical Research*, 18 (1939), No. 2, 199-211.

DeCew, John. [Canadian militia] "Reminiscences of the Late Capt. John DeCew," *Annual Transactions of the United Empire Loyalist Association*, 4 (1901), 93-99.

Douglas, John [Surgeon, 8th Foot]. *Medical Topography of Upper Canada*. London: 1819, reprinted Science Publications, Boston, 1985.

Dunlop, William [Surgeon, 89th Foot]. *Tiger Dunlop's Upper Canada*. Carleton University, Toronto, 1967.

Harris, Amelia [civilian]. "Memoir" in James J. Talman, ed. *Loyalist Narratives from Upper Canada*. Toronto: Champlain Society, 1946, 144-148.

Hay, George [100th Foot]. "Recollections of the War of 1812 by George Hay, Eighth Marquis of Tweeddale," ed. Lewis Einstein, *American Historical Review* 32 (1926), 69-78.

Heriot, George. *Travels through the Canadas*. London: Richards, Philips, 1807.

Howison, John. *Sketches of Upper Canada, Domestic, Local, and Characteristic*. Edinburgh: Oliver & Boyd, 1825.

Kilborn, John [Incorporated Militia]. "Biographical Sketch" in Thaddeus Leavitt, *History of Leeds and Grenville*, 68-71. Belleville: 1879, reprinted, Mika, 1972.

Lampman, John. [Incorporated Militia] "Memoirs of Captain John Lampman (1970) and his Wife Mary Secord (1797)," ed., R.I. Warner, *Welland County Historical Society, Papers and Records*, 3 (1927), 126-134.

Lighton, William B. *Narrative of the Life and Sufferings of a Young British Captive*. Concord, N.H. : author, 1836.

MacEwan, William [1st Regiment of Foot]. *Excerpts from Lieut. and Adjutant William MacEwan To His Wife, Canada 1813-1814.* N.p., n.d., ed. Arthur Brymner.

Maude, John. *Visit to the Falls of Niagara in 1800.* London: Longman, Rees, Orme, Browne & Green, 1826.

McCollom, W.A. [Canadian militia] "McCollom Memories," *Ontario Historical Society, Papers and Records* 6 (1909), 90.

Mercer, Cavalie. *Journal of the Waterloo Campaign.* London: Peter Davies, 1927.

Merritt, William Hamilton [Provincial Light Dragoons]. *Journal of Events Principally on the Detroit and Niagara Frontiers during the War of 1812.* St. Catharines: Historical Society of British North America, 1863.

Norton, John. [Indian Department] *The Journal of John Norton 1816,* eds. J.J. Talman & C.F. Klinck. Toronto: Champlain Society, 1970.

Raymond, W.O., ed. *Winslow Papers A.D. 1776-1826. Printed under the Auspices of the New Brunswick Historical Society.* Saint John, N.B.: Sun Printing Co., 1901.

Ruttan, Henry [Incorporated Militia]. "Memoir" in James J. Talman, ed., *Loyalist Narratives from Upper Canada.* Toronto: Champlain Society, 1946, 302-311.

Weld, Isaac. *Travels through the States of North America and the Province of Upper Canada during the Years 1795, 1796, and 1797.* London: Stockdale, 1799.

Wheeler, William. *The Letters of Private Wheeler, 1809-1828.* ed. B.H. Liddell-Hart. London: Michael Joseph, 1954.

Yarrow, David. "A Journal of the Walcheren Expedition, 1809," *Mariner's Mirror,* 61 (1975), 183-189.

PERIOD MILITARY REGULATIONS, TREATISES AND TECHNICAL LITERATURE

Adye, Ralph W. *The Bombardier and Pocket Gunner.* London:, T. Egerton, 1813.

The Army Register of the United States, Corrected Up to the 1st of June, 1814. Boston: Chester Stebbins, 1814.

Congreve, William. *The Details of the Rocket System.* London: J. Whiting, 1814, reprinted Museum Restoration Service, Ottawa, 1970.

De Lacroix, Irenée Amelot. *Rules and Regulations for the Field Exercises and Manoeuvres of the French Infantry.* Boston: T.B. Wait, 1810. 2 vols.

De Scheel, Henri Othon. *Treatise on Artillery.* Philadelphia: War Department, 1800, reprinted Museum Restoration Service, Bloomfield, Ontario, 1984.

Duane, William. *American Military Library, or, Compendium of the Modern Tactics.* Philadelphia: Author, 1809. 2 vols.

Gassendi, Jean-Jacques Basilien de. *Aide-Memoire, á l'usage des Officiers d'Artillerie de France.* Paris: Magimel, 1801. 2 vols.

Great Britain, Horse Guards. *Instructions to Regimental Surgeons for Regulating the Concerns of the Sick and of the Hospitals.* London: Horse Guards, 1808.

——. *General Regulations and Orders for the Army.* London: T. Egerton, 1811.

Great Britain, War Office. *A List of all the Officers of the Army and Royal Marines on Full and Half-pay.* London: War Office, 1814, 1815, 1819.

——. *Rules and Regulations for the Formation, Field-Exercise, and Movements of His Majesty's Forces.* London: T. Egerton, 1808.

James, Charles. *The Regimental Companion; Containing the Pay, Allowances and Relative Duties of Every Officer in the British Service.* London: T. Egerton, 1811. 2 vols.

The Royal Military Calendar, or Army Service and Commission Book. London: T. Egerton, 1815. 5 vols.

Smyth, Alexander. *Rules and Regulations for the Field Exercise, Manoeuvres and Conduct of the Infantry of the United States.* Philadelphia: T. & G. Palmer, 1812.

[Stoddard, Amos]. *Exercise for Garrison and Field Ordnance, Together with Manoeuvres of Horse Artillery, as Altered from the Manual of General Kosciusko, and Adapted for the Service of the United States.* Philadelphia: A. Finlay, 1812.

Tousard, Louis de. *American Artillerist's Companion, or Elements of Artillery.* Philadelphia, C. & A. Conrad, 1809. 2 vols.

PUBLISHED MAPS, PLANS, ATLASES

Melish, John. *A Military and Topographical Atlas of the United States; including the British Possessions and Florida*. Philadephia: G. Palmer, 1813.

Wilkinson, James. *Diagrams and Plans, Illustrative of the Principal Battles and Military Affairs Treated of in Memoirs of My Own Times*. Philadelphia: Abraham Small, 1816.

SECONDARY SOURCES – BOOKS

Adams, Henry. *History of the United States during the Administration of James Madison*. New York: A.C. Boni, 1930. 4 vols.

Address by Canon Houston, 25th July, 1893. Niagara Falls: Lundy's Lane Historical Society, 1893.

Askwith, W.H. *List of Officers of the Royal Regiment of Artillery From the Year 1716 to the Year 1899*. London: Royal Artillery Institution, 1900.

Auchinleck, Gilbert. *A History of the War between Great Britain and the United States in the years 1812-1814*. Toronto: Maclear, 1855.

Babcock, Louis. *The War of 1812 on the Niagara Frontier*. Buffalo: Buffalo Historical Society, 1927.

Bauer, K. Jack. *The Mexican War. 1846-1848*. New York: Macmillan, 1974.

Biddulph, John. *The Nineteenth and their Times; Being an Account of the Four Cavalry Regiments in the British Army That Have borne the Number Nineteen and of the Campaigns in Which They Served*. London: John Murray, 1899.

Biggar, C.L. *A Tale of Early Days on Lundy's Lane*. Niagara Falls, Canada: n.p., n.d.

Blackmore, Howard. *British Military Firearms, 1650-1850*. London: Herbert Jenkins, 1961.

Blanco, Richard. *Wellington's Surgeon General: Sir James McGrigor*. Durham, N.C.: Duke University, 1974.

Bond, Ray Corry. *Peninsula Village. The Story of Chippawa*. N.p., n.d. [c. 1963]

Bonnycastle, Richard. *Canada, As it was, Is, and May Be*. London: Colburn, 1852. 2 vols.

Brief Account of a Third Military Re-Interment at Lundy's Lane, Oct. 13th, 1899, with Notes, etc. Niagara Falls: Lundy's Lane Historical Society, 1899.

Browne, James. *England's Artillerymen: An Historical Narrative of the Services of the Royal Artillery*. London: Hall, Smart & Allen, 1865.

Calloway, Colin. *Crown and Calumet: British-Indian Relations, 1783-1815*. Norman: University of Oklahoma, 1987.

The Canadian Encyclopedia. Edmonton: Hurtig, 1985. 3 vols.

Cannon, Richard, compiler. *Historical Records of the First or Royal Regiment of Foot*. London: Parker, Furnivall & Parker, 1847.

——, compiler. *Historical Records of The Eighth, or, The King's Regiment of Foot*. London: Parker, Furnivall & Parker, 1844.

Carmichael-Smyth, James. *Precis of the Wars in Canada*. London: Tinsley Brothers, 1862.

Centenary Celebration of the Battle of Lundy's Lane. July Twenty-Fifth, Nineteen Hundred and Fourteen. Niagara Falls: Lundy's Lane Historical Society, 1919.

Chartrand, René. *Uniforms and Equipment of the United States Forces in the War of 1812*. Youngstown: Old Fort Niagara Association, 1992.

—— & Jack Summers. *Military Uniforms in Canada, 1665-1970*. Ottawa: National Museums, 1981.

Chichester, Henry and George Burgess-Short. *Records and Badges of the British Army*. London: Gale & Polden, 1902.

Colin, Jean. *L'Infanterie au XVIIIe siècle: La Tactique*. Paris: Berger-Levrault, 1907.

Cruikshank, Ernest A. *The Battle of Lundy's Lane, 25th July, 1814*. Welland: 3rd edition, 1893.

——. *History of the County of Welland*. Welland: Welland Tribune, 1887.

Cullum, George W. *Campaigns of the War of 1812-15; against Great Britain; with Brief Biographies of the American Engineers*. New York: James Miller, 1879.

Cunliffe, Marcus *The Royal Irish Fusiliers, 1793-1850*. London: Oxford University Press, 1950.

De Watteville, H. *The British Soldier: His Daily Life from Tudor to Modern Times*. London: J.M. Dent, 1954.

Dictionary of American Biography. New York: Scribner, 1958-1964. 22 vols.

Dictionary of Canadian Biography. Volumes V-IX. Toronto: University of Toronto, 1976-1988.

Dictionary of National Biography. London: Smith, Elder, 1885. 65 vols.

Edgar, Matilda. *Ten Years of Upper Canada in Peace and War, 1805-1815; Being the Ridout Letters with Annotations.* Toronto: William Briggs, 1890.

Edwards, R. David. *The Shawnee Prophet.* Lincoln: University of Nebraska, 1983.

Elliott, Charles W. *Winfield Scott: The Soldier and the Man.* New York: MacMillan, 1937.

Everest, Alan S. *The War of 1812 in the Champlain Valley.* Syracuse: Syracuse University Press, 1981.

Fitzgibbon, Mary Agnes. *A Veteran of 1812 ... The Life of James Fitzgibbon.* Toronto: William Briggs, 1894.

Fortescue, John. *A History of the British Army.* Volume X. London: Macmillan, 1920.

Fredriksen, John C. *Officers of the War of 1812 with Portraits and Anecdotes.* Lewiston: Edgar Mellen, 1989.

Glover, Michael. *Wellington as Military Commander.* London: Sphere, 1973.

Glover, Richard. *Peninsular Preparation. The Reform of the British Army, 1795-1809.* Cambridge: Cambridge University, 1963.

Goodhue, Josiah. *History of the Town of Shoreham, Vermont.* Middlebury: Published by the town, 1861.

Gourlay, Robert. *Statistical Account of Upper Canada Compiled with a View to a Grand System of Emigration.* London: Simpkin & Marshall, 1822. 2 vols.

Green, Ernest. *Some Graves in Lundy's Lane.* Ottawa: Niagara Historical Society Publications No. 22, 1911.

Greener, William. *The Gun; or, A Treatise on the Various Descriptions of Small Fire-Arms.* London: Longman, Rees, Orme, Brown, Green, and Longman, 1835.

Griffith, Paddy. *Forward into Battle: Fighting Techniques from Waterloo to Vietnam.* Strettington: Antony Bird, 1981.

Guthrie, George. *Commentaries on the Surgery of War.* London: Burgess & Hill, 1855.

——. *A Treatise on Gun-Shot Wounds.* London: Burgess & Hill, 1827.

Hannay, James. *History of the War of 1812 between Great Britain and the United States of America.* Saint John, N.B.: J.A. Bowles, 1901.

Haythornewaite, Philip. *Weapons and Equipment of the Napoleonic Wars.* Poole: Blandford, 1979.

Heitman, Francis B. *Historical Register and Dictionary of the U.S Army.* Washington: Government Printing Office, 1903. 2 vols.

Henderson, John L. *John Strachan, 1778-1867.* Toronto: University of Toronto, 1969.

Hennen, John. *Principles of Military Surgery.* London: Constable, 1820.

Hickey, Donald R. *The War of 1812: A Forgotten Conflict.* Chicago: University of Illinois, 1989.

Hicks, James. *Notes on U.S. Ordnance.* Green Farms, Conn.: Modern Books & Craft, 1971, reprint of 1940 edition. 2 vols.

Hitsman, J.M. *The Incredible War of 1812.* Toronto: University of Toronto, 1965.

Hough, Franklin B. *A History of Jefferson County.* Albany: Little, 1854.

Hughes, B.P. *Firepower: Weapons Effectiveness on the Battlefield, 1630-1850.* London: Arms and Armour, 1974.

——. *Open Fire. Artillery Tactics from Marlborough to Wellington.* Strettington: Antony Bird, 1983.

Ingersoll, Charles J. *Historical Sketches of the Second War between the United States of America and Great Britain.* Philadelphia: Lee, Blanchard, 1849. 2 vols.

Irving, L. Homfray. *Officers of the British Forces in Canada during the War of 1812-15.* Welland: Canadian Military Institute, 1908.

Jacobs, John G. *The Life and Times of Patrick Gass.* Wellsburg, Va.: Jacobs, Smith, 1859.

Jacobs, John R. *The Beginnings of the United States Army, 1783-1812.* Princeton: Princeton, 1947.

James, William. *A Full and Correct Account of the Military Occurrences of the Late War between Great Britain and the United States.* London: Black, 1818. 2 vols.

Jocelyn, Arthur. *Awards of Honour.* London: Adam & Charles Black, 1956.

Johnson, Rossiter, ed. *The Twentieth Century Biographical Dictionary of Notable Americans.* Boston: Biographical Society, 1904. 10 vols.

Jones, Robert J. *A History of the 15th (East Yorkshire) Regiment (The Duke of York's Own) 1685 to 1914.* Beverly: The Regiment, 1958.

Kampfoly-St. Angelo, Mabel & Velma Slagget-Rivard. *Historic Drummond Hill Cemetery Transcriptions (With Additional Notes).* St. David's, Ont.: Niagara Research, 1985.

Keegan, John. *Face of Battle.* New York: Viking, 1976.

Ketchum, William. *An Authentic and Comprehensive History of Buffalo.* Buffalo: Rockwell, Baker S. Hill, 1864. 2 vols.

Kiefer, Chester L. *Maligned General: The Biography of Thomas Sidney Jesup.* San Rafael: Presidio, 1979.

Lauerma, Matti. *L'artillerie de campagne francaise pendant les guerres de la Revolution.* Helsinki: Sumolaisen Tiedakatemian Tormituksia, 1958.

Laws, M.E.S. *Battery Records of the Royal Artillery. 1716-1859.* Woolwich: Royal Artillery Institute, 1952.

Lemmon, Sarah McCullough. *Frustrated Patriots: North Carolina and the War of 1812.* Chapel Hill: University of North Carolina, 1977.

Linn, John B. *Annals of Buffalo Valley, Pennsylvania, 1755-1855.* Harrisburg, Penn.: Lane & Haupt, 1877.

Livingston, John. *Sketches of Eminent Americans.* New York: Craighead, 1854.

Lossing, Benson J. *Pictorial Field Book of the War of 1812.* New York: Harpers, 1869.

Lucas, Charles P. *The Canadian War of 1812.* Oxford: Clarendon Press, 1906.

Lynn, John. *Bayonets of the Republic: Motivation and Tactics in the Army of Revolutionary France, 1791-1794.* Chicago: University of Illinois, 1984.

Mansfield, Edward D. *Life and Services of General Winfield Scott.* New York: A.S. Barnes, 1846.

McConnell, David. *British Smooth-Bore Artillery: A Technological Study.* Ottawa: Environment Canada, 1988.

McIntosh, Dave. *The Collectors: A History of Canadian Customs and Excise.* Ottawa: Revenue Canada, 1985.

McLeod, Donald. *A Brief Review of the Settlement of Upper Canada by the U.E. Loyalists and Scotch Highlanders.* Cleveland: author, 1841.

Memoir of General Scott from Records Contemporaneous with Events. Washington: C. Alexander, 1852.

Military Re-Interment of Eleven Soldiers (of the 89th and 103rd Regiments) killed in Battle at Lundy's Lane, July 25th, 1814. Niagara Falls, Canada: Lundy's Lane Historical Society, 1891.

Morden, James C. *Historic Niagara Falls.* Niagara Falls, Canada: Lundy's Lane Historical Society, 1932.

——. *Historical Monuments and Observatories of Lundy's Lane and Queenston Heights.* Niagara Falls, Canada: Lundy's Lane Historical Society, 1929.

National Cyclopedia of American Biography. Clifton, N.J.: J.T. White, 1891, reprinted 1967. 63 vols.

Norman, C.B. *Battle Honours of the British Army.* London: David & Charles, 1971.

Nosworthy, Brent. *Battle Tactics of Napoleon and His Enemies.* London: Constable, 1995.

Owen, David. *Fort Erie (1764-1823): An Historical Guide.* Fort Erie: Niagara Parks Commission, 1986.

Parsons, Horatio. *The Book of Niagara Falls.* Buffalo: Steele & Peck, 1838.

Peterson, Charles J. *The Military Heroes of the War of 1812.* Philadelphia: James B. Smith, 1858.

Pivka, Otto von. *Armies of the Napoleonic Period.* Newton Abbot: David & Charles, 1979.

Reilly, Robin. *The British at the Gates. The New Orleans Campaign in the War of 1812.* New York: G.P. Putnam, 1974.

[Richardson, James]. *The Letters of Veritas.* Montreal: Gray, 1815.

Rothenberg, Gunther. *The Art of Warfare in the Age of Napoleon.* Bloominton: University of Indiana, 1978.

Salisbury, George Cooke. *The Battle of Chrysler's Farm, War of 1812-1814.* Ottawa: Library of Parliament, n.d. [c. 1955].

Sawicki, James. *Infantry Regiments of the US Army.* Dumfries, Va.: Wyvern, 1981.

Skeen, Edward C. *John Armstrong Jr., 1758-1843: A Biography.* Syracuse, N.Y.: University of Syracuse, 1981.

Sketch of the Life of General Nathan Towson, U.S. Army. Baltimore: N. Hickman, 1842.

Spiller, Roger & Joseph Dawson, eds. *Dictionary of American Military Biography.* Westport, Conn.: Greenwood, 1984. 3 vols.

Squires, W. Austin. *The 104th Regiment of Foot (The New Brunswick Regiment) 1803-1817.* Fredericton: Brunswick Press, 1962.

Stagg, John. *Mr. Madison's War: Politics, Diplomacy, and Warfare in the Early American Republic.* Princeton: Princeton University, 1983.

Stanley, George. *The War of 1812. Land Operations.* Ottawa: National Museums of Canada, 1983.

Stevens, Joan. *Victorian Voices: An Introduction to the Papers of Sir John Le Couteur.* St. Helier, Jersey: Societé Jersiaise, 1969.

Stewart, Charles. *The Service of British Regiments in North America.* Ottawa: Department of National Defence Library, 1962.

——. *The Concise Lineages of the Canadian Army, 1855 to 1982.* Toronto: author, 1982.

Stone, William L. *The Life and Times of Red Jacket.* New York: Wiley, Putnam, 1841.

Strachan, Hew. *From Waterloo to Balaclava: Tactics, Technology and the British Army, 1815-1834.* Cambridge: Cambridge University Press, 1985.

Swinson, Arthur. *A Register of the Regiments and Corps of the British Army.* London: Arms & Armour, 1972.

Tancred, George. *Historical Record of Medals and Honorary Distinctions Conferred on the British Navy, Army & Auxiliary Forces.* London: Spink & Son, 1891.

Thomas, R. *The Glory of America; Comprising Memoirs of the Lives and Glorious Exploits of some of the Distinguished Officers Engaged in the Late War with Great Britain.* New York: Ezra Strong, 1836.

Thompson, David. *History of the Late War Between Great Britain and the United States of America.* Niagara, Canada: T. Sewell, 1832.

Thomson, John L. *Historical Sketches of the Late War.* Philadelphia: T. Donilever, 1817.

Tullibardine, Marchioness of, ed. *A Military History of Perthshire, 1660-1902.* Perthshire: R. & J. Hay, 1908. 2 vols.

Weigley, Russell F. *History of the United States Army.* New York: Macmillan, 1967.

Wickes, H.L. *Regiments of Foot.* London: Osprey, 1974.

Wilson, James & John Fiske, ed. *Appleton's Encyclopedia of American Biography.* New York: Appleton, 1888. 7 vols.

Wilson, Thomas. *The Biography of the Principal American Military and Naval Heroes.* New York: John Law, 1817, 1819. 2 vols.

Wright, Ross P. *The Burning of Dover.* Erie: author, 1948.

Zimmerman, James F. *Impressment of American Seamen.* New York: Columbia University, 1925.

SECONDARY SOURCES – ARTICLES

"Artillero Viejo," "How to Fight Brother Jonathan," *Museum of Foreign Literature, Science and Art,* 42 (May/August 1841), 210-214.

Bates, George C. "Reminiscences of the Brady Guards," *Michigan Pioneer* 13 (1888) 530-546.

"Biographical Sketch of Major Thomas Biddle," *Illinois Monthly Magazine* 1 (1831), 549-561.

"Biographical Sketch of Colonel Jacob Hindman of the United States' Army," *Portico,* 3 (1816), 38-52.

Brady, Hugh. "The Battle of Lundy's Lane," *Historical Magazine* 10 (1866), 272.

Carnochan, Janet. "Early Churches in the Niagara Peninsula, Stamford and Chippawa, with Marriage Records of Thomas Cummings and Extracts from the Cummings Papers," *Papers and Records Ontario Historical Society* 8 (1907), 149-225.

Cresswell, D.K.R. "A Near-Run Thing on the Niagara: The Battle of Lundy's Lane," in Corlene Taylor, ed., *Sharing Past and Future: Proceedings of the Ontario Genealogical Society,* 33-56. Toronto: Ontario Genealogical Society, 1988.

Cruikshank, Ernest A. "A Memoir of Colonel The Honourable James Kerby, His Life in letters," *Welland County Historical Society, Papers and Records* 4 (1931), 17-37.

——. "Record of the Services of Canadian Regiments in the War of 1812 – II. The Glengarry Light Infantry," *Selected Papers of the Canadian Military Institute*, 9 (1897-1899), 70-80.

——. "Record of the Services of Canadian Regiments in the War of 1812 – V. The Incorporated Militia," *Selected Papers of the Canadian Military Institute*, 6 (1894-1895), 9-23.

——. "Record of the Services of Canadian Regiments in the War of 1812 – XI. The Militia of Norfolk, Oxford and Middlesex," *Selected Papers of the Canadian Military Institute* 15 (1907), 47-71.

——. "The County of Norfolk in the War of 1812," *Proceedings of the Ontario Historical Society*, 20 (1923), 9-40.

Dudley, William. "Commodore Isaac Chauncey and U.S. Joint Operations on Lake Ontario, 1813-14," in William B. Cogar, ed., *New Interpretations in Naval History*. Annapolis: Naval Institute Press, 1990.

"Early Systems of Artillery," *U.S. Ordnance Notes* 25 (May 1874), 137-167.

"Eight Men were Sentenced to be 'Hanged-Drawn-Quartered'," *Cuesta* (Spring, 1981), 30-31.

Elting, John & H.C. McBarron. "Musicians, 1st U.S. Infantry, Winter Uniform, 1812-1813," *Military Collector & Historian*, 2 (1950), 24-25.

Fitzgibbon, Mary Agnes. *A Veteran of the War of 1812; the Life of James Fitzgibbon*. Toronto: Briggs, 1898.

Graves, Donald E. "A Note on British Field Artillery Equipments of the War of 1812," *Arms Collecting* 20 (1982), 127-129.

——. "'Dry Books of Tactics': U.S. Infantry Manuals of the War of 1812 and After," *Military Historian*, 38 (1986), No. 2, 50-61.

——. "Field Artillery of the War of 1812: Equipment, Organization, Tactics and Effectiveness," *Arms Collecting*, 30 (1992), No. 2, 39-48.

——. "'I have a handsome little army': A Re-examination of Winfield Scott's Camp at Buffalo in 1814," in R.A. Bowler, ed., *War Along the Niagara: Essays on the War of 1812 and its Legacy*, 38-52. Lewiston: Old Fort Niagara Association, 1991.

——. "William Drummond and the Battle of Fort Erie," *Canadian Military History* 1 (1992), 1-18.

Grazebrook, R.M. "The Wearing of Equipment, 1801," *Journal of the Society for Army Historical Research* 24 (1946), 38.

Green, Ernest. "Township No. 2. Mount Dorchester, Stamford," *Papers and Records of the Ontario Historical Society* 25 (1929), 248-338.

——. "Canadians at Lundy's Lane," undated newspaper article (c. 1940) in History Room, Public Library, Niagara Falls, Canada.

Hallahan, John M. "No Doubt Blamable: The Transformations of Captain Winfield Scott," *Virginia Cavalcade*, 40 (Spring, 1991), 160-171.

Hare, John S. "Military Punishments in the War of 1812," *Journal of the American Military Institute*, 4 (Winter 1940), No. 4, 225-239.

Heller, Charles F. "Those are Regulars, by God!," *Army* 37 (1987), 52-54.

Hitsman, J.M. "Sir George Prevost's Conduct of the Canadian War of 1812," *Canadian Historical Association Report* 1962, 34-43.

Hofschromb, Peter. "Flintlocks in Battle," *Military Illustrated*, No. 1 (June/July 1986), 29-36.

Holden, Robert J. "James Miller, Collector of the Port of Salem," *Essex Institute Collections* 104 (1968), 253-302.

McBarron, H.C. & John Elting, "Musicians, 1st U.S. Infantry, Winter Uniforms, 1812-1813," *Military Collector & Historian* 2 (1950), 24-25.

"Memoirs of General Ripley," *Portfolio*, 14 (1815), 108-136.

Parker, Henry S. "Henry Leavenworth, Pioneer General," *Military Review*, 50 (1970), 56-68.

Patterson, William. "A Forgotten Hero in a Forgotten War," *Journal of the Society For Army Historical Research* 68 (1990) 7-21.

Phalen, James. "Landmarks in Surgery. Surgeon James Mann, U.S. Army; Observations on Battlefield Amputations," *Surgery* 66 (1938), 1072-1073.

"Recollections of Lundy's Lane," *The Army and Navy Chronicle*, 3 (1836), No. 14.

Riddell, William R. "The Ancaster 'Bloody Assize' of 1814," *Papers and Records of the Ontario Historical Society* 20 (1923), 108-125.

Robertson, H.H. "Major Titus Geer Simons at Lundy's Lane," *Transactions of the Wentworth County Historical Society* 11 (1899), 49-54.

——. "Some Historical and Biographical Notes on the Militia within the limits now constituting the County of Wentworth in the years 1804, 1821, 1830, 1838 and 1839 with the Lists of the Officers," *Journal and Transactions of the Wentworth County Historical Society* 4 (1905), 25-65.

Roland, Charles G. "War Amputations in Upper Canada," *Archivaria*, 10 (1980), 73-84.

Scarborough, W. Frances. "William Jenkins Worth – Soldier," *Americana (American Historical Magazine)* 23 (1929), 276-297.

Simons, John R. "The Fortunes of a United Empire Loyalist Family," *Ontario Historical Society Papers and Records* 23 (1926), 470-482.

Stacey, C.P. "Upper Canada at War: Captain Armstrong Reports," *Ontario History* 48 (1956), 37-42.

Stagg, John. "Enlisted Men in the United States Army, 1812-1815: A Preliminary Survey," *William and Mary Quarterly*, 3rd Series, 43 (1986), 616-645.

——. "The Politics of Ending the War of 1812," in R.A. Bowler, ed., *War Along the Niagara. Essays on the War of 1812 and Its Legacy*, 93-104. Youngstown, NY: Old Fort Niagara Association, 1991.

Warner, Mabel V. "Memorials at Lundy's Lane," *Ontario History* 51 (1959), 43-49.

Way, Ronald. "The Day of Crysler's Farm," *Canadian Geographical Journal*, 62 (1961), 184-217.

Whitehorne, Joseph, "The Battle of Fort Erie. Reconstruction of a War of 1812 Battle," *Prologue* 22 (1990), 129-148.

"Winfield Scott," *Harper's Magazine*, 451-466.

SECONDARY SOURCES – UNPUBLISHED

Couture, Paul. "The Non-Regular Military Forces on the Niagara Frontier: 1812-1814," Canadian Parks Service, Microfiche Report Series, No. 193, Ottawa, 1985.

Graves, Donald E. "Joseph Willcocks and the Canadian Volunteers: An Account of Political Disaffection in Upper Canada during the War of 1812," M.A. Thesis, Carleton University, Ottawa, Canada, 1982.

Hein, Edward B. "The Niagara Frontier and the War of 1812," PhD. dissertation, University of Ottawa, 1949.

Kimball, Jeffrey. "Strategy on the Northern Frontier, 1814," PhD. dissertation, University of Louisiana at Baton Rouge, 1969.

Morris, John. "General Jacob Brown," Unpublished paper read before the 50th Anniversay Commemorative Conference, Siena College, NY, 1987.

Walker, Charles. "Engineers in the War of 1812," Typescript, Historical Division, Engineer School, Fort Belvoir, Va.

ADDENDUM TO THE BIBLIOGRAPHY

Since the appearance of the first edition of this book in 1993, there has been much new material published on the War of 1812 that will be useful for the reader interested in that conflict and in the Niagara campaign. In addition, many of the sources cited above, that were in manuscript form when the first edition of this book appeared, have since been published.

Published Sources

Graves, Donald E., "From Steuben to Scott: The Adoption of French Infantry Tactics by the U.S. Army, 1807-1816," *Acta* No. 13, International Commission on Military History, Helsinki, 1991, 223-235.

——, ed, *Merry Hearts Make Light Days: The War of 1812 Journal of Lieutenant John Le Couteur, 104th Foot.* Ottawa: Carleton University Press, 1993.

——. "American Ordnance of the War of 1812: A Preliminary Investigation." *Arms Collecting*, Volume 31, No. 4 (November 1993): 111-120

——. "The War of 1812 along the Lake Ontario and St. Lawrence Borders – A Canadian Perspective." In Jan Saltzgaber, ed., *Essays on the Historical Legacy of Sackett's Harbor and Madison Barracks.* Ithaca, N.Y.: Ithaca College, 1993, 115-131.

——. *Red Coats and Grey Jackets: The Battle of Chippawa, 1814.* Toronto: Dundurn Press, 1994.

——, ed. *Soldiers of 1814: American Enlisted Men's Memoirs of the Niagara Campaign.* Youngstown, N.Y.: Old Fort Niagara Association, 1995. Contains the memoirs of Jarvis Hanks, Amasiah Ford and Alexander McMullen who fought at Lundy's Lane.

Gray, William, *Soldiers of the King: The Upper Canadian Militia 1812-1815. A Reference Guide.* Toronto: Boston Mills, 1995.

Litt, Paul, and Ronald Williamson and Joseph Whitehorne, eds., *Death at Snake Hill: Secrets from a War of 1812 Cemetary.* Toronto: Dundurn Press, 1993.

Malcomson, Robert, "HMS St. Lawrence: Commodore Yeo's Unique First-Rate," *Freshwater,* 6 (1991), 27-36.

——. *The Battle of Queenston Heights.* The Friends of Fort George, 1994.

——. "War on Lake Ontario: A Costly Victory at Oswego, 1814," *The Beaver,* 75 (1995), 4-13.

McGurty, Michael S. "Notes on the Flank Companies of the Left Division 1814." *Military Collector & Historian* Vol XLV, No. 3 (Fall 1993): 117.

Pfeiffer, Susan and Ronald Williamson, eds. *Snake Hill. An Investigation of a Military Cemetery from the War of 1812.* Toronto: Dundurn Press, 1991.

Sheppard, George. *Plunder, Profit, and Paroles. A Social History of the War of 1812 in Upper Canada.* Kingston: McGill-Queens, 1994.

Whitehorne, Joseph. *While Washington Burned: The Battle for Fort Erie, 1814.* Baltimore: Nautical & Aviation Publishing, 1992.

——. *The Battle for Baltimore.* Baltimore: Nautical & Aviation Publishing, 1997.

Wilder, Patrick. *The Battle of Sackett's Harbor, 1813.* Baltimore: Nautical & Aviation Publishing, 1995.

Index